JavaScript from Beg
Professional

Learn JavaScript quickly by building fun, interactive,
and dynamic web apps, games, and pages

Laurence Lars Svekis

Maaike van Putten

Rob Percival

BIRMINGHAM – MUMBAI

JavaScript from Beginner to Professional

Producer: Tushar Gupta

Acquisition Editor – Peer Reviews: Divya Mudaliar

Project Editor: Namrata Katare

Content Development Editor: Edward Doxey

Copy Editor: Safis Editing

Technical Editor: Karan Sonawane

Proofreader: Safis Editing

Indexer: Sejal Dsilva

Presentation Designer: Pranit Padwal

First published: December 2021

Production reference: 3141022

Published by Packt Publishing Ltd.
Livery Place
35 Livery Street
Birmingham
B3 2PB, UK.

ISBN 978-1-80056-252-3

www.packt.com

Contributors

About the authors

Laurence Lars Svekis is an innovative technology expert with a wide range of expertise and real-world experience in web development, having worked on various web development projects, both large and small, since 1999. He has been a top course instructor since 2015, and has a passion for bringing ideas to life online. Teaching and helping others has been an amazing opportunity for him, as he enjoys sharing knowledge with others. He has an enthusiasm for education and a desire to help others experience the joy of application development and web design.

Thanks to Alexis and Sebastian for all their support.

Maaike van Putten is a software developer and trainer with a passion for software development and helping others get to the next level in their career. Some of her favorite languages are JavaScript, Java, and Python. She participates as a developer in software development projects and as a trainer in various topics, ranging from IT for dummies to advanced topics for senior software developers. Next to that, she loves to create online content for diverse platforms to help larger audiences.

Rob Percival is a highly regarded web developer and Udemy instructor with over 1.7 million students. Over 500,000 of them have taken Rob's Complete Web Developer Course 2.0, as well as his Android Developer and iOS Developer courses.

About the reviewer

Chris Minnick is a prolific author, blogger, trainer, speaker, and web developer. His company, *WatzThis?*, is dedicated to finding better ways to teach computer and programming skills to beginners.

Chris has been a full-stack developer for over 25 years and a trainer for over 10 years. He has taught web development, ReactJS, and advanced JavaScript at many of the world's largest companies, as well as at public libraries, co-working spaces, and meetups.

Minnick has authored and co-authored over a dozen technical books for adults and kids, including *React JS Foundations, HTML and CSS for Dummies, Coding with JavaScript for Dummies, JavaScript for Kids, Adventures in Coding,* and *Writing Computer Code.*

Join our book's Discord space

Join the book's Discord workspace for a monthly *Ask me Anything* session with the authors: `https://packt.link/JSBook`

Table of Contents

Preface

JavaScript is an amazing multi-functional language that is used a lot for web development (among other things). Any interaction that happens on web pages is JavaScript in action. In fact, all modern browsers understand JavaScript—and soon you will understand it too.

This book deals with everything you need to know to create JavaScript applications and use JavaScript on web pages. By the time you finish this book, you'll be capable of creating interactive web pages, dynamic applications, and a lot more as you progress on your professional JavaScript journey!

Who this book is for

To get started with this book, you don't need any JavaScript experience. However, if you do have some coding experience, you're likely to go through the book and exercises with a bit more ease. Basic familiarity with HTML and CSS would be of benefit. If you're a first-time programmer, we are honored to welcome you to the world of programming in this book. It may seem difficult in the beginning, but we'll guide you right through it.

What this book covers

Chapter 1, Getting Started with JavaScript, covers some fundamentals of the JavaScript language that you'll have to know to understand the rest of the book.

Chapter 2, JavaScript Essentials, deals with essentials such as variables, data types, and operators.

Chapter 3, JavaScript Multiple Values, covers how to store multiple values in one variable using arrays and objects.

Chapter 4, Logic Statements, is where the real fun starts: we are going to use logic statements to make decisions for us!

Chapter 5, Loops, accounts for situations when it is necessary to repeat a block of code, which is what we use loops for. We are using different types of loops, such as the `for` and the `while` loop.

Chapter 6, Functions, introduces a very useful block for repeating code snippets: functions! This enables us to invoke a specified code block at any time in our script to do something for us. This will help you to not repeat yourself, which is one of the fundamental principles of writing clean code.

Chapter 7, Classes, continues with building blocks of JavaScript that help us to structure our application better. We have already seen how to create objects, and with classes we learn how to create a template for objects that we can reuse anytime we need that particular type of object.

Chapter 8, Built-In JavaScript Methods, deals with some great built-in functionality. Functions are something we can write ourselves, but we'll find ourselves using the built-in JavaScript functions often whenever we need to do common tasks, such as checking whether something is a number or not.

Chapter 9, The Document Object Model, dives into the browser object model and document object model (DOM). This is going to enrich the way we can use JavaScript by a lot. We'll learn what the DOM is, and how we can affect it with JavaScript and change our websites by doing so.

Chapter 10, Dynamic Element Manipulation Using the DOM, demonstrates how to manipulate the elements of the DOM dynamically, which will enable you to create modern user experiences. We can change our website as a response to user behavior such as clicking on a button.

Chapter 11, Interactive Content and Event Listeners, takes our responses to the user to the next level. For example, we are going to learn how to respond to events such as the cursor leaving an input box and the mouse of the user moving.

Chapter 12, Intermediate JavaScript, deals with topics that you'll need to write intermediate JavaScript code, such as regular expressions, recursion, and debugging, to boost the performance of your code.

Chapter 13, Concurrency, introduces the topic of concurrency and asynchronous programming, which will allow our code to do multiple things at the same time and be truly flexible.

Chapter 14, HTML5, Canvas, and JavaScript, focuses on HTML5 and JavaScript. We'll have seen a lot of both HTML and JavaScript in the previous chapters, but here we'll be focusing on the HTML5-specific features, such as the canvas element.

Chapter 15, Next Steps, explores the next steps you could take after you've gotten all the fundamental features of JavaScript down and you are able to write nifty programs using JavaScript. We'll take a look at some of the famous JavaScript libraries and development frameworks, such as Angular, React, and Vue, and we'll have a look at Node.js to see how the backend can be written in JavaScript.

To get the most out of this book

Previous coding experience will help, but is definitely not required. If you have a computer with a text editor (such as Notepad or TextEdit, not Word!) and a browser, you can get started with this book. We encourage you to engage with the exercises and projects, and experiment continually while you go through the chapters, to ensure you are comfortable with each concept before moving on.

Download the example code files

The code bundle for the book is hosted on GitHub at `https://github.com/PacktPublishing/JavaScript-from-Beginner-to-Professional`. We also have other code bundles from our rich catalog of books and videos available at `https://github.com/PacktPublishing/`. Check them out!

Download the color images

We also provide a PDF file that has color images of the screenshots/diagrams used in this book. You can download it here: `https://static.packt-cdn.com/downloads/9781800562523_ColorImages.pdf`.

Conventions used

There are a number of text conventions used throughout this book.

`CodeInText`: Indicates code words in text, database table names, folder names, filenames, file extensions, pathnames, dummy URLs, user input, and Twitter handles. For example; "We also need to let the browser know what kind of document we're working on with the `<!DOCTYPE>` declaration."

A block of code is set as follows:

```html
<html>
  <script type="text/javascript">
    alert("Hi there!");
  </script>
</html>
```

Any command-line input or output is written as follows:

```
console.log("Hello world!")
```

Bold: Indicates a new term, an important word, or words that you see on the screen, for example, in menus or dialog boxes, also appear in the text like this. For example: "If you right-click and select **Inspect** on macOS systems, you will see a screen appear, similar to the one in the following screenshot."

Warnings or important notes appear like this.

Tips and tricks appear like this.

Get in touch

Feedback from our readers is always welcome.

General feedback: Email feedback@packtpub.com, and mention the book's title in the subject of your message. If you have questions about any aspect of this book, please email us at questions@packtpub.com.

Errata: Although we have taken every care to ensure the accuracy of our content, mistakes do happen. If you have found a mistake in this book we would be grateful if you would report this to us. Please visit, http://www.packtpub.com/submit-errata, selecting your book, clicking on the Errata Submission Form link, and entering the details.

Piracy: If you come across any illegal copies of our works in any form on the Internet, we would be grateful if you would provide us with the location address or website name. Please contact us at copyright@packtpub.com with a link to the material.

If you are interested in becoming an author: If there is a topic that you have expertise in and you are interested in either writing or contributing to a book, please visit http://authors.packtpub.com.

Share Your Thoughts

Once you've read *JavaScript from Beginner to Professional*, we'd love to hear your thoughts! Scan the QR code below to go straight to the Amazon review page for this book and share your feedback.

https://packt.link/r/1800562527

Your review is important to us and the tech community and will help us make sure we're delivering excellent quality content.

Download a free PDF copy of this book

Thanks for purchasing this book!

Do you like to read on the go but are unable to carry your print books everywhere? Is your eBook purchase not compatible with the device of your choice?

Don't worry, now with every Packt book you get a DRM-free PDF version of that book at no cost.

Read anywhere, any place, on any device. Search, copy, and paste code from your favorite technical books directly into your application.

The perks don't stop there, you can get exclusive access to discounts, newsletters, and great free content in your inbox daily

Follow these simple steps to get the benefits:

1. Scan the QR code or visit the link below

https://packt.link/free-ebook/9781800562523

2. Submit your proof of purchase
3. That's it! We'll send your free PDF and other benefits to your email directly

1

Getting Started with JavaScript

It appears you have decided to start learning JavaScript. Excellent choice! JavaScript is a programming language that can be used on both the server side and client side of applications. The server side of an application is the backend logic that usually runs on computers in data centers and interacts with the database, while the client side is what runs on the device of the user, often the browser for JavaScript.

It is not unlikely that you have used functionality written in JavaScript. If you have used a web browser, such as Chrome, Firefox, Safari, or Edge, then you definitely have. JavaScript is all over the web. If you enter a web page and it asks you to accept cookies and you click OK, the popup disappears. This is JavaScript in action. And if you want to navigate a website and a sub-menu opens up, that means more JavaScript. Often, when you filter products in a web shop, this involves JavaScript. And what about these chats that start talking to you after you have been on a website for a certain number of seconds? Well, you guessed it—JavaScript!

Pretty much any interaction we have with web pages is because of JavaScript; the buttons you are clicking, birthday cards you are creating, and calculations you are doing. Anything that requires more than a static web page needs JavaScript.

In this chapter, we will cover the following topics:

- Why should you learn JavaScript?
- Setting up your environment
- How does the browser understand JavaScript?

- Using the browser console
- Adding JavaScript to a web page
- Writing JavaScript code

 Note: exercise, project and self-check quiz answers can be found in the *Appendix*.

Why should you learn JavaScript?

There are many reasons why you should want to learn JavaScript. JavaScript originates from 1995, and is often considered the most widely used programming language. This is because JavaScript is the language that web browsers support and understand. You have everything you need to interpret it already installed on your computer if you have a web browser and text editor. There are better setups, however, and we will discuss these later in this chapter.

It is a great programming language for beginners, and most advanced software developers will know at least some JavaScript because they will have run into it at some point. JavaScript is a great choice for beginners for a number of reasons. The first reason is that you can start building really cool apps using JavaScript sooner than you could imagine. By the time you get to *Chapter 5, Loops*, you will be able to write quite complex scripts that interact with users. And by the end of the book, you will be able to write dynamic web pages to do all sorts of things.

JavaScript can be used to write many different types of applications and scripts. It can be used for programming for the web browser, but also the logic layer of code that we cannot see (such as communication with the database) of an application can be programmed in JavaScript, along with games, automation scripts, and a plethora of other purposes. JavaScript can also be used for different programming styles, by which we mean ways to structure and write code. How you would go about this depends on the purpose of your script. If you've never coded before, you may not quite grasp these concepts, and it's not entirely necessary to at this stage, but JavaScript can be used for (semi) object-oriented, functional, and procedural programming, which are just different programming paradigms.

There are a ton of libraries and frameworks you can use once you get the basics of JavaScript down. These libraries and frameworks will really enhance your software life and make it a lot easier and possible to get more done in less time. Examples of these great libraries and frameworks include React, Vue.js, jQuery, Angular, and Node.js. Don't worry about these for now; just see them as a bonus for later. We will cover some of them briefly at the very end of this book.

Finally, we'll mention the JavaScript community. JavaScript is a very popular programming language, and many people are using it. As a beginner in particular, there won't be a problem for which you cannot find a solution on the internet.

The community of JavaScript is huge. The popular Stack Overflow forum contains lots of help for all sorts of coding issues and has an enormous section on JavaScript. You'll find yourself running into this web page a lot while googling problems and tips and tricks.

If JavaScript is your first programming language, you are new to the whole software community and you are in for a treat. Software developers, no matter the language, love to help one another. There are forums and tutorials online and you can find answers to almost all your questions. As a beginner, it can be hard to understand all the answers though. Just hang in there, keep trying and learning, and you will understand it soon enough.

Setting up your environment

There are many ways in which you can set up a JavaScript coding environment. For starters, your computer probably already has all the minimal things you will need to code JavaScript. We recommend you make your life a little bit easier and use an IDE.

Integrated Development Environment

An **Integrated Development Environment** (IDE) is a special application that is used to write, run, and debug code. You can just open it like you would any program. For example, to write a text document, you need to open the program, select the right file, and start to write. Coding is similar. You open the IDE and write the code. If you want to execute the code, the IDE often has a special button for this. Pressing this button will run the code from inside the IDE. For JavaScript, you might find yourself opening your browser manually in certain cases though.

An IDE does do more than that though; it usually has syntax highlighting. This means that certain elements in your code will have a certain color, and you can easily see when something is going wrong. Another great feature is the autosuggest feature, where the editor helps you with the options you have at the place where you are coding. This is often called code completion. Many IDEs have special plugins so you can make working with other tools more intuitive and add features to it, for example, a hot reload in the browser.

There are many IDEs out there and they differ in what they have to offer. We use Visual Studio Code throughout the book, but that's a personal preference. Other popular ones at the time of writing include Atom, Sublime Text, and WebStorm.

There are many IDEs and they keep on appearing, so chances are the most popular one at the time you are reading is not on this list. There are many other options. You can do a quick search on the web for JavaScript IDEs. There are a few things to pay attention to when selecting an IDE. Make sure that it supports syntax highlighting, debugging, and code completion for JavaScript.

Web browser

You will also need a web browser. Most browsers are perfectly fine for this, but it's better not to use Internet Explorer, which doesn't support the latest JavaScript features. Two good options would be Chrome and Firefox. They support the latest JavaScript features and helpful plugins are available.

Extra tools

There are many extra things you can use while coding, for example, browser plugins that will help you to debug or make things easier to look at. You don't really need any of them at this point, but keep an open mind whenever you come across a tool that others are very excited about.

Online editor

It may be the case that you don't have access to a computer, perhaps just a tablet, or that you cannot install anything on your laptop. There are great online editors out there for these scenarios as well. We don't name any, since they are evolving rapidly and probably will be old by the time you are reading this. But if you do a web search for `online JavaScript IDE`, you will find plenty of online options where you can just start coding JavaScript and hit a button to run it.

How does the browser understand JavaScript?

JavaScript is an interpreted language, which means that the computer understands it while running it. Some languages get processed before running, this is called compiling, but not JavaScript. The computer can just interpret JavaScript on the fly. The "engine" that understands JavaScript will be called the interpreter here.

A web page isn't just JavaScript. Web pages are written in three languages: HTML, CSS, and JavaScript.

HTML determines what is on the page; the content of the page is in there. If there is a paragraph on the page, the HTML of the page contains a paragraph. And if there is a heading, HTML was used to add a heading, and so forth. HTML consists of elements, also called tags. They specify what is on the page. Here is a little sample that will create a web page with the text Hello world on it:

```
<html>
  <body>
    Hello world!
  </body>
</html>
```

In *Chapter 9, The Document Object Model,* we have a little crash course in HTML, so don't worry if you have never seen it.

CSS is the layout of the web page. So for example, if the text color is blue, this is done by CSS. Font size, font family, and position on the page are all determined by CSS. JavaScript is the final piece in the puzzle, which defines what the web page can do and how it can interact with the user or the backend.

When dealing with JavaScript, you will come across the term **ECMAScript** sooner or later. This is the specification or standardization for the JavaScript language. The current standard is **ECMAScript 6** (also referred to as **ES6**). Browsers use this specification to support JavaScript (in addition to some other topics such as **Document Object Model (DOM)**, which we'll see later). JavaScript has many implementations that might differ slightly, but ECMAScript can be considered the basic specification that the JavaScript implementation will definitely include.

Using the browser console

You may have seen this already, or not, but web browsers have a built-in option to see the code that makes the web page you are on possible. If you hit *F12* on a Windows computer while you are in the web browser, or you right-click and select **Inspect** on macOS systems, you will see a screen appear, similar to the one in the following screenshot.

It might work slightly differently on your browser on your machine, but right-clicking and selecting **Inspect** generally does the trick:

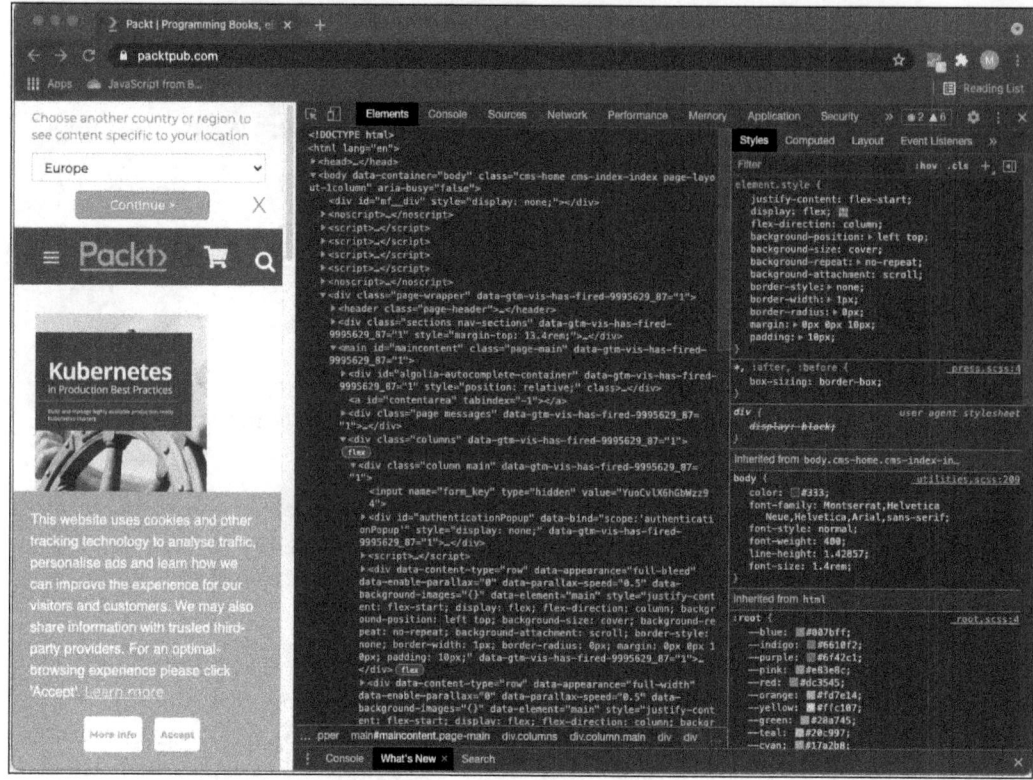

Figure 1.1: Browser console on the Packt website

This screenshot contains multiple tabs at the top. We are now looking at the element tabs, which contain all the HTML and CSS (remember those?). If you click on the console tab, you will find at the bottom of the panel a place where you can insert some code directly. You may see some warnings or error messages in this tab. This is not uncommon, and don't worry about it if the page is working.

The console is used by developers to log what is going on and do any debugging. Debugging is finding the problem when an application is not displaying the desired behavior. The console gives some insights as to what is happening if you log sensible messages. This is actually the first command we are going to learn:

```
console.log("Hello world!");
```

If you click on this console tab, enter the first JavaScript code above, and then hit *Enter*, this will show you the output of your code therein. It will look like the following screenshot:

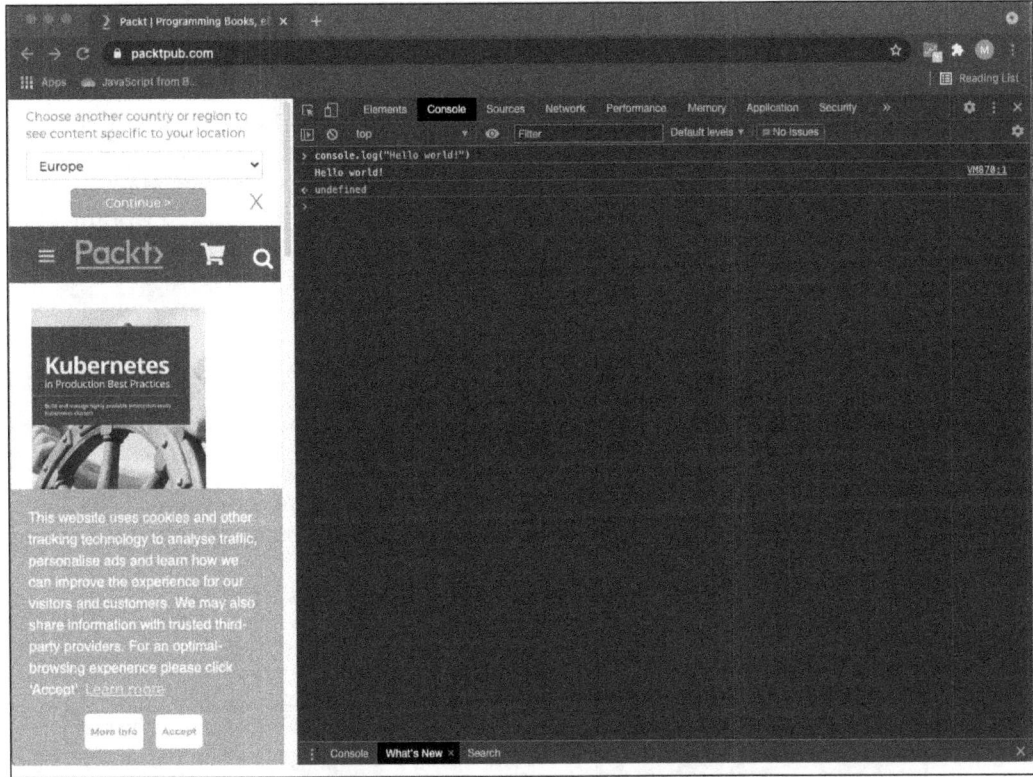

Figure 1.2: JavaScript in the browser console

You will be working with the `console.log()` statement a lot throughout the book in your code to test your code snippets and see the results. There are also other console methods, such as `console.table()`, that create a table when the inputted data can be presented as a table. Another console method is `console.error()`, which will log the inputted data, but with a styling that draws attention to the fact that it's an error.

Practice exercise 1.1

Working with the console:

1. Open the browser console, type `4 + 10`, and press *Enter*. What do you see as the response?

2. Use the `console.log()` syntax, placing a value within the rounded brackets. Try entering your name with quotes around it (this is to indicate the fact that it's a text string—we'll get to this in the next chapter).

Adding JavaScript to a web page

There are two ways to link JavaScript to a web page. The first way is to type the JavaScript directly in the HTML between two `<script>` tags. In HTML, the first tag, `<script>`, is to declare that the following script will be executed. Then we have the content that should be inside this element. Next, we close the script with the same tag, but preceded by a forward slash, `</script>`. Or you can link a JavaScript file to the HTML file using the script tag at the head of the HTML page.

Directly in HTML

Here is an example of how to write a very simple web page that will give a pop-up box saying `Hi there!`:

```
<html>
  <script type="text/javascript">
    alert("Hi there!");
  </script>
</html>
```

If you store this as a `.html` file, and open the file in your browser, you will get something like the following screenshot. We will be storing this one as `Hi.html`:

Figure 1.3: JavaScript made this popup with the text "Hi there!" appear

The `alert` command will create a popup that provides a message. This message is specified between the parentheses behind the alert.

Right now, we have the content directly within our `<html>` tags. This is not a best practice. We will need to create two elements inside `<html>`—`<head>` and `<body>`. In the head element, we write metadata and we also use this part later to connect external files to our HTML file. In the body, we have the content of the web page.

We also need to let the browser know what kind of document we're working on with the `<!DOCTYPE>` declaration. Since we're writing JavaScript inside an HTML file, we need to use `<!DOCTYPE html>`. Here's an example:

```
<!DOCTYPE html>
<html>

<head>
  <title>This goes in the tab of your browser</title>
</head>

<body>
The content of the webpage
  <script>
    console.log("Hi there!");
  </script>
</body>

</html>
```

This example web page will display the following: The content of the webpage. If you look in the browser console, you'll find a surprise! It has executed the JavaScript as well and logs Hi there! in the console.

Practice exercise 1.2

JavaScript in an HTML page:

1. Open your code editor and create an HTML file.
2. Within your HTML file, set up the HTML tags, doctype, HTML, head, and body, and then proceed and add the script tags.
3. Place some JavaScript code within the script tags. You can use console.log("hello world!").

Linking an external file to our web page

You could also link an external file to the HTML file. This is considered a better practice, as it organizes code better and you can avoid very lengthy HTML pages due to the JavaScript. In addition to these benefits, you can reuse the JavaScript on other web pages of your website without having to copy and paste. Say that you have the same JavaScript on 10 pages and you need to make a change to the script. You would only have to change one file if you did it in the way we are showing you in this example.

First, we are going to create a separate JavaScript file. These files have the postfix `.js`. I'm going to call it `ch1_alert.js`. This will be the content of our file:

```
alert("Saying hi from a different file!");
```

Then we are going to create a separate HTML file (using the postfix `.html` again). And we are going to give it this content:

```
<html>
  <script type="text/javascript" src="ch1_alert.js"></script>
</html>
```

Make sure that you put the files in the same location, or that you specify the path to the JavaScript file in your HTML. The names are case-sensitive and should match exactly.

You have two options. You can use a relative path and an absolute path. Let's cover the latter first since that is the easiest to explain. Your computer has a root. For Linux and macOS, it is `/`, and for Windows, it is often `C:/`. The path to the file starting from the root is the absolute path. This is the easiest to add because it will work on your machine. But there is a catch: on your machine, if this website folder later gets moved to a server, the absolute path will no longer work.

The second, safer option is relative paths. You specify how to get there from the file you are in at that time. So if it's in the same folder, you will only have to insert the name. If it's in a folder called "example" that is inside the folder that your file is in, you will have to specify `example/nameOfTheFile.js`. And if it's a folder up, you would have to specify `../nameOfTheFile.js`.

If you open the HTML file, this is what you should get:

Figure 1.4: Popup created by JavaScript in a different file

Practice exercise 1.3

Linking to a JS JavaScript file:

1. Create a separate file called app with the extension .js.
2. Within the .js file, add some JavaScript code.
3. Link to the separate .js file within the HTML file you created in *Practice exercise 1.2*.
4. Open the HTML file within your browser and check to see whether the JavaScript code ran properly.

Writing JavaScript code

So, we now have lots of context, but how do you actually write JavaScript code? There are some important things to keep in mind, such as how to format the code, using the right indentation level, using semicolons, and adding comments. Let's start with formatting code.

Formatting code

Code needs to be formatted well. If you have a long file with many lines of code and you didn't stick to a few basic formatting rules, it is going to be hard to understand what you've written. So, what are the basic formatting rules? The two most important for now are indentations and semicolons. There are also naming conventions, but these will be addressed for every topic that is yet to come.

Indentations and whitespace

When you are writing code, often a line of code belongs to a certain code block (code between two curly brackets { like this }) or parent statement. If that is the case, you give the code in that block one indentation to make sure that you can see easily what is part of the block and when a new block starts. You don't need to understand the following code snippet, but it will demonstrate readability with and without indentations.

Without new lines:

```
let status = "new"; let scared = true; if (status === "new") { console.
log("Welcome to JavaScript!");  if (scared) { console.log("Don't worry
you will be fine!"); } else { console.log("You're brave! You are going
to do great!"); } } else { console.log("Welcome back, I knew you'd like
it!"); }
```

With new lines but without indentation:

```
let status = "new";
let scared = true;
if (status === "new") {
console.log("Welcome to JavaScript!");
if (scared) {
console.log("Don't worry you will be fine!");
} else {
console.log("You're brave! You are going to do great!");
}
} else {
console.log("Welcome back, I knew you'd like it!");
}
```

With new lines and indentation:

```
let status = "new";
let scared = true;
if (status === "new") {
    console.log("Welcome to JavaScript!");
    if (scared) {
        console.log("Don't worry you will be fine!");
    } else {
        console.log("You're brave! You are going to do great!");
    }
} else {
    console.log("Welcome back, I knew you'd like it!");
}
```

As you can see, you can now easily see when the code blocks end. This is where the if has a corresponding } at the same indentation level. In the example without indentations, you would have to count the brackets to determine when the if block would end. Even though it is not necessary for working code, make sure to use indentation well. You will thank yourself later.

Semicolons

After every statement, you should insert a semicolon. JavaScript is very forgiving and will understand many situations in which you have forgotten one, but develop the habit of adding one after every line of code early. When you declare a code block, such as an if statement or loop, you should not end with a semicolon. It is only for the separate statements.

Code comments

With comments, you can tell the interpreter to ignore some lines of the file. They won't get executed if they are comments. It is often useful to be able to avoid executing a part of the file. This could be for the following reasons:

1. You do not want to execute a piece of code while running the script, so you comment it out so it gets ignored by the interpreter.

2. Metadata. Adding some context to the code, such as the author, and a description of what the file covers.

3. Adding comments to specific parts of the code to explain what is happening or why a certain choice has been made.

There are two ways to write comments. You can either write single-line comments or multi-line comments. Here is an example:

```
// I'm a single line comment
// console.log("single line comment, not logged");

/* I'm a multi-line comment. Whatever is between the slash asterisk and
the asterisk slash will not get executed.
console.log("I'm not logged, because I'm a comment");
*/
```

In the preceding code snippet, you see both commenting styles. The first one is single-line. This can also be an inline comment at the end of the line. Whatever comes after the // on the line will get ignored. The second one is multiline; it is written by starting with /* and ending with */.

Practice exercise 1.4

Adding comments:

1. Add a new statement to your JavaScript code by setting a variable value. Since we will cover this in the next chapter, you can use the following line:

   ```
   let a = 10;
   ```

2. Add a comment at the end of the statement indicating that you set a value of 10.

3. Print the value using `console.log()`. Add a comment explaining what this will do.

4. At the end of your JavaScript code, use a multiple-line comment. In a real production script, you might use this space to add a brief outline of the purpose of the file.

Prompt

Another thing we would like to show you here is also a command prompt. It works very much like an alert, but instead, it takes input from the user. We will learn how to store variables very soon, and once you know that, you can store the result of this prompt function and do something with it. Go ahead and change the `alert()` to a `prompt()` in the `Hi.html` file, for example, like this:

```
prompt("Hi! How are you?");
```

Then, go ahead and refresh the HTML. You will get a popup with an input box in which you can enter text, as follows:

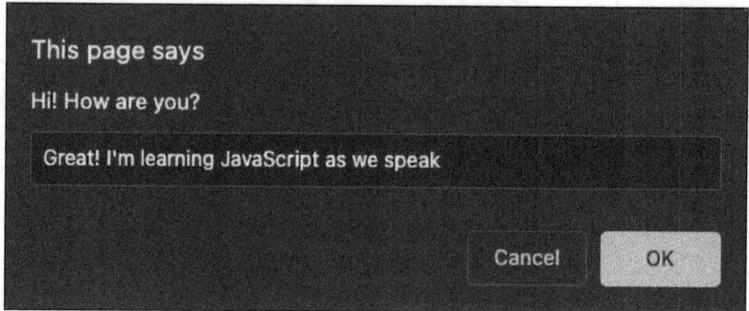

Figure 1.5: Page prompting for use input

The value you (or any other user) enter will be returned to the script, and can be used in your code! This is great for getting user input to shape the way your code works.

Random numbers

For the purpose of fun exercises in the early chapters of this book, we would like you to know how to generate a random number in JavaScript. It is absolutely fine if you don't really understand what is going on just yet; just know that this is the command to create a random number:

```
Math.random();
```

We can do it in the console and see the result appear if we log it:

```
console.log(Math.random());
```

This number will be a decimal between 0 and 1. If we want a number between 0 and 100, we can multiply it by 100, like this:

```
console.log(Math.random() * 100);
```

 Don't worry, we will cover mathematic operators in *Chapter 2, JavaScript Essentials*.

If we don't want to have a decimal result, we can use the `Math.floor` function on it, which is rounding it down to the nearest integer:

```
console.log(Math.floor(Math.random() * 100));
```

Don't worry about not getting this yet. This will be explained in more detail further on in the book. In *Chapter 8, Built-In JavaScript Methods*, we will discuss built-in methods in more detail. Until then, just trust us that this does generate a random number between 0 and 100.

Chapter project

Creating an HTML file and a linked JavaScript file

Create an HTML file and create a separate JavaScript file. Then, connect to the JavaScript file from the HTML file.

1. In the JavaScript file, output your name into the console and add a multiple-line comment to your code.

2. Try commenting out the console message in your JavaScript file so that nothing shows in the console.

Self-check quiz

1. What is the HTML syntax to add an external JavaScript file?
2. Can you run JavaScript in a file with a JS extension in your browser?
3. How do you write a multiple-line comment in JavaScript?
4. What is the best way to remove a line of code from running that you might want to keep as you debug?

Summary

Nicely done! You have made a start with JavaScript! In this chapter, we have discussed a lot of context, which you will need to know before starting to code JavaScript. We saw that we can use JavaScript for many purposes, and one of the most popular use cases is the web. Browsers can work with JavaScript because they have a special part, called an interpreter, that can process JavaScript. We saw that we have multiple options for writing JavaScript on our computer. We will need an IDE, a program that we can use to write and run our code.

Adding JavaScript to a web page can be done in several ways. We saw how to include it in the script element and how to add a separate JavaScript file to a page. We ended this chapter with some important general notes on how to write well-structured, readable, and easy-to-maintain code that is well documented with comments. We also saw that we can write to the console with our `console.log()` method and ask for user input using `prompt()`. Lastly, we also saw that we can generate random numbers with the `Math.random()` function.

Next, we'll look at JavaScript's basic data types and the operators that can be used to manipulate them!

Join our book's Discord space

Join the book's Discord workspace for a monthly *Ask me Anything* session with the authors: `https://packt.link/JSBook`

2

JavaScript Essentials

In this chapter, we will be dealing with some essential building blocks of JavaScript: variables and operators. We will start with variables, what they are, and which different variable data types exist. We need these basic building blocks to store and work with variable values in our scripts, making them dynamic.

Once we've got the variables covered, we will be ready to deal with operators. Arithmetic, assignment, and conditional and logical operators will be discussed at this stage. We need operators to modify our variables or to tell us something about these variables. This way we can do basic calculations based on factors such as user input.

Along the way, we'll cover the following topics:

- Variables
- Primitive data types
- Analyzing and modifying data types
- Operators

 Note: exercise, project, and self-check quiz answers can be found in the *Appendix*.

Variables

Variables are the first building block you will be introduced to when learning most languages. Variables are values in your code that can represent different values each time the code runs. Here is an example of two variables in a script:

```
firstname = "Maaike";
x = 2;
```

And they can be assigned a new value while the code is running:

```
firstname = "Edward";
x = 7;
```

Without variables, a piece of code would do the exact same thing every single time it was run. Even though that could still be helpful in some cases, it can be made much more powerful by working with variables to allow our code to do something different every time we run it.

Declaring variables

The first time you create a variable, you declare it. And you need a special word for that: let, var, or const. We'll discuss the use of these three arguments shortly. The second time you call a variable, you only use the name of the existing variable to assign it a new value:

```
let firstname = "Maria";
firstname = "Jacky";
```

In our examples, we will be assigning a value to our variables in the code. This is called "hardcoded" since the value of your variable is defined in your script instead of coming dynamically from some external input. This is something you won't be doing that often in actual code, as more commonly the value comes from an external source, such as an input box on a website that a user filled out, a database, or some other code that calls your code. The use of variables coming from external sources instead of being hardcoded into a script is actually the reason that scripts are adaptable to new information, without having to rewrite the code.

We have just established how powerful the variable building block is in code. Right now, we are going to hardcode variables into our scripts, and they therefore will not vary until a coder changes the program. However, we will soon learn how to make our variables take in values from outside sources.

let, var, and const

A variable definition consists of three parts: a variable-defining keyword (let, var, or const), a name, and a value. Let's start with the difference between let, var, or const. Here you can see some examples of variables using the different keywords:

```
let nr1 = 12;
var nr2 = 8;
const PI = 3.14159;
```

let and var are both used for variables that might have a new value assigned to them somewhere in the program. The difference between let and var is complex. It is related to scope.

 If you understand the following sentences on scope, that is great, but it is totally fine if you do not get it. You will understand it soon enough as you keep working your way through the book.

var has **global scope** and let has **block scope**. var's global scope means that you can use the variables defined with var in the entire script. On the other hand, let's block scope means you can only use variables defined with let in the specific block of code in which they were defined. Remember, a block of code will always start with { and end with }, which is how you can recognize them.

On the other hand, const is used for variables that only get a value assigned once—for example, the value of pi, which will not change. If you try reassigning a value declared with const, you will get an error:

```
const someConstant = 3;
someConstant = 4;
```

This will result in the following output:

```
Uncaught TypeError: Assignment to constant variable.
```

We will be using let in most of our examples—for now, trust us that you should use let in most cases.

Naming variables

When it comes to naming variables, there are some conventions in place:

- Variables start with a lowercase letter, and they should be descriptive. If something holds an age, do not call it x, but age. This way, when you read your script later, you can easily understand what you did by just reading your code.

- Variables cannot contain spaces, but they can use underscores. If you use a space, JavaScript doesn't recognize it as a single variable.

> We will be using camel case here. This means that when we want to use multiple words to describe a variable, we will start with a lowercase word, then use a capital for every new word after the first word—for example: ageOfBuyer.
>
> Whatever the convention is in the place you are working, the key is consistency. If all naming is done in a similar format, the code will look cleaner and more readable, which makes it a lot easier to make a small change later.

The value of your variable can be anything. Let's start with the easiest thing variables can be: primitives.

Primitive data types

Now you know what variables are and why we need them in our code, it is time to look at the different types of values we can store in variables. Variables get a value assigned. And these values can be of different types. JavaScript is a loosely typed language. This means that JavaScript determines the type based on the value. The type does not need to be named explicitly. For example, if you declared a value of 5, JavaScript will automatically define it as a number type.

A distinction exists between primitive data types and other, more complex data types. In this chapter, we will cover the primitive type, which is a relatively simple data structure. Let's say for now that they just contain a value and have a type. JavaScript has seven primitives: String, Number, BigInt, Boolean, Symbol, undefined, and null. We'll discuss each of them in more detail below.

String

A string is used to store a text value. It is a sequence of characters. There are different ways to declare a string:

- Double quotes
- Single quotes
- Backticks: special template strings in which you can use variables directly

The single and double quotes can both be used like so:

```
let singleString = 'Hi there!';
let doubleString = "How are you?";
```

 You can use the option you prefer, unless you are working on code in which one of these options has already been chosen. Again, consistency is key.

The main difference between single quotes and double quotes is that you can use single quotes as literal characters in double-quoted strings, and vice versa. If you declare a string with single quotes, the string will end as soon as a second quote is detected, even if it's in the middle of a word. So for example, the following will result in an error, because the string will be ended at the second single quote within let's:

```
let funActivity = 'Let's learn JavaScript';
```

Let will be recognized as a string, but after that, the bunch of characters that follow cannot be interpreted by JavaScript. However, if you declare the string using double quotes, it will not end the string as soon as it hits the single quote, because it is looking for another double quote. Therefore, this alternative will work fine:

```
let funActivity = "Let's learn JavaScript";
```

In the same way with double quotes, the following would not work:

```
let question = "Do you want to learn JavaScript? "Yes!"";
```

Again, the compiler will not distinguish between double quotes used in different contexts, and will output an error.

In a string using backticks, you can point to variables and the variable's value will be substituted into the line. You can see this in the following code snippet:

```
let language = "JavaScript";
let message = `Let's learn ${language}`;
console.log(message);
```

As you can see, you will have to specify these variables with a rather funky syntax—don't be intimidated! Variables in these template strings are specified between ${nameOfVariable}. The reason that it's such an intense syntax is that they want to avoid it being something you would normally use, which would make it unnecessarily difficult to do so. In our case, the console output would be as follows:

```
Let's learn JavaScript
```

As you can see, the language variable gets replaced with its value: JavaScript.

Escape characters

Say we want to have double quotes, single quotes, and backticks in our string. We would have a problem, as this cannot be done with just the ingredients we have now. There is an elegant solution to this problem. There is a special character that can be used to tell JavaScript, "do not take the next character as you normally would." This is the escape character, a backslash.

In this example, the backslash can be used to ensure your interpreter doesn't see the single or double quote marks and end either string too early:

```
let str = "Hello, what's your name? Is it \"Mike\"?";
console.log(str);
let str2 = 'Hello, what\'s your name? Is it "Mike"?';
console.log(str2);
```

This logs the following to the console:

```
Hello, what's your name? Is it "Mike"?
Hello, what's your name? Is it "Mike"?
```

As you can see, both types of quote marks inside the strings have been logged without throwing an error. This is because the backslash before the quote character gives the quote character a different meaning. In this case, the meaning is that it should be a literal character instead of an indicator to end the string.

The escape character has even more purposes. You can use it to create a line break with \n, or to include a backslash character in the text with \\:

```
let str3 = "New \nline.";
let str4 = "I'm containing a backslash: \\!";
console.log(str3);
console.log(str4);
```

The output of these lines is as follows:

```
New
line.
I'm containing a backslash: \!
```

There are some more options, but we will leave them for now. Let's get back to primitive data types by looking at the number type.

Number

The number data type is used to represent, well, numbers. In many languages, there is a very clear difference between different types of numbers. The developers of JavaScript decided to go for one data type for all these numbers: number. To be more precise, they decided to go for a 64-bit floating-point number. This means that it can store rather large numbers and both signed and unsigned numbers, numbers with decimals, and more.

However, there are different kinds of numbers it can represent. First of all, integers, for example: 4 or 89. But the number data type can also be used to represent decimals, exponentials, octal, hexadecimal, and binary numbers. The following code sample should speak for itself:

```
let intNr = 1;
let decNr = 1.5;
let expNr = 1.4e15;
let octNr = 0o10; //decimal version would be 8
let hexNr = 0x3E8; //decimal version would be 1000
let binNr = 0b101; //decimal version would be 5
```

You don't need to worry about these last three if you're not familiar with them. These are just different ways to represent numbers that you may encounter in the broader field of computer science. The takeaway here is that all the above numbers are of the number data type. So integers are numbers, like these ones:

```
let intNr2 = 3434;
let intNr3 = -111;
```

And the floating points are numbers as well, like this one:

```
let decNr2 = 45.78;
```

And binary numbers are of the number data type as well, for example, this one:

```
let binNr2 = 0b100; //decimal version would be 4
```

We have just seen the number data type, which is very commonly used. But in some special cases, you will need an even bigger number.

BigInt

The limits of the number data type are between $2^{53}-1$ and $-(2^{53}-1)$. In case you were to need a bigger (or smaller) number, BigInt comes into play. A BigInt data type can be recognized by the postfix n:

```
let bigNr = 90071992547409920n;
```

Let's see what happens when we start to do some calculations between our previously made integer Number, intNr, and BigInt, bigNr:

```
let result = bigNr + intNr;
```

The output will be as follows:

```
Uncaught TypeError: Cannot mix BigInt and other types, use explicit
conversions
```

Uh-oh, a TypeError! It is very clear about what is going wrong. We cannot mix BigInt with the Number data type to perform operations. This is something to keep in mind for later when actually working with BigInt—you can only operate on BigInt with other BigInts.

Boolean

The Boolean data type can hold two values: `true` and `false`. There is nothing in between. This Boolean is used a lot in code, especially expressions that evaluate to a Boolean:

```
let bool1 = false;
let bool2 = true;
```

In the preceding example, you can see the options we have for the Boolean data type. It is used for situations in which you want to store a `true` or a `false` value (which can indicate on/off or yes/no). For example, whether an element is deleted:

```
let objectIsDeleted = false;
```

Or, whether the light is on or off:

```
let lightIsOn = true;
```

These variables suggest respectively that the specified object is not deleted, and that the specific light is on.

Symbol

Symbol is a brand new data type introduced in ES6 (we mentioned ECMA Script 6, or ES6, in *Chapter 1, Getting Started with JavaScript*). Symbol can be used when it is important that variables are not equal, even though their value and type are the same (in this case, they would both be of the symbol type). Compare the following string declarations to the symbol declarations, all of equal value:

```
let str1 = "JavaScript is fun!";
let str2 = "JavaScript is fun!";
console.log("These two strings are the same:", str1 === str2);

let sym1 = Symbol("JavaScript is fun!");
let sym2 = Symbol("JavaScript is fun!");
console.log("These two Symbols are the same:", sym1 === sym2);
```

And the output:

```
These two strings are the same: true
These two Symbols are the same: false
```

In the first half, JavaScript concludes that the strings are the same. They have the same value, and the same type. However, in the second part, each symbol is unique. Therefore, although they contain the same string, they are not the same, and output `false` when compared. These symbol data types can be very handy as properties of objects, which we will see in *Chapter 3, JavaScript Multiple Values*.

Undefined

JavaScript is a very special language. It has a special data type for a variable that has not been assigned a value. And this data type is undefined:

```
let unassigned;
console.log(unassigned);
```

The output here will be:

```
Undefined
```

We can also purposefully assign an `undefined` value. It is important you know that it is possible, but it is even more important that you know that manually assigning undefined is a bad practice:

```
let terribleThingToDo = undefined;
```

Alright, this can be done, but it is recommended to not do this. This is for a number of reasons—for example, checking whether two variables are the same. If one variable is undefined, and your own variable is manually set to undefined, they will be considered equal. This is an issue because if you are checking for equality, you would want to know whether two values are actually equal, not just that they are both undefined. This way, someone's pet and their last name might be considered equal, whereas they are actually both just empty values.

null

In the last example, we saw an issue that can be solved with a final primitive type, null. null is a special value for saying that a variable is empty or has an unknown value. This is case sensitive. You should use lowercase for null:

```
let empty = null;
```

To solve the issue we encountered with setting a variable as undefined, note that if you set it to null, you will not have the same problem. This is one of the reasons it is better to assign null to a variable when you want to say it is empty and unknown at first:

```
let terribleThingToDo = undefined;
let lastName;
console.log("Same undefined:", lastName === terribleThingToDo);

let betterOption = null;
console.log("Same null:", lastName === betterOption);
```

This outputs the following:

```
Same undefined: true
Same null: false
```

This shows that an automatically undefined variable, lastName, and a deliberately undefined variable, terribleThingToDo, are considered equal, which is problematic. On the other hand, lastName and betterOption, which was explicitly declared with a value of null, are not equal.

Analyzing and modifying data types

We have seen the primitive data types. There are some built-in JavaScript methods that will help us deal with common problems related to primitives. Built-in methods are pieces of logic that can be used without having to write JavaScript logic yourself.

 We've seen one built-in method already: console.log().

There are many of these built-in methods, and the ones you will be meeting in this chapter are just the first few you will encounter.

Working out the type of a variable

Especially with null and undefined, it can be hard to determine what kind of data type you are dealing with. Let's have a look at typeof. This returns the type of the variable. You can check the type of a variable by entering typeof, then either a space followed by the variable in question, or the variable in question in brackets:

```
testVariable = 1;
variableTypeTest1 = typeof testVariable;
variableTypeTest2 = typeof(testVariable);
console.log(variableTypeTest1);
console.log(variableTypeTest2);
```

As you might assume, both methods will output number. Brackets aren't required because technically, typeof is an operator, not a method, unlike console.log. But, sometimes you may find that using brackets makes your code easier to read. Here you can see it in action:

```
let str = "Hello";
let nr = 7;
let bigNr = 12345678901234n;
let bool = true;
let sym = Symbol("unique");
let undef = undefined;
let unknown = null;

console.log("str", typeof str);
console.log("nr", typeof nr);
console.log("bigNr", typeof bigNr);
console.log("bool", typeof bool);
console.log("sym", typeof sym);
console.log("undef", typeof undef);
console.log("unknown", typeof unknown);
```

Here, in the same console.log() print command, we are printing the name of each variable (as a string, declared with double quotes), then its type (using typeof). This will produce the following output:

```
str string
nr number
bigNr bigint
bool boolean
```

```
sym symbol
undef undefined
unknown object
```

There is an odd one out, and that is the null type. In the output you can see that typeof null returns object, while in fact, null truly is a primitive and not an object. This is a bug that has been there since forever and now cannot be removed due to backward compatibility problems. Don't worry about this bug, as it won't affect our programs—just be aware of it, since it will go nowhere anytime soon, and it has the potential to break applications.

Converting data types

The variables in JavaScript can change types. Sometimes JavaScript does this automatically. What do you think the result of running the following code snippet will be?

```
let nr1 = 2;
let nr2 = "2";
console.log(nr1 * nr2);
```

We try to multiply a variable of type Number with a variable of type String. JavaScript does not just throw an error (as many languages would), but first tries to convert the string value to a number. If that can be done, it can execute without any problem as if two numbers were declared. In this case, console.log() will write 4 to the console.

But this is dangerous! Guess what this code snippet does:

```
let nr1 = 2;
let nr2 = "2";
console.log(nr1 + nr2);
```

This one will log 22. The plus sign can be used to concatenate strings. Therefore, instead of converting a string to a number, it is converting a number to a string in this example, and clubbing the two strings together—"2" and "2" make "22". Luckily, we do not need to rely on JavaScript's behavior when converting data types. There are built-in functions we can use to convert the data type of our variable.

There are three conversion methods: String(), Number(), and Boolean(). The first one converts a variable to type String. It pretty much takes any value, including undefined and null, and puts quotes around it.

The second one tries to convert a variable to a number. If that cannot be done logically, it will change the value into NaN (not a number). `Boolean()` converts a variable to a Boolean. This will be true for everything except for null, undefined, 0 (number), an empty string, and NaN. Let's see them in action:

```
let nrToStr = 6;
nrToStr = String(nrToStr);
console.log(nrToStr, typeof nrToStr);

let strToNr = "12";
strToNr = Number(strToNr);
console.log(strToNr, typeof strToNr);

let strToBool = "any string will return true";
strToBool = Boolean(strToBool);
console.log(strToBool, typeof strToBool);
```

This will log the following:

```
6 string
12 number
true boolean
```

This might seem pretty straightforward, but not all of the options are equally obvious. These, for example, are not what you might think:

```
let nullToNr = null;
nullToNr = Number(nullToNr);
console.log("null", nullToNr, typeof nullToNr);

let strToNr = "";
strToNr = Number(strToNr);
console.log("empty string", strToNr, typeof strToNr);
```

The preceding code snippet will log the following to the console:

```
null 0 number
empty string 0 number
```

As you can see, an empty string and null will both result in the number 0. This is a choice that the makers of JavaScript made, which you will have to know—it can come in handy at times when you want to convert a string to 0 when it is empty or null.

Next, enter the following snippet:

```
let strToNr2 = "hello";
strToNr2 = Number(strToNr2);
console.log(strToNr2, typeof strToNr2);
```

The result that will be logged to the console is:

```
NaN number
```

Here, we can see that anything that can't be interpreted as a number by simply removing the quotes will evaluate as NaN (not a number).

Let's continue with the following code:

```
let strToBool2 = "false";
strToBool2 = Boolean(strToBool2);
console.log(strToBool2, typeof strToBool2);

let strToBool = "";
strToBool = Boolean(strToBool);
console.log(strToBool, typeof strToBool);
```

Finally, this one will log the following:

```
true boolean
false boolean
```

This output shows that any string will return true when converted to a Boolean, even the string "false"! Only an empty string, null, and undefined will lead to a Boolean value of false.

Let's tease your brain a little bit more. What do you think this one will log?

```
let nr1 = 2;
let nr2 = "2";
console.log(nr1 + Number(nr2));
```

This one logs 4! The string gets converted to a number before it executes the plus operation, and therefore it is a mathematical operation and not a string concatenation. In the next sections of this chapter, we will discuss operators in more depth.

Practice exercise 2.1

What are the types of these variables listed below? Verify this with `typeof` and output the result to the console:

```
let str1 = 'Laurence';
let str2 = "Svekis";
let val1 = undefined;
let val2 = null;
let myNum = 1000;
```

Operators

After seeing quite a few data types and some ways to convert them, it is time for the next major building block: operators. These come in handy whenever we want to work with the variables, modify them, perform calculations on them, and compare them. They are called operators because we use them to operate on our variables.

Arithmetic operators

Arithmetic operators can be used to perform operations with numbers. Most of these operations will feel very natural to you because they are the basic mathematics you will have come across earlier in life already.

Addition

Addition in JavaScript is very simple, we have seen it already. We use + for this operation:

```
let nr1 = 12;
let nr2 = 14;
let result1 = nr1 + nr2;
```

However, this operator can also come in very handy for concatenating strings. Note the added space after "Hello" to ensure the end result contains space characters:

```
let str1 = "Hello ";
let str2 = "addition";
let result2 = str1 + str2;
```

The output of printing `result1` and `result2` will be as follows:

```
26
Hello addition
```

As you can see, adding numbers and strings lead to different results. If we add two different strings, it will concatenate them into a single string.

Practice exercise 2.2

Create a variable for your name, another one for your age, and another one for whether you can code JavaScript or not.

Log to the console the following sentence, where name, age and `true`/`false` are variables:

```
Hello, my name is Maaike, I am 29 years old and I can code JavaScript:
true.
```

Subtraction

Subtraction works as we would expect it as well. We use - for this operation. What do you think gets stored in the variable in this second example?

```
let nr1 = 20;
let nr2 = 4;
let str1 = "Hi";
let nr3 = 3;
let result1 = nr1 - nr2;
let result2 = str1 - nr3;
console.log(result1, result2);
```

The output is as follows:

```
16 NaN
```

The first result is 16. And the second result is more interesting. It gives NaN, not an error, but just simply the conclusion that a word and a number subtracted is not a number. Thanks for not crashing, JavaScript!

Multiplication

We can multiply two numeric values with the * character. Unlike some other languages, we cannot successfully multiply a number and a string in JavaScript.

The result of multiplying a numeric and a non-numeric value is NaN:

```javascript
let nr1 = 15;
let nr2 = 10;
let str1 = "Hi";
let nr3 = 3;
let result1 = nr1 * nr2;
let result2 = str1 * nr3;
console.log(result1, result2);
```

Output:

```
150 NaN
```

Division

Another straightforward operator is division. We can divide two numbers with the / character:

```javascript
let nr1 = 30;
let nr2 = 5;
let result1 = nr1 / nr2;
console.log(result1);
```

The output is as follows:

```
6
```

Exponentiation

Exponentiation means raising a certain base number to the power of the exponent, for example, x^y. This can be read as x to the power of y. It means that we will multiply x by itself y number of times. Here is an example of how to do this in JavaScript—we use ** for this operator:

```javascript
let nr1 = 2;
let nr2 = 3;
let result1 = nr1 ** nr2;
console.log(result1);
```

We get the following output:

```
8
```

The result of this operation is 2 to the power of 3 (2 * 2 * 2), which is 8. We're going to avoid going into a mathematics lesson here, but we can also find the root of a number by using fractional exponents: for example, the square root of a value is the same as raising it to the power of 0.5.

Modulus

This is one that often requires a little explanation. Modulus is the operation in which you determine how much is left after dividing a number by another number in its entirety. The amount of times the number can fit in the other number does not matter here. The outcome will be the remainder, or what is left over. The character we use for this operation is the % character. Here are some examples:

```
let nr1 = 10;
let nr2 = 3;
let result1 = nr1 % nr2;
console.log(`${nr1} % ${nr2} = ${result1}`);

let nr3 = 8;
let nr4 = 2;
let result2 = nr3 % nr4;
console.log(`${nr3} % ${nr4} = ${result2}`);

let nr5 = 15;
let nr6 = 4;
let result3 = nr5 % nr6;
console.log(`${nr5} % ${nr6} = ${result3}`);
```

And the output:

```
10 % 3 = 1
8 % 2 = 0
15 % 4 = 3
```

The first one is 10 % 3, where 3 fits 3 times into 10, and then 1 is left. The second one is 8 % 2. This results in 0, because 2 can fit 4 times into 8 without having anything left. The last one is 15 % 4, where 4 fits 3 times into 15. And then we have 3 left as a result.

This is something that would happen in your head automatically if I asked you to add 125 minutes to the current time. You will probably do two things: integer division to determine how many whole hours fit into 125 minutes, and then 125 modulo 60 (in JavaScript terms, 125 % 60) to conclude that you'll have to add 5 more minutes to the current time. Say our current time is 09:59, you will probably start by adding 2 hours, and get to 11:59, and then add 5 minutes, and then you will perform another modulus operation with 59 and 5, adding 1 more hour to the total and having 4 minutes left: 12:04.

Unary operators: increment and decrement

The last two operators of our arithmetic operator section are probably new to you, if you are new to programming (or only familiar with another programming language). These are the increment and decrement operators. A term we use here is **operand**. Operands are subject to the operator. So, if we say x + y, *x* and *y* are operands.

We only need one operand for these operators, and therefore we also call them unary operators. If we see x++, we can read this as $x = x + 1$. The same is true for the decrement operators: x-- can be read as $x = x - 1$:

```
let nr1 = 4;
nr1++;
console.log(nr1);

let nr2 = 4;
nr2--;
console.log(nr2);
```

The output is as follows:

```
5
3
```

Prefix and postfix operators

We can have the increment operator after the operand (x++), in which case we call this the **postfix unary operator**. We can also have it before (++x), which is the **prefix unary operator**. This does something different though—the next few lines might be complicated, so do not worry if you need to read it a few times and have a good look at the examples here.

The postfix gets executed after sending the variable through, and then after that, the operation gets executed. In the following example, nr gets incremented by 1 *after* logging. So the first logging statement is still logging the old value because it has not been updated yet. It has been updated for the second log statement:

```
let nr = 2;
console.log(nr++);
console.log(nr);
```

The output is as follows:

```
2
3
```

The prefix gets executed *before* sending the variable through, and often this is the one you will need. Have a look at the following example:

```
let nr = 2;
console.log(++nr);
```

We get the following output:

```
3
```

Alright, if you can figure out what the next code snippets logs to the console, you should really have a handle on it:

```
let nr1 = 4;
let nr2 = 5;
let nr3 = 2;
console.log(nr1++ + ++nr2 * nr3++);
```

It outputs 16. It will do the multiplication first, according to the basic mathematical order of operations. For multiplying, it uses 6 (prefix, so 5 is incremented before multiplying) and 2 (postfix, so 2 is only incremented after execution, meaning it won't affect our current calculation). This comes down to 12. And then nr1 is a postfix operator, so this one will execute after the addition. Therefore, it will add 12 to 4 and become 16.

Combining the operators

These operators can be combined, and it works just as it does in math. They get executed in a certain order, and not necessarily from left to right. This is due to a phenomenon called operator precedence.

There is one more thing to take into account here, and that is grouping. You can group using (and). The operations between the parentheses have the highest precedence. After that, the order of the operations takes place based on the type of operation (highest precedence first) and if they are of equal precedence, they take place from left to right:

Name	Symbol	Example
Grouping	(...)	(x + y)
Exponentiation	**	x ** y
Prefix increment and decrement	--, ++	--x, ++y
Multiplication, division, modulus	*, /, %	x * y, x / y, x % y
Addition and subtraction	+, -	x + y, x - y

Practice exercise 2.3

Write some code to calculate the hypotenuse of a triangle using the Pythagorean theorem when given the values of the other two sides. The theorem specifies that the relation between the sides of a right-angled triangle is $a^2 + b^2 = c^2$.

 The Pythagorean theorem only applies to right-angled triangles. The sides connected to the 90-degree angle are called the adjacent and opposite sides, represented by a and b in the formula. The longest side, not connected to the 90-degree angle, is called the hypotenuse, represented by c.

You can use `prompt()` to get the value for a and b. Write code to get the value from the user for a and b. Then square the values of both a and b before adding them together and finding the square root. Print your answer to the console.

Assignment operators

We have seen one assignment operator already when we were assigning values to variables. The character for this basic assignment operation is =. There are a few others available. Every binary arithmetic operator has a corresponding assignment operator to write a shorter piece of code. For example, x += 5 means $x = x + 5$, and x **= 3 means $x = x ** 3$ (x to the power of 3).

In this first example we declare a variable x, and set it to 2 as an initial value:

```
let x = 2;
x += 2;
```

After this assignment operation, the value of x becomes 4, because $x += 2$ is the same as $x = x + 2$:

In the next assignment operation, we will subtract 2:

```
x -= 2;
```

So, after this operation the value of x becomes 2 again ($x = x - 2$). In the next operation, we are going to multiply the value by 6:

```
x *= 6;
```

When this line has been executed, the value of x is no longer 2, but becomes 12 ($x = x * 6$). In the next line, we are going to use an assignment operator to perform a division:

```
x /= 3;
```

After dividing x by 3, the new value becomes 4. The next assignment operator we will use is exponentiation:

```
x **= 2;
```

The value of x becomes 16, because the old value was 4, and 4 to the power of 2 equals 16 (4 * 4). The last assignment operator we will talk about is the modulus assignment operator:

```
x %= 3;
```

After this assignment operation, the value of x is 1, because 3 can fit 5 times into 16 and then leaves 1.

Practice exercise 2.4

Create variables for three numbers: *a*, *b*, and *c*. Update these variables with the following actions using the assignment operators:

- Add *b* to *a*
- Divide *a* by *c*

- Replace the value of c with the modulus of *c* and *b*
- Print all three numbers to the console

Comparison operators

Comparison operators are different from the operators we have seen so far. The outcome of the comparison operators is always a Boolean, true, or false.

Equal

There are a few equality operators that determine whether two values are equal. They come in two flavors: equal value only, or equal value and data type. The first one returns true when the values are equal, even though the type is different, while the second returns true only when the value and the type are the same:

```
let x = 5;
let y = "5";
console.log(x == y);
```

The double equals operator, two equal signs, means that it will only check for equal value and not for data type. Both have the value 5, so it will log true to the console. This type of equality is sometimes called loose equality.

The triple equals operator, written as three equal signs, means that it will evaluate both the value and the data type to determine whether both sides are equal or not. They both need to be equal in order for this statement to be true, but they are not and therefore the following statement outputs false:

```
console.log(x === y);
```

This is sometimes also called strict equality. This triple equals operator is the one you should most commonly be using when you need to check for equality, as only with this one can you be sure that both variables are really equal.

Not equal

Not equal is very similar to equal, except it does the opposite—it returns true when two variables are not equal, and false when they are equal. We use the exclamation mark for not equal:

```
let x = 5;
let y = "5";
console.log(x != y);
```

This will log `false` to the console. If you are wondering what is going on here, take a look again at the double and triple equals operators, because it is the same here. However, when there is only one equals sign in a not-equal operator, it is comparing loosely for non-equality. Therefore, it concludes that they are equal and therefore not equal should result in false. The one with two equals signs is checking for strict non-equality:

```
console.log(x !== y);
```

This will conclude that since x and y have different data types, they are not the same, and will log `true` to the console.

Greater than and smaller than

The greater than operator returns true if the left-hand side is greater than the right-hand side of the operation. We use the > character for this. We also have a greater than or equal to operator, >=, which returns `true` if the left-hand side is greater than or equal to the right-hand side.

```
let x = 5;
let y = 6;
console.log(y > x);
```

This one will log `true`, because y is greater than x.

```
console.log(x > y);
```

Since x is not greater than y, this one will log `false`.

```
console.log(y > y);
```

y is not greater than y, so this one will log `false`.

```
console.log(y >= y);
```

This last one is looking at whether y is greater than or equal to y, and since it is equal to itself, it will log `true`.

It might not surprise you that we also have smaller than (<) and smaller than or equal to operators (<=). Let's have a look at the smaller than operator, as it is very similar to the previous ones.

```
console.log(y < x);
```

This first one will be `false`, since y is not smaller than x.

```
console.log(x < y);
```

So, this second one will log `true`, because x is smaller than y.

```
console.log(y < y);
```

y is not smaller than y, so this one will log `false`.

```
console.log(y <= y);
```

This last one looks at whether y is smaller than or equal to y. It is equal to y, so it will log `true`.

Logical operators

Whenever you want to check two conditions in one, or you need to negate a condition, the logical operators come in handy. You can use and, or, and not.

And

The first one we will have a look at is and. If you want to check whether x is greater than y and y is greater than z, you would need to be able to combine two expressions. This can be done with the && operator. It will only return `true` if both expressions are true:

```
let x = 1;
let y = 2;
let z = 3;
```

With these variables in mind, we are going to have a look at the logical operators:

```
console.log(x < y && y < z);
```

This will log `true`, you can read it like this: if x is smaller than y and y is smaller than z, it will log `true`. That is the case, so it will log `true`. The next example will log `false`:

```
console.log(x > y && y < z);
```

Since x is not greater than y, one part of the expression is not true, and therefore it will result in `false`.

Or

If you want to get true if either one of the expressions is true, you use or. The operator for this is ||. These pipes are used to see if either one of these two is true, in which case the whole expression evaluates to `true`. Let's have a look at the or operator in action:

```
console.log(x > y || y < z);
```

This will result in `true`, whereas it was `false` with `&&`. This is because only one of the two sides needs to be true in order for the whole expression to evaluate to `true`. This is the case because y is smaller than z.

When both sides are false, it will log `false`, which is the case in the next example:

```
console.log(x > y || y > z);
```

Not

In some cases you will have to negate a Boolean. This will make it the opposite value. It can be done with the exclamation mark, which reads as not:

```
let x = false;
console.log(!x);
```

This will log true, since it will simply flip the value of the Boolean. You can also negate an expression that evaluates to a Boolean, but you would have to make sure that the expression gets evaluated first by grouping it.

```
let x = 1;
let y = 2;
console.log(!(x < y));
```

x is smaller than y, so the expression evaluates to `true`. But, it gets negated due to the exclamation mark and prints `false` to the console.

Chapter project

Miles-to-kilometers converter

Create a variable that contains a value in miles, convert it to kilometers, and log the value in kilometers in the following format:

```
The distance of 130 kms is equal to 209.2142 miles
```

For reference, 1 mile equals 1.60934 kilometers.

BMI calculator

Set values for height in inches and weight in pounds, then convert the values to centimeters and kilos, outputting the results to the console:

- 1 inch is equal to 2.54 cm
- 2.2046 pounds is equal to 1 kilo

Output the results. Then, calculate and log the BMI: this is equal to weight (in kilos) divided by squared height (in meters). Output the results to the console.

Self-check quiz

1. What data type is the following variable?

   ```
   const c = "5";
   ```

2. What data type is the following variable?

   ```
   const c = 91;
   ```

3. Which one is generally better, line 1 or line 2?

   ```
   let empty1 = undefined; //line 1
   let empty2 = null; //line 2
   ```

4. What is the console output for the following?

   ```
   let a = "Hello";
   a = "world";
   console.log(a);
   ```

5. What will be logged to the console?

   ```
   let a = "world";
   let b = `Hello ${a}!`;
   console.log(b);
   ```

6. What is the value of a?

   ```
   let a = "Hello";
   a = prompt("world");
   console.log(a);
   ```

7. What is the value of b output to the console?

```
let a = 5;
let b = 70;
let c = "5";
b++;
console.log(b);
```

8. What is the value of result?

```
let result = 3 + 4 * 2 / 8;
```

9. What is the value of total and total2?

```
let firstNum = 5;
let secondNum = 10;
firstNum++;
secondNum--;
let total = ++firstNum + secondNum;
console.log(total);
let total2 = 500 + 100 / 5 + total--;
console.log(total2);
```

10. What is logged to the console here?

```
const a = 5;
const b = 10;
console.log(a > 0 && b > 0);
console.log(a == 5 && b == 4);
console.log(true ||false);
console.log(a == 3 || b == 10);
console.log(a == 3 || b == 7);
```

Summary

In this chapter, we dealt with the first two programming building blocks: variables and operators. Variables are special fields that have a name and contain values. We declare a variable by using one of the special variable-defining words: let, var, or const. Variables enable us to make our scripts dynamic, store values, access them later, and change them later. We discussed some primitive data types, including strings, numbers, Booleans, and Symbols, as well as more abstract types such as undefined and null. You learned how to determine the type of a variable using the typeof word. And you saw how you can convert the data type by using the built-in JavaScript methods Number(), String(), and Boolean().

Then we moved on and discussed operators. Operators enable us to work with our variables. They can be used to perform calculations, compare variables, and more. The operators we discussed included arithmetic operators, assignment operators, comparison operators, and logical operators.

After this chapter, you are ready to deal with more complex data types, such as arrays and objects. We'll cover these in the next chapter.

Join our book's Discord space

Join the book's Discord workspace for a monthly *Ask me Anything* session with the authors: https://packt.link/JSBook

3
JavaScript Multiple Values

The basic data types have been dealt with in the previous chapter. Now it's time to look at a slightly more complicated topic: arrays and objects. In the previous chapter, you saw variables that held just a single value. To allow for more complex programming, objects and arrays can contain multiple values.

You can look at objects as a collection of properties and methods. Properties can be thought of as variables. They can be simple data structures such as numbers and strings, but also other objects. Methods perform actions; they contain a certain number of lines of code that will be executed when the method gets called. We'll explain methods in more detail later in this book and focus on properties for now. An example of an object can be a real-life object, for example, a dog. It has properties, such as name, weight, color, and breed.

We will also discuss arrays. An array is a type of object, which allows you to store multiple values. They are a bit like lists. So, you could have an array of items to buy at the grocery store, which might contain the following values: apples, eggs, and bread. This list would take the form of a single variable, holding multiple values.

Along the way, we will cover the following topics:

- Arrays and their properties
- Array methods
- Multidimensional arrays
- Objects in JavaScript
- Working with objects and arrays

Let's start with arrays.

 Note: exercise, project and self-check quiz answers can be found in the *Appendix*.

Arrays and their properties

Arrays are lists of values. These values can be of all data types and one array can even contain different data types. It is often very useful to store multiple values inside one variable; for example, a list of students, groceries, or test scores. Once you start writing scripts, you'll find yourself needing to write arrays very often; for example, when you want to keep track of all the user input, or when you want to have a list of options to present to the user.

Creating arrays

You might be convinced by now that arrays are great, so let's see how we can make them. There is actually a right way and a wrong way to do it. Here are both. Which one do you think is the right one?

```
arr1 = new Array("purple", "green", "yellow");
arr2 = ["black", "orange", "pink"];
```

If you guessed the second option, using square brackets, you are right. This is the best and most readable way to create a new array. On the other hand, the first option can do unexpected things. Look at both lines of code here. What do you think they will do?

```
arr3 = new Array(10);
arr4 = [10];
```

Probably, you sense that something is up here. They do not both create an array with one value, 10. The second one, arr4, does. The first option creates an array with 10 undefined values. If we log the values like this:

```
console.log(arr3);
console.log(arr4);
```

Here is what it logs:

```
[ <10 empty items> ]
[ 10 ]
```

Thanks, JavaScript! That was very helpful. So, unless that is what you need to do, please use the square brackets!

As I already mentioned, we can have mixed arrays and arrays can hold any type of variable. The values of the array won't be converted to a single data type or anything like that. JavaScript simply stores all the variables with their own data type and value in the array:

```
let arr = ["hi there", 5, true];
console.log(typeof arr[0]);
console.log(typeof arr[1]);
console.log(typeof arr[2]);
```

This will output to the console:

```
string
number
boolean
```

The last array fun fact we will go over here is what happens if you define an array using const. You can change the values of a constant array, but you cannot change the array itself. Here is a piece of code to demonstrate:

```
const arr = ["hi there"];
arr[0] = "new value";
console.log(arr[0]);

arr = ["nope, now you are overwriting the array"];
```

The new value for the first element of the array is going fine, but you cannot assign a new value to the full array. Here is what it will output:

```
new value
TypeError: Assignment to constant variable.
```

Accessing elements

This beautiful array we just made would become much more powerful if we could access its elements. We can do this by referencing the array's index. This is something we did not specify when we created the array, and we did not need to either. JavaScript assigns an index to every value of the array. The first value is assigned the position of 0, the second 1, the third 2, and so on. If we want to call a specific value based on its position in the array, we can use the name of our array, add square brackets to the end, and put the index we want to access between the square brackets, like this:

```
cars = ["Toyota", "Renault", "Volkswagen"];
console.log(cars[0]);
```

This log statement will write Toyota to the console because we called for the position 0 of the array, which outputs the first value in the list.

```
console.log(cars[1]);
```

Calling index position 1 is giving us the second element in the array, which is Renault. This will be logged to the console.

```
console.log(cars[2]);
```

The third element in our array has index 2, so this one will log Volkswagen. What do you think will happen if we use a negative index or an index that is higher than the number of values we get?

```
console.log(cars[3]);
console.log(cars[-1]);
```

We didn't assign a value to the negative or non-existent index, so when we ask for it, the value is undefined. As such, the log output will be undefined. JavaScript does not throw an error because of this.

Overwriting elements

The elements in an array can be overwritten. This can be done by accessing a certain element using the index and assigning a new value:

```
cars[0] = "Tesla";
console.log(cars[0]);
```

The output of this log is Tesla because it has overwritten the old value, Toyota. If we output the whole array:

```
console.log(cars);
```

It will output the following:

```
[ 'Tesla', 'Renault', 'Volkswagen' ]
```

What happens if you try to overwrite an element that does not exist?

```
cars[3] = "Kia";
```

Or even a negative index?

```
cars[-1] = "Fiat";
```

Let's see what happens when we try to write the values to the console:

```
console.log(cars[3]);
console.log(cars[-1]);
```

And the output:

```
Kia
Fiat
```

Ha! They suddenly exist. How is that you may wonder? We will discuss this in the next section. For now, just remember that this is not the right way to add values to the array. We will discuss the right way when we explain arrays in the *Array methods* section.

Built-in length property

Arrays have a very useful built-in property: length. This will return the number of values that the array has:

```
colors = ["black", "orange", "pink"]
booleans = [true, false, false, true];
emptyArray = [];

console.log("Length of colors:", colors.length);
console.log("Length of booleans:", booleans.length);
console.log("Length of empty array:", emptyArray.length);
```

The first `console.log` call returns 3, indicating that the colors array contains 3 values. The second one returns 4, and the last one is an empty array with a length of 0:

```
Length of colors: 3
Length of booleans: 4
Length of empty array: 0
```

So, be aware that the length is one higher than the maximum index because the index of the array starts at 0, but when determining the length, we look at the number of elements and there are four separate elements. This is why the maximum index is 3 when the length is 4. Hence, the positional value of the last element in the array will be one fewer than the total number of elements.

Take a moment and try to figure out how you can use the length to access the last element of the array:

```
lastElement = colors[colors.length - 1];
```

You get the highest index by subtracting 1 from the length because, as you know, arrays are zero-indexed. So, the positional value of the last element in the array will be one fewer than the total number of elements.

So, this might seem pretty straightforward. Remember the non-existent index position we called in the previous section? Let's see what happens in this example:

```
numbers = [12, 24, 36];
numbers[5] = 48;
console.log(numbers.length);
```

The length of the array is only counting the integer numbers starting from 0 up to the highest filled index. If there are elements in the middle of the sequence that do not have a value, they will still get counted. In this case, the length becomes 6. If we log the array, we can see why:

```
console.log("numbers", numbers);
```

The output will be as follows:

```
numbers [ 12, 24, 36, <2 empty items>, 48 ]
```

Because we added an element, 48, at index 5, it also created 2 elements at index positions 3 and 4 containing empty values. For now, let's have a look at array methods and find out the right way to add to an array.

Practice exercise 3.1

1. Create an array to use as your shopping list with 3 items: "Milk," "Bread," and "Apples."
2. Check your list length in the console.
3. Update "Bread" to "Bananas."
4. Output your entire list to the console.

Array methods

We have just seen the built-in length property. We also have a few built-in methods. Methods are functions on a certain object. Instead of holding a value, like properties, they perform actions. We will cover functions in-depth in *Chapter 6, Functions*. For now, all you need to know is that you can call methods and functions, and when you do, some code that is specified inside that function gets executed.

We just accidentally saw we could add elements using new indices. This is not the proper way to do it as it is easy to make mistakes and accidentally overwrite a certain value or skip a certain index. The right way is to do this with a special method. Similarly, we can also delete elements and sort the elements in the array.

Adding and replacing elements

We can add elements with the push() method:

```
favoriteFruits = ["grapefruit", "orange", "lemon"];
favoriteFruits.push("tangerine");
```

The value gets added to the end of the array. The push method returns the new length of the array, four in this case. You can store this length in a variable like this:

```
let lengthOfFavoriteFruits = favoriteFruits.push("lime");
```

The value 5 gets stored in the lengthOfFavoriteFruits variable. If we log our array, favoriteFruits, like this:

```
console.log(favoriteFruits);
```

Here is the new array:

```
[ 'grapefruit', 'orange', 'lemon', 'tangerine', 'lime' ]
```

This was easy right? But what if you would want to add elements at a certain index? You can use the `splice()` method. This one is slightly more difficult:

```
let arrOfShapes = ["circle", "triangle", "rectangle", "pentagon"];
arrOfShapes.splice(2, 0, "square", "trapezoid");
console.log(arrOfShapes);
```

After this, the output containing the array is as follows:

```
[
  'circle',
  'triangle',
  'square',
  'trapezoid',
  'rectangle',
  'pentagon'
]
```

First, let's point out the different layouts of this output. This might depend on the interpreter you are using, but at some point, it will decide it is too long for a single line and apply an automatic format to the array to make it more readable. It doesn't change the value of the array; it is just a different representation of the same values were they to be on a single line.

As you can see, the square and trapezoid get inserted on index 2. The rest of the array is shifting to the right. The `splice()` method takes multiple parameters. The first parameter, 2 in our case, is the index of the array on which we want to start inserting. The second parameter, 0 in our case, is the number of elements we want to delete starting at our previously defined starting index. The parameters after these first two, square and trapezoid in our case, are whatever should be inserted starting at the start index.

So, had we said this instead:

```
arrOfShapes.splice(2, 2, "square", "trapezoid");
console.log(arrOfShapes);
```

It would have replaced the elements rectangle and pentagon and added square and trapezoid in their place, as follows:

```
[ 'circle', 'triangle', 'square', 'trapezoid' ]
```

If you were to increase the second parameter to a number higher than our array, it would not affect the result as JavaScript would simply stop as soon as it runs out of values to delete. Try the following code:

```
arrOfShapes.splice(2, 12, "square", "trapezoid");
console.log(arrOfShapes);
```

This would also have had this output:

```
[ 'circle', 'triangle', 'square', 'trapezoid' ]
```

You can also add another array to your array. This can be done with the `concat()` method. This way, you can create a new array that consists of a concatenation of both arrays. The elements of the first array will be first, and the elements of the argument of `concat()` will be concatenated to the end:

```
let arr5 = [1, 2, 3];
let arr6 = [4, 5, 6];
let arr7 = arr5.concat(arr6);
console.log(arr7);
```

And here is the output:

```
[ 1, 2, 3, 4, 5, 6 ]
```

This `concat()` method can do even more! We can use it to add values as well. We can add a single value, or we can comma-separate multiple values:

```
let arr8 = arr7.concat(7, 8, 9);
console.log(arr8);
```

The new value of the array will be as follows:

```
[ 1, 2, 3, 4, 5, 6, 7, 8, 9 ]
```

Deleting elements

There are several ways in which you can delete elements from an array. Removing the last element is done with `pop()`:

```
arr8.pop();
```

Logging the array after executing pop() results in this:

```
[ 1, 2, 3, 4,   5, 6, 7, 8 ]
```

Deleting the first element can be done with shift(). This causes all other indices to be reduced by one:

```
arr8.shift();
```

The new array will be:

```
[ 2, 3, 4, 5,   6, 7, 8 ]
```

Remember splice()? This is a very special method because we can also use it to delete values. We specify the index from where we want to start deleting, and then the number of elements we want to delete.

```
arr8.splice(1, 3);
```

After this, the value of the array is as follows:

```
[ 2, 6, 7, 8 ]
```

As you can see, 3 elements starting from the second positional index have been deleted. The values 3, 4, and 5 are gone. If you do not wish to change any of the later indices, you can also use the operator delete. This is not a method, but you can use it to change the value of a certain position of the array to undefined:

```
delete arr8[0];
```

The array then becomes:

```
[ <1 empty item>, 6, 7, 8 ]
```

This is useful when you are relying on index or length for some reason. For example, if you are keeping user input, and you want to determine the number of user inputs based on an array that the user is pushing to, deleting would decrease the number of inputs, whereas that might not be what you would want.

Finding elements

If you want to check whether a value is present in an array, you can use the find() method. What will go in the find() method is somewhat different. It is actually a function. This function will be executed on every element in the array until it finds a match, and if it does not, then it will return undefined.

Do not worry if this is too difficult for now; it will become clear soon enough. We are writing the function in two different ways in the following code snippet. They are actually doing the same, except that the first one is checking for an element being equal to 6, and the second for an element being equal to 10:

```
arr8 = [ 2, 6, 7, 8 ];
let findValue = arr8.find(function(e) { return e === 6});
let findValue2 = arr8.find(e => e === 10);
console.log(findValue, findValue2);
```

The log statement will log 6 and undefined because it can find an element that matches for 6, but not one that matches for 10.

A function can take a certain input. In this case, it takes the element of the array as an input. When the element of the array equals 6 (findValue) or 10 (findValue2), it returns the element. In *Chapter 6, Functions*, we will cover functions in much more detail. It is a lot for a beginner to take in, so you can review this a bit later if it is unclear for now.

Often, you do not only want to find the element, but you want to know what position it is on. This can be done with the indexOf() method. This method returns the index on which the value is found. If a value occurs in an array more than once, it will return the first occurrence. If the value is not found, it will return -1:

```
arr8 = [ 2, 6, 7, 8 ];
let findIndex = arr8.indexOf(6);
let findIndex2 = arr8.indexOf(10);
console.log(findIndex, findIndex2);
```

So, the first one will return 1 since that is the index position of 6 in the array. The second one will return -1 because the array does not contain 10.

If you want to find the next occurrence of the specified number, you can add a second argument to indexOf(), specifying from which position it should start searching:

```
arr8 = [ 2, 6, 7, 8 ];
let findIndex3 = arr8.indexOf(6, 2);
```

In this case, the value of findIndex3 will be -1, because 6 cannot be found starting from index 2.

The last occurrence can also be found. This is done with the `lastIndexOf()` method:

```
let animals = ["dog", "horse", "cat", "platypus", "dog"];
let lastDog = animals.lastIndexOf("dog");
```

The value of `lastDog` will be 4 because that is the last occurrence of `dog` in the array.

Sorting

There is also a built-in method for sorting arrays. It sorts numbers from small to high and strings A-Z. You can call `sort()` on an array and the order of the values of the array will change to a sorted order:

```
let names = ["James", "Alicia", "Fatiha", "Maria", "Bert"];
names.sort();
```

The value of names after sorting is as follows:

```
[ 'Alicia', 'Bert', 'Fatiha', 'James', 'Maria' ]
```

As you can see, the array is now sorted alphabetically. For numbers, it is sorting them in ascending order, as you can see in the following code snippet:

```
let ages = [18, 72, 33, 56, 40];
ages.sort();
```

After executing this `sort()` method, the value of ages is:

```
[ 18, 33, 40, 56, 72 ]
```

Reversing

The elements of the array can be reversed by calling the built-in method, `reverse()`, on an array. It puts the last element first, and the first element last. It does not matter whether the array is sorted or not; it just reverses the order.

The value of names before reversing is as follows:

```
[ 'Alicia', 'Bert', 'Fatiha', 'James', 'Maria' ]
```

Now we are going to call the `reverse()` method:

```
names.reverse();
```

The new order will be:

```
[ 'Maria', 'James', 'Fatiha', 'Bert', 'Alicia' ]
```

Practice exercise 3.2

1. Create an empty array to use as a shopping list.
2. Add Milk, Bread, and Apples to your list.
3. Update "Bread" with Bananas and Eggs.
4. Remove the last item from the array and output it into the console.
5. Sort the list alphabetically.
6. Find and output the index value of Milk.
7. After Bananas, add Carrots and Lettuce.
8. Create a new list containing Juice and Pop.
9. Combine both lists, adding the new list twice to the end of the first list.
10. Get the last index value of Pop and output it to the console.
11. Your final list should look like this:

```
["Bananas", "Carrots", "Lettuce", "Eggs", "Milk", "Juice",
"Pop", "Juice", "Pop"]
```

Multidimensional arrays

Earlier, we established already that arrays can contain any data type. This means that arrays can also contain other arrays (which, in turn, can contain… other arrays!). This is called a multidimensional array. It sounds complicated, but it is just an array of arrays: a list of lists:

```
let someValues1 = [1, 2, 3];
let someValues2 = [4, 5, 6];
let someValues3 = [7, 8, 9];

let arrOfArrays = [someValues1, someValues2, someValues3];
```

So, we can create an array of already existing arrays. This is called a two-dimensional array. We can write it like this:

```
let arrOfArrays2 = [[1, 2, 3], [4, 5, 6], [7, 8, 9]];
```

If you want to access elements of the inner arrays, you will have to specify an index twice:

```
let value1 = arrOfArrays[0][1];
```

The statement will grab the first array because it has an index position of 0. From this first array, it will take the second value, because it has an index position of 1. Then it stores this value in value1. That means the value of value1 will be 2. Can you figure out what the value of the next one will be?

```
let value2 = arrOfArrays[2][2];
```

It takes the third array, and from this third array, it takes the third value. Thus, 9 will be stored in value2. And it does not stop here; it can go many levels deep. Let's show that by creating an array of our array of arrays. We are simply going to store this array three times in another array:

```
arrOfArraysOfArrays = [arrOfArrays, arrOfArrays, arrOfArrays];
```

This is what the array looks like in terms of values:

```
[
    [ [ 1, 2, 3 ], [ 4, 5, 6 ], [ 7, 8, 9 ] ],
    [ [ 1, 2, 3 ], [ 4, 5, 6 ], [ 7, 8, 9 ] ],
    [ [ 1, 2, 3 ], [ 4, 5, 6 ], [ 7, 8, 9 ] ]
]
```

Let's get the middle element of this array, which is the value 5, belonging to the second array of arrays. It is done like this:

```
let middleValue = arrOfArraysOfArrays[1][1][1];
```

The first step is to get the second array of arrays, so index 1. Then we need to get the second array of this one, which again is index 1. Now we reach the level of the values, and we need the second value, so again we use index 1. This is useful in many situations, for example, when you want to work with matrices.

Practice exercise 3.3

1. Create an array containing three values: 1, 2, and 3.
2. Nest the original array into a new array three times.
3. Output the value 2 from one of the arrays into the console.

Objects in JavaScript

Now it is time to have a look at another complex data structure that can contain more than one value: objects! Objects are very useful and can be used to describe real-life objects as well as more complex abstract concepts that allow for more flexibility in your code.

Secretly, you have just been introduced to objects already, because arrays are a very special type of object. Arrays are objects with indexed properties. All the other objects, and also the objects we will see here, are objects with named properties. This means that instead of an automatically generated index number, we will give it a custom descriptive name.

As we can tell from the following code, arrays are defined by JavaScript as being of the object type:

```
let arr = [0, 1, 2];
console.log(typeof arr);
```

The output of the preceding code is as follows:

```
Object
```

Objects are not too dissimilar to real-world objects. They *have* properties and they *can perform* actions, methods. Here, we will only deal with the properties. We will cover methods in *Chapter 7, Classes*, after we have seen functions. An object is a chance to group multiple variables into one. This is done with curly brackets: { and }. Let's have a look at this object of a dog here:

```
let dog = { dogName: "JavaScript",
            weight: 2.4,
            color: "brown",
            breed: "chihuahua",
            age: 3,
            burglarBiter: true
          };
```

We created a variable, dog, and we gave this an object as a value. We can recognize that this is an object by seeing the { and }. In between the curly braces, we see a bunch of properties and their values.

If you have ever wondered whether something should be a property, just try the following template sentence in your head:

objectname has a(n) *property name*

For example, a dog has a name, a dog has a color, and a dog has a weight. This is slightly different for the Boolean properties, for which you can use "is" or "is not" instead of "has".

We can access the properties of this object in a very similar way as we would with the array. This time, we are not using the index number, but the name of the property, to get the value:

```
let dogColor1 = dog["color"];
```

There is another way to do this. Instead of the square brackets, the property name can also be added to the object name with a dot in between:

```
let dogColor2 = dog.color;
```

This might look familiar. Do you remember how we got the length of an array with the built-in property length? Yes—the same way! The difference between properties and methods is the lack of parentheses for properties.

Updating objects

We can change the value of the properties of the objects. Again, this is similar to an array because an array is an object as well, but for properties, we have two options:

```
dog["color"] = "blue";
dog.weight = 2.3;
```

This has changed the properties of our chihuahua JavaScript. The color gets updated to blue and it has lost a little bit of weight since the new weight is 0.1 lower. So if we log our dog:

```
console.log(dog);
```

We will get the following:

```
{
    dogName: 'JavaScript',
    weight: 2.3,
    color: 'blue',
```

```
  breed: 'chihuahua',
  age: 3,
  burglarBiter: true
}
```

It's useful to note that if we change the data type of one of our properties, for example:

```
dog["age"] = "three";
```

This is not a problem. JavaScript will just change the whole value and data type to the new situation.

Another element to note is that we are now using the literal string values to refer to the object's properties, but we can also work with variables to achieve this. So, for example:

```
let variable = "age";
console.log(dog[variable]);
```

This will still output three, as we just changed the value of age to three. If we change the value of the variable to another dog property, we will be accessing another property, like this:

```
variable = "breed";
console.log(dog[variable]);
```

This will print chihuahua. And when we update the value accessing this way, it is the exact same as when we would have accessed it with the literal string:

```
dog[variable] = "dachshund";
console.log(dog["breed"]);
```

So, this will log dachshund to the console.

Practice exercise 3.4

1. Create a new myCar object for a car. Add some properties, including, but not limited to, make and model, and values for a typical car or your car. Feel free to use booleans, strings, or numbers.

2. Create a variable that can hold the string value `color`. This variable containing a string value color can now be used to reference the property name within `myCar`. Then, use the variable within the square bracket notation to assign a new value to the color property in `myCar`.

3. Use that same variable and assign a new property string value to it, such as `forSale`. Use the bracket notation once again to assign a new value to the `forSale` property to indicate whether the car is available for purchase.

4. Output `make` and `model` into the console.

5. Output the value of `forSale` into the console.

Working with objects and arrays

When working with objects and arrays, you will see these often combined. In the last section of this chapter, we will deal with combining objects and arrays, and also objects inside objects.

Objects in objects

Let's say we want to have an object for a company. This company will have an address. And an address is another object. If we give our company an address, we are using an object inside an object:

```
let company = { companyName: "Healthy Candy",
            activity: "food manufacturing",
            address: {
                street: "2nd street",
                number: "123",
                zipcode: "33116",
                city: "Miami",
                state: "Florida"
            },
            yearOfEstablishment: 2021
        };
```

As you can see, our company object has an address object with values. This can go very many levels deep if necessary.

To access or modify one of the properties of the address here, we can use two approaches:

```
company.address.zipcode = "33117";
company["address"]["number"] = "100";
```

As you can see, this is very similar to the array. We first need to select the address and then do the same thing to access the property we want to change.

Arrays in objects

Our company might have a range of activities instead of one. We can simply replace the activity from our previous sample with an array:

```
company = { companyName: "Healthy Candy",
            activities: ["food manufacturing",
"improving kids' health", "manufacturing toys"],
            address: {
                street: "2nd street",
                number: "123",
                zipcode: "33116",
                city: "Miami",
                state: "Florida"
            },
            yearOfEstablishment: 2021
        };
```

We have now used an array in our company object. You can simply use an array with the square braces after the property. Retrieving the individual values is very similar. The second value of the activities array can be fetched using this statement:

```
let activity = company.activities[1];
```

Here, we call the object we're interested in, company, then the relevant array, activities, with reference to the index position of the variable we're looking for within the array, which is 1.

Objects in arrays

It is very possible that instead of one address, our company has a list of addresses. We can accomplish this by creating an array of address objects. In this case, we will create an array of two:

```
let addresses = [{
    street: "2nd street",
    number: "123",
    zipcode: "33116",
    city: "Miami",
    state: "Florida"
},
{
    street: "1st West avenue",
    number: "5",
    zipcode: "75001",
    city: "Addison",
    state: "Texas"
}];
```

So, the arrays can be recognized by the square brackets and the objects by the curly brackets. The street name of the first object can be fetched using this statement:

```
let streetName = addresses[0].street;
```

Here, we call the array we're interested in, `addresses`, with reference to the index position of the object we're looking for within the array, `0`, and then the required variable from within the object, which is `street`. This may seem complicated, but you may notice that this simply reverses the syntax required to retrieve a variable from an array inside an object from the previous section. It's worth practicing calling variables from nested arrays and objects until you're comfortable with it!

Objects in arrays in objects

Just to show that this can go as many levels as we would need, we are going to give our company object an array of address objects. So, let's add this array of address objects to our company object. This way, our company has an array of addresses:

```
company = { companyName: "Healthy Candy",
                activities: [ "food manufacturing",
 "improving kids' health",
```

```
"manufacturing toys"],
                  address: [{
                      street: "2nd street",
                      number: "123",
                      zipcode: "33116",
                      city: "Miami",
                      state: "Florida"
                  },
                  {
                      street: "1st West avenue",
                      number: "5",
                      zipcode: "75001",
                      city: "Addison",
                      state: "Texas"
                  }],
                  yearOfEstablishment: 2021
              };
```

To access elements of increasingly nested objects and arrays, we simply extend the same logic you have seen in the previous sections. To access the street name of Healthy Candy's first address, we can use the following code:

```
let streetName = company.address[0].street;
```

As you see, we can stack object and array element requests indefinitely.

We will not make it any more complicated than this for now. Whenever you need a list of something, you will be using an array. Whenever you want to represent something with properties that have descriptive names, it is better to use an object. Just remember that object properties can be of any type.

Practice exercise 3.5

1. Create an object named `people` that contains an empty array that is called `friends`.

2. Create three variables, each containing an object, that contain one of your friend's first names, last names, and an ID value.

3. Add the three friends to the `friend` array.

4. Output it to the console.

Chapter projects

Manipulating an array

Take the following array:

```
const theList = ['Laurence', 'Svekis', true, 35, null, undefined,
{test: 'one', score: 55}, ['one', 'two']];
```

Manipulate your array using various methods, such as pop(), push(), shift(), and unshift(), and transform it into the following:

```
["FIRST", "Svekis", "MIDDLE", "hello World", "LAST"]
```

You can take the following steps, or adopt your own approach:

- Remove the first item and the last item.
- Add FIRST to the start of the array.
- Assign hello World to the fourth item value.
- Assign MIDDLE to the third index value.
- Add LAST to the last position in the array.
- Output it to the console.

Company product catalog

In this project, you will implement a data structure for a product catalog and create queries to retrieve data.

1. Create an array to hold an inventory of store items.
2. Create three items, each having the properties of name, model, cost, and quantity.
3. Add all three objects to the main array using an array method, and then log the inventory array to the console.
4. Access the quantity element of your third item, and log it to the console. Experiment by adding and accessing more elements within your data structure.

Self-check quiz

1. Can you use `const` and update values within an array?

2. Which property in an array gives the number of items contained in the array?

3. What is the output in the console?

```
const myArr1 = [1,3,5,6,8,9,15];
console.log(myArr1.indexOf(0));
console.log(myArr1.indexOf(3));
```

4. How do you replace the second element in an array `myArr = [1,3,5,6,8,9,15]` with the value 4?

5. What is the output in the console?

```
const myArr2 = [];
myArr2[10] = 'test'
console.log(myArr2);
console.log(myArr2[2]);
```

6. What is the output in the console?

```
const myArr3 = [3,6,8,9,3,55,553,434];
myArr3.sort();
myArr3.length = 0;
console.log(myArr3[0]);
```

Summary

So, in this chapter, we have seen arrays and objects. Arrays are a list of values. These could be values of the same type, but also values of different types. Every element of the array gets an index. The index of the first element is 0. We can access the elements of the array using this index. We can also use this index to change and delete the element.

We then saw that it is also possible to have arrays containing other arrays; these are multidimensional arrays. To access the elements of a multidimensional array, you would need to use as many indices as you have nested arrays.

Then, we covered objects and learned that arrays are a special kind of object. Objects contain properties and methods. We looked at the properties of objects and saw that these properties are given a name and can be accessed and modified using this name.

We ended this module by looking at how arrays can contain objects, and how objects can contain arrays and more. This enables us to create complex object structures, which will be of great use in designing real-life applications.

Join our book's Discord space

Join the book's Discord workspace for a monthly *Ask me Anything* session with the authors: https://packt.link/JSBook

4
Logic Statements

Up to this point, our code has been rather static. It will do the same thing every time we execute it. In this chapter, that is all going to change. We will be dealing with logical statements. Logical statements allow us to make multiple paths in our code. Depending on the outcome of a certain expression, we will follow one code path or another.

There are different logic statements, and we will go over them in this chapter. We will start with if and if else statements. After that, we will be dealing with the ternary operator, and the final one we will be dealing with is the switch statement.

Along the way, we will cover the following topics:

- if and if else statements
- else if statements
- Conditional ternary operators
- switch statements

Note: exercise, project and self-check quiz answers can be found in the *Appendix*.

if and if else statements

We can make decisions in our code using if and if else statements. It is very much like this template:

if *some condition is true*, then *a certain action will happen*, else *another action will happen*

For example, *if* it is raining then, I will take my umbrella, *else* I will leave my umbrella at home. It is not that much different in code:

```
let rain = true;

if(rain){
  console.log("** Taking my umbrella when I need to go outside **");
} else {
  console.log("** I can leave my umbrella at home **");
}
```

In this case, the value of rain is true. And therefore, it will log to the console:

```
** Taking my umbrella when I need to go outside **
```

But let's first take a step back and look at the syntax. We start with the word "if." After this, we get something within parentheses. Whatever is between these parantheses will be translated to a Boolean. If the value of this Boolean is true, it will execute the block of code associated with if. You can recognize this block by the curly braces.

The next block is optional; it is an else block. It starts with the word "else" and is only executed in case of the Boolean having the value false. If there is no else block and the condition evaluates to false, the program will just skip ahead to the code underneath the if.

Only one of these two blocks will be executed; the if block when the expression is true, and the else block when the expression is false:

```
if(expression) {
  // code associated with the if block
  // will only be executed if the expression is true
} else {
  // code associated with the else block
  // we don't need an else block, it is optional
  // this code will only be executed if the expression is false
}
```

Here is another example. If the age is below 18, log to the console that access is denied, otherwise log to the console that the person is allowed to come in:

```
if(age < 18) {
   console.log("We're very sorry, but you can't get in under 18");
} else {
   console.log("Welcome!");
}
```

There is a common coding mistake related to if statements. I have made it in the following code snippet. Can you see what this code does?

```
let hobby = "dancing";

if(hobby = "coding"){
   console.log("** I love coding too! **");
} else {
   console.log("** Can you teach me that? **");
}
```

It will log the following:

```
** I love coding too! **
```

That might surprise you. The problem here is the single equal sign in the if statement. Instead of evaluating the condition, it is assigning coding to hobby. And then it is converting coding to a Boolean, and since it is not an empty string, it will become true, so the if block will be executed. So, always remember to use the double equal sign in this case.

Let's test our knowledge with a practice exercise.

Practice exercise 4.1

1. Create a variable with a Boolean value.
2. Output the value of the variable to the console.
3. Check whether the variable is true and if so, output a message to the console, using the following syntax:

```
if(myVariable){
//action
}
```

4. Add another if statement with an ! in front of the variable to check whether the condition is *not* true, and create a message that will be printed to the console in that instance. You should have two if statements, one with an ! and the other without. You could also use an if and an else statement instead — experiment!

5. Change the variable to the opposite to see how the result changes.

else if statements

A variation of the if statement is an if statement with multiple else if blocks. This can be more efficient in certain situations because you are always only going to execute one or zero blocks. If you have many if else statements underneath one another, they are going to be evaluated and possibly executed even though one of the ones above already had a condition evaluate to true and proceeded to execute the associated code block.

Here is the written template:

*If *a value falls into a certain category*, then *a certain action will happen*, else if *the value falls into a different category than the previous statement*, then *a certain action will happen*, else if *the value falls into a different category than either of the previous brackets*, then *a certain action will happen**

For example, take this statement, to determine what the ticket price should be. If a person is younger than 3, then access is free, else if a person is older than 3 and younger than 12, then access is 5 dollars, else if a person is older than 12 and younger than 65, then access is 10 dollars, else if a person is 65 or older, then access is 7 dollars:

```
let age = 10;
let cost = 0;
let message;
if (age < 3) {
    cost = 0;
    message = "Access is free under three.";
} else if (age >= 3 && age < 12) {
    cost = 5;
    message ="With the child discount, the fee is 5 dollars";
} else if (age >= 12 && age < 65) {
    cost = 10;
    message ="A regular ticket costs 10 dollars.";
```

```
} else {
    cost = 7;
    message ="A ticket is 7 dollars.";
}

console.log(message);
console.log("Your Total cost "+cost);
```

Chances are that you will think the code is easier to read than the written template. In that case, nicely done! You are really starting to think like a JavaScript developer already.

The code gets executed top to bottom, and only one of the blocks will be executed. As soon as a true expression is encountered, the other ones will be ignored. This is why we can also write our sample like this:

```
if(age < 3){
  console.log("Access is free under three.");
} else if(age < 12) {
  console.log("With the child discount, the fee is 5 dollars");
} else if(age < 65) {
  console.log("A regular ticket costs 10 dollars.");
} else if(age >= 65) {
  console.log("A ticket is 7 dollars.");
}
```

Practice exercise 4.2

1. Create a prompt to ask the user's age

2. Convert the response from the prompt to a number

3. Declare a message variable that you will use to hold the console message for the user

4. If the input age is equal to or greater than 21, set the message variable to confirm entry to a venue and the ability to purchase alcohol

5. If the input age is equal to or greater than 19, set the message variable to confirm entry to the venue but deny the purchase of alcohol

6. Provide a default else statement to set the message variable to deny entry if none are true

7. Output the response message variable to the console

Conditional ternary operators

We did not actually discuss this very important operator in our section on operators in *Chapter 2, JavaScript Essentials*. This is because it helps to understand the if else statement first. Remember that we had a unary operator that was called a unary operator because it only had one operand? This is why our ternary operator has its name; it has three operands. Here is its template:

```
operand1 ? operand2 : operand3;
```

operand1 is the expression that is to be evaluated. If the value of the expression is true, operand2 gets executed. If the value of the expression is false, operand3 gets executed. You can read the question mark as "then" and the colon as "else" here:

```
expression ? statement for true : statement associated with false;
```

The template for saying it in your head should be:

if *operand1*, then *operand2*, else *operand3*

Let's have a look at a few examples:

```
let access = age < 18 ? "denied" : "allowed";
```

This little code snippet will assign a value to access. *If* age is lower than 18, *then* it will assign the value denied, *else* it will assign the value allowed. You can also specify an action in a ternary statement, like this:

```
age < 18 ? console.log("denied") : console.log("allowed");
```

This syntax can be confusing at first. The template of what to say in your head while reading it can really come to the rescue here. You can only use these ternary operators for very short actions, so it's best practice to use the ternary operator in these instances as it makes code easier to read. However, if the logic contains multiple comparison arguments, you'll have to use the regular if-else.

Practice exercise 4.3

1. Create a Boolean value for an ID variable
2. Using a ternary operator, create a message variable that will check whether their ID is valid and either allow a person into a venue or not
3. Output the response to the console

switch statements

If else statements are great for evaluating Boolean conditions. There are many things you can do with them, but in some cases, it is better to replace them with a switch statement. This is especially the case when evaluating more than four or five values.

We are going to see how switch statements can help us and what they look like. First, have a look at this if else statement:

```
if(activity === "Get up") {
    console.log("It is 6:30AM");
} else if(activity === "Breakfast") {
    console.log("It is 7:00AM");
} else if(activity === "Drive to work") {
    console.log("It is 8:00AM");
} else if(activity === "Lunch") {
    console.log("It is 12.00PM");
} else if(activity === "Drive home") {
    console.log("It is 5:00PM")
} else if(activity === "Dinner") {
    console.log("It is 6:30PM");
}
```

It is determining what the time is based on what we are doing. It would be better to implement this using a switch statement. The syntax of a switch statement looks like this:

```
switch(expression) {
    case value1:
        // code to be executed
        break;
    case value2:
        // code to be executed
        break;
    case value-n:
        // code to be executed
        break;
}
```

You can read it in your head as follows: If the expression equals value1, do whatever code is specified for that case. If the expression equals value2, do whatever code is specified for that case, and so on.

Here is how we can rewrite our long if else statement in a much cleaner manner using a switch statement:

```javascript
switch(activity) {
  case "Get up":
    console.log("It is 6:30AM");
    break;
  case "Breakfast":
    console.log("It is 7:00AM");
    break;
  case "Drive to work":
    console.log("It is 8:00AM");
    break;
  case "Lunch":
    console.log("It is 12:00PM");
    break;
  case "Drive home":
    console.log("It is 5:00PM");
    break;
  case "Dinner":
    console.log("It is 6:30PM");
    break;
}
```

If our activity has the value Lunch it will output the following to the console:

```
It is 12:00PM
```

What's up with all these breaks, you may be wondering? If you do not use the command break at the end of a case, it will execute the next case as well. This will be done from the case where it has a match, until the end of the switch statement or until we encounter a break statement. This is what the output of our switch statement would be without breaks for the Lunch activity:

```
It is 12:00PM
It is 5:00PM
It is 6:30PM
```

One last side note. switch uses strict type checking (the triple equals strategy) to determine equality, which checks for both a value and a data type.

The default case

There is one part of switch that we have not worked with yet, and that is a special case label, namely, default. This works a lot like the else part of an if else statement. If it does not find a match with any of the cases and a default case is present, then it will execute the code associated with the default case. Here is the template of a switch statement with a default case:

```
switch(expression) {
  case value1:
    // code to be executed
    break;
  case value2:
    // code to be executed
    break;
  case value-n:
    // code to be executed
    break;
  default:
    // code to be executed when no cases match
    break;
}
```

The convention is to have the default case as the last case in the switch statement, but the code will work just fine when it is in the middle or the first case. However, we recommend you stick to the conventions and have it as a last case, since that is what other developers (and probably your future self) will expect when dealing with your code later.

Let's say our long if statement has an else statement associated with it that looks like this:

```
if(…) {
  // omitted to avoid making this unnecessarily long
} else {
  console.log("I cannot determine the current time.");
}
```

The switch statement would then look like this:

```
switch(activity) {
  case "Get up":
    console.log("It is 6:30AM");
```

```
      break;
   case "Breakfast":
     console.log("It is 7:00AM");
     break;
   case "Drive to work":
     console.log("It is 8:00AM");
     break;
   case "Lunch":
     console.log("It is 12:00PM");
     break;
   case "Drive home":
     console.log("It is 5:00PM");
     break;
   case "Dinner":
     console.log("It is 6:30PM");
     break;
   default:
     console.log("I cannot determine the current time.");
     break;
 }
```

If the value of the activity was to be something that is not specified as a case, for example, "Watch Netflix," it would log the following to the console:

```
I cannot determine the current time.
```

Practice exercise 4.4

As discussed in *Chapter 1, Getting Started with JavaScript*, the JavaScript function `Math.random()` will return a random number in the range of 0 to less than 1, including 0 but not 1. You can then scale it to the desired range by multiplying the result and using `Math.floor()` to round it down to the nearest whole number; for example, to generate a random number between 0 and 9:

```
// random number between 0 and 1
let randomNumber = Math.random();
// multiply by 10 to obtain a number between 0 and 10
randomNumber = randomNumber * 10;
// removes digits past decimal place to provide a whole number
RandomNumber = Math.floor(randomNumber);
```

In this exercise, we'll create a Magic 8-Ball random answer generator:

1. Start by setting a variable that gets a random value assigned to it. The value is assigned by generating a random number 0-5, for 6 possible results. You can increase this number as you add more results.

2. Create a prompt that can get a string value input from a user that you can repeat back in the final output.

3. Create 6 responses using the switch statement, each assigned to a different value from the random number generator.

4. Create a variable to hold the end response, which should be a sentence printed for the user. You can assign different string values for each case, assigning new values depending on the results from the random value.

5. Output the user's original question, plus the randomly selected case response, to the console after the user enters their question.

Combining cases

Sometimes, you would want to do the exact same thing for multiple cases. In an if statement, you would have to specify all the different *or* (| |) clauses. In a switch statement, you can simply combine them by putting them on top of each other like this:

```
switch(grade){
  case "F":
  case "D":
    console.log("You've failed!");
    break;
  case "C":
  case "B":
    console.log("You've passed!");
    break;
  case "A":
    console.log("Nice!");
    break;
  default:
    console.log("I don't know this grade.");
}
```

For the values F and D, the same thing is happening. This is also true for C and B. When the value of grade is either C or B, it will log the following to the console:

```
You've passed!
```

This is more readable than the alternative if-else statement:

```javascript
if(grade === "F" || grade === "D") {
  console.log("You've failed!");
} else if(grade === "C" || grade === "B") {
  console.log("You've passed!");
} else if(grade === "A") {
  console.log("Nice!");
} else {
  console.log("I don't know this grade.");
}
```

Practice exercise 4.5

1. Create a variable called prize and use a prompt to ask the user to set the value by selecting a number between 0 and 10

2. Convert the prompt response to a number data type

3. Create a variable to use for the output message containing the value "My Selection: "

4. Using the switch statement (and creativity), provide a response back regarding a prize that is awarded depending on what number is selected

5. Use the switch break to add combined results for prizes

6. Output the message back to the user by concatenating your prize variable strings and the output message string

Chapter projects

Evaluating a number game

Ask the user to enter a number and check whether it's greater than, equal to, or less than a dynamic number value in your code. Output the result to the user.

Friend checker game

Ask the user to enter a name, using the switch statement to return a confirmation that the user is a friend if the name selected is known in the case statements. You can add a default response that you don't know the person if it's an unknown name. Output the result into the console.

Rock Paper Scissors game

This is a game between a player and the computer, where both will make a random selection of either Rock, Paper, or Scissors (alternatively, you could create a version using real player input!). Rock will beat out Scissors, Paper will beat out Rock, and Scissors will beat out Paper. You can use JavaScript to create your own version of this game, applying the logic with an if statement. Since this project is a little more difficult, here are some suggested steps:

1. Create an array that contains the variables Rock, Paper, and Scissors.

2. Set up a variable that generates a random number 0-2 for the player and then do the same for the computer's selection. The number represents the index values in the array of the 3 items.

3. Create a variable to hold a response message to the user. This can show the random results for the player and then also the result for the computer of the matching item from the array.

4. Create a condition to handle the player and computer selections. If both are the same, this results in a tie.

5. Use conditions to apply the game logic and return the correct results. There are several ways to do this with the condition statements, but you could check which player's index value is bigger and assign the victory accordingly, with the exception of Rock beating Scissors.

6. Add a new output message that shows the player selection versus the computer selection and the result of the game.

Self-check quiz

1. What will be outputted to the console in this instance?

```
const q = '1';
switch (q) {
    case '1':
        answer = "one";
```

```
            break;
        case 1:
            answer = 1;
            break;
        case 2:
            answer = "this is the one";
            break;
        default:
            answer = "not working";
    }
    console.log(answer);
```

2. What will be outputted to the console in this instance?

```
const q = 1;

switch (q) {
    case '1':
        answer = "one";
    case 1:
        answer = 1;
    case 2:
        answer = "this is the one";
        break;
    default:
        answer = "not working";
}
console.log(answer);
```

3. What will be outputted to the console in this instance?

```
let login = false;
let outputHolder = "";
let userOkay = login ? outputHolder = "logout" : outputHolder =
"login";
console.log(userOkay);
```

4. What will be outputted to the console in this instance?

```
const userNames = ["Mike", "John", "Larry"];
const userInput = "John";
let htmlOutput = "";
if (userNames.indexOf(userInput) > -1) {
    htmlOutput = "Welcome, that is a user";
```

```
    } else {
        htmlOutput = "Denied, not a user ";
    }
    console.log(htmlOutput + ": " + userInput);
```

5. What will be outputted to the console in this instance?

```
    let myTime = 9;
    let output;
    if (myTime >= 8 && myTime < 12) {
        output = "Wake up, it's morning";
    } else if (myTime >= 12 && myTime < 13) {
        output = "Go to lunch";
    } else if (myTime >= 13 && myTime <= 16) {
        output = "Go to work";
    } else if (myTime > 16 && myTime < 20) {
        output = "Dinner time";
    } else if (myTime >= 22) {
        output = "Time to go to sleep";
    } else {
        output = "You should be sleeping";
    }
    console.log(output);
```

6. What will be outputted to the console in this instance?

```
    let a = 5;
    let b = 10;
    let c = 20;
    let d = 30;
    console.log(a > b || b > a);
    console.log(a > b && b > a);
    console.log(d > b || b > a);
    console.log(d > b && b > a);
```

7. What will be outputted to the console in this instance?

```
    let val = 100;
    let message = (val > 100) ? `${val} was greater than 100` :
    `${val} was LESS or Equal to 100`;
    console.log(message);
    let check = (val % 2) ? `Odd` : `Even`;
    check = `${val} is ${check}`;
    console.log(check);
```

Summary

Now, let's wrap things up. In this chapter, we have covered conditional statements. We started with if else statements. Whenever the condition associated with the if is true, the if block gets executed. If the condition is false and there is an else block present, that will be executed. We have also seen ternary operators and the funky syntax they bring to the table. It is a short way of writing an if-else statement if you only need one statement per block.

And lastly, we have seen switch statements and how they can be used to optimize our conditional code. With the switch statement, we can compare one condition with many different cases. When they are equal (value and type), the code associated with the case gets executed.

In the next chapter, we are going to add loops to the mix! This is going to help us write more efficient code and algorithms.

Join our book's Discord space

Join the book's Discord workspace for a monthly *Ask me Anything* session with the authors: https://packt.link/JSBook

5

Loops

We are starting to get a good basic grasp of JavaScript. This chapter will focus on a very important control flow concept: loops. Loops execute a code block a certain number of times. We can use loops to do many things, such as repeating operations a number of times and iterating over data sets, arrays, and objects. Whenever you feel the need to copy a little piece of code and place it right underneath where you copied it from, you should probably be using a loop instead.

We will first discuss the basics of loops, then continue to discuss nesting loops, which is basically using loops inside loops. Also, we will explain looping over two complex constructs we have seen, arrays and objects. And finally, we will introduce two keywords related to loops, break and continue, to control the flow of the loop even more.

 There is one topic that is closely related to loops that is not in this chapter. This is the built-in foreach method. We can use this method to loop over arrays, when we can use an arrow function. Since we won't discuss these until the next chapter, foreach is not included here.

These are the different loops we will be discussing in this chapter:

- while loop
- do while loop
- for loop
- for in
- for of loop

Note: exercise, project, and self-check quiz answers can be found in the *Appendix*.

while loops

The first loop we will discuss is the **while loop**. A `while` loop executes a certain block of code as long as an expression evaluates to `true`. The snippet below demonstrates the syntax of the `while` loop:

```
while (condition) {
    // code that gets executed as long as the condition is true
}
```

The `while` loop will only be executed as long as the condition is `true`, so if the condition is `false` to begin with, the code inside will be skipped.

Here is a very simple example of a `while` loop printing the numbers 0 to 10 (excluding 10) to the console:

```
let i = 0;
while (i < 10) {
    console.log(i);
    i++;
}
```

The output will be as follows:

```
1
2
3
4
5
6
7
8
9
```

These are the steps happening here:

1. Create a variable, i, and set its value to zero

2. Start the `while` loop and check the condition that the value of i is smaller than 10

3. Since the condition is true, the code logs i and increases i by 1

4. The condition gets evaluated again; 1 is still smaller than 10

5. Since the condition is true, the code logs i and increases i by 1

6. The logging and increasing continues until i becomes 10

7. 10 is not smaller than 10, so the loop ends

We can have a `while` loop that looks for a value in an array, like this:

```
let someArray = ["Mike", "Antal", "Marc", "Emir", "Louiza", "Jacky"];
let notFound = true;

while (notFound && someArray.length > 0) {
  if (someArray[0] === "Louiza") {
    console.log("Found her!");
    notFound = false;
  } else {
    someArray.shift();
  }
}
```

It checks whether the first value of the array is a certain value, and when it is not, it deletes that value from the array using the `shift` method. Remember this method? It removes the first element of the array. So, by the next iteration, the first value has changed and is checked again. If it stumbles upon the value, it will log this to the console and change the Boolean `notFound` to `false`, because it has found it. That was the last iteration and the loop is done. It will output:

```
Found her!
false
```

Why do you think the `&& someArray.length > 0` is added in the `while` condition? If we were to leave it out, and the value we were looking for was not in the array, we would get stuck in an infinite loop. This is why we make sure that we also end things if our value is not present, so our code can continue.

But we can also do more sophisticated things very easily with loops. Let's see how easy it is to fill an array with the Fibonacci sequence using a loop:

```
let nr1 = 0;
let nr2 = 1;
let temp;
```

```
fibonacciArray = [];

while (fibonacciArray.length < 25) {
  fibonacciArray.push(nr1);
  temp = nr1 + nr2;
  nr1 = nr2;
  nr2 = temp;
}
```

In the Fibonacci sequence, each value is the sum of the two previous values, starting with the values 0 and 1. We can do this in a while loop as stated above. We create two numbers and they change every iteration. We have limited our number of iterations to the length of the fibonacciArray, because we don't want an infinite loop. In this case the loop will be done as soon as the length of the array is no longer smaller than 25.

We need a temporary variable that stores the next value for nr2. And every iteration we push the value of the first number to the array. If we log the array, you can see the numbers getting rather high very quickly. Imagine having to generate these values one by one in your code!

```
[
      0,      1,      1,      2,      3,
      5,      8,     13,     21,     34,
     55,     89,    144,    233,    377,
    610,    987,   1597,   2584,   4181,
   6765,  10946,  17711,  28657,  46368
]
```

Practice exercise 5.1

In this exercise we will create a number guessing game that takes user input and replies based on how accurate the user's guess was.

1. Create a variable to be used as the max value for the number guessing game.

2. Generate a random number for the solution using Math.random() and Math.floor(). You will also need to add 1 so that the value is returned as 1-[whatever the set max value is]. You can log this value to the console for development to see the value as you create the game, then when the game is complete you can comment out this console output.

3. Create a variable that will be used for tracking whether the answer is correct or not and set it to a default Boolean value of `false`. We can update it to be `true` if the user guess is a match.

4. Use a `while` loop to iterate a prompt that asks the user to enter a number between 1 and 5, and convert the response into a number in order to match the data type of the random number.

5. Inside the `while` loop, check using a condition to see if the prompt value is equal to the solution number. Apply logic such that if the number is correct, you set the status to `true` and break out of the loop. Provide the player with some feedback as to whether the guess was high or low, and initiate another prompt until the user guesses correctly. In this way we use the loop to keep asking until the solution is correct, and at that point we can stop the iteration of the block of code.

do while loops

In some cases, you really need the code block to be executed at least once. For example, if you need valid user input, you need to ask at least once. The same goes for trying to connect with a database or some other external source: you will have to do so at least once in order for it to be successful. And you will probably need to do so as long as you did not get the result you needed. In these cases, you can use a **do while loop**.

Here is what the syntax looks like:

```
do {
    // code to be executed if the condition is true
} while (condition);
```

It executes what is within the `do` block, and then after that it evaluates the `while`. If the condition is `true`, it will execute what is in the `do` block again. It will continue to do so until the condition in the `while` changes to `false`.

We can use the `prompt()` method to get user input. Let's use a `do while` loop to ask the user for a number between 0 and 100.

```
let number;
do {
    number = prompt("Please enter a number between 0 and 100: ");
} while (!(number >= 0 && number < 100));
```

Here is the output; you will have to enter the number in the console yourself here.

```
Please enter a number between 0 and 100: > -50
Please enter a number between 0 and 100: > 150
Please enter a number between 0 and 100: > 34
```

 Everything behind the > is user input here. The > is part of the code; it is added by the console to make the distinction between console output (Please enter a number between 0 and 100) and the console input (-50, 150, and 34) clearer.

It asks three times, because the first two times the number was not between 0 and 100 and the condition in the while block was true. With 34, the condition in the while block became false and the loop ended.

Practice exercise 5.2

In this exercise, we will create a basic counter that will increase a dynamic variable by a consistent step value, up to an upper limit.

1. Set the starting counter to 0
2. Create a variable, step, to increase your counter by
3. Add a do while loop, printing the counter to the console and incrementing it by the step amount each loop
4. Continue to loop until the counter is equal to 100 or more than 100

for loops

for loops are special loops. The syntax might be a little bit confusing at first, but you will find yourself using them soon, because they are very useful.

Here is what the syntax looks like:

```
for (initialize variable; condition; statement) {
  // code to be executed
}
```

Between the parentheses following the for statement, there are three parts, separated by semi-colons. The first one initializes the variables that can be used in the for loop. The second one is a condition: as long as this condition is true, the loop will keep on iterating. This condition gets checked after initializing the variables before the first iteration (this will only take place when the condition evaluates to true). The last one is a statement. This statement gets executed after every iteration. Here is the flow of a for loop:

1. Initialize the variables.
2. Check the condition.
3. If the condition is true, execute the code block. If the condition is false, the loop will end here.
4. Perform the statement (the third part, for example, i++).
5. Go back to step 2.

This is a simple example that logs the numbers 0 to 10 (excluding 10) to the console:

```
for (let i = 0; i < 10; i++) {
  console.log(i);
}
```

It starts by creating a variable, i, and sets this to 0. Then it checks whether i is smaller than 10. If it is, it will execute the log statement. After this, it will execute i++ and increase i by one.

 If we don't increase i, we will get stuck in an infinite loop, since the value of i would not change and it would be smaller than 10 forever. This is something to look out for in all loops!

The condition gets checked again. And this goes on until i reaches a value of 10. 10 is not smaller than 10, so the loop is done executing and the numbers 0 to 9 have been logged to the console.

We can also use a for loop to create a sequence and add values to an array, like this:

```
let arr = [];
for (let i = 0; i < 100; i++) {
  arr.push(i);
}
```

This is what the array looks like after this loop:

```
[
    0,  1,  2,  3,  4,  5,  6,  7,  8,  9, 10, 11,
   12, 13, 14, 15, 16, 17, 18, 19, 20, 21, 22, 23,
   24, 25, 26, 27, 28, 29, 30, 31, 32, 33, 34, 35,
   36, 37, 38, 39, 40, 41, 42, 43, 44, 45, 46, 47,
   48, 49, 50, 51, 52, 53, 54, 55, 56, 57, 58, 59,
   60, 61, 62, 63, 64, 65, 66, 67, 68, 69, 70, 71,
   72, 73, 74, 75, 76, 77, 78, 79, 80, 81, 82, 83,
   84, 85, 86, 87, 88, 89, 90, 91, 92, 93, 94, 95,
   96, 97, 98, 99
]
```

Since the loop ran the block of code 100 times, starting with an initial value of 0 for i, the block of code will add the incrementing value into the array at the end of the array. This results in an array that has a count of 0–99 and a length of 100 items. Since arrays start with an index value of zero, the values in the array will actually match up with the index values of the items in the array.

Or we could create an array containing only even values:

```
let arr = [];
for (let i = 0; i < 100; i = i + 2) {
  arr.push(i);
}
```

Resulting in this array:

```
[
    0,  2,  4,  6,  8, 10, 12, 14, 16, 18, 20,
   22, 24, 26, 28, 30, 32, 34, 36, 38, 40, 42,
   44, 46, 48, 50, 52, 54, 56, 58, 60, 62, 64,
   66, 68, 70, 72, 74, 76, 78, 80, 82, 84, 86,
   88, 90, 92, 94, 96, 98
]
```

Most commonly, you will see i++ as the third part of the for loop, but please note that you can write any statement there. In this case, we are using i = i + 2 to add 2 to the previous value every time, creating an array with only even numbers.

Practice exercise 5.3

In this exercise we will use a for loop to create an array that holds objects. Starting with creating a blank array, the block of code within the loop will create an object that gets inserted into the array.

1. Setup a blank array, myWork.

2. Using a for loop, create a list of 10 objects, each of which is a numbered lesson (e.g. Lesson 1, Lesson 2, Lesson 3....) with an alternating true/false status for every other item to indicate whether the class will be running this year. For example:

    ```
    name: 'Lesson 1', status: true
    ```

3. You can specify the status by using a ternary operator that checks whether the modulo of the given lesson value is equal to zero and by setting up a Boolean value to alternate the values each iteration.

4. Create a lesson using a temporary object variable, containing the name (lesson with the numeric value) and predefined status (which we set up in the previous step).

5. Push the objects to the myWork array.

6. Output the array to the console.

Nested loops

Sometimes it can be necessary to use a loop inside a loop. A loop inside a loop is called a nested loop. Often it is not the best solution to the problem. It could even be a sign of poorly written code (sometimes called "code smell" among programmers), but every now and then it is a perfectly fine solution to a problem.

Here is what it would look like for while loops:

```
while (condition 1) {
  // code that gets executed as long as condition 1 is true
  // this loop depends on condition 1 being true
    while (condition 2) {
      // code that gets executed as long as condition 2 is true
    }
}
```

Nesting can also be used with `for` loops, or with a combination of both `for` and `while`, or even with all kinds of loops; they can go several levels deep.

An example in which we might use nested loops would be when we want to create an array of arrays. With the outer loop, we create the top-level array, and with the inner loop we add the values to the array.

```
let arrOfArrays = [];
for (let i = 0; i < 3; i++){
  arrOfArrays.push([]);
  for (let j = 0; j < 7; j++) {
    arrOfArrays[i].push(j);
  }
}
```

When we log this array like this:

```
console.log(arrOfArrays);
```

We can see that the output is an array of arrays with values from 0 up to 6.

```
[
  [
    0, 1, 2, 3, 4, 5, 6
  ],
  [
    0, 1, 2, 3, 4, 5, 6
  ],
  [
    0, 1, 2, 3, 4, 5, 6
  ]
]
```

We used the nested loops to create an array in an array, meaning we can work with rows and columns after having created this loop. This means nested loops can be used to create tabular data. We can show this output as a table using the `console.table()` method instead, like so:

```
console.table(arrOfArrays);
```

This will output:

```
| (index) | 0 | 1 | 2 | 3 | 4 | 5 | 6 |

|    0    | 0 | 1 | 2 | 3 | 4 | 5 | 6 |
|    1    | 0 | 1 | 2 | 3 | 4 | 5 | 6 |
|    2    | 0 | 1 | 2 | 3 | 4 | 5 | 6 |
```

Let's put this into practice in the next exercise.

Practice exercise 5.4

In this exercise we will be generating a table of values. We will be using loops to generate rows and also columns, which will be nested within the rows. Nested arrays can be used to represent rows in a table. This is a common structure in spreadsheets, where each row is a nested array within a table and the contents of these rows are the cells in the table. The columns will align as we are creating an equal number of cells in each row.

1. To create a table generator, first create an empty array, myTable, to hold your table data.

2. Set variable values for the number of rows and columns. This will allow us to dynamically control how many rows and columns we want within the table. Separating the values from the main code helps make updates to the dimensions easier.

3. Set up a counter variable with an initial value of 0. The counter will be used to set the content and count the values of the cells within the table.

4. Create a for loop with conditions to set the number of iterations, and to construct each row of the table. Within it, set up a new temporary array (tempTable) to hold each row of data. The columns will be nested within the rows, generating each cell needed for the column.

5. Nest a second loop within the first to count the columns. Columns are run within the row loop so that we have a uniform number of columns within the table.

6. Increment the main counter each iteration of the inner loop, so that we track a master count of each one of the cells and how many cells are created.

7. Push the counter values to the temporary array, `tempTable`. Since the array is a nested array representing a table, the values of the counter can also be used to illustrate the cell values next to each other in the table. Although these are separate arrays representing new rows, the value of the counter will help illustrate the overall sequence of cells in the final table.

8. Push the temporary array to the main table. As each iteration builds a new row of array items, this will continue to build the main table in the array.

9. Output into the console with `console.table(myTable)`. This will show you a visual representation of the table structure.

Loops and arrays

If you are not convinced of how extremely useful loops are by now, have a look at loops and arrays. Loops make life with arrays a lot more comfortable.

We can combine the `length` property and the condition part of the `for` loop or `while` loop to loop over arrays. It would look like this in the case of a `for` loop:

```
let arr = [some array];
for (initialize variable; variable smaller than arr.length; statement)
{
    // code to be executed
}
```

Let's start with a simple example that is going to log every value of the array:

```
let names = ["Chantal", "John", "Maxime", "Bobbi", "Jair"];
for (let i = 0; i < names.length; i ++){
    console.log(names[i]);
}
```

This will output:

```
Chantal
John
Maxime
Bobbi
Jair
```

We use the `length` property to determine the maximum value of our index. The index starts counting at 0, but the length does not. The index is always one smaller than the length. Hence, we loop over the values of the array by increasing the length.

In this case we aren't doing very interesting things yet; we are simply printing the values. But we could be changing the values of the array in a loop, for example, like this:

```
let names = ["Chantal", "John", "Maxime", "Bobbi", "Jair"];
for (let i = 0; i < names.length; i ++){
  names[i] = "hello " + names[i];
}
```

We have concatenated `hello` with the beginnings of our names. The array is changed in the loop and the array will have this content after the loop has executed:

```
[
  'hello Chantal',
  'hello John',
  'hello Maxime',
  'hello Bobbi',
  'hello Jair'
]
```

The possibilities are endless here. When an array comes in somewhere in the application, data can be sent to the database per value. Data can be modified by value, or even filtered, like this:

```
let names = ["Chantal", "John", "Maxime", "Bobbi", "Jair"];
for (let i = 0; i < names.length; i ++){
  if(names[i].startsWith("M")){
    delete names[i];
    continue;
  }
  names[i] = "hello " + names[i];
}
console.log(names);
```

The `startsWith()` method just checks whether the string starts with a certain character. In this case it checks whether the name starts with the string `M`.

Don't worry, we will cover this function and many more in detail in *Chapter 8, Built-in JavaScript Methods*.

The output is:

```
[
  'hello Chantal',
  'hello John',
  <1 empty item>,
  'hello Bobbi',
  'hello Jair'
]
```

You'll have to be careful here though. If we were to remove the item instead of deleting it and leaving an empty value, we would accidentally skip the next value, since that value gets the index of the recently deleted one and i is incremented and moves on to the next index.

What do you think this one does:

```
let names = ["Chantal", "John", "Maxime", "Bobbi", "Jair"];
for (let i = 0; i < names.length; i++){
  names.push("...")
}
```

Your program gets stuck in an infinite loop here. Since a value gets added every iteration, the length of the loop grows with every iteration and i will never be bigger than or equal to length.

Practice exercise 5.5

Explore how to create a table grid that contains nested arrays as rows within a table. The rows will each contain the number of cells needed for the number of columns set in the variables. This grid table will dynamically adjust depending on the values for the variables.

1. Create a grid array variable.

2. Set a value of 64 for the number of cells.

3. Set a counter to 0.

4. Create a global variable to be used for the row array.

5. Create a loop that will iterate up to the number of cells you want in the array, plus one to include the zero value. In our example, we would use 64+1.

6. Add an outer `if` statement, which uses modulo to check if the main counter is divisible by 8 or whatever number of columns you want.

7. Inside the preceding `if` statement, add another `if` statement to check if the row is undefined, indicating whether it is the first run or whether the row is complete. If the row has been defined, then add the row to the main grid array.

8. To finish off the outer `if` statement, if the counter is divisible by 8, clear the row array—it has already been added to the grid by the inner `if` statement.

9. At the end of the for loop, increment of the main counter by 1.

10. Set up a temporary variable to hold the value of the counter and push it to the row array.

11. Within the loop iteration, check if the value of the counter is equal to the total number of columns you want; if it is, then add the current row to the grid.

12. Please note that the extra cell will not be added to the grid since there aren't enough cells to make a new row within the condition that adds the rows to the grid. An alternative solution would be to remove the +1 from the loop condition and add `grid.push(row)` after the loop is completed, both of which will provide the same solution output.

13. Output the grid into the console.

for of loop

There is another loop we can use to iterate over the elements of an array: the **for of loop**. It cannot be used to change the value associated with the index as we can do with the regular loop, but for processing values it is a very nice and readable loop.

Here is what the syntax looks like:

```
let arr = [some array];
for (let variableName of arr) {
  // code to be executed
  // value of variableName gets updated every iteration
  // all values of the array will be variableName once
}
```

So you can read it like this: "For every value of the array, call it `variableName` and do the following." We can log our `names` array using this loop:

```
let names = ["Chantal", "John", "Maxime", "Bobbi", "Jair"];
for (let name of names){
   console.log(name);
}
```

We need to specify a temporary variable; in this case we called it `name`. This is used to put the value of the current iteration in, and after the iteration, it gets replaced with the next value. This code results in the following output:

```
Chantal
John
Maxime
Bobbi
Jair
```

There are some limitations here; we cannot modify the array, but we could write all the elements to a database or a file, or send it somewhere else. The advantage of this is that we cannot accidentally get stuck in an infinite loop or skip values.

Practice exercise 5.6

This exercise will construct an array as it loops through the incrementing values of x. Once the array is done, this exercise also will demonstrate several ways to output array contents.

1. Create an empty array
2. Run a loop 10 times, adding a new incrementing value to the array
3. Log the array into the console
4. Use the `for` loop to iterate through the array (adjust the number of iterations to however many values are in your array) and output into the console
5. Use the `for` of loop to output the value into the console from the array

Loops and objects

We have just seen how to loop over the values of an array, but we can also loop over the properties of an object. This can be helpful when we need to go over all the properties but don't know the exact properties of the object we are iterating over.

Looping over an object can be done in a few ways. We can use the `for in` loop to loop over the object directly, or we can convert the object to an array and loop over the array. We'll consider both in the following sections.

for in loop

Manipulating objects with loops can also be done with another variation of the `for` loop, the **for in loop**. The `for in` loop is somewhat similar to the `for of` loop. Again here, we need to specify a temporary name, also referred to as a key, to store each property name in. We can see it in action here:

```
let car = {
   model: "Golf",
   make: "Volkswagen",
   year: 1999,
   color: "black",
};

for (let prop in car){
   console.log(car[prop]);
}
```

We need to use the prop of each loop iteration to get the value out of the `car` object. The output then becomes:

```
Golf
Volkswagen
1999
black
```

If we just logged the prop, like this:

```
for (let prop in car){
   console.log(prop);
}
```

This is what our output would look like:

```
model
make
year
color
```

As you can see, all the names of the properties get printed, and not the values. This is because the `for in` loop is getting the property names (keys) and not the values. The `for of` is doing the opposite; it is getting the values and not the keys.

This `for in` loop can also be used on arrays, but it is not really useful. It will only return the indices, since these are the "keys" of the values of the arrays. Also, it should be noted that the order of execution cannot be guaranteed, even though this is usually important for arrays. It is therefore better to use the approaches mentioned in the section on loops and arrays.

Practice exercise 5.7

In this exercise, we will experiment with looping over objects and internal arrays.

1. Create a simple object with three items in it.
2. Using the `for in` loop, get the properties' names and values from the object and output them into the console.
3. Create an array containing the same three items. Using either the `for` loop or the `for in` loop, output the values from the array into the console.

Looping over objects by converting to an array

You can use any loop on objects, as soon as you convert the object to an array. This can be done in three ways:

- Convert the keys of the object to an array
- Convert the values of the object to an array
- Convert the key-value entries to an array (containing arrays with two elements: object key and object value)

Let's use this example:

```
let car = {
  model: "Golf",
  make: "Volkswagen",
  year: 1999,
  color: "black",
};
```

If we want to loop over the keys of the object, we can use the for in loop, as we saw in the previous section, but can also use the for of loop if we convert it to an array first. We do so by using the `Object.keys(nameOfObject)` built-in function. This takes an object and grabs all the properties of this object and converts them to an array.

To demonstrate how this works:

```
let arrKeys = Object.keys(car);
console.log(arrKeys);
```

This will output:

```
[ 'model', 'make', 'year', 'color' ]
```

We can loop over the properties of this array like this using the for of loop:

```
for(let key of Object.keys(car)) {
    console.log(key);
}
```

And this is what it will output:

```
model
make
year
color
```

Similarly, we can use the for of loop to loop over the values of the object by converting the values to an array. The main difference here is that we use `Object.values(nameOfObject)`:

```
for(let key of Object.values(car)) {
    console.log(key);
}
```

You can loop over these arrays in the same way you loop over any array. You can use the length and index strategy like this in a regular for loop:

```
let arrKeys = Object.keys(car);
for(let i = 0; i < arrKeys.length; i++) {
    console.log(arrKeys[i] + ": " + car[arrKeys[i]]);
}
```

And this will output:

```
model: Golf
make: Volkswagen
year: 1999
color: black
```

More interesting is how to loop over both arrays at the same time using the `for of` loop. In order to do so, we will have to use `Object.entries()`. Let's demonstrate what it does:

```
let arrEntries = Object.entries(car);
console.log(arrEntries);
```

This will output:

```
[
  [ 'model', 'Golf' ],
  [ 'make', 'Volkswagen' ],
  [ 'year', 1999 ],
  [ 'color', 'black' ]
]
```

As you can see, it is returning a two-dimensional array, containing key-value pairs. We can loop over it like this:

```
for (const [key, value] of Object.entries(car)) {
  console.log(key, ":", value);
}
```

And this will output:

```
model : Golf
make : Volkswagen
year : 1999
color : black
```

Alright, you have seen many ways to loop over objects now. Most of them come down to converting the object to an array. We can imagine that at this point you could use a break. Or maybe you'd just like to continue?

break and continue

break and **continue** are two keywords that we can use to control the flow of execution of the loop. break will stop the loop and move on to the code below the loop. continue will stop the current iteration and move back to the top of the loop, checking the condition (or in the case of a for loop, performing the statement and then checking the condition).

We will be using this array of car objects to demonstrate break and continue:

```
let cars = [
  {
    model: "Golf",
    make: "Volkswagen",
    year: 1999,
    color: "black",
  },
  {
    model: "Picanto",
    make: "Kia",
    year: 2020,
    color: "red",
  },
  {
    model: "Peugeot",
    make: "208",
    year: 2021,
    color: "black",
  },
  {
    model: "Fiat",
    make: "Punto",
    year: 2020,
    color: "black",
  }
];
```

We will first have a closer look at break.

break

We have already seen **break** in the switch statement. When break was executed, the switch statement ended. This is not very different when it comes to loops: when the break statement is executed, the loop will end, even when the condition is still true.

Here is a silly example to demonstrate how break works:

```
for (let i = 0; i < 10; i++) {
  console.log(i);
  if (i === 4) {
    break;
  }
}
```

It looks like a loop that will log the numbers 0 to 10 (again excluding 10) to the console. There is a catch here though: as soon as i equals 4, we execute the break command. break ends the loop immediately, so no more loop code gets executed afterward.

We can also use break to stop looping through the array of cars when we have found a car that matches our demands.

```
for (let i = 0; i < cars.length; i++) {
  if (cars[i].year >= 2020) {
    if (cars[i].color === "black") {
      console.log("I have found my new car:", cars[i]);
      break;
    }
  }
}
```

As soon as we run into a car with the year 2020 or later and the car is black, we will stop looking for other cars and just buy that one. The last car in the array would also have been an option, but we did not even consider it because we found one already. The code snippet will output this:

```
I have found my new car: { model: 'Peugeot', make: '208', year: 2021,
color: 'black' }
```

However, often it is not a best practice to use break. If you can manage to work with the condition of the loop to break out of the loop instead, this is a much better practice. It prevents you getting stuck in an infinite loop, and the code is easier to read.

If the condition of the loop is not an actual condition, but pretty much a run-forever kind of statement, the code gets hard to read.

Consider the following code snippet:

```
while (true) {
    if (superLongArray[0] != 42 && superLongArray.length > 0) {
        superLongArray.shift();
    } else {
        console.log("Found 42!");
        break;
    }
}
```

This would be better to write without break and without something terrible like while(true); you could do it like this:

```
while (superLongArray.length > 0 && notFound) {
    if (superLongArray[0] != 42) {
        superLongArray.shift();
    } else {
        console.log("Found 42!");
        notFound = false;
    }
}
```

With the second example, we can see the conditions of the loop easily, namely the length of the array and a notFound flag. However, with while(true) we are kind of misusing the while concept. You want to specify the condition, and it should evaluate to true or false; this way your code is nice to read. If you say while(true), you're actually saying forever, and the reader of your code will have to interpret it line by line to see what is going on and when the loop is ended by a workaround break statement.

continue

break can be used to quit the loop, and **continue** can be used to move on to the next iteration of the loop. It quits the current iteration and moves back up to check the condition and start a new iteration.

Here you can see an example of continue:

```
for (let car of cars){
    if(car.color !== "black"){
```

```
      continue;
   }
   if (car.year >= 2020) {
      console.log("we could get this one:", car);
   }
}
```

The approach here is to just skip every car that is not black and consider all the others that are not older than make year 2020 or later. The code will output this:

```
we could get this one: { model: 'Peugeot', make: '208', year: 2021,
color: 'black' }
we could get this one: { model: 'Fiat', make: 'Punto', year: 2020,
color: 'black' }
```

Be careful with `continue` in a `while` loop. Without running it, what do you think the next code snippet does?

```
// let's only log the odd numbers to the console
let i = 1;
while (i < 50) {
   if (i % 2 === 0){
      continue;
   }
   console.log(i);
   i++;
}
```

It logs 1, and then it gets you stuck in an infinite loop, because `continue` gets hit before the value of i changes, so it will run into `continue` again, and again, and so on. This can be fixed by moving the `i++` up and subtracting 1 from i, like this:

```
let i = 1;
while (i < 50) {
   i++;
   if ((i-1) % 2 === 0){
      continue;
   }
   console.log(i-1);
}
```

But again, there is a better way without `continue` here. The chance of error is a lot smaller:

```
for (let i = 1; i < 50; i = i + 2) {
  console.log(i);
}
```

And as you can see it is even shorter and more readable. The value of `break` and `continue` usually comes in when you are looping over large data sets, possibly coming from outside your application. Here you'll have less influence to apply other types of control. Using `break` and `continue` is not a best practice for simple basic examples, but it's a great way to get familiar with the concepts.

Practice exercise 5.8

This exercise will demonstrate how to create a string with all the digits as it loops through them. We can also set a value to skip by adding a condition that will use `continue`, skipping the matching condition. A second option is to do the same exercise and use the `break` keyword.

1. Set up a string variable to use as output.
2. Select a number to skip, and set that number as a variable.
3. Create a `for` loop that counts to 10.
4. Add a condition to check if the value of the looped variable is equal to the number that should be skipped.
5. If the number is to be skipped in the condition, `continue` to the next number.
6. As you iterate through the values, append the new count value to the end of the main output variable.
7. Output the main variable after the loop completes.
8. Reuse the code, but change the `continue` to `break` and see the difference. It should now stop at the skip value.

break, continue, and nested loops

`break` and `continue` can be used in nested loops as well, but it is important to know that when `break` or `continue` is used in a nested loop, the outer loop will not break.

We will use this array of arrays to discuss break and continue in nested loops:

```
let groups = [
  ["Martin", "Daniel", "Keith"],
  ["Margot", "Marina", "Ali"],
  ["Helen", "Jonah", "Sambikos"],
];
```

Let's break down this example. We are looking for all the groups that have two names starting with an M. If we find such a group, we will log it.

```
for (let i = 0; i < groups.length; i++) {
  let matches = 0;

  for (let j = 0; j < groups[i].length; j++) {
    if(groups[i][j].startsWith("M")){
        matches++;
      } else {
        continue;
      }
    if (matches === 2){
        console.log("Found a group with two names starting with an M:");
        console.log(groups[i]);
        break;
      }
    }
  }
}
```

We first loop over the top-level arrays and set a counter, matches, with a start value of 0, and for each of these top-level arrays, we are going to loop over the values. When a value starts with an M, we increase matches by one and check whether we have found two matches already. If we find two Ms, we break out of the inner loop and continue in our outer loop. This one will move on to the next top-level array, since nothing is happening after the inner loop.

If the name does not start with an M, we do not need to check for matches being 2, and we can continue to the next value in the inner array.

Take a look at this example: what do you think it will log?

```
for (let group of groups){
  for (let member of group){
    if (member.startsWith("M")){
      console.log("found one starting with M:", member);
```

```
        break;
      }
    }
  }
```

It will loop over the arrays, and for every array it will check the value to see if it starts with an M. If it does, the inner loop will break. So, if one of the arrays in the array contains multiple values starting with M, only the first one will be found, since the iteration over that array breaks and we continue to the next array.

This one will output:

```
found one starting with M: Martin
found one starting with M: Margot
```

We can see that it finds Margot, the first one from the second array, but it skips Marina, because it is the second one in the array. And it breaks after having found one group, so it won't loop over the other elements in the inner array. It will continue with the next array, which doesn't contain names starting with an M.

If we wanted to find groups that have a member with a name that starts with an M, the previous code snippet would have been the way to go, because we are breaking the inner loop as soon as we find a hit. This can be useful whenever you want to make sure that an array in a data set contains at least one of something. Because of the nature of the for of loop, it won't give the index or place where it found it. It will simply break, and you have the value of the element of the array to use. If you need to know more, you can work with counters, which are updated every iteration.

If we want to see whether only one of all the names in the array of arrays starts with an M, we would have to break out of the outer loop. This is something we can do with labeled loops.

break and continue and labeled blocks

We can break out of the outer loop from inside the inner loop, but only if we give a label to our loop. This can be done like this:

```
outer:
for (let group of groups) {
  inner:
  for (let member of group) {
    if (member.startsWith("M")) {
      console.log("found one starting with M:", member);
```

```
      break outer;
    }
  }
}
```

We are giving our block a label by putting a word and a colon in front of a code block. These words can be pretty much anything (in our case, "outer" and "inner"), but not JavaScript's own reserved words, such as for, if, break, else, and others.

This will only log the first name starting with an M:

```
found one starting with M: Martin
```

It will only log one, because it is breaking out of the outer loop and all the loops end as soon as they find one. In a similar fashion you can continue the outer loop as well.

Whenever you want to be done as soon as you find one hit, this is the option to use. So, for example, if you want check for errors and quit if there aren't any, this would be the way to go.

Chapter project

Math multiplication table

In this project, you will create a math multiplication table using loops. You can do this using your own creativity or by following some of the following suggested steps:

1. Set up a blank array to contain the final multiplication table.
2. Set a value variable to specify how many values you want to multiply with one another and show the results for.
3. Create an outer for loop to iterate through each row and a temp array to store the row values. Each row will be an array of cells that will be nested into the final table.
4. Add an inner for loop for the column values, which will push the multiplied row and column values to the temp array.
5. Add the temporary row data that contains the calculated solutions to the main array of the final table. The final result will add a row of values for the calculations.

Self-check quiz

1. What is the expected output for the following code?

```
let step = 3;

for (let i = 0; i < 1000; i += step) {
    if (i > 10) {
        break;
    }
    console.log(i);
}
```

2. What is the final value for myArray, and what is expected in the console?

```
const myArray = [1,5,7];
for(el in myArray){
    console.log(Number(el));
    el = Number(el) + 5;
    console.log(el);
}
console.log(myArray);
```

Summary

In this chapter we introduced the concept of loops. Loops enable us to repeat a certain block of code. We need some sort of condition when we loop, and as long as that condition is true, we'll keep looping. As soon as it changes to false, we end our loop.

We have seen the while loop, in which we just insert a condition, and as long as that condition is true we keep looping. If the condition is never true, we won't even execute the loop code once.

This is different for the do while loop. We always execute the code once, and then we start to check a condition. If this condition is true, we execute the code again and do so until the condition becomes false. This can be useful when working with input from outside, such as user input. We would need to request it once, and then we can keep on requesting it again until it is valid.

Then we saw the `for` loop, which has a slightly different syntax. We have to specify a variable, check a condition (preferably using that variable, but this is not mandatory), and then specify an action to be executed after every iteration. Again, it's preferable for the action to include the variable from the first part of the `for` loop. This gives us code that is to be executed as long as a condition is true.

We also saw two ways to loop over arrays and objects, `for in` and `for of`. The `for in` loop loops over keys and `for of` loops over values. They go over every element in a collection. The advantage of these loops is that JavaScript controls the execution: you can't miss an element or get stuck in an infinite loop.

Lastly, we saw `break` and `continue`. We can use the `break` keyword to end a loop immediately and the `continue` keyword to end the current iteration and go back to the top and start the next iteration, if the condition is still true, that is.

In the next chapter we are going to be adding a really powerful tool to our JavaScript toolbox: functions! They allow us to take our coding skills to the next level and structure our code better.

Join our book's Discord space

Join the book's Discord workspace for a monthly *Ask me Anything* session with the authors: `https://packt.link/JSBook`

6
Functions

You have seen quite a lot of JavaScript already, and now you are ready for functions. Soon you will see that you have been using functions already, but now it is time to learn how to start writing your own. Functions are a great building block that will reduce the amount of code you will need in your app. You can call a function whenever you need it, and you can write it as a kind of template with variables. So, depending on how you've written it, you can reuse it in many situations.

They do require you to think differently about the structure of your code and this can be hard, especially in the beginning. Once you have got the hang of this way of thinking, functions will really help you to write nicely structured, reusable, and low-maintenance code. Let's dive into this new abstraction layer!

Along the way, we will cover the following topics:

- Basic functions
- Function arguments
- Return
- Variable scope in functions
- Recursive functions
- Nested functions
- Anonymous functions
- Function callbacks

 Note: exercise, project and self-check quiz answers can be found in the *Appendix*.

Basic functions

We have been calling functions for a while already. Remember `prompt()`, `console.log()`, `push()`, and `sort()` for arrays? These are all functions. Functions are a group of statements, variable declarations, loops, and so on that are bundled together. Calling a function means an entire group of statements will get executed.

First, we are going to have a look at how we can invoke functions, and then we will see how to write functions of our own.

Invoking functions

We can recognize functions by the parentheses at the end. We can invoke functions like this:

```
nameOfTheFunction();
functionThatTakesInput("the input", 5, true);
```

This is invoking a function called `nameOfTheFunction` with no arguments, and a function called `functionThatTakesInput` with three required arguments. Let's have a look at what functions can look like when we start writing them.

Writing functions

Writing a function can be done using the `function` keyword. Here is the template syntax to do so:

```
function nameOfTheFunction() {
    //content of the function
}
```

The above function can be called like this:

```
nameOfTheFunction();
```

Let's write a function that asks for your name and then greets you:

```
function sayHello() {
  let you = prompt("What's your name? ");
  console.log("Hello", you + "!");
}
```

We add a space after the question mark to ensure the user starts typing their answer one space away from the question mark, rather than directly afterward. We call this function like this:

```
sayHello();
```

It will prompt:

```
What's your name? >
```

Let's go ahead and enter our name. The output will be:

```
Hello Maaike!
```

Take a moment to consider the relationship between functions and variables. As you have seen, functions can contain variables, which shape how they operate. The opposite is also true: variables can contain functions. Still with me? Here you can see an example of a variable containing a function (`varContainingFunction`) and a variable inside a function (`varInFunction`):

```
let varContainingFunction = function() {
    let varInFunction = "I'm in a function.";
    console.log("hi there!", varInFunction);
};

varContainingFunction();
```

Variables contain a certain value and *are* something; they do not *do* anything. Functions are actions. They are a bundle of statements that can be executed when they get called. JavaScript will not run the statements when the functions do not get invoked. We will return to the idea of storing functions in variables, and consider some of the benefits, in the *Anonymous functions* section, but for now let's move on to look at the best way to name your functions.

Naming functions

Giving your function a name might seem like a trivial task, but there are some best practices to keep in mind here. To keep it short:

- Use camelCase for your functions: this means that the first word starts with a lowercase letter and new words start with a capital. That makes it a lot easier to read and keeps your code consistent.

- Make sure that the name describes what the function is doing: it's better to call a number addition function `addNumbers` than `myFunc`.

- Use a verb to describe what the function is doing: make it an action. So instead of hiThere, call it sayHi.

Practice exercise 6.1

See if you can write a function for yourself. We want to write a function that adds two numbers.

1. Create a function that takes two parameters, adds the parameters together, and returns the result.
2. Set up two different variables with two different values.
3. Use your function on the two variables, and output the result using console.log.
4. Create a second call to the function using two more numbers as arguments sent to the function.

Practice exercise 6.2

We are going to create a program that will randomly describe an inputted name.

1. Create an array of descriptive words.
2. Create a function that contains a prompt asking the user for a name.
3. Select a random value from the array using Math.random.
4. Output into the console the prompt value and the randomly selected array value.
5. Invoke the function.

Parameters and arguments

You may have noticed that we are talking about parameters and arguments. Both terms are commonly used to mean the information that is passed into a function:

```
function tester(para1, para2){
    return para1 + " " + para2;
}
const arg1 = "argument 1";
const arg2 = "argument 2";
tester(arg1, arg2);
```

A parameter is defined as the variable listed inside the parentheses of the function definition, which defines the scope of the function. They are declared like so:

```
function myFunc(param1, param2) {
  // code of the function;
}
```

A practical example could be the following, which takes x and y as parameters:

```
function addTwoNumbers(x, y) {
   console.log(x + y);
}
```

When called, this function will simply add the parameters and log the result. However, to do this, we can call the function with arguments:

```
myFunc("arg1", "arg2");
```

We have seen various examples of arguments; for example:

```
console.log("this is an argument");
prompt("argument here too");

let arr = [];
arr.push("argument");
```

Depending on the arguments you are calling with the function, the outcome of the function can change, which makes the function a very powerful and flexible building block. A practical example using our addTwoNumbers() function looks like this:

```
addTwoNumbers(3, 4);
addTwoNumbers(12,-90);
```

This will output:

```
7
-78
```

As you can see, the function has a different outcome for both calls. This is because we call it with different arguments, which take the place of x and y, that are sent to the function to be used within the function scope.

Practice exercise 6.3

Create a basic calculator that takes two numbers and one string value indicating an operation. If the operation equals add, the two numbers should be added. If the operation equals subtract, the two numbers should be subtracted from one another. If there is no option specified, the value of the option should be add.

The result of this function needs to be logged. Test your function by invoking it with different operators and no operator specified.

1. Set up two variables containing number values.

2. Set up a variable to hold an operator, either + or -.

3. Create a function that retrieves the two values and the operator string value within its parameters. Use those values with a condition to check if the operator is + or -, and add or subtract the values accordingly (remember if not presented with a valid operator, the function should default to addition).

4. Within `console.log()`, call the function using your variables and output the response to the console.

5. Update the operator value to be the other operator type—either plus or minus—and call to the function again with the new updated arguments.

Default or unsuitable parameters

What happens if we call our `addTwoNumbers()` function without any arguments? Take a moment and decide what you think this should do:

```
addTwoNumbers();
```

Some languages might crash and cry, but not JavaScript. JavaScript just gives the variables a default type, which is undefined. And `undefined + undefined` equals:

```
NaN
```

Instead, we could tell JavaScript to take different default parameters. And that can be done like this:

```
function addTwoNumbers(x = 2, y = 3) {
    console.log(x + y);
}
```

If you call the function with no arguments now, it will automatically assign 2 to x and 3 to y, unless you override them by calling the function with arguments. The values that are used for invoking are prioritized over hardcoded arguments. So, given the above function, what will the output of these function calls be?

```
addTwoNumbers();
addTwoNumbers(6, 6);
addTwoNumbers(10);
```

The output will be:

```
5
12
13
```

The first one has the default values, so x is 2 and y is 3. The second one assigns 6 to both x and y. The last one is a bit less obvious. We are only giving one argument, so which one will be given this value? Well, JavaScript does not like to overcomplicate things. It simply assigns the value to the first parameter, x. Therefore, x becomes 10 and y gets its default value 3, and together that makes 13.

If you call a function with more arguments than parameters, nothing will happen. JavaScript will just execute the function using the first arguments that can be mapped to parameters. Like this:

```
addTwoNumbers(1,2,3,4);
```

This will output:

```
3
```

It is just adding 1 and 2 and ignoring the last two arguments (3 and 4).

Special functions and operators

There are a few special ways of writing functions, as well as some special operators that will come in handy. We are talking about arrow functions and the spread and rest operators here. Arrow functions are great for sending functions around as parameters and using shorter notations. The spread and rest operators make our lives easier and are more flexible when sending arguments and working with arrays.

Arrow functions

Arrow functions are a special way of writing functions that can be confusing at first. Their use looks like this:

```
(param1, param2) => body of the function;
```

Or for no parameters:

```
() => body of the function;
```

Or for one parameter (no parentheses are needed here):

```
param => body of the function;
```

Or for a multiline function with two parameters:

```
(param1, param2) => {
  // line 1;
  // any number of lines;
};
```

Arrow functions are useful whenever you want to write an implementation on the spot, such as inside another function as an argument. This is because they are a shorthand notation for writing functions. They are most often used for functions that consist of only one statement. Let's start with a simple function that we will rewrite to an arrow function:

```
function doingStuff(x) {
    console.log(x);
}
```

To rewrite this as an arrow function, you will have to store it in a variable or send it in as an argument if you want to be able to use it. We use the name of the variable to execute the arrow function. In this case we only have one parameter, so it's optional to surround it with parentheses. We can write it like this:

```
let doingArrowStuff = x => console.log(x);
```

And invoke it like this:

```
doingArrowStuff("Great!");
```

This will log `Great!` to the console. If there is more than one argument, we will have to use parentheses, like this:

```
let addTwoNumbers = (x, y) => console.log(x + y);
```

We can call it like this:

```
addTwoNumbers(5, 3);
```

And then it will log `8` to the console. If there are no arguments, you must use the parentheses, like this:

```
let sayHi = () => console.log("hi");
```

If we call `sayHi()`, it will log `hi` to the console.

As a final example, we can combine the arrow function with certain built-in methods. For example, we can use the `foreach()` method on an array. This method executes a certain function for every element in the array. Have a look at this example:

```
const arr = ["squirrel", "alpaca", "buddy"];
arr.forEach(e => console.log(e));
```

It outputs:

```
squirrel
alpaca
buddy
```

For every element in the array, it takes the element as input and executing the arrow function for it. In this case, the function is to log the element. So the output is every single element in the array.

Using arrow functions combined with built-in functions is very powerful. We can do something for every element in the array, without counting or writing a complicated loop. We'll see more examples of great use cases for arrow functions later on.

Spread operator

The spread operator is a special operator. It consists of three dots used before a referenced expression or string, and it spreads out the arguments or elements of an array.

This might sound very complicated, so let's look at a simple example:

```
let spread = ["so", "much", "fun"];
let message = ["JavaScript", "is", ...spread, "and", "very",
               "powerful"];
```

The value of this array becomes:

```
['JavaScript', 'is', 'so', 'much', 'fun', 'and', 'very', 'powerful']
```

As you can see, the elements of the spread operator become individual elements in the array. The spread operator spreads the array to individual elements in the new array. It can also be used to send multiple arguments to a function, like this:

```
function addTwoNumbers(x, y) {
   console.log(x + y);
}
let arr = [5, 9];
addTwoNumbers(...arr);
```

This will log 14 to the console, since it is the same as calling the function with:

```
addTwoNumbers(5, 9);
```

This operator avoids having to copy a long array or string into a function, which saves time and reduces code complexity. You can call a function with multiple spread operators. It will use all the elements of the arrays as input. Here's an example:

```
function addFourNumbers(x, y, z, a) {
   console.log(x + y + z + a);
}
let arr = [5, 9];
let arr2 = [6, 7];
addFourNumbers(...arr, ...arr2);
```

This will output 27 to the console, calling the function like this:

```
addFourNumbers(5, 9, 6, 7);
```

Rest parameter

Similar to the spread operator, we have the rest parameter. It has the same symbol as the spread operator, but it is used inside the function parameter list. Remember what would happen if we were to send an argument too many times, as here:

```
function someFunction(param1, param2) {
  console.log(param1, param2);
}
someFunction("hi", "there!", "How are you?");
```

That's right. Nothing really: it would just pretend we only sent in two arguments and log hi there!. If we use the rest parameter, it allows us to send in any number of arguments and translate them into a parameter array. Here is an example:

```
function someFunction(param1, ...param2) {
  console.log(param1, param2);
}
someFunction("hi", "there!", "How are you?");
```

This will log:

```
hi [ 'there!', 'How are you?' ]
```

As you can see, the second parameter has changed into an array, containing our second and third arguments. This can be useful whenever you are not sure what number of arguments you will get. Using the rest parameter allows you to process this variable number of arguments, for example, using a loop.

Returning function values

We are still missing a very important piece to make functions as useful as they are: the return value. Functions can give back a result when we specify a return value. The return value can be stored in a variable. We have done this already – remember prompt()?

```
let favoriteSubject = prompt("What is your favorite subject?");
```

Functions

We are storing the result of our `prompt()` function in the variable `favoriteSubject`, which in this case would be whatever the user specifies. Let's see what happens if we store the result of our `addTwoNumbers()` function and log that variable:

```
let result = addTwoNumbers(4, 5);
console.log(result);
```

You may or may not have guessed it—this logs the following:

```
9
undefined
```

The value `9` is written to the console because `addTwoNumbers()` contains a `console.log()` statement. The `console.log(result)` line outputs `undefined`, because nothing is inserted into the function to store the result, meaning our function `addTwoNumbers()` does not send anything back. Since JavaScript does not like to cause trouble and crash, it will assign `undefined`. To counter this, we can rewrite our `addTwoNumbers()` function to actually return the value instead of logging it. This is much more powerful because we can store the result and continue working with the result of this function in the rest of our code:

```
function addTwoNumbers(x, y) {
    return x + y;
}
```

`return` ends the function and sends back whatever value comes after `return`. If it is an expression, like the one above, it will evaluate the expression to one result and then return that to where it was called (the `result` variable, in this instance):

```
let result = addTwoNumbers(4, 5);
console.log(result);
```

With these adjustments made, the code snippet logs 9 to the terminal.

What do you think this code does?

```
let resultsArr = [];

for(let i = 0; i < 10; i ++){
    let result = addTwoNumbers(i, 2*i);
    resultsArr.push(result);
}

console.log(resultsArr);
```

It logs an array of all the results to the screen. The function is being called in a loop. The first iteration, i, equals 0. Therefore, the result is 0. The last iteration, i, equals 9, and therefore the last value of the array equals 27. Here are the results:

```
[
    0,   3,   6,   9,  12,
   15,  18,  21,  24,  27
]
```

Practice exercise 6.4

Modify the calculator that you made in *Practice exercise 6.2* to return added values instead of printing them. Then, call the function 10 or more times in a loop, and store the results in an array. Once the loop finishes, output the final array into the console.

1. Set up an empty array to store the values that will be calculated within the loop.
2. Create a loop that runs 10 times, incrementing by 1 each time, creating two values each iteration. For the first value, multiply the value of the loop count by 5. For the second value, multiply the value of the loop counter by itself.
3. Create a function that returns the value of the two parameters passed into the function when it is called. Add the values together, returning the result.
4. Within the loop, call the calculation function, passing in the two values as arguments into the function and storing the returned result in a response variable.
5. Still within the loop, push the result values into the array as it iterates through the loop.
6. After the loop is complete, output the value of the array into the console.
7. You should see the values [0, 6, 14, 24, 36, 50, 66, 84, 104, 126] for the array in the console.

Returning with arrow functions

If we have a one-line arrow function, we can return without using the keyword return. So if we want to rewrite the function, we can write it like this to make an arrow function out of it:

```
let addTwoNumbers = (x, y) => x + y;
```

And we can call it and store the result like this:

```
let result = addTwoNumbers(12, 15);
console.log(result);
```

This will then log 27 to the console. If it's a multiline function, you will have to use the keyword `return` as demonstrated in the previous section. So, for example:

```
let addTwoNumbers = (x, y) => {
    console.log("Adding...");
    return x + y;
}
```

Variable scope in functions

In this section, we will discuss a topic that is often considered challenging. We will talk about scope. Scope defines where you can access a certain variable. When a variable is *in scope*, you can access it. When a variable is *out of scope*, you cannot access the variable. We will discuss this for both local and global variables.

Local variables in functions

Local variables are only in scope within the function they are defined. This is true for `let` variables and `var` variables. There is a difference between them, which we will touch upon here as well. The function parameters (they do not use `let` or `var`) are also local variables. This might sound very vague, but the next code snippet will demonstrate what this means:

```
function testAvailability(x) {
    console.log("Available here:", x);
}

testAvailability("Hi!");
console.log("Not available here:", x);
```

This will output:

```
Available here: Hi!
ReferenceError: x is not defined
```

When called inside the function, x will be logged. The statement outside of the function fails, because x is a local variable to the function `testAvailability()`. This is showing that the function parameters are not accessible outside of the function.

They are out of scope outside the function and in scope inside the function. Let's have a look at a variable defined inside a function:

```
function testAvailability() {
    let y = "Local variable!";
    console.log("Available here:", y);
}


testAvailability();
console.log("Not available here:", y);
```

This shows the following on the console:

```
Available here: Local variable!
ReferenceError: y is not defined
```

Variables defined inside the function are not available outside the function either.

For beginners, it can be confusing to combine local variables and return. Right now, we're telling you the local variables declared inside a function are not available outside of the function, but with return you can make their values available outside the function. So if you need their values outside a function, you can return the values. The key word here is *values*! You cannot return the variable itself. Instead, a value can be caught and stored in a different variable, like this:

```
function testAvailability() {
    let y = "I'll return";
    console.log("Available here:", y);
    return y;
}


let z = testAvailability();
console.log("Outside the function:", z);
console.log("Not available here:", y);
```

So, the returned value I'll return that was assigned to local variable y gets returned and stored in variable z.

 This variable z could actually also have been called y, but that would have been confusing since it still would have been a different variable.

The output of this code snippet is as follows:

```
Available here: I'll return
Outside the function: I'll return
ReferenceError: y is not defined
```

let versus var variables

The difference between let and var is that var is function-scoped, which is the concept we described above. let is actually not function-scoped but block-scoped. A block is defined by two curly braces { }. The code within those braces is where let is still available.

Let's see this distinction in action:

```
function doingStuff() {
  if (true) {
    var x = "local";
  }
  console.log(x);
}

doingStuff();
```

The output of this snippet will be:

```
local
```

If we use var, the variable becomes function-scoped and is available anywhere in the function block (even before defining with the value undefined). Thus, after the if block has ended, x can still be accessed.

Here is what happens with let:

```
function doingStuff() {
  if (true) {
    let x = "local";
  }
  console.log(x);
}

doingStuff();
```

This will produce the following output:

```
ReferenceError: x is not defined
```

Here we get the error that x is not defined. Since let is only block-scoped, x goes out of scope when the if block ends and can no longer be accessed after that.

A final difference between let and var relates to the order of declaration in a script. Try using the value of x before having defined it with let:

```
function doingStuff() {
  if (true) {
    console.log(x);
    let x = "local";
  }
}

doingStuff();
```

This will give a ReferenceError that x is not initialized. This is because variables declared with let cannot be accessed before being defined, even within the same block. What do you think will happen for a var declaration like this?

```
function doingStuff() {
  if (true) {
    console.log(x);
    var x = "local";
  }
}

doingStuff();
```

This time, we won't get an error. When we use a var variable before the define statement, we simply get undefined. This is due to a phenomenon called hoisting, which means using a var variable before it's been declared results in the variable being undefined rather than giving a ReferenceError.

 Hoisting, and how to negate its effects if needed, are more complex topics that we will cover in *Chapter 12, Intermediate JavaScript*.

const scope

Constants are block-scoped, just like let. This is why the scope rules here are similar to those for let. Here is an example:

```
function doingStuff() {
  if (true) {
```

```
      const X = "local";
  }
  console.log(X);
}

doingStuff();
```

This will produce the following output:

```
ReferenceError: X is not defined
```

Using a `const` variable before having defined it will also give a `ReferenceError`, just as it does for a `let` variable.

Global variables

As you might have guessed, global variables are variables declared outside a function and not in some other code block. Variables are accessible in the scope (either function or block) where they're defined, plus any "lower" scopes. So, a variable defined outside of a function is available within the function as well as inside any functions or other code blocks inside that function. A variable defined at the top level of your program is therefore available everywhere in your program. This concept is called a global variable. You can see an example here:

```
let globalVar = "Accessible everywhere!";
console.log("Outside function:", globalVar);

function creatingNewScope(x) {
  console.log("Access to global vars inside function." , globalVar);
}

creatingNewScope("some parameter");

console.log("Still available:", globalVar);
```

This will output:

```
Outside function: Accessible everywhere!
Access to global vars inside function. Accessible everywhere!
Still available: Accessible everywhere!
```

As you can see, global variables are accessible from everywhere because they are not declared in a block. They are *always* in scope after they have been defined — it doesn't matter where you use them. However, you can hide their accessibility inside a function by specifying a new variable with the same name inside that scope; this can be done for `let`, `var`, and `const`. (This is not changing the value of the `const` variable; you are creating a new `const` variable that is going to override the first one in the inner scope.) In the same scope, you cannot specify two `let` or two `const` variables with the same name. You can do so for `var`, but you shouldn't do so, in order to avoid confusion.

If you create a variable with the same name inside a function, that variable's value will be used whenever you refer to that variable name within the scope of that particular function. Here you can see an example:

```
let x = "global";

function doingStuff() {
  let x = "local";
  console.log(x);
}

doingStuff();
console.log(x);
```

This will output:

```
local
global
```

As you can see, the value of x inside the `doingStuff()` function is `local`. However, outside the function the value is still `global`. This means that you'll have to be extra careful about mixing up names in local and global scopes. It is usually better to avoid this.

The same is also true for parameter names. If you have the same parameter name as a global variable, the value of the parameter will be used:

```
let x = "global";

function doingStuff(x) {
  console.log(x);
}

doingStuff("param");
```

This will log param.

There is a danger in relying on global variables too much. This is something you will come across soon when your applications grow. As we just saw, local variables override the value of global variables. It is best to work with local variables in functions; this way, you have more control over what you are working with. This might be a bit vague for now, but it will become clear when coding in the wild as things get bigger and more lines and files of code get involved.

There is only one more very important point to be made about scopes for now. Let's start with an example and see if you can figure out what this should log:

```
function confuseReader() {
  x = "Guess my scope...";
  console.log("Inside the function:", x);
}


confuseReader();
console.log("Outside of function:", x);
```

Answer ready? Here is the output:

```
Inside the function: Guess my scope...
Outside of function: Guess my scope...
```

Do not close the book—we'll explain what is going on. If you look carefully, the x in the function gets defined without the keyword let or var. There is no declaration of x above the code; this is all the code of the program. JavaScript does not see let or var and then decides, "this must be a global variable." Even though it gets defined inside the function, the declaration of x within the function gets global scope and can still be accessed outside of the function.

We really want to emphasize that this is a terrible practice. If you need a global variable, declare it at the top of your file.

Immediately invoked function expression

The **immediately invoked function expression (IIFE)** is a way of expressing a function so that it gets invoked immediately. It is anonymous, it doesn't have a name, and it is self-executing.

This can be useful when you want to initialize something using this function. It is also used in many design patterns, for example, to create private and public variables and functions.

This has to do with where functions and variables are accessible from. If you have an IIFE in the top-level scope, whatever is in there is not accessible from outside even though it is top level.

Here is how to define it:

```
(function () {
    console.log("IIFE!");
})();
```

The function itself is surrounded by parentheses, which makes it create a function instance. Without these parentheses around it, it would throw an error because our function does not have a name (this is worked around by assigning the function to a variable, though, where the output can be returned to the variable).

(); executes the unnamed function—this must be done immediately following a function declaration. If your function were to require a parameter, you would pass it in within these final brackets.

You could also combine IIFE with other function patterns. For example, you could use an arrow function here to make the function even more concise:

```
(()=>{
    console.log("run right away");
})();
```

Again, we use (); to invoke the function that you created.

Practice exercise 6.5

Use IIFE to create a few immediately invoked functions and observe how the scope is affected.

1. Create a variable value with let and assign a string value of 1000 to it.
2. Create an IIFE function and within this function scope assign a new value to a variable of the same name. Within the function, print the local value to the console.
3. Create an IIFE expression, assigning it to a new result variable, and assign a new value to a variable of the same name within this scope. Return this local value to the result variable and invoke the function. Print the result variable, along with the variable name you've been using: what value does it contain now?

4. Lastly, create an anonymous function that has a parameter. Add logic that will assign a passed-in value to the same variable name as the other steps, and print it as part of a string sentence. Invoke the function and pass in your desired value within the rounded brackets.

Recursive functions

In some cases, you want to call the same function from inside the function. It can be a beautiful solution to rather complex problems. There are some things to keep in mind though. What do you think this will do?

```
function getRecursive(nr) {
  console.log(nr);
  getRecursive(--nr);
}


getRecursive(3);
```

It prints 3 and then counts down and never stops. Why is it not stopping? Well, we are not saying when it should stop. Look at our improved version:

```
function getRecursive(nr) {
  console.log(nr);
  if (nr > 0) {
    getRecursive(--nr);
  }
}


getRecursive(3);
```

This function is going to call itself until the value of the parameter is no longer bigger than 0. And then it stops.

What happens when we call a function recursively is that it goes one function deeper every time. The first function call is done last. For this function it goes like this:

- getRecursive(3)
  - getRecursive(2)
    - getRecursive(1)
      - getRecursive(0)
      - done with getRecursive(0) execution

- done with getRecursive(1) execution
- done with getRecursive(2) execution
- done with getRecursive(3) execution

The next recursive function will demonstrate that:

```
function logRecursive(nr) {
  console.log("Started function:", nr);
  if (nr > 0) {
    logRecursive(nr - 1);
  } else {
      console.log("done with recursion");
  }
  console.log("Ended function:", nr);
}

logRecursive(3);
```

It will output:

```
Started function: 3
Started function: 2
Started function: 1
Started function: 0
done with recursion
Ended function: 0
Ended function: 1
Ended function: 2
Ended function: 3
```

Recursive functions can be great in some contexts. When you feel the need to call the same function over and over again in a loop, you should probably consider recursion. An example could also be searching for something. Instead of looping over everything inside the same function, you can split up inside the function and call the function repeatedly from the inside.

However, it must be kept in mind that in general, the performance of recursion is slightly worse than the performance of regular iteration using a loop. So if this causes a bottleneck situation that would really slow down your application, then you might want to consider another approach.

Have a look at calculating the factorial using recursive functions in the following exercise.

Practice exercise 6.6

A common problem that we can solve with recursion is calculating the factorial.

 Quick mathematics refresher about factorials:

The factorial of a number is the product of all positive integers bigger than 0, up to the number itself. So for example, the factorial of seven is 7 * 6 * 5 * 4 * 3 * 2 * 1. You can write this as 7!.

How are recursive functions going to help us calculate the factorial? We are going to call the function with a lower number until we reach 0. In this exercise, we will use recursion to calculate the factorial result of a numeric value set as the argument of a function.

1. Create a function that contains a condition within it checking if the argument value is 0.

2. If the parameter is equal to 0, it should return the value of 1. Otherwise, it should return the value of the argument multiplied by the value returned from the function itself, subtracting one from the value of the argument that is provided. This will result in running the block of code until the value reaches 0.

3. Invoke the function, providing an argument of whatever number you want to find the factorial of. The code should run whatever number is passed initially into the function, decreasing all the way to 0 and outputting the results of the calculation to the console. It could also contain a `console.log()` call to print the current value of the argument in the function as it gets invoked.

4. Change and update the number to see how it affects the results.

Nested functions

Just as with loops, `if` statements, and actually all other building blocks, we can have functions inside functions. This phenomenon is called nested functions:

```
function doOuterFunctionStuff(nr) {
  console.log("Outer function");
  doInnerFunctionStuff(nr);
  function doInnerFunctionStuff(x) {
    console.log(x + 7);
```

```
    console.log("I can access outer variables:", nr);
  }
}
doOuterFunctionStuff(2);
```

This will output:

```
Outer function
9
I can access outer variables: 2
```

As you can see, the outer function is calling its nested function. This nested function has access to the variables of the parent. The other way around, this is not the case. Variables defined inside the inner function have function scope. This means they are accessible inside the function where they are defined, which is in this case the inner function. Thus, this will throw a ReferenceError:

```
function doOuterFunctionStuff(nr) {
  doInnerFunctionStuff(nr);
  function doInnerFunctionStuff(x) {
    let z = 10;
  }
  console.log("Not accessible:", z);
}

doOuterFunctionStuff(2);
```

What do you think this will do?

```
function doOuterFunctionStuff(nr) {
  doInnerFunctionStuff(nr);
  function doInnerFunctionStuff(x) {
    let z = 10;
  }
}

doInnerFunctionStuff(3);
```

This will also throw a ReferenceError. Now, doInnerFunctionStuff() is defined inside the outer function, which means that it is only in scope inside doOuterFunctionStuff(). Outside this function, it is out of scope.

Practice exercise 6.7

Create a countdown loop starting at a dynamic value of 10.

1. Set the start variable at a value of 10, which will be used as the starting value for the loop.
2. Create a function that takes one argument, which is the countdown value.
3. Within the function, output the current value of the countdown into the console.
4. Add a condition to check if the value is less than 1; if it is, then return the function.
5. Add a condition to check if the value of the countdown is not less than 1, then continue to loop by calling the function within itself.
6. Make sure you add a decrement operator on the countdown so the preceding condition eventually will be true to end the loop. Every time it loops, the value will decrease until it reaches 0.
7. Update and create a second countdown using a condition if the value is greater than 0. If it is, decrease the value of the countdown by 1.
8. Use return to return the function, which then invokes it again and again until the condition is no longer true.
9. Make sure, when you send the new countdown value as an argument into the function, that there is a way out of the loop by using the return keyword and a condition that continues the loop if met.

Anonymous functions

So far, we have been naming our functions. We can also create functions without names if we store them inside variables. We call these functions anonymous. Here is a non-anonymous function:

```
function doingStuffAnonymously() {
  console.log("Not so secret though.");
}
```

Here is how to turn the previous function into an anonymous function:

```
function () {
  console.log("Not so secret though.");
};
```

As you can see, our function has no name. It is anonymous. So you may wonder how you can invoke this function. Well actually, you can't like this!

We will have to store it in a variable in order to call the anonymous function; we can store it like this:

```
let functionVariable = function () {
    console.log("Not so secret though.");
};
```

An anonymous function can be called using the variable name, like this:

```
functionVariable();
```

It will simply output `Not so secret though.`.

This might seem a bit useless, but it is a very powerful JavaScript construct. Storing functions inside variables enables us to do very cool things, like passing in functions as parameters. This concept adds another abstract layer to coding. This concept is called callbacks, and we will discuss it in the next section.

Practice exercise 6.8

1. Set a variable name and assign a function to it. Create a function expression with one parameter that outputs a provided argument to the console.

2. Pass an argument into the function.

3. Create the same function as a normal function declaration.

Function callbacks

Here is an example of passing a function as an argument to another function:

```
function doFlexibleStuff(executeStuff) {
    executeStuff();
    console.log("Inside doFlexibleStuffFunction.");
}
```

If we call this new function with our previously made anonymous function, `functionVariable`, like this:

```
doFlexibleStuff(functionVariable);
```

It will output:

```
Not so secret though.
Inside doFlexibleStuffFunction.
```

But we can also call it with another function, and then our `doFlexibleStuff` function will execute this other function. How cool is that?

```
let anotherFunctionVariable = function() {
   console.log("Another anonymous function implementation.");
}

doFlexibleStuff(anotherFunctionVariable);
```

This will produce the following output:

```
Another anonymous function implementation.
Inside doFlexibleStuffFunction.
```

So what happened? We created a function and stored it in the `anotherFunctionVariable` variable. We then sent that in as a function parameter to our `doFlexibleStuff()` function. And this function is simply executing whatever function gets sent in.

At this point you may wonder why the writers are so excited about this callback concept. It probably looks rather lame in the examples you have seen so far. Once we get to asynchronous functions later on, this concept is going to be of great help. To still satisfy your need for a more concrete example, we will give you one.

In JavaScript, there are many built-in functions, as you may know by now. One of them is the `setTimeout()` function. It is a very special function that is executing a certain function after a specified amount of time that it will wait first. It is also seemingly responsible for quite a few terribly performing web pages, but that is definitely not the fault of this poor misunderstood and misused function.

This code is really something you should try to understand:

```
let youGotThis = function () {
   console.log("You're doing really well, keep coding!");
};

setTimeout(youGotThis, 1000);
```

It is going to wait for 1000ms (one second) and then print:

```
You're doing really well, keep coding!
```

If you need more encouragement, you can use the setInterval() function instead. It works very similarly, but instead of executing the specified function once, it will keep on executing it with the specified interval:

```
setInterval(youGotThis, 1000);
```

In this case, it will print our encouraging message every second until you kill the program.

This concept of the function executing the function after having been called itself is very useful for managing asynchronous program execution.

Chapter projects

Create a recursive function

Create a recursive function that counts up to 10. Invoke the function with different start numbers as the arguments that are passed into the function. The function should run until the value is greater than 10.

Set timeout order

Use the arrow format to create functions that output the values one and two to the console. Create a third function that outputs the value three to the console, and then invokes the first two functions.

Create a fourth function that outputs the word four to the console and also use setTimeout() to invoke the first function immediately and then the third function.

What does your output look like in the console? Try to get the console to output:

```
Four
Three
One
Two
One
```

Self-check quiz

1. What value is output into the console?

```
let val = 10;
function tester(val){
    val += 10;
    if(val < 100){
        return tester(val);
    }
    return val;
}
tester(val);
console.log(val);
```

2. What will be output into the console by the below code?

```
let testFunction = function(){
    console.log("Hello");
}();
```

3. What will be output to the console?

```
(function () {
    console.log("Welcome");
})();
(function () {
    let firstName = "Laurence";
})();
let result = (function () {
    let firstName = "Laurence";
    return firstName;
})();
console.log(result);
(function (firstName) {
    console.log("My Name is " + firstName);
})("Laurence");
```

4. What will be output to the console?

```
let test2 = (num) => num + 5;
console.log(test2(14));
```

5. What will be output to the console?

```
var addFive1 = function addFive1(num) {
return num + 2;
};
let addFive2 = (num) => num + 2;
console.log(addFive1(14));
```

Summary

In this chapter, we have covered functions. Functions are a great JavaScript building block that we can use to reuse lines of code. We can give our functions parameters, so that we can change the code depending on the arguments a function gets invoked with. Functions can return a result; we do so using the `return` keyword. And we can use `return` at the place where we call a function. We can store the result in a variable or use it in another function, for example.

We then met with variable scopes. The scope entails the places from where variables are accessible. Default `let` and `const` variables can be accessed inside the block where they're defined (and the inner blocks of that block) and `var` is just accessible from the line where it was defined.

We can also use recursive functions to elegantly solve problems that can be solved recursively by nature, such as calculating the factorial. Nested functions were the next topic we studied. They are not a big deal, just functions inside functions. Basic functions inside functions are not considered very pretty, but anonymous functions and arrow functions are not uncommon to see. Anonymous functions are functions without a name and arrow functions are a special case of anonymous functions, where we use an arrow to separate the parameters and the body.

In the next chapter, we'll consider classes, another powerful programming construct!

Join our book's Discord space

Join the book's Discord workspace for a monthly *Ask me Anything* session with the authors: https://packt.link/JSBook

7

Classes

In this chapter, we are going to discuss JavaScript classes. We have seen JavaScript objects already, and classes are a blueprint or template for object creation. So, many of the things discussed here should not sound too unfamiliar or revolutionary.

Classes enable object-oriented programming, which was one of the most important design advancements in software development. This development reduced the complexity of applications and increased maintainability by a huge margin.

So, object-oriented programming and classes are of great importance for computer science in general. This is not necessarily the case when we apply it to JavaScript though. JavaScript classes are something special compared to other programming languages. Beneath the surface, classes are wrapped in some sort of special function. This means that they are actually an alternative syntax for defining objects using a constructor function. In this chapter, we will learn what classes are and how we can create and use them. Along the way, we will cover the following topics:

- Object-oriented programming
- Classes and objects
- Classes
- Inheritance
- Prototypes

 Note: exercise, project, and self-check quiz answers can be found in the *Appendix*.

Object-oriented programming

Before we start diving right into the fun of classes, let's briefly say something about **object-oriented programming (OOP)**. OOP is a very important programming paradigm wherein code is structured in objects, leading to more maintainable and reusable code. Working with OOP teaches you to really try to think of all sorts of topics in objects, by bundling properties in such a way that they can be wrapped in a blueprint called a class. This in turn might be inheriting properties from a parent class.

For example, if we are thinking of an animal, we can come up with certain properties: name, weight, height, maximum speed, colors, and a lot more. And then if we think of a specific species of fish, we can reuse all the properties of "animal" and add a few fish-specific properties in there as well. The same for dogs; if we then think of a dog, we can reuse all the properties of "animal" and add a few dog-specific ones to it. This way we have reusable code of our animal class. And when we realize we forgot a very important property for the many animals in our application, we only need to add it to the animal class.

This is very important for Java, .NET, and other classic object-oriented ways of writing code. JavaScript doesn't necessarily revolve around objects. We will need them and we will use them, but they are not the star of our code, so to speak.

Classes and objects

As a quick refresher, objects are a collection of properties and methods. We saw them in *Chapter 3, JavaScript Multiple Values*. The properties of an object should have sensible names. So for example, if we have a person object, this object could have properties called age and lastName that contain values. Here is an example of an object:

```
let dog = { dogName: "JavaScript",
            weight: 2.4,
            color: "brown",
            breed: "chihuahua"
          };
```

Classes in JavaScript encapsulate data and functions that are part of that class. If you create a class, you can later create objects using that class using the following syntax:

```
class ClassName {
  constructor(prop1, prop2) {
    this.prop1 = prop1;
```

```
      this.prop2 = prop2;
  }
}

let obj = new ClassName("arg1", "arg2");
```

This code defines a class with `ClassName` as a name, declares an `obj` variable, and initializes this with a new instance of the object. Two arguments are provided. These arguments will be used by the constructor to initialize the properties. As you can see, the parameters of the constructor and the properties of the class (`prop1` and `prop2`) have the same name. The properties of the class can be recognized by the `this` keyword in front of them. The `this` keyword refers to the object it belongs to, so it is the first property of the instance of `ClassName`.

Remember we said that classes are just some special function beneath the surface. We could create the object with a special function like this:

```
function Dog(dogName, weight, color, breed) {
  this.dogName = dogName;
  this.weight = weight;
  this.color = color;
  this.breed = breed;
}

let dog = new Dog("Jacky", 30, "brown", "labrador");
```

The dog example could have been made using a class syntax as well. It would have looked like this:

```
class Dog {
  constructor(dogName, weight, color, breed) {
    this.dogName = dogName;
    this.weight = weight;
    this.color = color;
    this.breed = breed;
  }
}

let dog = new Dog("JavaScript", 2.4, "brown", "chihuahua");
```

This results in an object with the same properties. If we do some logging as follows, we will be able to see it:

```
console.log(dog.dogName, "is a", dog.breed, "and weighs", dog.weight,
"kg.");
```

This will output:

```
JavaScript is a chihuahua and weighs 2.4 kg.
```

In the next section, we will dive into all the parts of classes.

Classes

You may wonder, if classes do the exact same thing as simply defining an object, why do we even need classes? The answer is that classes are essentially blueprints for object creation. This means that we need to do much less typing if we need to create 20 dogs when we have a dog class. If we have to create the objects, we will have to specify all the properties' names each time. And it would be easy to make a typo and misspell a property name. Classes come in handy in these sorts of situations.

As shown in the previous section, we use the `class` keyword to tell JavaScript we want to create a class. Next, we give the class a name. It is the convention to start class names with a capital letter.

Let's have a look at all the different elements of a class.

Constructors

The `constructor` method is a special method that we use to initialize objects with our class blueprint. There can only be one constructor in a class. This constructor contains properties that will be set when initiating the class.

Here you can see an example of a constructor in a `Person` class:

```
class Person {
  constructor(firstname, lastname) {
    this.firstname = firstname;
    this.lastname = lastname;
  }
}
```

Beneath the surface, JavaScript creates a special function based on this constructor. This function gets the class name, and it will create an object with the given properties. With this special function, you can create instances (objects) of the class.

Here is how you can create a new object from the Person class:

```
let p = new Person("Maaike", "van Putten");
```

The new word is what tells JavaScript to look for the special constructor function in the Person class and create a new object. The constructor gets called and returns an instance of the person object with the specified properties. This object gets stored in the p variable.

If we use our new p variable in a logging statement, you can see that the properties are really set:

```
console.log("Hi", p.firstname);
```

This outputs:

```
Hi Maaike
```

What do you think will happen when we create a class without all of the properties? Let's find out:

```
let p = new Person("Maaike");
```

Many languages would crash, but not JavaScript. It just sets the remaining properties to undefined. You can see what happens by logging it:

```
console.log("Hi", p.firstname, p.lastname);
```

This results in:

```
Hi Maaike undefined
```

You can specify default values in constructor. You would do it like this:

```
constructor(firstname, lastname = "Doe") {
    this.firstname = firstname;
    this.lastname = lastname;
}
```

This way, it would not have printed Hi Maaike undefined, but Hi Maaike Doe.

Practice exercise 7.1

Take the following steps to create a person class, and print instances of friends' names:

1. Create a class for `Person` including the constructor for `firstname` and `lastname`.

2. Create a variable and assign a value of the new `Person` object using your friend's first and last names.

3. Now add a second variable with another friend's name using their first name and last name.

4. Output both friends into the console with a greeting of `hello`.

Methods

In a class, we can specify functions. This means that our object can start doing things using the object's own properties — for example, printing a name. Functions on a class are called methods. When defining these methods, we don't use the `function` keyword. We start directly with the name:

```
class Person {
  constructor(firstname, lastname) {
    this.firstname = firstname;
    this.lastname = lastname;
  }

  greet() {
    console.log("Hi there! I'm", this.firstname);
  }
}
```

We can call the `greet` method on a `Person` object like this:

```
let p = new Person("Maaike", "van Putten");
p.greet();
```

It will output:

```
Hi there! I'm Maaike
```

You can specify as many methods on a class as you want. In this example, we are using the `firstname` property. We do so by saying `this.property`. If we had a person with a different value for the `firstname` property, for example, Rob, it would have printed:

```
Hi there! I'm Rob
```

Just like functions, methods can also take parameters and return results:

```
class Person {
  constructor(firstname, lastname) {
    this.firstname = firstname;
    this.lastname = lastname;
  }

  greet() {
    console.log("Hi there!");
  }

  compliment(name, object) {
    return "That's a wonderful " + object + ", " + name;
  }
}
```

The `compliment` function does not output anything itself, so we are logging it

```
let compliment = p.compliment("Harry", "hat");
console.log(compliment);
```

The output will be:

```
That's a wonderful hat, Harry
```

In this case we are sending parameters into our method, because you don't usually compliment your own properties (that's a nice sentence, Maaike!). However, whenever the method doesn't require external input but only the properties of the object, no parameters will work and the method can use its object's properties. Let's do an exercise and then move on to using the properties of classes outside the class.

Practice exercise 7.2

Get your friend's full name:

1. Using the `Person` class from *Practice exercise 7.1*, add a method called
    `fullname`, which returns the concatenated value of `firstname` and `lastname`
    when invoked.
2. Create values for `person1` and `person2` using two friends' first and last names.
3. Using the `fullname` method within the class, return the full name of one or
    both people.

Properties

Properties, sometimes also called fields, hold the data of the class. We have seen one
kind of property already, when we created them in our constructors:

```
class Person {
  constructor(firstname, lastname) {
    this.firstname = firstname;
    this.lastname = lastname;
  }
}
```

Here, the `Person` class gets two properties from the constructor: `firstname` and
`lastname`. Properties can be added or removed just like we did for objects. These
properties can be accessed from outside the class, as we saw when we logged them
outside the class by accessing them on the instance:

```
let p = new Person("Maaike", "van Putten");
console.log("Hi", p.firstname);
```

Often, it is not desirable to provide direct access to our properties. We want our class
to be in control of the values of properties for several reasons—perhaps we want to
do validation on a property to assure it has a certain value. For example, imagine
wanting to validate an age as not being lower than 18. We can achieve this by
making direct access to the property from outside the class impossible.

This is how to add properties that aren't accessible from outside. We prefix them
with a # symbol:

```
class Person {
  #firstname;
  #lastname;
```

```
  constructor(firstname, lastname) {
    this.#firstname = firstname;
    this.#lastname = lastname;
  }
}
```

Right now, the `firstname` and `lastname` properties cannot be accessed from outside the class. This is done by adding # in front of the property. If we try it:

```
let p = new Person("Maria", "Saga");
console.log(p.firstname);
```

We'll get:

```
undefined
```

If we wanted to make sure we could only create objects with names starting with an "M," we could modify our constructor a bit:

```
constructor(firstname, lastname) {
    if(firstname.startsWith("M")){
      this.#firstname = firstname;
    } else {
      this.#firstname = "M" + firstname;
    }
    this.#lastname = lastname;
  }
```

Now when you try to create a person that has a `firstname` value that doesn't start with an "M," it will add an M in front. So for example, the value of the following first name is `Mkay`:

```
let p = new Person("kay", "Moon");
```

This is a very silly example of validation. At this point, we cannot access it from outside the class at all after the constructor. We can only access it from inside the class. This is where getters and setters come into play.

Getters and setters

Getters and setters are special properties that we can use to get data from a class and to set data fields on the class. Getters and setters are computed properties. So, they are more like properties than they are like functions. We call them accessors. They do look a bit like functions, because they have () behind them, but they are not!

These accessors start with the get and set keywords. It is considered good practice to make fields private as much as possible and provide access to them using getters and setters. This way, the properties cannot be set from outside without the object itself being in control. This principle is called **encapsulation**. The class encapsulates the data, and the object is in control of its own fields.

Here is how to do it:

```
class Person {
  #firstname;
  #lastname;
  constructor(firstname, lastname) {
    this.#firstname = firstname;
    this.#lastname = lastname;
  }

  get firstname() {
    return this.#firstname;
  }

  set firstname(firstname) {
    this.#firstname = firstname;
  }

  get lastname() {
    return this.#lastname;
  }

  set lastname(lastname) {
    this.#lastname = lastname;
  }
}
```

The getter is used to get the property. Therefore, it doesn't take any parameters, but simply returns the property. The setter is the other way around: it takes a parameter, assigns this new value to the property, and returns nothing. The setter can contain more logic, for example, some validation, as we'll see below. The getter can be used outside the object as if it were a property. The properties are no longer directly accessible from outside the class, but can be accessed via the getter to get the value and via the setter to update the value. Here is how to use it outside the class instance:

```
let p = new Person("Maria", "Saga");
console.log(p.firstname);
```

This will output:

```
Maria
```

We have created a new `Person` object with a first name of `Maria` and last name of `Saga`. The output is showing the first name, which is only possible because we have a getter accessor. We can also set the value to something else, because there is a setter. Here is how to update the first name, so the name is no longer `Maria`, but `Adnane`.

```
p.firstname = "Adnane";
```

At this point, nothing special is happening in the setter. We could do a similar validation as in the constructor before, like this:

```
set firstname(firstname) {
    if(firstname.startsWith("M")){
       this.#firstname = firstname;
    } else {
       this.#firstname = "M" + firstname;
    }
  }
```

This will check whether `firstname` starts with an `M`, and if it does it will update the value to whatever the `firstname` parameter is. If it doesn't, it will concatenate an `M` in front of the parameter.

Please note that we do not access `firstname` as if it was a function. If you put two parentheses `()` after it, you would actually get an error telling you that it is not a function.

Inheritance

Inheritance is one of the key concepts of OOP. It is the concept that classes can have child classes that inherit the properties and methods from the parent class. For example, if you needed all sorts of vehicle objects in your application, you could specify a class named `Vehicle` in which you specify some shared properties and methods of vehicles. You would then go ahead and create the specific child classes based on this `Vehicle` class, for example, `boat`, `car`, `bicycle`, and `motorcycle`.

This could be a very simple version of the `Vehicle` class:

```
class Vehicle {
  constructor(color, currentSpeed, maxSpeed) {
    this.color = color;
```

```
      this.currentSpeed = currentSpeed;
      this.maxSpeed = maxSpeed;
    }


    move() {
      console.log("moving at", this.currentSpeed);
    }


    accelerate(amount) {
      this.currentSpeed += amount;
    }
  }
```

Here we have two methods in our `Vehicle` class: move and `accelerate`. And this could be a `Motorcyle` class inheriting from this class using the extends keyword:

```
class Motorcycle extends Vehicle {
  constructor(color, currentSpeed, maxSpeed, fuel) {
    super(color, currentSpeed, maxSpeed);
    this.fuel = fuel;
  }
  doWheelie() {
    console.log("Driving on one wheel!");
  }
}
```

With the extends keyword we specify that a certain class is the child of another class. In this case, `Motorcycle` is a child class of `Vehicle`. This means that we'll have access to properties and methods from `Vehicle` in our `Motorcycle` class. We have added a special doWheelie() method. This is not something that makes sense to add to the `Vehicle` class, because this is an action that is specific to certain vehicles.

The `super` word in the constructor is calling the constructor from the parent, the `Vehicle` constructor in this case. This makes sure that the fields from the parent are set as well and that the methods are available without having to do anything else: they are automatically inherited. Calling super() is not optional, you must do it when you are in a class that is inheriting from another class, else you will get a `ReferenceError`.

Because we have access to the fields of `Vehicle` in `Motorcycle`, this will work:

```
let motor = new Motorcycle("Black", 0, 250, "gasoline");
console.log(motor.color);
```

```
motor.accelerate(50);
motor.move();
```

And this is what it will output:

```
Black
moving at 50
```

We cannot access any `Motorcycle` specific properties or methods in our `Vehicle` class. This is because not all vehicles are motorcycles, so we cannot be sure that we would have the properties or methods from a child.

Right now, we don't use any getters and setters here, but we clearly could. If there are getters and setters in the parent class, they are inherited by the child class as well. This way we could influence which properties could be fetched and changed (and how) outside our class. This is generally a good practice.

Prototypes

A prototype is the mechanism in JavaScript that makes it possible to have objects. When nothing is specified when creating a class, the objects inherit from the `Object.prototype` prototype. This is a rather complex built-in JavaScript class that we can use. We don't need to look at how this is implemented in JavaScript, as we can consider it the base object that is always on top of the inheritance tree and therefore always present in our objects.

There is a `prototype` property available on all classes, and it is always named "prototype." We can access it like this:

```
ClassName.prototype
```

Let's give an example of how to add a function to a class using the `prototype` property. In order to do so, we'll be using this `Person` class:

```
class Person {
  constructor(firstname, lastname) {
    this.firstname = firstname;
    this.lastname = lastname;
  }

  greet() {
    console.log("Hi there!");
  }
}
```

And here is how to add a function to this class using `prototype`:

```
Person.prototype.introduce = function () {
    console.log("Hi, I'm", this.firstname);
};
```

`prototype` is a property holding all the properties and methods of an object. So, adding a function to `prototype` is adding a function to the class. You can use `prototype` to add properties or methods to an object, like we did in the above example in our code with the `introduce` function. You can also do this for properties:

```
Person.prototype.favoriteColor = "green";
```

And then you can call them from instances of `Person`:

```
let p = new Person("Maria", "Saga");
console.log(p.favoriteColor);
p.introduce();
```

It will output:

```
green
Hi, I'm Maria
```

And it will be as if you had defined the class with a favorite color holding a default value, and a function, `introduce`. They have been added to the class and are available for all instances and future instances.

So the methods and properties defined via `prototype` are really as if they were defined in the class. This means that overwriting them for a certain instance doesn't overwrite them for all instances. For example, if we were to have a second `Person` object, this person could overwrite the `favoriteColor` value and this wouldn't change the value for our object with `firstname` as `Maria`.

This is something you should not be using when you have control over the class code and you want to change it permanently. In that case, just change the class. However, you can expand existing objects like this and even expand existing objects conditionally. It is also important to know that the JavaScript built-in objects have prototypes and inherit from `Object.prototype`. However, be sure not to modify this prototype since it will affect how our JavaScript works.

Practice exercise 7.3

Create a class that contains properties for different animal species and the sound that each species makes, and create two (or more) animals:

1. Create a method that prints a given animal and its sound.
2. Add a prototype with another action for the animal.
3. Output an entire animal object into the console.

Chapter projects

Employee tracking app

Create a class to track the employees of a company:

1. Use first names, last names, and the number of years worked as values in the constructor.
2. Create two or more people with values for their first names, last names, and the number of years they've worked at the company. Add the people into an array.
3. Set up a prototype to return the details of the person's first and last names and how long they've worked at the company.
4. Iterate the contents of the array to output the results into the console, adding some text to make the output a full sentence.

Menu items price calculator

Create a class which will allow you to work out the combined price of a number of items, and interact with it to work out the total cost of different orders.

1. Create a class that contains the prices of two menu items as private field declarations.
2. Use the constructor in the class to get the argument values (how many of each item are being bought).
3. Create a method to calculate and return the total cost depending on how many of each item the user selects.
4. Use a getter property to grab the value output by the calculation method.
5. Create two or three objects with different combinations of menu selections, and output the total cost in the console.

Self-check quiz

1. What is the keyword used to create a class?

2. How would you set up a class for a person's first and last names that could include `first` and `last` as initial properties?

3. What is the concept of one thing gaining the properties and behaviors of another thing called?

4. Which of the following are true about the `constructor` method?

   - It gets executed automatically when a new object is created.

   - It should only be added afterward.

   - It has to include the `constructor` keyword.

   - It is used to initialize object properties.

   - It can be used when you have multiple values.

5. Troubleshoot the following code so that the prototype outputs the first and last name of the `Person` into the console. Which is the correct syntax for the `Person` prototype?

   ```
   function Person(first,last) {
     this.first = first;
     this.last = last;
   }
   // What should go here: A, B, or C?
   const friend1 = new Person("Laurence", "Svekis");
   console.log(friend1.getName());
   ```

   A)

   ```
   Person.prototype.getName = (first,last) {
     return this.first + " " + this.last;
   };
   ```

   B)

   ```
   Person.prototype.getName = function getName() {
   return this.first + " " + this.last;
   };
   ```

   C)

   ```
   Person.prototype = function getName() {
   return this.first + " " + this.last;
   };
   ```

Summary

In this chapter, we introduced you to the concept of OOP. This means that we structure our code in such a way that objects are the central players of the logic. Classes are blueprints for objects. We can make a template for an object and create an instance easily by using the new keyword.

We then saw that classes can inherit from each other by using the extends keyword. Classes that extend from another class will have to call the constructor of this class with super() and will then automatically have access to all the properties and methods of the parent. This is great for reusable and highly maintainable code.

Lastly, we encountered prototypes. This is the built-in JavaScript concept that makes classes possible. By adding properties and methods to a class using prototype, we can modify the blueprint of that class.

In the next chapter, we will consider some of JavaScript's built-in methods, which can be used to manipulate and add complexity to your code!

Join our book's Discord space

Join the book's Discord workspace for a monthly *Ask me Anything* session with the authors: https://packt.link/JSBook

8

Built-In JavaScript Methods

We have just covered most of the basic building blocks in JavaScript. Now it's time to look at some powerful built-in methods that will make your life easier that we haven't seen yet. Built-in methods are functionality that we get out of the box with JavaScript. We can use these methods without having to code them first. This is something we have done a lot already, for example, `console.log()` and `prompt()`.

Many built-in methods belong to built-in classes as well. These classes and their methods can be used at any time because JavaScript has already defined them. These classes exist for our convenience, since they are very common things to need, such as the `Date`, `Array`, and `Object` classes.

The ability to harness the capabilities that are already built into JavaScript can improve the effectiveness of the code, save time, and comply with various best practices for developing solutions. We are going to address some of the common uses for such functions, such as manipulating text, mathematical computations, dealing with date and time values, interactions, and supporting robust code. Here are the topics covered in this chapter:

- Global JavaScript methods
- String methods
- Math methods
- Date methods
- Array methods
- Number methods

Note: exercise, project and self-check quiz answers can be found in the *Appendix*.

Introduction to built-in JavaScript methods

We have seen many built-in JavaScript methods already. Any method that we didn't define ourselves is a built-in method. Some examples include console.log(), Math. random(), prompt(), and many more—think about methods on arrays for example. The difference between a method and a function is that a function is defined anywhere in the script, and a method is defined inside a class. So methods are pretty much functions on classes and instances.

Methods can often be chained as well; this is only true for methods returning a result. The next method will then be performed on the result. So for example:

```
let s = "Hello";
console.log(
    s.concat(" there!")
    .toUpperCase()
    .replace("THERE", "you")
    .concat(" You're amazing!")
);
```

We create a variable, s, and we store Hello in there on the first line. Then we want to be logging something. This code has been divided over different lines for readability, but it's actually one statement. We first perform a concat() method on our s variable, which appends a string to our string. So after that first operation the value is Hello there!. Then we transform this to uppercase with the next method. At that point the value is HELLO THERE!. Then we proceed to replace THERE with you. After that, the value becomes HELLO you!. We then append a string to it again and finally the value will be logged:

```
HELLO you! You're amazing!
```

We need to log or store the output in this example, because the original string value will not be updated by just calling methods on a string.

Global methods

The global JavaScript methods can be used without referring to the built-in object they are part of. This means that we can just use the method name as if it is a function that has been defined inside the scope we are in, without the "object" in front of it. For example, instead of writing:

```
let x = 7;
console.log(Number.isNaN(x));
```

You can also write:

```
console.log(isNaN(x));
```

So, the Number can be left out, because isNaN is made globally available without referring to the class it belongs to (in this instance, the Number class). In this case, both of these console.log statements will log false (they are doing the exact same thing), because isNaN returns true when it isn't a number. And 7 is a number, so it will log false.

JavaScript has been built to have these available directly, so to achieve this, some magic is going on beneath the surface. The JavaScript creators chose the methods that they thought were most common. So the reasons why some of them are available as global methods and others are not might seem a bit arbitrary. It's just the choice of some very bright developers at a certain point in time.

We'll address the most common global methods below. We start with decoding and encoding URIs, escaped and unescaped, followed by parsing numbers, and finally evaluate.

Decoding and encoding URIs

Sometimes you will need to encode or decode a string. Encoding is simply converting from one shape to another. In this case we will be dealing with percent encoding, also called URL encoding. Before we start, there might be some confusion on the URI and URL meaning. A **URI (uniform resource identifier)** is an identifier of a certain resource. **URL (uniform resource locator)** is a subcategory of URI that is not only an identifier, but also holds the information on how to access it (location).

Let's talk about encoding and decoding these URIs (and also URLs, since they are a subset). An example of when you'd need this is when you are sending variables over the URL using the get method in a form. These variables that you are sending via the URL are called query parameters.

If something contains a space, this will be decoded, because you cannot use spaces in your URL. They will be converted to `%20`. The URL might look something like:

`www.example.com/submit?name=maaike%20van%20putten&love=coding`

All characters can be converted to some %-starting format. However, this is not necessary in most cases. URIs can contain a certain number of alphanumeric characters. The special characters need to be encoded. An example, before encoding, is:

`https://www.example.com/submit?name=maaike van putten`

The same URL after encoding is:

`https://www.example.com/submit?name=maaike%20van%20putten`

There are two pairs of encode and decode methods. We will discuss them and their use cases here. You cannot have a URI with spaces, so working with these methods is crucial in order to work with variables containing spaces.

decodeUri() and encodeUri()

The `decodeUri()` and `encodeUri()` are actually not really encoding and decoding, they are more so fixing broken URIs. It is like the previous example with the spaces. This method pair is really good at fixing broken URIs and decoding them back into a string. Here you can see them in action:

```
let uri = "https://www.example.com/submit?name=maaike van putten";
let encoded_uri = encodeURI(uri);
console.log("Encoded:", encoded_uri);
let decoded_uri = decodeURI(encoded_uri);
console.log("Decoded:", decoded_uri);
```

And here is the output:

```
Encoded: https://www.example.com/submit?name=maaike%20van%20putten
Decoded: https://www.example.com/submit?name=maaike van putten
```

As you can see, it has replaced the spaces in the encoded version and removed them again in the decoded version. All the other characters get to stay the same — this encode and decode do not take special characters into account, and therefore leave them in the URI. Colons, question marks, equal signs, slashes, and ampersands can be expected.

This is great for fixing broken URIs, but it's actually a bit useless whenever you need to encode strings that contain any of these characters: / , ? : @ & = + $ #. These can be used in URIs as part of the URI and are therefore skipped. This is where the next two built-in methods come in handy.

decodeUriComponent() and encodeUriComponent()

So, the methods decodeURI() and encodeURI() can be very useful to fix a broken URI, but they are useless when you only want to encode or decode a string that contains a character with a special meaning, such as = or &. Take the following example:

https://www.example.com/submit?name=this&that=some thing&code=love

Weird value, we can agree on that, but it will demonstrate our problem. Using encodeURI on this will leave us with:

https://www.example.com/submit?name=this&that=some%20thing&code=love

There are actually 3 variables in here according to URI standards:

- name (value is this)
- that (value is some thing)
- code (value is love)

While we intended to send in one variable, name, with the value this&that=some thing&code=love.

In this case, you will need decodeUriComponent() and encodeUriComponent(), because you would need the = and & in the variable part encoded as well. Right now, this is not the case and it will actually cause problems in interpreting the query parameters (the variables after the ?). We only wanted to send in one parameter: name. But instead we sent in three.

Let's have a look at another example. Here is what the example of the previous section would have done with this component encoding:

```
let uri = "https://www.example.com/submit?name=maaike van putten";
let encoded_uri = encodeURIComponent(uri);
console.log("Encoded:", encoded_uri);
let decoded_uri = decodeURIComponent(encoded_uri);
console.log("Decoded:", decoded_uri);
```

The resulting output is as follows:

```
Encoded: https%3A%2F%2Fwww.example.com%2Fsubmit%3Fname%3Dmaaike%20
van%20putten
Decoded: https://www.example.com/submit?name=maaike van putten
```

Clearly, you don't want this as your URI, but the component methods are useful to encode, for example, a URL variable. If the URL variable were to contain a special character, like = and &, this would change the meaning and break the URI if these characters don't get encoded.

Encoding with escape() and unescape()

These are still global methods available to do something similar to encode (escape) and decode (unescape). Both methods are strongly discouraged to use and they might actually disappear from future JavaScript versions or may not be supported by browsers for good reasons.

Practice exercise 8.1

Output the decodeURIComponent() for the string How's%20it%20going%3F to the console. Also, encode the string How's it going? to be output into the console. Create a web URL and encode the URI:

1. Add the strings as variables in the JavaScript code
2. Using encodeURIComponent() and decodeURIComponent() output the results into the console
3. Create a web URI with request parameters http://www.basescripts.com?=Hello World";
4. Encode and output the web URI into the console

Parsing numbers

There are different ways to parse strings to numbers. In many situations you will have to translate a string to a number, for example reading input boxes from an HTML web page. You cannot calculate with strings, but you can with numbers. Depending on what exactly you need to do, you will need either one of these methods.

Making integers with parseInt()

With the method parseInt() a string will be changed to an integer. This method is part of the Number class, but it is global and you can use it without the Number in front of it. Here you can see it in action:

```
let str_int = "6";
let int_int = parseInt(str_int);
console.log("Type of ", int_int, "is", typeof int_int);
```

We start off with a string containing a 6. Then we convert this string to an integer using the `parseInt` method, and when we log the result, we will get in the console:

```
Type of 6 is number
```

You can see that the type has changed from `string` to `number`. At this point, you may wonder what will happen if `parseInt()` tries to parse other types of numbers, like string versions of floats or binary numbers. What do you think will happen when we do this?

```
let str_float = "7.6";
let int_float = parseInt(str_float);
console.log("Type of", int_float, "is", typeof int_float);

let str_binary = "0b101";
let int_binary = parseInt(str_binary);
console.log("Type of", int_binary, "is", typeof int_binary);
```

This will log:

```
Type of 7 is number
Type of 0 is number
```

Can you figure out the logic here? First of all, JavaScript doesn't like crashing or using errors as a way out, so it is trying to make it work to the best of its abilities. The `parseInt()` method simply stops parsing when it runs into a non-numeric character. This is the specified behavior, and you need to keep that in mind while working with `parseInt()`. In the first case, it stops parsing as soon as it finds the dot, so the result is 7. And in the binary number case, it stops parsing as soon as it hits the b, and the result is 0. By now you can probably figure out what this does:

```
let str_nan = "hello!";
let int_nan = parseInt(str_nan);
console.log("Type of", int_nan, "is", typeof int_nan);
```

Since the first character is non-numeric, JavaScript will convert this string to `NaN`. Here is the result that you will get in the console:

```
Type of NaN is number
```

So `parseInt()` can be a bit quirky, but it's very valuable. In the real world, it is used a lot to combine the input of users via web pages and calculations.

Making floats with parseFloat()

Similarly, we can use `parseFloat()` to parse a string to a float. It works exactly the same, except it can also understand decimal numbers and it doesn't quit parsing as soon as it runs into the first dot:

```
let str_float = "7.6";
let float_float = parseFloat(str_float);
console.log("Type of", float_float, "is", typeof float_float);
```

This will log:

```
Type of 7.6 is number
```

With the `parseInt()`, this value became 7, because it would stop parsing as soon as it finds a non-numeric character. However, `parseFloat()` can deal with one dot in the number, and the numbers after that are interpreted as decimals. Can you guess what happens when it runs into a second dot?

```
let str_version_nr = "2.3.4";
let float_version_nr = parseFloat(str_version_nr);
console.log("Type of", float_version_nr, "is", typeof float_version_
nr);
```

This will log:

```
Type of 2.3 is number
```

The strategy is similar to the `parseInt()` function. As soon as it finds a character it cannot interpret, a second dot in this case, it will stop parsing and just return the result so far. Then one more thing to note. It is not going to append a `.0` to integers, so `6` is not going to become `6.0`. This example:

```
let str_int = "6";
let float_int = parseFloat(str_int);
console.log("Type of", float_int, "is", typeof float_int);
```

Will log:

```
Type of 6 is number
```

Lastly, the behavior for binary numbers and strings is the same. It is going to stop parsing as soon as it runs into a character it cannot interpret:

```
let str_binary = "0b101";
let float_binary = parseFloat(str_binary);
console.log("Type of", float_binary, "is", typeof float_binary);

let str_nan = "hello!";
let float_nan = parseFloat(str_nan);
console.log("Type of", float_nan, "is", typeof float_nan);
```

This will log:

```
Type of 0 is number
Type of NaN is number
```

You will use the parseFloat() whenever you need a decimal number. However, it will not work with binary, hexadecimal, and octal values, so whenever you really need to work with these values or integers you'll have to use parseInt().

Executing JavaScript with eval()

This global method executes the argument as a JavaScript statement. This means that it will just do whatever JavaScript is inserted in there, as if that JavaScript were written directly on the spot instead of eval(). This can be convenient for working with injected JavaScript, but injected code comes with great risks. We'll deal with these risks later; let's first explore an example. Here is a fabulous website:

```
<html>
  <body>
    <input onchange="go(this)"></input>
    <script>
      function go(e) {
        eval(e.value);
      }
    </script>
  </body>
</html>
```

This is a basic HTML web page with an input box on it.

> You'll learn more about HTML in *Chapter 9, The Document Object Model*.

Whatever you insert in the input box will get executed. If we were to write this in the input box:

```
document.body.style.backgroundColor = "pink";
```

The website background would change to pink. That looks like fun, right? However, we cannot stress enough how careful you should be using `eval()`. They might as well have called it *evil* according to many developers. Can you reason why this might be?

The answer is security! Yes, this is probably the worst thing security-wise you can do in most situations. You are going to execute external code. This code could be malicious. It is a method for supporting code injection. The well-respected **OWASP (Open Web Application Security Project)** Foundation creates top 10s for security threats every 3 years. Code injection has been on it since their first top 10 and it is still in the OWASP top 10 security threats now. Running it server side can cause your server to crash and your website to go down, or worse. There are almost always better solutions to what you want to do than using `eval()`. Next to the security risks, it is terrible performance-wise. So just for this reason already you might want to avoid using it.

Alright, so one last note on this. If you know what you are doing you might want to use it in very specific cases. Even though it is "evil", it has a lot of power. It can be okay to use in certain cases, for example when you are creating template engines, your own interpreter, and all other JavaScript core tools. Just beware of the danger and control access to this method carefully. And one last bonus tip, when you feel like you really have to use eval, do a quick search on the web. Chances are that you will find a better approach.

Array methods

We have seen arrays already — they can contain multiple items. We have also seen quite a few built-in methods on arrays, like `shift()` and `push()`. Let's look at a few more in the following sections.

Performing a certain action for every item

There is a reason we are starting with this method. You might be thinking of loops at this point, but there is a built-in method that you can use to execute a function for every element in the array. This is the `forEach()` method. We mentioned this briefly in *Chapter 6, Functions*, but let's consider it in some more detail. It takes the function that needs to be executed for every element as input. Here you can see an example:

```
let arr = ["grapefruit", 4, "hello", 5.6, true];

function printStuff(element, index) {
    console.log("Printing stuff:", element, "on array position:", index);
}

arr.forEach(printStuff);
```

This code snippet will write to the console:

```
Printing stuff: grapefruit on array position: 0
Printing stuff: 4 on array position: 1
Printing stuff: hello on array position: 2
Printing stuff: 5.6 on array position: 3
Printing stuff: true on array position: 4
```

As you can see, it called the printStuff() function for every element in the array. And we can also use the index, it is the second parameter. We don't need to control the flow of the loop here and we cannot get stuck at a certain point. We just need to specify what function needs to be executed for every element. And the element will be input for this function. This is used a lot, especially for a more functional programming style in which many methods get chained, for example, to process data.

Filtering an array

We can use the built-in filter() method on an array to alter which values are in the array. The filter method takes a function as an argument, and this function should return a Boolean. If the Boolean has the value true, the element will end up in the filtered array. If the Boolean has the value false, the element will be left out. You can see how it works here:

```
let arr = ["squirrel", 5, "Tjed", new Date(), true];

function checkString(element, index) {
    return typeof element === "string";
}

let filterArr = arr.filter(checkString);
console.log(filterArr);
```

This will log to the console:

```
[ 'squirrel', 'Tjed' ]
```

It is important to realize that the original array has not changed, the `filter()` method returns a new array with the elements that made it through the filter. We capture it here in the variable `filterArr`.

Checking a condition for all elements

You can use the `every()` method to see whether something is true for all elements in the array. If that is the case, the `every()` method will return `true`, else it will return `false`. We are using the `checkString()` function and array from the previous example here:

```
console.log(arr.every(checkString));
```

This will log `false`, since not all elements are of type `string` in the array.

Replacing part of an array with another part of the array

The `copyWithin()` method can be used to replace a part of the array with another part of the array. In the first example we specify 3 arguments. The first one is the target position, to which the values get copied. The second one is the start of what to copy to the target position and the last one is the end of the sequence that will be copied to the target position; this last index is not included. Here we are only going to override position 0 with whatever is in position 3:

```
arr = ["grapefruit", 4, "hello", 5.6, true];
arr.copyWithin(0, 3, 4);
```

`arr` becomes:

```
[ 5.6, 4, 'hello', 5.6, true ]
```

If we specify a range with length 2, the first two elements after the starting position get overridden:

```
arr = ["grapefruit", 4, "hello", 5.6, true];
arr.copyWithin(0, 3, 5);
```

And now `arr` becomes:

```
[ 5.6, true, 'hello', 5.6, true ]
```

We can also not specify an end at all; it will take the range to the end of the string:

```
let arr = ["grapefruit", 4, "hello", 5.6, true, false];
arr.copyWithin(0, 3);
console.log(arr);
```

This will log:

```
[ 5.6, true, false, 5.6, true, false ]
```

It is important to keep in mind that this function changes the *content* of the original array, but will never change the *length* of the original array.

Mapping the values of an array

Sometimes you'll need to change all the values in an array. With the array `map()` method you can do just that. This method will return a new array with all the new values. You'll have to say how to create these new values. This can be done with the arrow function. It is going to execute the arrow function for every element in the array, so for example:

```
let arr = [1, 2, 3, 4];
let mapped_arr = arr.map(x => x + 1);
console.log(mapped_arr);
```

This is what the console output with the new mapped array looks like:

```
[ 2, 3, 4, 5 ]
```

Using the arrow function, the `map()` method has created a new array, in which each of the original array values has been increased by 1.

Finding the last occurrence in an array

We can find occurrences with `indexOf()` as we have seen already. To find the last occurrence, we can use the `lastIndexOf()` method on an array, just as we did for `string`.

It will return the index of the last element with that value, if it can find it at all:

```
let bb = ["so", "bye", "bye", "love"];
console.log(bb.lastIndexOf("bye"));
```

This will log 2, because the index 2 holds the last bye variable. What do you think you'll get when you ask for the last index of something that's not there?

```
let bb = ["so", "bye", "bye", "love"];
console.log(bb.lastIndexOf("hi"));
```

That's right (hopefully)! It's -1.

Practice exercise 8.2

Remove duplicates from the array using `filter()` and `indexOf()`. The starting array is:

```
["Laurence", "Mike", "Larry", "Kim", "Joanne", "Laurence", "Mike",
"Laurence", "Mike", "Laurence", "Mike"]
```

Using the array `filter()` method, this will create a new array using the elements that pass the test condition implemented by the function. The final result will be:

```
[ 'Laurence', 'Mike', 'Larry', 'Kim', 'Joanne' ]
```

Take the following steps:

1. Create an array of names of people. Make sure you include duplicates. The exercise will remove the duplicate names.

2. Using the `filter()` method, assign the results of each item from the array as arguments within an anonymous function. Using the value, index, and array arguments, return the filtered result. You can set the return value to `true` temporarily as this will build the new array with all the results in the original array.

3. Add a `console.log` call within the function that will output the index value of the current item in the array. Also add the value so you can see the results of the item value that has the current index number and the first matching result from the array's index value.

4. Using `indexOf()` the current value returns the index value of the item and applies the condition to check to see if it matches the original index value. This condition will only be true on the first result so all subsequent duplicates will be false and not get added to the new array. `false` will not return the value into the new array. The duplicates will all be false since the `indexof()` only gets the first match in the array.

5. Output the new, unique value array onto the console.

Practice exercise 8.3

Using the array `map()` method, update an array's contents. Take the following steps:

1. Create an array of numbers.
2. Using the array map method and an anonymous function, return an updated array, multiplying all the numbers in the array by 2. Output the result into the console.
3. As an alternative method, use the arrow function format to multiply each element of the array by 2 with the array `map()` method in one line of code.
4. Log the result onto the console.

String methods

We have worked with strings already and chances are that you have run into some of the methods on strings by now. There are a few we didn't address specifically just yet and we are going to discuss them in this section.

Combining strings

When you want to concatenate strings, you can use the `concat()` method. This does not change the original string(s); it returns the combined result as a string. You will have to capture the result in a new variable, else it will get lost:

```
let s1 = "Hello ";
let s2 = "JavaScript";
let result = s1.concat(s2);
console.log(result);
```

This will log:

```
Hello JavaScript
```

Converting a string to an array

With the `split()` method we can convert a string to an array. Again, we will have to capture the result; it is not changing the original string. Let's use the previous result containing `Hello JavaScript`. We will have to tell the `split` method on what string it should split. Every time it encounters that string, it will create a new array item:

```
let result = "Hello JavaScript";
let arr_result = result.split(" ");
console.log(arr_result);
```

This will log:

```
[ 'Hello', 'JavaScript' ]
```

As you can see, it creates an array of all the elements separated by a space. We can split by any character, for example a comma:

```
let favoriteFruits = "strawberry,watermelon,grapefruit";
let arr_fruits = favoriteFruits.split(",");
console.log(arr_fruits);
```

This will log:

```
[ 'strawberry', 'watermelon', 'grapefruit' ]
```

It has now created an array with 3 items. You can split on anything, and the string you are splitting on is left out of the result.

Converting an array to a string

With the `join()` method you can convert an array to a string. Here is a basic example:

```
let letters = ["a", "b", "c"];
let x = letters.join();
console.log(x);
```

This will log:

```
a,b,c
```

The type of x is `string`. If you want something else other than a comma, you can specify that, like this:

```
let letters = ["a", "b", "c"];
let x = letters.join('-');
console.log(x);
```

This will use the – instead of the comma. This is the result:

```
a-b-c
```

This can be nicely combined with the `split()` method that we covered in the previous section, which does the reverse and converts a string into an array.

Working with index and positions

Being able to find out what index a certain substring is at within your string is very useful. For example, when you need to search for a certain word through the user input of a log file and create a substring starting at that index. Here is an example of how to find the index of a string. The `indexOf()` method returns the index, a single number, of the first character of the substring:

```
let poem = "Roses are red, violets are blue, if I can do JS, then you
           can too!";
let index_re = poem.indexOf("re");
console.log(index_re);
```

This is logging 7 to the console, because the first occurrence of re is in are, and the re begins at index 7. When it can't find an index, it will return -1, like this example:

```
let indexNotFound = poem.indexOf("python");
console.log(indexNotFound);
```

It is logging -1 to indicate that the string we are searching for doesn't occur in the target string. Often you will write an `if` check to see whether it's -1 before dealing with the result. For example:

```
if(poem.indexOf("python") != -1) {
  // do stuff
}
```

An alternative way of searching for a particular substring within a string is to use the `search()` method:

```
let searchStr = "When I see my fellow, I say hello";
let pos = searchStr.search("lo");
console.log(pos);
```

This will log 17, because that is the index of `lo` in `fellow`. Much like `indexOf()`, if it cannot find it, it will return -1. This is the case for this example:

```
let notFound = searchStr.search("JavaScript");
console.log(notFound);
```

`search()` will accept a regex format as input, whereas `indexOf()` just takes a string. `indexOf()` is faster than the `search()` method, so if you just need to look for a string, use `indexOf()`. If you need to look for a string pattern, you'll have to use the `search()` method.

 Regex is a special syntax for defining string patterns, with which you can replace all occurrences, but we'll deal with that in *Chapter 12, Intermediate JavaScript*.

Moving on, the `indexOf()` method is returning the index of the first occurrence, but similarly, we also have a `lastIndexOf()` method. It returns the index where the argument string occurs last. If it cannot find it, it returns -1. Here is an example:

```
let lastIndex_re = poem.lastIndexOf("re");
console.log(lastIndex_re);
```

This returns 24; this is the last time `re` appears in our poem. It is the second `are`.

Sometimes you will have to do the reverse; instead of looking for what index a string occurs at, you will want to know what character is at a certain index position. This is where the `charAt(index)` method comes in handy, where the specified index position is taken as an argument:

```
let pos1 = poem.charAt(10);
console.log(pos1);
```

This is logging `r`, because the character at index 10 is the `r` of `red`. If you are asking for the position of an index that is out of the range of the string, it will return an empty string, as is happening in this example:

```
let pos2 = poem.charAt(1000);
console.log(pos2);
```

This will log an empty line to the screen, and if you ask for the type of pos2, it will return string.

Creating substrings

With the slice(start, end) method we can create substrings. This does not alter the original string, but returns a new string with the substring. It takes two parameters, the first is the index at which it starts and the second is the end index. If you leave out the second index it will just continue until the end of the string from the start. The end index is not included in the substring. Here is an example:

```
let str = "Create a substring";
let substr1 = str.slice(5);
let substr2 = str.slice(0,3);
console.log("1:", substr1);
console.log("2:", substr2);
```

This will log:

```
1: e a substring
2: Cre
```

The first one only has one argument, so it starts at index 5 (which holds an e) and grabs the rest of the string from there. The second one has two arguments, 0 and 3. C is at index 0 and a is at index 3. Since the last index is not included in the substring, it will only return Cre.

Replacing parts of the string

If you need to replace a part of the string, you can use the replace(old, new) method. It takes two arguments, one string to look for in the string and one new value to replace the old value with. Here is an example:

```
let hi = "Hi buddy";
let new_hi = hi.replace("buddy", "Pascal");
console.log(new_hi);
```

This will log to the console Hi Pascal. If you don't capture the result, it is gone, because the original string will not get changed. If the string you are targeting doesn't appear in the original string, the replacement doesn't take place and the original string will be returned:

```
let new_hi2 = hi.replace("not there", "never there");
console.log(new_hi2);
```

This logs Hi buddy.

One last note here, it is only changing the first occurrence by default. So this example will only replace the first hello in the new string:

```
let s3 = "hello hello";
let new_s3 = s3.replace("hello", "oh");
console.log(new_s3);
```

This logs oh hello. If we wanted to replace all the occurences, we could use the replaceAll() method. This will replace all occurrences with the specified new string, like this:

```
let s3 = "hello hello";
let new_s3 = s3.replaceAll("hello", "oh");
console.log(new_s3);
```

This logs oh oh.

Uppercase and lowercase

We can change the letters of a string with the toUpperCase() and toLowerCase() built-in methods on string. Again, this is not changing the original string, so we'll have to capture the result:

```
let low_bye = "bye!";
let up_bye = low_bye.toUpperCase();
console.log(up_bye);
```

This logs:

```
BYE!
```

It converts all the letters to uppercase. We can do the opposite with `toLowerCase()`:

```
let caps = "HI HOW ARE YOU?";
let fixed_caps = caps.toLowerCase();
console.log(fixed_caps);
```

This will log:

```
hi how are you?
```

Let's make it a bit more complicated and say that we'd like the first letter of the sentence to be capitalized. We can do this by combining some of the methods we have seen already right now:

```
let caps = "HI HOW ARE YOU?";
let fixed_caps = caps.toLowerCase();
let first_capital = fixed_caps.charAt(0).toUpperCase().concat(fixed_
caps.slice(1));
console.log(first_capital);
```

We are chaining the methods here; we first grab the first character of `fixed_caps` with `charAt(0)` and then make it uppercase by calling `toUpperCase()` on it. We then need the rest of the string and we get it by concatenating `slice(1)`.

The start and end of a string

Sometimes you would want to check what a string starts or ends with. You've guessed it, there are built-in methods for this on `string`. We can imagine this chapter is tough to work through, so here is a little encouragement and an example at the same time:

```
let encouragement = "You are doing great, keep up the good work!";
let bool_start = encouragement.startsWith("You");
console.log(bool_start);
```

This will log `true` to the console, because the sentence starts with `You`. Careful here, because it is case sensitive. So the following example will log `false`:

```
let bool_start2 = encouragement.startsWith("you");
console.log(bool_start2);
```

If you don't care about uppercase or lowercase, you can use the previously discussed `toLowerCase()` method here, so that it will not take uppercase or lowercase into account:

```
let bool_start3 = encouragement.toLowerCase().startsWith("you");
console.log(bool_start3);
```

We are now converting the string to lowercase first, so we know we are only working with lowercase characters here. However, an important side note here is that this will affect performance for huge strings.

 Again, a more performance-friendly alternative is to use regex. Getting excited for *Chapter 12, Intermediate JavaScript*, yet?

To end this section, we can do the same thing for checking whether a string ends with a certain string. You can see it in action here:

```
let bool_end = encouragement.endsWith("Something else");
console.log(bool_end);
```

Since it doesn't end with `Something else`, it will return `false`.

Practice exercise 8.4

Using string manipulation, create a function that will return a string with the first letter of all the words capitalized and the rest of the letters in lowercase. You should transform the sentence `thIs will be capITalized for each word` into `This Will Be Capitalized For Each Word`:

1. Create a string with several words that have letters with different cases, a mix of upper and lowercase words.
2. Create a function that gets a string as an argument, which will be the value that we will manipulate.
3. In the function first transform everything to lowercase letters.
4. Create an empty array that can hold the values of the words when we capitalize them.
5. Convert the phrase into words in an array using the `split()` method.
6. Loop through each one of the words that are now in the new array, so you can select each one independently. You can use `forEach()` for this.

7. Using `slice()` isolate the first letter in each word, then transform it to uppercase. Again using `slice()`, get the remaining value of the word without including the first letter. Then concatenate the two together to form the word that is now capitalized.

8. Add the new capitalized word into the blank array that you created. By the end of the loop you should have an array with all the words as separate items in the new array.

9. Take the array of updated words and using the `join()` method, transform them back into a string with spaces between each word.

10. Return the value of the newly updated string with capitalized words that can then be output into the console.

Practice exercise 8.5

Using the `replace()` string method, complete this vowel replacer exercise by replacing the vowels in a string with numbers. You can start with this string:

```
I love JavaScript
```

And turn it into something like the following:

```
2 13v1 j0v0scr2pt
```

Take the following steps:

1. Create the previously specified string, and convert it to lowercase.

2. Create an array containing the vowels: a, e, i, o, u.

3. Loop through each letter you have in the array, and output the current letter into the console so that you can see which letter will be converted.

4. Within the loop, using `replaceAll()` update each vowel substring with the index value of the letter from the vowel array.

 Using `replace()` will only replace the first occurrence; if you use `replaceAll()` this will update all matching results.

5. Once the loop completes output the result of the new string into the console.

Number methods

Let's move on to some built-in methods on the Number object. We have seen a few already, these are so popular that some of them have been made into global methods.

Checking if something is (not) a number

This can be done with isNaN(). We have seen this already when we talked about global methods, we can use this method without Number in front of it. Often you will want to do the opposite, you can negate the function with an ! in front of it:

```
let x = 34;
console.log(isNaN(x));
console.log(!isNaN(x));
let str = "hi";
console.log(isNaN(str));
```

This will log to the console:

```
false
true
true
```

Since x is a number, isNaN will be false. But this result negated becomes true, since x is a number. The string hi is not a number, so it will become false. And this one?

```
let str1 = "5";
console.log(isNaN(str1));
```

Some funky stuff is going on here, even though 5 is between quotation marks, JavaScript still sees that it's a 5 and it will log false. At this point, I'm sure you'd wish your partner, family, and coworkers are as understanding and forgiving as JavaScript.

Checking if something is finite

By now you might be able to guess the name of the method on Number that checks whether something is finite. It is a very popular one and has been made into a global method as well, and its name is isFinite(). It returns false for NaN, Infinity, and undefined, and true for all other values:

```
let x = 3;
let str = "finite";
console.log(isFinite(x));
console.log(isFinite(str));
console.log(isFinite(Infinity));
console.log(isFinite(10 / 0));
```

This will log:

```
true
false
false
false
```

The only finite number in this list is x. The others are not finite. A string is a not a number and is therefore not finite. `Infinity` is not finite and `10` divided by `0` returns `Infinity` (not an error).

Checking if something is an integer

Yes, this is done with `isInteger()`. Unlike `isNaN()` and `isFinite()`, `isInteger()` has not been made global and we will have to refer to the `Number` object to use it. It really does what you think it would: it returns `true` if the value is an integer and `false` when it's not:

```
let x = 3;
let str = "integer";
console.log(Number.isInteger(x));
console.log(Number.isInteger(str));
console.log(Number.isInteger(Infinity));
console.log(Number.isInteger(2.4));
```

This will log:

```
true
false
false
false
```

Since the only integer in the list is x.

Specifying a number of decimals

We can tell JavaScript how many decimals to use with the `toFixed()` method. This is different from the rounding methods in `Math`, since we can specify the number of decimals here. It doesn't change the original value, so we'll have to store the result:

```
let x = 1.23456;
let newX = x.toFixed(2);
```

This will only leave two decimals, so the value of `newX` will be `1.23`. It rounds the number normally; you can see this when we ask for one more decimal:

```
let x = 1.23456;
let newX = x.toFixed(3);
console.log(x, newX);
```

This logs `1.23456  1.235` as output.

Specifying precision

There is also a method to specify precision. Again this is different from the rounding methods in the `Math` class, since we can specify the total number of numbers to look at. This comes down to JavaScript looking at the total number of numbers. It is also counting the ones before the dot:

```
let x = 1.23456;
let newX = x.toPrecision(2);
```

So the value of newX will be `1.2` here. And also here, it is rounding the numbers:

```
let x = 1.23456;
let newX = x.toPrecision(4);
console.log(newX);
```

This will log `1.235`.

Now, let's move on and talk about some related mathematical methods!

Math methods

The `Math` object has many methods that we can use to do calculations and operations on numbers. We will go over the most important ones here. You can see all the available ones when you use an editor that shows suggestions and options during typing.

Finding the highest and lowest number

There is a built-in method max() to find the highest number among the arguments. You can see it here:

```
let highest = Math.max(2, 56, 12, 1, 233, 4);
console.log(highest);
```

It logs 233, because that's the highest number. In a similar way, we can find the lowest number:

```
let lowest = Math.min(2, 56, 12, 1, 233, 4);
console.log(lowest);
```

This will log 1, because that is the lowest number. If you try to do this with non-numeric arguments, you will get NaN as a result:

```
let highestOfWords = Math.max("hi", 3, "bye");
console.log(highestOfWords);
```

It is not giving 3 as output, because it is not ignoring the text but concluding that it cannot determine whether hi should be higher or lower than 3. So it returns NaN instead.

Square root and raising to the power of

The method sqrt() is used to calculate the square root of a certain number. Here you can see it in action:

```
let result = Math.sqrt(64);
console.log(result);
```

This will log 8, because the square root of 64 is 8. This method works just like the mathematics you learned in school. In order to raise a number to a certain power (base^{exponent}, for example 2^3), we can use the pow(base, exponent) function. Like this:

```
let result2 = Math.pow(5, 3);
console.log(result2);
```

We are raising 5 to the power of 3 here (5^3), so the result will be 125, which is the result of 5*5*5.

Turning decimals into integers

There are different ways to turn decimals into integers. Sometimes you will want to round a number. This you can do with the round() method:

```
let x = 6.78;
let y = 5.34;

console.log("X:", x, "becomes", Math.round(x));
console.log("Y:", y, "becomes", Math.round(y));
```

This will log:

```
X: 6.78 becomes 7
Y: 5.34 becomes 5
```

As you can see it is using normal rounding here. It is also possible that you don't want to round down, but up. For example, if you need to calculate how many wood boards you need and you conclude that you need 1.1, 1 is not going to be enough to do the job. You'll need 2. In this case, you can use the ceil() method (referring to ceiling):

```
console.log("X:", x, "becomes", Math.ceil(x));
console.log("Y:", y, "becomes", Math.ceil(y));
```

This will log:

```
X: 6.78 becomes 7
Y: 5.34 becomes 6
```

The ceil() method is always rounding up to the first integer it encounters. We have used this before when we were generating random numbers! Careful with negative numbers here, because -5 is higher than -6. This is how it works, as you can see in this example:

```
let negativeX = -x;
let negativeY = -y;

console.log("negativeX:", negativeX, "becomes", Math.ceil(negativeX));
console.log("negativeY:", negativeY, "becomes", Math.ceil(negativeY));
```

This will log:

```
negativeX: -6.78 becomes -6
negativeY: -5.34 becomes -5
```

The `floor()` method is doing the exact opposite of the `ceil()` method. It rounds down to the nearest integer number, as you can see here:

```
console.log("X:", x, "becomes", Math.floor(x));
console.log("Y:", y, "becomes", Math.floor(y));
```

This will log:

```
X: 6.78 becomes 6
Y: 5.34 becomes 5
```

Again, careful with negative numbers here, because it can feel counterintuitive:

```
console.log("negativeX:", negativeX, "becomes", Math.floor(negativeX));
console.log("negativeY:", negativeY, "becomes", Math.floor(negativeY));
```

This logs:

```
negativeX: -6.78 becomes -7
negativeY: -5.34 becomes -6
```

And then one last method, `trunc()`. This gives the exact same result as `floor()` for positive numbers, but it gets to these results differently. It is not rounding down, it is simply only returning the integer part:

```
console.log("X:", x, "becomes", Math.trunc(x));
console.log("Y:", y, "becomes", Math.trunc(y));
```

This will log:

```
X: 6.78 becomes 6
Y: 5.34 becomes 5
```

When we use negative numbers for `trunc()` we can see the difference:

```
negativeX: -6.78 becomes -6
negativeY: -5.34 becomes -5
```

So whenever you need to round down, you'll have to use `floor()`, if you need the integer part of the number, you'll need `trunc()`.

Exponent and logarithm

The exponent is the number to which a base is being raised. We use e (Euler's number) a lot in mathematics, this is what the exp() method in JavaScript does. It returns the number to which e must be raised to get the input. We can use the exp() built-in method of Math to calculate the exponent, and the log() method to calculate the natural logarithm. You can see an example here:

```
let x = 2;
let exp = Math.exp(x);
console.log("Exp:", exp);
let log = Math.log(exp);
console.log("Log:", log);
```

This will log:

```
Exp: 7.38905609893065
Log: 2
```

Don't worry if you can't follow along mathematically at this point. You'll figure this out whenever you'll need it for your programming.

Practice exercise 8.6

Experiment with the Math object with these steps:

1. Output the value of PI into the console using Math.
2. Using Math get the ceil() value of 5.7, get the floor() value of 5.7, get the round value of 5.7, and output it into the console.
3. Output a random value into the console.
4. Use Math.floor() and Math.random() to get a number from 0 to 10.
5. Use Math.floor() and Math.random() to get a number from 1 to 10.
6. Use Math.floor() and Math.random() to get a number from 1 to 100.
7. Create a function to generate a random number using the parameters of min and max. Run that function 100 times, returning into the console a random number from 1 to 100 each time.

Date methods

In order to work with dates in JavaScript we use the built-in Date object. This object contains a lot of built-in functions to work with dates.

Creating dates

There are different ways to create a date. One way to create dates is by using the different constructors. You can see some examples here:

```
let currentDateTime = new Date();
console.log(currentDateTime);
```

This will log the current date and time, in this case:

```
2021-06-05T14:21:45.625Z
```

But, this way we are not using the built-in method, but the constructor. There is a built-in method, `now()`, that returns the current date and time, similar to what the no argument constructor does:

```
let now2 = Date.now();
console.log(now2);
```

This will log the current time, represented in seconds since January 1st 1970. This is an arbitrary date representing the Unix epoch. In this case:

```
1622902938507
```

We can add 1,000 milliseconds to the Unix epoch time:

```
let milliDate = new Date(1000);
console.log(milliDate);
```

It will log:

```
1970-01-01T00:00:01.000Z
```

JavaScript can also convert many string formats to a date. Always mind the order in which days and months of dates are presented in the date format and the interpreter of JavaScript. This can vary depending on the region:

```
let stringDate = new Date("Sat Jun 05 2021 12:40:12 GMT+0200");
console.log(stringDate);
```

This will log:

```
2021-06-05T10:40:12.000Z
```

And lastly, you can also specify a certain date using the constructor:

```
let specificDate = new Date(2022, 1, 10, 12, 10, 15, 100);
console.log(specificDate);
```

This will log:

```
2022-02-10T12:10:15.100Z
```

Please mind this very important detail here, the second parameter is the month. 0 is for January and 11 is for December.

Methods to get and set the elements of a date

Now we have seen how to create dates, we'll learn how to get certain parts of dates. This can be done with one of the many get methods. Which you will use depends on the part you need:

```
let d = new Date();
console.log("Day of week:", d.getDay());
console.log("Day of month:", d.getDate());
console.log("Month:", d.getMonth());
console.log("Year:", d.getFullYear());
console.log("Seconds:", d.getSeconds());
console.log("Milliseconds:", d.getMilliseconds());
console.log("Time:", d.getTime());
```

This will log right now:

```
Day of week: 6
Day of month: 5
Month: 5
Year: 2021
Seconds: 24
Milliseconds: 171
Time: 1622903604171
```

The time is so high because it's the number of milliseconds since January 1st 1970. You can change the date in a similar way with a set method. Important to note here is that the original date object gets changed with these set methods:

```
d.setFullYear(2010);
console.log(d);
```

We have changed the year of our date object to 2010. This will output:

```
2010-06-05T14:29:51.481Z
```

We can also change the month. Let's add the below snippet to our change of the year code. This will change it to October. Please mind that while I'm doing this, I run the code again and again, so the minutes and smaller units of time will vary in the examples when I haven't set these yet:

```
d.setMonth(9);
console.log(d);
```

It will log:

```
2010-10-05T14:30:39.501Z
```

This is a weird one, in order to change the day, we have to call the setDate() method and not the setDay() method. There is no setDay() method, since the day of the week is deducted from the specific date. We cannot change that September 5th 2021 is a Sunday. We can change the number of days of the month though:

```
d.setDate(10);
console.log(d);
```

This will log:

```
2010-10-10T14:34:25.271Z
```

We can also change the hours:

```
d.setHours(10);
console.log(d);
```

Now it will log:

```
2010-10-10T10:34:54.518Z
```

Remember how JavaScript doesn't like to crash? If you call setHours() with a number higher than 24, it will roll over to the next date (1 per 24 hours) and after using the modulo operator, whatever is left over from hours % 24 will be the hours. The same process applies for minutes, seconds, and milliseconds.

The `setTime()` actually overrides the complete date with the inserted epoch time:

```
d.setTime(1622889770682);
console.log(d);
```

This will log:

```
2021-06-05T10:42:50.682Z
```

Parsing dates

With the built-in `parse()` method we can parse epoch dates from strings. It accepts many formats, but again you will have to be careful with the order of days and months:

```
let d1 = Date.parse("June 5, 2021");
console.log(d1);
```

This will log:

```
1622851200000
```

As you can see it ends with many zeros, because no time or seconds are specified in our string. And here is another example of a completely different format:

```
let d2 = Date.parse("6/5/2021");
console.log(d2);
```

This will also log:

```
1622851200000
```

The input for the parse is ISO formats of dates. Quite a few formats can be parsed to string, but you'll have to be careful. The result might depend on the exact implementation. Make sure that you know what the format of the incoming string is, so that you don't confuse months and days, and make sure that you know the behavior of the implementations. This can only be done reliably if you know what the string format is. So for example when you need to convert data coming from your own database or website's date picker.

Converting a date to a string

We can also convert dates back to strings. For example with these methods:

```
console.log(d.toDateString());
```

This will log the day in written format:

```
Sat Jun 05 2021
```

This is another method that converts it differently:

```
console.log(d.toLocaleDateString());
```

It will log:

```
6/5/2021
```

Practice exercise 8.7

Output the date with the full month name into the console. When converting to or from arrays, remember that they are zero-based:

1. Set up a date object, which can be any date in the future or past. Log the date out into the console to see how it is typically output as a date object.
2. Set up an array with all the named months of the year. Keep them in sequential order so that they will match the date month output.
3. Get the day from the date object value, using `getDate()`.
4. Get the year from the date object value, using `getFullYear()`.
5. Get the month of the date object value, using `getMonth()`.
6. Set up a variable to hold the date of the date object and output the month using the numeric value as the index for the array month name. Due to arrays being zero-based and the month returning a value of 1-12, the result needs to be subtracted by one.
7. Output the result into the console.

Chapter projects

Word scrambler

Create a function that returns a value of a word and scrambles the letter order with `Math.random()`:

1. Create a string that will hold a word value of your choice.
2. Create a function that can intake a parameter of the string word value.

3. Just like an array, strings also have a length by default. You can use this length to set the loop maximum value. You will need to create a separate variable to hold this value as the length of the string will be decreasing as the loop continues.

4. Create an empty temporary string variable that you can use to hold the new scrambled word value.

5. Create a for loop that will iterate the number of letters within the string parameter starting at 0 and iterating until the original length value of the string is reached.

6. Create a variable that will randomly select one letter using its index value, with Math.floor() and Math.random() multiplied by the current length of the string.

7. Add the new letter to the new string and remove it from the original string.

8. Using console.log() output the newly constructed string from the random letters and output to the console both the original string and the new one as the loop continues.

9. Update the original string by selecting the substring from the index value and adding it to the remaining string value from the index plus one onward. Output the new original string value with the removed characters.

10. As you loop through the content you will see a countdown of the remaining letters, the new scrambled version of the word as it is built, and the decreasing letters in the original word.

11. Return the final result and invoke the function with the original string word as an argument. Output this to the console.

Countdown timer

Create code for a countdown timer that can be executed in the console window, and will show the total milliseconds, days, hours, minutes, and seconds remaining until a target date is reached:

1. Create an end date that you want to count down to. Format it in a date type format within a string.

2. Create a countdown function that will parse the endDate() and subtract the current date from that end date. This will show the total in milliseconds. Using Date.parse() you can convert a string representation of a date to a numeric value as a number of milliseconds since January 1, 1970, 00:00:00 UTC.

3. Once you have the total milliseconds, to get the days, hours, minutes, and seconds you can take the following steps:

   - To get days you can divide the number of milliseconds in a date, removing the remainder with `Math.floor()`.

   - To get hours you can use modulus to capture just the remainder once the total days are removed.

   - To get minutes you can use the value of milliseconds in a minute and using the modulus capture the remainder.

   - Do the same for seconds by dividing the number by seconds in milliseconds and getting the remainder. If you use `Math.floor()` you can round down removing any remaining decimal places that will be shown in the lower values.

4. Return all the values within an object with property names indicating what the unit of time the values refer to.

5. Create a function to use a `setTimeout()` to run the `update()` function every second (1,000 milliseconds). The `update()` function will create a variable that can temporarily hold the object return values of `countdown()`, and create an empty variable that will be used to create the output values.

6. Within the same function, using the `for` loop get all the properties and values of the `temp` object variable. As you iterate through the object update the output string to contain the property name and property value.

7. Using `console.log()`, print the output result string into the console.

Self-check quiz

1. Which method will decode the following?

   ```
   var c = "http://www.google.com?id=1000&n=500";
   var e = encodeURIComponent(c);
   ```

   a. `decodeURIComponent(e)`

   b. `e.decodeUriComponent()`

   c. `decoderURIComponent(c)`

   d. `decoderURIComponent(e)`

2. What will be output into the console from the following syntax?

   ```
   const arr = ["hi","world","hello","hii","hi","hi World","Hi"];
   console.log(arr.lastIndexOf("hi"));
   ```

3. What is the result of the below code in the console?

```
const arr = ["Hi","world","hello","Hii","hi","hi World","Hi"];
arr.copyWithin(0, 3, 5);
console.log(arr);
```

4. What is the result of the below code in the console?

```
const arr = ["Hi","world","hello","Hii","hi","hi World","Hi"];
const arr2 = arr.filter((element,index)=>{
    const ele2 = element.substring(0, 2);
    return (ele2 == "hi");
});
console.log(arr2);
```

Summary

In this chapter we have dealt with many built-in methods. These are methods that are handed to us by JavaScript and that we can use for things that we'll often need. We went over the most used global built-in methods, which are so common they can be used without being prepended by the object they belong to.

We also discussed array methods, string methods, number methods, math methods, and date methods. You'll find yourself using these methods a lot and chaining them (whenever they return a result) when you get more comfortable with JavaScript.

Now we've become familiar with many of JavaScript's core features, we'll spend the next couple of chapters diving into how it works alongside HTML and the browser to bring web pages to life!

Join our book's Discord space

Join the book's Discord workspace for a monthly *Ask me Anything* session with the authors: https://packt.link/JSBook

9

The Document Object Model

The **Document Object Model (DOM)** is a lot more exciting than it may sound at first. In this chapter, we will introduce you to the DOM. This is a fundamental concept you will need to understand before working with JavaScript on web pages. It grabs an HTML page and turns it into a logical tree. If you do not know any HTML, no worries. We start with an HTML crash course section that you can skip if you are familiar with HTML.

Once we are sure that we are on the same page with HTML knowledge, we will introduce you to the **Browser Object Model (BOM)**. The BOM holds all the methods and properties for JavaScript to interact with the browser. This is information related to previous pages visited, the size of the window of the browser, and also the DOM.

The DOM contains the HTML elements on the web page. With JavaScript, we can select and manipulate parts of the DOM. This leads to interactive web pages instead of static ones. So, long story short, being able to work with the DOM means you're able to create interactive web pages!

We will cover the following topics:

- HTML crash course
- Introducing the BOM
- Introducing the DOM
- Types of DOM elements
- Selecting page elements

We can imagine you cannot wait to get started, so let's dive into it.

Note: exercise, project and self-check quiz answers can be found in the *Appendix*.

HTML crash course

Hyper-Text Markup Language (HTML) is the language that shapes the content of web pages. Web browsers understand HTML code and represent it in the format we are used to seeing: web pages. Here is a little very basic HTML example:

```
<!DOCTYPE html>
<html>
  <head>
    <title>Tab in the browser</title>
  </head>
  <body>
    <p>Hello web!</p>
  </body>
</html>
```

This is what this basic web page looks like:

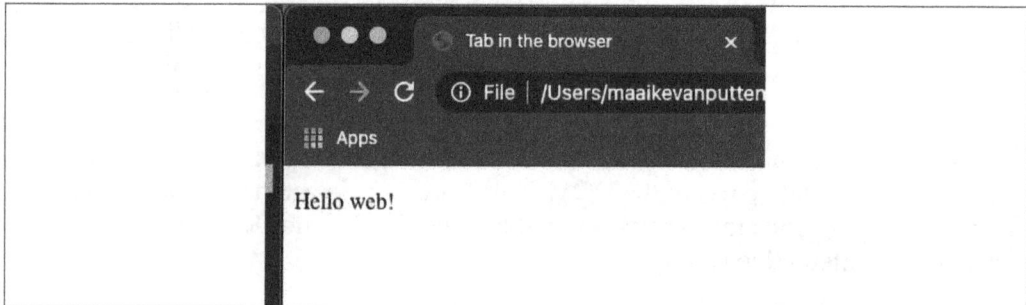

Figure 9.1: Basic website

HTML code consists of elements. These elements contain a tag and attributes. We will explain these fundamental concepts in the coming sections.

HTML elements

As you can see, HTML consists of words between `<angle brackets>`, or elements. Any element that gets opened needs to be closed. We open with `<elementname>` and we close with `</elementname>`.

Everything in between that is part of the element. There are a few exceptions with regards to the closing, but you will run into them at your own pace. In the previous example we had multiple elements, including these two. It is an element with the tag body and an inner element with the tag p:

```
<body>
   <p>Hello web!</p>
</body>
```

So elements can contain inner elements. Elements can only be closed if all inner elements have been closed. Here is an example to demonstrate that. Here is the right way:

```
<outer>
  <sub>
    <inner>
    </inner>
  </sub>
</outer>
```

And here is the wrong way:

```
<outer>
  <sub>
    <inner>
  </sub>
    </inner>
</outer>
```

Please note, these are just made-up element names. In the last example, we close sub before we have closed the inner element. This is wrong; you must always close the inner elements before closing the outer element. We call inner elements child elements, and outer elements parent elements. Here is some correct HTML:

```
<body>
  <div>
    <p>
    </p>
  </div>
</body>
```

This isn't correct HTML, because the div is closed before its inner element p:

```
<body>
  <div>
    <p>
  </div>
    </p>
</body>
```

The different elements represent different pieces of layout. The p we just saw represents paragraphs. And another common one is h1, which represents a big title. What is more important is to know the three major building elements of every HTML page. The HTML element, the head element, and the body element.

In the HTML element, all the HTML takes place. You can only have one of these in your HTML page. It is the outer element, and all other elements are housed in it. It contains the other two top-level elements: head and body. If you are ever confused about the order of head and body, just think of a human; the head is on top of the body.

In the head element, we arrange a lot of things that are meant for the browser and not for the user. You can think of certain metadata, such as which JavaScript scripts and which stylesheets need to be included, and what the searching engine should use as a description on the search result page. We will not really be doing a lot with the head element as JavaScript developers, other than including scripts.

Here's an example of a basic head element:

```
<head>
    <title>This is the title of the browser tab</title>
    <meta name="description" content="This is the preview in google">
<script src="included.js"></script>
</head>
```

The body element is mostly the content that will appear on the web page. There can only be one body element in the HTML element. Titles, paragraphs, images, lists, links, buttons, and many more are all elements that we can come across in the body. They have their own tag, so for example, img for image and a for a link. Here is a table including common tags for in the body. It is definitely not an exhaustive list.

Tag to open	Tag to end	Description
`<p>`	`</p>`	Used to create a paragraph.
`<h1>`	`</h1>`	Used to create a header; smaller headers are h2 to h6.
`<span>`	`</span>`	Generic inline container for content that needs to be separated, for example, for layout purposes.
`<a>`	`</a>`	Used for hyperlinks.
`<button>`	`</button>`	Used for buttons.
`<table>`	`</table>`	Creates a table.
`<tr>`	`</tr>`	Creates a table row, must be used inside a table.
`<td>`	`</td>`	Creates a table data cell inside a row.
`<ul>`	`</ul>`	Unordered lists, with bullet points, for example.
`<ol>`	`</ol>`	Ordered lists with numbers.
`<li>`	`</li>`	List items for inside ordered and unordered lists.
`<div>`	`</div>`	Section inside the HTML page. It is often used as a container for other styles or sections and can easily be used for special layouts.
`<form>`	`<form>`	Creates an HTML form.
`<input>`	`</input>`	Creates an input field in which the user can enter information. These can be textboxes, checkboxes, buttons, passwords, numbers, dropdowns, radio buttons, and much more.
`<input />`	None	Same as input, but written without a closing tag, the / at the end makes it self-closing. This is only possible for a few elements.
` `	None	Used to make a line break (go to a new line). It does not need an end tag and is therefore an exception.

Can you figure out what this HTML example does:

```
<html>

<head>
    <title>Awesome</title>
</head>

<body>
    <h1>Language and awesomeness</h1>
    <table>
```

```
        <tr>
            <th>Language</th>
            <th>Awesomeness</th>
        </tr>
        <tr>
            <td>JavaScript</td>
            <td>100</td>
        </tr>
        <tr>
            <td>HTML</td>
            <td>100</td>
        </tr>
    </table>
</body>

</html>
```

It creates a web page, with Awesome in the tab title. And on the page, it has a big header saying Language and awesomeness. Then there is a table with three rows and two columns. The first row contains the headers Language and Awesomeness. The second row holds the values JavaScript and 100, and the third row holds the values HTML and 100.

HTML attributes

The last part of HTML that we will discuss in this crash course is HTML attributes. Attributes influence the element they are specified on. They exist inside the element they are specified on and are assigned a value using an equal sign. For example, the attribute of a (which indicates a hyperlink) is the href. This specifies where the link is redirecting to:

```
<a href="https://google.com">Ask Google</a>
```

This displays a link with the text Ask Google. And when you click it, you will be sent to Google, which can be told by the value of the href attribute. This modifies the a element. There are many attributes out there, but for now you just need to know that they modify the element they are specified on.

Here is a table with an overview of the most important attributes to get started with HTML and JavaScript. Why these are important will unfold somewhere in the next chapter.

Attribute name	Description	Can be used on which element?
id	Gives an element a unique ID, such as age.	All of them
name	Used to give a custom name to an element.	input, button, form, and quite a few we haven't seen yet
class	Special metadata that can be added to an element. This can result in a certain layout or JavaScript manipulation.	Almost all of them inside body
value	Sets the initial value of the element it is added to.	button, input, li, and a few we haven't seen yet
style	Gives a specified layout to the HTML element it is added to.	All of them

We will introduce you to other attributes when you will need them for practicing your JavaScript magic.

Okay, this has been one of the more brief HTML crash courses out there. There are many great resources to find more information. If you need more information or explanation at this point, create and open an HTML file like the following and take it from there!

```
<!DOCTYPE html >
<html>

<body>
    <a href="https://google.com">Ask google</a>
</body>

</html>
```

We will now go ahead and have a look at the BOM and the different parts of the BOM.

The BOM

The BOM, sometimes also called the **window browser object,** is the amazing "magic" element that makes it possible for your JavaScript code to communicate with the browser.

The window object contains all the properties required to represent the window of the browser, so for example, the size of the window and the history of previously visited web pages. The window object has global variables and functions, and these can all be seen when we explore the window object. The exact implementation of the BOM depends on the browser and the version of the browser. This is important to keep in mind while working your way through these sections.

Some of the most important objects of the BOM we will look into in this chapter are:

- History
- Navigator
- Location

As well as the preceding useful objects, we will also consider the DOM in more detail. But first, we can explore the BOM and see the objects of it with the command `console.dir(window)`. We will enter this in the console of our browser. Let's discuss how to get there first.

We can access the HTML elements and the JavaScript if we go to the inspection panel of our browser. It differs a bit in how you get there, but often the *F12* button while in the browser will do the trick, or else a right-click on the website you want to see the console for and clicking on **Inspect element** or **Inspect** on a macOS device.

You should see a side panel (or if you have changed your settings, a separate window) pop up.

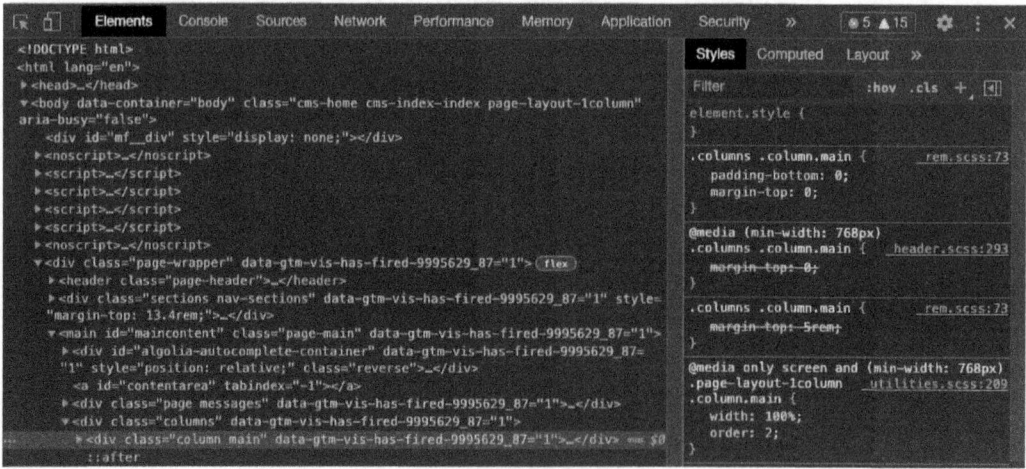

Figure 9.2: Inspecting a page in the browser

Navigate to the **Console** tab, which is next to the **Elements** tab in the image above. You can type the following command and press *Enter* to get information about the window object:

```
console.dir(window);
```

This command will produce a view like the following:

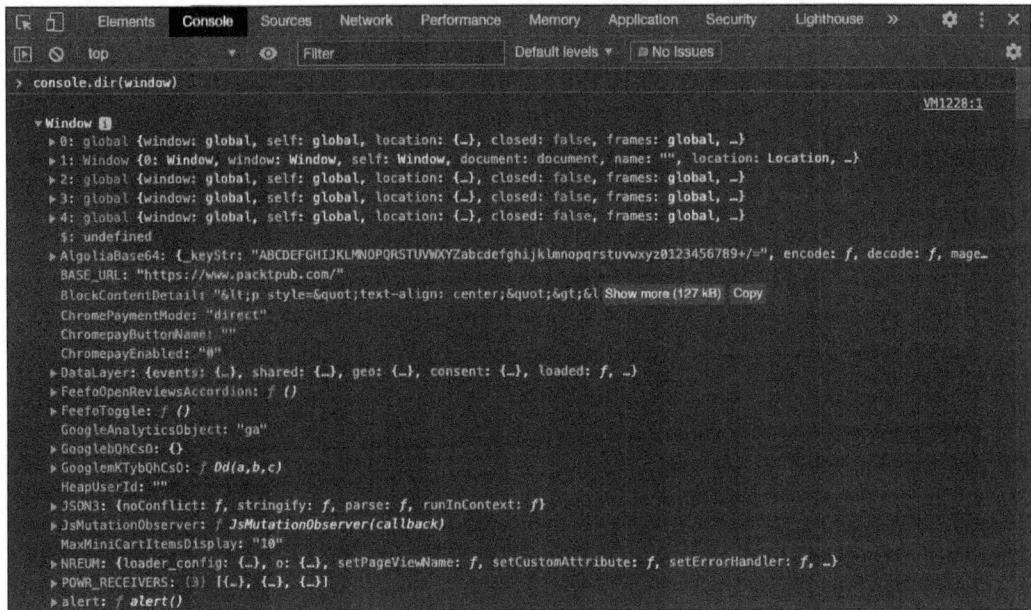

Figure 9.3: Part of the output of console.dir(window) showing the window browser object

The console.dir() method shows a list of all the properties of the specified object. You can click on the little triangles to open the objects and inspect them even more.

The BOM contains many other objects. We can access these like we saw when we dealt with objects, so for example, we can get the length of the history (in my browser) accessing the history object of the window and then the length of the history object, like this:

```
window.history.length;
```

After the exercise, we will learn more about the history object.

Practice exercise 9.1

1. Go back to the website you were just viewing and execute the command `console.dir(window)`.

2. Can you find the `document` object that is nested within the `window` object? Under the root of the `window` object in the console, you can navigate down to the object that is named `document`.

3. Can you find the height and width (in pixels) of your window? You can return the inner and outer window.

Window history object

The window browser object also contains a `history` object. This object can actually be written without the prefix of `window` because it has been made globally available, so we can get the exact same object by using the `console.dir(window.history)` or simply the `console.dir(history)` command in the console:

Figure 9.4: History object

This object is actually what you can use to go back to a previous page. It has a built-in function for that called go. What happens when you execute this command?

```
window.history.go(-1);
```

Go ahead and try it for yourself in the console of your browser (make sure that you did visit multiple pages in that tab).

Window navigator object

In the window object that we just saw, there is a navigator property. This property is particularly interesting because it contains information about the browser we are using, such as what browser it is and what version we are using, and what operating system the browser is running on.

This can be handy for customizing the website for certain operating systems. Imagine a download button that will be different for Windows, Linux, and macOS.

You can explore it using this command in the console:

```
console.dir(window.navigator);
```

As you can see, we start with accessing the window, because navigator is an object of the window object. So it is a property of the window object, which we specify with the dot in between. In other words, we access these window objects in the same way we do any other object. But, in this case, as navigator is also globally available, we can also access this without window in front of it with this command:

```
console.dir(navigator);
```

Here is what the navigator object might look like:

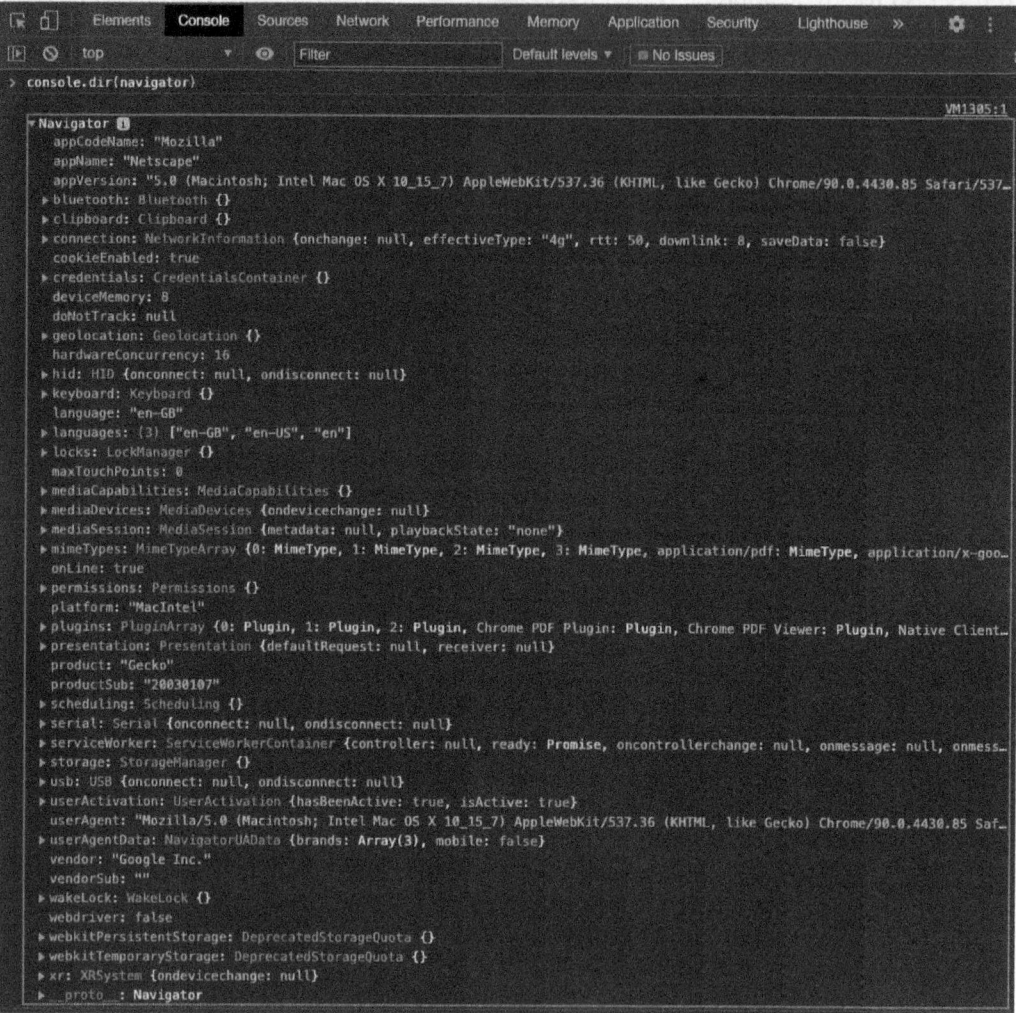

Figure 9.5: The navigator object

Window location object

Another rather interesting and unique property of window is the location object. This contains the URL of the current web page. If you override (parts of) that property, you force the browser to go to a new page! How to do this exactly differs per browser, but the next exercise will guide you through this.

The `location` object consists of a few properties. You can see them by using the command `console.dir(window.location)` or `console.dir(location)` in the console. Here is what the output will look like:

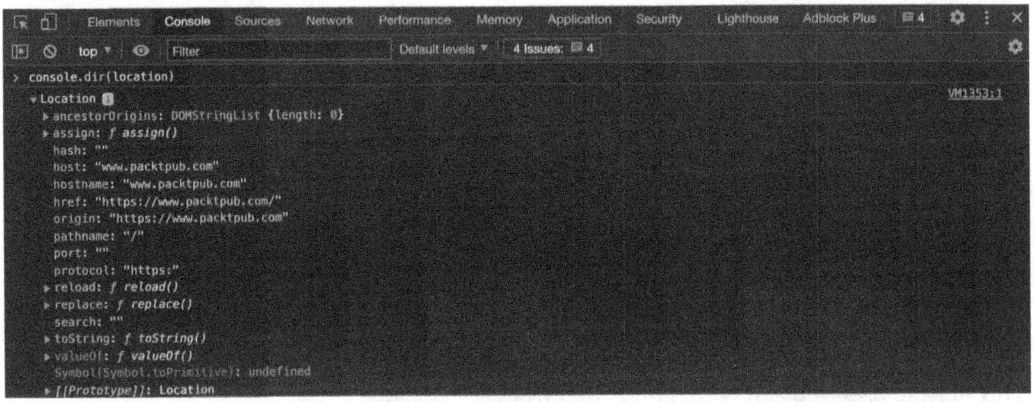

Figure 9.6: The location object

There are many objects on the `location` object, just as with the others we have seen. We can access the nested objects and properties using dot notation (like for other objects we have seen). So, for example, in this browser I can enter the following:

```
location.ancestorOrigins.length;
```

This will get the length of the `ancestorOrigins` object, which represents how many browsing contexts our page is associated with. This can be useful to determine whether the web page is framed in an unexpected context. Not all browsers have this object though; again, this BOM and all the elements of it vary per browser.

Follow the steps in the practice exercise to do such magic yourself.

Practice exercise 9.2

Travel through the `window` object to get to the `location` object, then output the values of the `protocol` and `href` properties of the current file, into the console.

The DOM

The DOM is actually not very complicated to understand. It is a way of displaying the structure of an HTML document as a logical tree. This is possible because of the very important rule that inner elements need to be closed before outer elements get closed.

Here is an HTML snippet:

```
<html>
  <head>
    <title>Tab in the browser</title>
  </head>
  <body>
    <h1>DOM</h1>
    <div>
      <p>Hello web!</p>
      <a href="https://google.com">Here's a link!</a>
    </div>
  </body>
</html>
```

And here is how we can translate it to a tree:

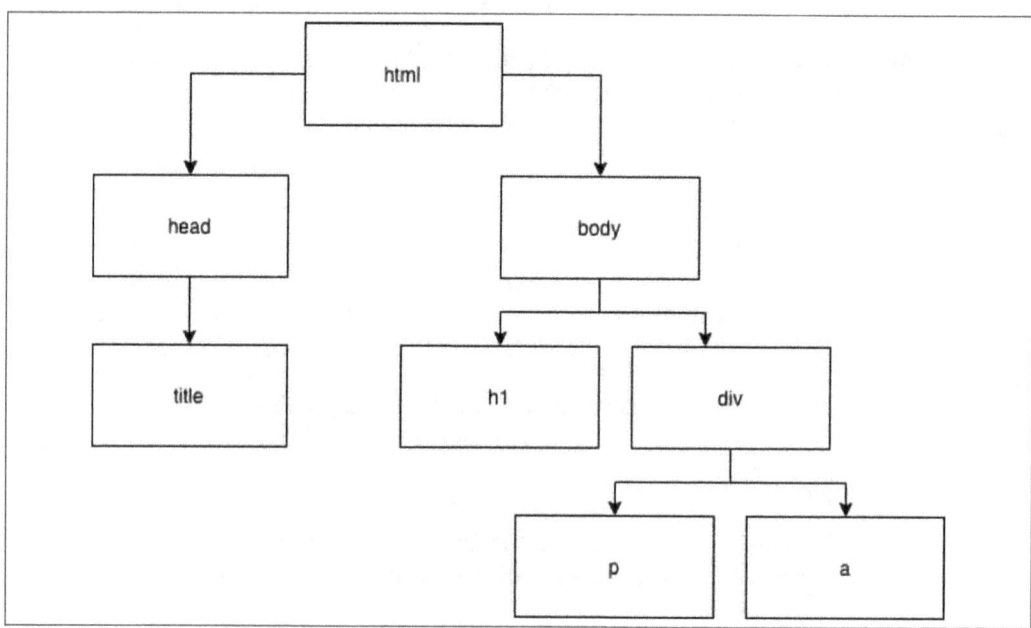

Figure 9.7: Tree structure of the DOM of a very basic web page

As you can see, the most outer element, **html**, is at the top of the tree. The next levels, **head** and **body**, are its children. **head** has only one child: **title**. **body** has two children: **h1** and **div**. And **div** has two children: **p** and **a**. These are typically used for paragraphs and links (or buttons). Clearly, complex web pages have complicated trees. This logical tree and a bunch of extra properties make up a web page's DOM.

The DOM of a real web page wouldn't fit on a page in this book. But if you can draw trees like these in your head, it will be of great help soon.

Additional DOM properties

We can inspect the DOM in a similar fashion as we did the others. We execute the following command in the console of our website (again, the document object is globally accessible, so accessing it through the window object is possible but not necessary):

```
console.dir(document);
```

In this case, we want to see the document object, which represents the DOM:

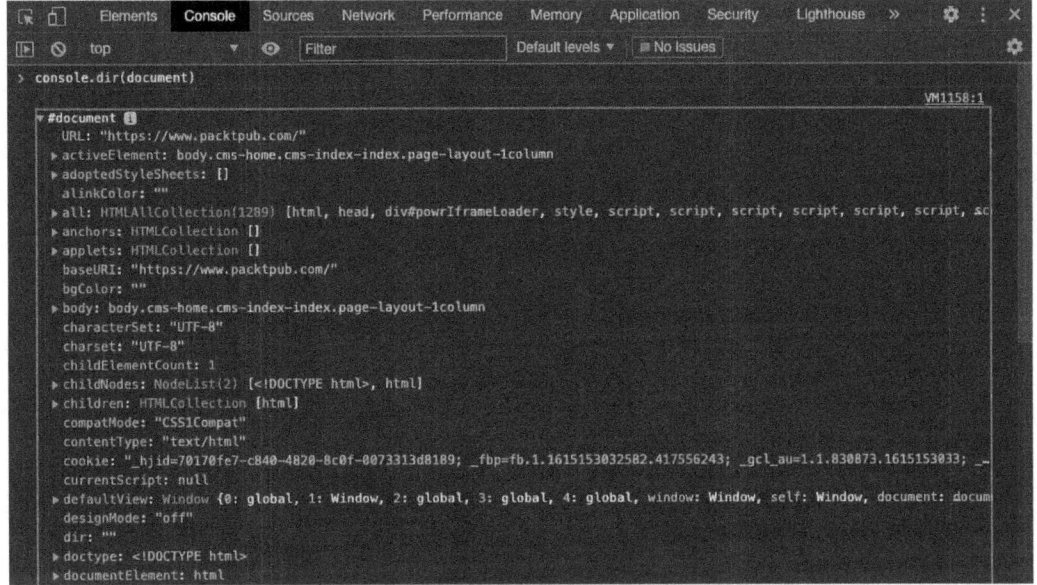

Figure 9.8: The DOM

You really do not need to understand everything you are seeing here, but it is showing many things, among which are the HTML elements and JavaScript code.

Great, right now you have got the basics of the BOM down, and its child object that is most relevant to us right now, the DOM. We saw many properties of the DOM earlier already. For us, it is most relevant to look at the HTML elements in the DOM. The DOM contains all the HTML elements of a web page.

These basics of DOM elements, combined with some knowledge of manipulating and exploring the DOM, will open up so many possibilities.

In the next chapter, we will focus on traversing the DOM, finding elements in the DOM, and manipulating the DOM. The code we will be writing there will really start to look like proper projects.

Selecting page elements

The `document` object contains many properties and methods. In order to work with elements on the page, you'll first have to find them. If you need to change the value of a certain paragraph, you'll have to grab this paragraph first. We call this selecting the paragraph. After selecting, we can start changing it.

To select page elements to use within your JavaScript code and in order to manipulate elements, you can use either the `querySelector()` or `querySelectorAll()` method. Both of these can be used to select page elements either by tag name, ID, or class.

The `document.querySelector()` method will return the first element within the document that matches the specified selectors. If no matching page elements are found, the result `null` is returned. To return multiple matching elements, you can use the method `document.querySelectorAll()`.

The `querySelectorAll()` method will return a static `NodeList`, which represents a list of the document's elements that match the specified group of selectors. We will demonstrate the usage of both `querySelector()` and `querySelectorAll()` with the following HTML snippet:

```
<!doctype html>
<html>
  <head>
    <title>JS Tester</title>
  </head>
  <body>
    <h1 class="output">Hello World</h1>
    <div class="output">Test</div>
  </body>
</html>
```

We are going to select the h1 element with `querySelector()`. Therefore, if there is more than one, it will just grab the first:

```
const ele1 = document.querySelector("h1");
console.dir(ele1);
```

If you want to select multiple elements, you can use `querySelectorAll()`. This method is going to return all the elements that match the selector in an array. In this example, we are going to look for instances of the output class, which is done by prepending the class name with a dot.

```
const eles = document.querySelectorAll(".output");
console.log(eles);
```

After selecting, you can start using the dynamic features of the DOM: you can manipulate the elements using JavaScript. Content can be changed in the same way a variable's contents can be, elements can be removed or added, and styles can be adjusted. This can all be done with JavaScript and the way the user interacts with the page can affect this. We have seen the two most common methods to select in the DOM here, `querySelector()` and `querySelectorAll()`. You can actually select any element you might need with these. There are lots more, which you'll encounter in the next chapter, along with many of the ways the DOM can be manipulated.

Practice exercise 9.3

Select a page element and update the content, change the style, and add attributes. Create an HTML file containing a page element with a class of output using the following code template:

```
<!DOCTYPE html >
<html>

<div class="output"></div>
    <script>
    </script>

</html>
```

Within the `script` tags, make the following changes to the output element:

1. Select the page element as a JavaScript object.
2. Update the `textContent` property of the selected page element.
3. Using the `classList.add` object method, add a class of red to the element.
4. Update the `id` property of the element to `tester`.
5. Through the `style` object, add a `backgroundColor` property of red to the page element.

6. Get the document URL via `document.URL` and update the text of the output element to contain the value of the document URL. You can log it in the console first to ensure you have the correct value.

Chapter project

Manipulating HTML elements with JavaScript

Take the HTML code below:

```
<div class="output">
    <h1>Hello</h1>
    <div>Test</div>
    <ul>
        <li id="one">One</li>
        <li class="red">Two</li>
    </ul>
    <div>Test</div>
</div>
```

Take the following steps (and experiment further) to understand how HTML elements can be manipulated with JavaScript code.

1. Select the element with the class `output`.
2. Create another JavaScript object called `mainList` and select only the `ul` tag that is within the `output` element. Update the ID of that `ul` tag to `mainList`.
3. Search for the `tagName` of each `div`, and output them into the console as an array.
4. Using a `for` loop, set the ID of each of the `div` tags to `id` with a numeric value of the order they appear within output. Still within the loop, alternate the color of the contents of each element in `output` to be red or blue.

Self-check quiz

1. Go to your favorite website and open the browser console. Type `document.body`. What do you see in the console?
2. As we know, with objects, we can write to the property value and assign a new value with the assignment operator. Update the `textContent` property of the `document.body` object on a web page of your choosing to contain the string `Hello World`.

3. Use what we learned about objects to list out BOM object properties and values. Try it on the `document` object.

4. Now do the same for the `window` object.

5. Create an HTML file with an `h1` tag. Use JavaScript and select the page element with the `h1` tag and assign the element into a variable. Update the `textContent` property of the variable to `Hello World`.

Summary

We started this chapter with the basics of HTML. We learned that HTML consists of elements and that these elements can contain other elements. Elements have a tag that specifies the type of element they are and they can have attributes that alter the element or add some metadata to the element. These attributes can be used by JavaScript.

We then had a look at the BOM, which represents the window of the browser that is being used for the web page and contains other objects, such as the `history`, `location`, `navigator`, and `document` objects. The `document` object is referred to as the DOM, which is what you are most likely to be working with. The document contains the HTML elements of the web page.

We also started to consider how we can select document elements and use these to manipulate the web page. This is what we'll continue exploring in the next chapter!

Join our book's Discord space

Join the book's Discord workspace for a monthly *Ask me Anything* session with the authors: `https://packt.link/JSBook`

10

Dynamic Element Manipulation Using the DOM

Learning the difficult concepts of the previous chapter will be rewarded in this chapter. We will take our DOM knowledge one step further and learn how to manipulate the DOM elements on the page with JavaScript. First, we need to learn how to navigate the DOM and select the elements we want. We will learn how we can add and change attributes and values, and how to add new elements to the DOM.

You will also learn how to add style to elements, which can be used to make items appear and disappear. Then we will introduce you to events and event listeners. We will start easy, but by the end of this chapter you will be able to manipulate web pages in many ways, and you will have the knowledge to create basic web apps. The sky is the limit after getting this skill down.

Along the way, we will cover the following topics:

- Basic DOM traversing
- Accessing elements in the DOM
- Element click handler
- This and the DOM
- Manipulating element style
- Changing the classes of an element
- Manipulating attributes
- Event listeners on elements
- Creating new elements

Note: exercise, project and self-check quiz answers can be found in the *Appendix*.

We have learned a lot about the DOM already. In order to interact with our web page and create a dynamic web page, we have to connect our JavaScript skills to the DOM.

Basic DOM traversing

We can traverse the DOM using the document object that we saw in the previous chapter. This document object contains all the HTML and is a representation of the web page. Traversing over these elements can get you to the element you need in order to manipulate it.

This is not the most common way to do it, but this will help understand how it works later. And sometimes, you might actually find yourself needing these techniques as well. Just don't panic: there are other ways to do it, and they will be revealed in this chapter!

Even for a simple HTML piece there are already multiple ways to traverse the DOM. Let's go hunting for treasure in our DOM. We start with this little HTML snippet:

```
<!DOCTYPE html>
<html>
  <body>
    <h1>Let's find the treasure</h1>
    <div id="forest">
      <div id="tree1">
        <div id="squirrel"></div>
        <div id="flower"></div>
      </div>
      <div id="tree2">
        <div id="shrubbery">
          <div id="treasure"></div>
        </div>
        <div id="mushroom">
          <div id="bug"></div>
        </div>
      </div>
    </div>
  </body>
</html>
```

We now want to traverse the DOM of this snippet to find the treasure. We can do this by stepping into the document object and navigating our way from there onwards. It is easiest to do this exercise in the console in the browser, because that way you'll get direct feedback about where in the DOM you are.

We can start by using the body property from the document. This contains everything that's inside the body element. In the console, we'll type:

```
console.dir(document.body);
```

We should get a really long object. There are a few ways from this object to get to our treasure. To do so, let's discuss the children and childNodes property.

 childNodes is more a complete term than children. Children just contain all the HTML elements, so are really the nodes. childNodes also contain text nodes and comments. With children, however, you can use the ID, and therefore they are easier to use.

To get to the treasure using children you would have to use:

```
console.dir(document.body.children.forest.children.tree2.children.
shrubbery.children.treasure);
```

As you can see, on every element we select, we have to select the children again. So, first, we grab the children from the body, then we select forest from these children. Then from forest, we want to grab its children again, and from these children we want to select tree2. From tree2 we want to grab the children again, from these children we need shrubbery. And then finally, we can grab the children from shrubbery and select treasure.

To get to the treasure using childNodes you would have to use your console a lot because text and comment nodes are also in there. childNodes is an array, so you will have to select the right index to select the right child. There is one advantage here: it is a lot shorter because you won't need to select the name separately.

```
console.dir(document.body.childNodes[3].childNodes[3].childNodes[1].
childNodes[1]);
```

You could also combine them:

```
console.dir(document.body.childNodes[3].childNodes[3].childNodes[1].
children.treasure);
```

There are many ways to traverse the document. Depending on what you need, you might have to use one specific way. For tasks that require DOM traversing, it is usually the case that if it is works, it is a good solution.

So far, we have seen how we can move down the DOM, but we can also move up. Every element knows its parent. We can use the `parentElement` property to move back up. For example, if we use the treasure HTML sample and type this into the console:

```
document.body.children.forest.children.tree2.parentElement;
```

We are back at `forest`, since that is the parent element of `tree2`. This can be very useful, in particular when combined with functions such as `getElementById()`, which we will see later in more detail.

Not only can we move up and down, we can also move sideways. For example, if we select `tree2` like this:

```
document.body.children.forest.children.tree2;
```

We can get to `tree1` using:

```
document.body.children.forest.children.tree2.previousElementSibling;
```

And from `tree1` we can get to `tree2` using:

```
document.body.children.forest.children.tree1.nextElementSibling;
```

As an alternative to `nextElementSibling`, which returns the next node that is an element, you could use `nextSibling`, which will return the next node of any type.

Practice exercise 10.1

In this exercise, experiment with traversing the DOM hierarchy. You can use this sample HTML website:

```
<!doctype html>
<html><head><title>Sample Webpage</title></head>
<body>
    <div class="main">
        <div>
            <ul >
                <li>One</li>
                <li>Two</li>
```

```
        <li>Three</li>
      </ul>
    </div>
    <div>blue</div>
    <div>green</div>
    <div>yellow</div>
    <div>Purple</div>
  </div>
</body>
</html>
```

Take the following steps:

1. Create and open the above sample web page, or visit your favorite website, and open the document body in the console with `console.dir(document)`.

2. In the `body.children` property, select some of the child elements. View how they match the page content.

3. Navigate to and output the next nodes or elements into the console.

Selecting elements as objects

Now we know how to traverse the DOM, we can make changes to the elements. Instead of using `console.dir()`, we can just type in the path to the element we want to change. We now have the element as a JavaScript object, and we can make changes to all its properties. Let's use a simpler HTML page for this one.

```
<!DOCTYPE html>
<html>
  <body>
    <h1>Welcome page</h1>
    <p id="greeting">
      Hi!
    </p>
  </body>
</html>
```

We can traverse to the p element, for example, by using this code:

```
document.body.children.greeting;
```

This gives us the power to manipulate the properties of the element, and the element itself, directly! Let's execute this newly gained power in the next section.

Changing innerText

The `innerText` property focuses on the text between the opening and closing of the element, like so:

```
<element>here</element>
```

The retrieved value would be `here` as plain text. For example, if we go to the console and we type:

```
document.body.children.greeting.innerText = "Bye!";
```

The message that is displayed on the page changes from `Hi!` to `Bye!` immediately. `innerText` returns the content of the element as plain text, which is not a problem in this case because there is only text in there. However, if there is any HTML inside the element you need to select, or if you want to add HTML, you cannot use this method. It will interpret the HTML as text and just output it on the screen. So if we executed this:

```
document.body.children.greeting.innerText = "<p>Bye!</p>";
```

It will output to the screen `<p>Bye!</p>`, with the HTML around it, as if it was intended as a text string. To get around this, you need to use `innerHTML`.

Changing innerHTML

If you did not only want to work with plain text, or perhaps specify some HTML formatting with your value, you could use the `innerHTML` property instead. This property doesn't just process be plain text, it can also be inner HTML elements:

```
document.body.children.greeting.innerHTML = "<b>Bye!</b>";
```

This will display **Bye!** in bold on the screen, having taken the b element into account rather than just printing it as if it were a single string value.

You were already promised that you could access elements in a more convenient way than traversing the DOM. Let's see how exactly in the next section.

Accessing elements in the DOM

There are multiple methods to select elements from the DOM. After getting the elements, we are able to modify them. In the following sections, we will discuss how to get elements by their ID, tag name, and class name, and by CSS selector.

Instead of traversing it step by step as we just did, we are going to use built-in methods that can go through the DOM and return the elements that match the specifications.

We are going to use the following HTML snippet as an example:

```
<!DOCTYPE html>
<html>
  <body>
    <h1>Just an example</h1>
    <div id="one" class="example">Hi!</div>
    <div id="two" class="example">Hi!</div>
    <div id="three" class="something">Hi!</div>
  </body>
</html>
```

Let's start by accessing elements by ID.

Accessing elements by ID

We can grab elements by ID with the `getElementById()` method. This returns one element with the specified ID. IDs should be unique, as only one result will be returned from the HTML document. There are not a lot of rules for valid IDs; they cannot contain spaces and must be at least one character. As with the conventions for naming variables, it is a best practice to make it descriptive and avoid special characters.

If we want to select the element with an ID of two right away, we could use:

```
document.getElementById("two");
```

This would return the full HTML element:

```
<div id="two" class="example">Hi!</div>
```

To reiterate, if you have more than one element with the same ID, it will just give you back the first one it encounters. You should avoid this situation in your code though.

This is what the full file looks like with the JavaScript inside the HTML page, instead of simply querying the browser console:

```
<html>
  <body>
```

```
    <h1 style="color:pink;">Just an example</h1>
    <div id="one" class="example">Hi!</div>
    <div id="two" class="example">Hi!</div>
    <div id="three" class="something">Hi!</div>
  </body>
  <script>
    console.log(document.getElementById("two"));
  </script>
</html>
```

In this case, it would log the full HTML `div` with `id="two"` to the console.

Practice exercise 10.2

Try experimenting with getting elements by their IDs:

1. Create an HTML element and assign an ID in the element attribute.
2. Select the page element using its ID.
3. Output the selected page element into the console.

Accessing elements by tag name

If we ask for elements by tag name, we get an array as a result. This is because there could be more than one element with the same tag name. It will be a collection of HTML elements, or `HTMLCollection`, which is a special JavaScript object. It's basically just a list of nodes. Execute the following command in the console:

```
document.getElementsByTagName("div");
```

It will give back:

```
HTMLCollection(3) [div#one.example, div#two.example, div#three.
something, one: div#one.example, two: div#two.example, three:
div#three.something]
```

As you can see, all the elements in the DOM with the `div` tag are returned. You can read what the ID is and what the class is from the syntax. The first ones in the collection are the objects: `div` is the name, `#` specifies the ID, and `.` specifies the class. If there are multiple dots, there are multiple classes. Then you can see the elements again (`namedItems`), this time as key-value pairs with their ID as the key.

We can access them using the `item()` method to access them by index, like this:

```
document.getElementsByTagName("div").item(1);
```

This will return:

```
<div id="two" class="example">Hi!</div>
```

We can also access them by name, using the `namedItem()` method, like this:

```
document.getElementsByTagName("div").namedItem("one");
```

And this will return:

```
<div id="one" class="example">Hi!</div>
```

When there is only one match, it will still return an `HTMLCollection`. There is only one h1 tag, so let's demonstrate this behavior:

```
document.getElementsByTagName("h1");
```

This will output:

```
HTMLCollection [h1]
```

Since h1 doesn't have an ID or class, it is only h1. And since it doesn't have an ID, it is not a `namedItem` and is only in there once.

Practice exercise 10.3

Use JavaScript to select page elements via their tag name:

1. Start by creating a simple HTML file.
2. Create three HTML elements using the same tag.
3. Add some content within each element so you can distinguish between them
4. Add a script element to your HTML file, and within it select the page elements by tag name and store them in a variable as an array
5. Using the index value, select the middle element and output it into the console.

Accessing elements by class name

We can do something very similar for class names. In our example HTML, we have two different class names: example and something. If you get elements by class name, it gives back an HTMLCollection containing the results. The following will get all the elements with the class example:

```
document.getElementsByClassName("example");
```

This returns:

```
HTMLCollection(2) [div#one.example, div#two.example, one: div#one.
example, two: div#two.example]
```

As you can see, it only returned the div tags with the example class. It left out the div with the something class.

Practice exercise 10.4

Select all matching page elements using the class name of the element.

1. Create a simple HTML file to work on.

2. Add three HTML elements adding the same class to each. You can use different tags as long as the same element class is included. Add some content within each element so you can distinguish between them.

3. Add a script element to your file, and within it select the page elements by class name. Assign the resulting HTMLCollection values to a variable.

4. You can use an index value to select the individual HTMLCollection items, just as you would for array items. Starting with an index of 0, select one of the page elements with the class name and output the element into the console.

Accessing elements with a CSS selector

We can also access elements using a CSS selector. We do this with querySelector() and querySelectorAll(). We then give the CSS selector as an argument, and this will filter the items in the HTML document and only return the ones that satisfy the CSS selector.

The CSS selector might look a bit different than you might think at first. Instead of looking for a certain layout, we use the same syntax as we use when we want to specify a layout for certain elements. We haven't discussed this yet, so we will cover it here briefly.

If we state p as a CSS selector, it means all the elements with tag p. This would look like this:

```
document.querySelectorAll("p");
```

If we say `p.example`, it means all the p tag elements with `example` as the class. They can also have other classes; as long as `example` is in there, it will match. We can also say #one, which means select all with an ID of one.

This method is the same result as `getElementById()`. Which one to use is a matter of taste when all you really need to do is select by ID—this is great input for a discussion with another developer. `querySelector()` allows for more complicated queries, and some developers will state that `getElementById()` is more readable. Others will claim that you might as well use `querySelector()` everywhere for consistency. It doesn't really matter at this point, but try to be consistent.

Don't worry too much about all these options for now; there are many, and you'll figure them out when you need them. This is how you can use the CSS selectors in JavaScript.

Using querySelector()

This first option will select the first element that matches the query. So, enter the following in the console, still using the HTML snippet introduced at the start of the section:

```
document.querySelector("div");
```

It should return:

```
<div id="one" class="example">Hi!</div>
```

It only returns the first `div`, because that's the first one it encounters. We could also ask for an element with the class .`something`. If you recall, we select classes using dot notation like this:

```
document.querySelector(".something");
```

This returns:

```
<div id="three" class="something">Hi!</div>
```

With this method, you can only use valid CSS selectors: elements, classes, and IDs.

Practice exercise 10.5

Use querySelector() to enable single element selection:

1. Create another simple HTML file.

2. Create four HTML elements adding the same class to each. They can be different tag names as long as they have the class within the element attribute.

3. Add some content within each element so you can distinguish between them.

4. Within a script element, use querySelector() to select the first occurrence of the elements with that class and store it in a variable. If there is more than one matching result in querySelector(), it will return the first one.

5. Output the element into the console.

Using querySelectorAll()

Sometimes it is not enough to return only the first instance, but you want to select all the elements that match the query. For example when you need to get all the input boxes and empty them. This can be done with querySelectorAll():

```
document.querySelectorAll("div");
```

This returns:

```
NodeList(3) [div#one.example, div#two.example, div#three.something]
```

As you can see, it is of object type NodeList. It contains all the nodes that match the CSS selector. With the item() method we can get them by index, just as we did for the HTMLCollection.

Practice exercise 10.6

Use querySelectorAll() to select all matching elements in an HTML file:

1. Create an HTML file and add four HTML elements, adding the same class to each one.

2. Add some content within each element so you can distinguish between them.

3. Within a script element, use QuerySelectorAll() to select all the matching occurrences of the elements with that class and store them in a variable.

4. Output all the elements into the console, first as an array and then looping through them to output them one by one.

Element click handler

HTML elements can do something when they are clicked. This is because a JavaScript function can be connected to an HTML element. Here is one snippet in which the JavaScript function associated with the element is specified in the HTML:

```
<!DOCTYPE html>
<html>
  <body>
    <div id="one" onclick="alert('Ouch! Stop it!')">Don't click here!
    </div>
  </body>
</html>
```

Whenever the text in the div gets clicked, a pop up with the text Ouch! Stop it! opens. Here, the JavaScript is specified directly after onclick, but if there is JavaScript on the page, you can also refer to a function that's in that JavaScript like this:

```
<!DOCTYPE html>
<html>
  <body>
    <script>
      function stop(){
        alert("Ouch! Stop it!");
      }
    </script>
    <div id="one" onclick="stop()">Don't click here!</div>
  </body>
</html>
```

This code is doing the exact same thing. As you can imagine, with bigger functions this would be a better practice. The HTML can also refer to scripts that get loaded into the page.

There is also a way to add a click handler using JavaScript. We select the HTML element we want to add the click handler to, and we specify the onclick property.

Here is a HTML snippet:

```
<!DOCTYPE html>
<html>
  <body>
```

```
        <div id="one">Don't click here!</div>
    </body>
</html>
```

This code is at the moment not doing anything if you click it. If we want to dynamically add a click handler to the div element, we can select it and specify the property via the console:

```
document.getElementById("one").onclick = function () {
alert("Auch! Stop!");
}
```

As it's been added in the console, this functionality will be gone when you refresh the page.

This and the DOM

The this keyword always has a relative meaning; it depends on the exact context it is in. In the DOM, the special this keyword refers to the element of the DOM it belongs to. If we specify an onclick to send this in as an argument, it will send in the element the onclick is in.

Here is a little HTML snippet with JavaScript in the script tag:

```
<!DOCTYPE html>
<html>
    <body>
        <script>
            function reveal(el){
                console.log(el);
            }
        </script>
        <button onclick="reveal(this)">Click here!</button>
    </body>
</html>
```

And this is what it will log:

```
<button onclick="reveal(this)">Click here!</button>
```

As you can see, it is logging the element it is in, the button element.

We can access the parent of `this` with a function like this:

```
function reveal(el){
    console.log(el.parentElement);
}
```

In the above example, the body is the parent of the button. So if we click the button with the new function, it will output:

```
<body>
    <script>
      function reveal(el.parentElement){
        console.log(el);
      }
    </script>
    <button onclick="reveal(this)">Click here!</button>
  </body>
```

We could output any other property of the element the same way; for example, `console.log(el.innerText);` would print the inner text value as we saw in the *Changing innerText* section.

So, the `this` keyword is referring to the element, and from this element we can traverse the DOM like we just learned. This can be very useful, for example, when you need to get the value of an input box. If you send `this`, then you can read and modify the properties of the element that triggered the function.

Practice exercise 10.7

Create a button within a basic HTML document and add the `onclick` attribute. The example will demonstrate how you can reference object data with `this`:

1. Create a function to handle a click within your JavaScript code. You can name the function `message`.

2. Add this to the `onclick` function parameters sending the current element object data using `this`.

3. Within the `message` function, use `console.dir()` to output in the console the element object data that was sent to the function using `onclick` and `this`.

4. Add a second button to the page also invoking the same function on the click.

5. When the button is clicked, you should see the element that triggered the click in the console, like so:

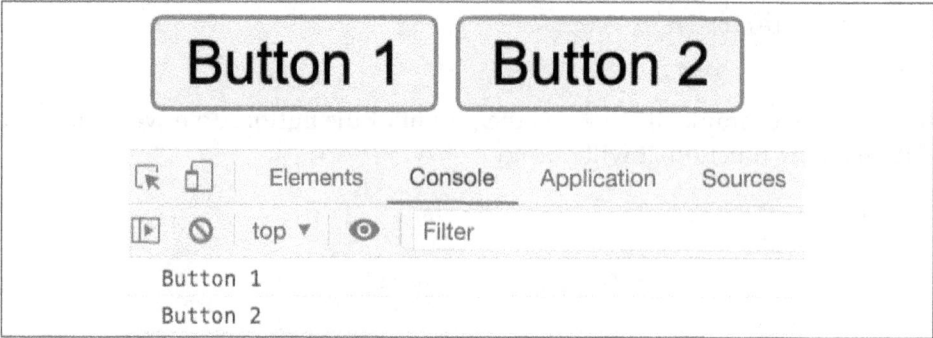

Figure 10.1: Implementing the onclick attribute

Manipulating element style

After selecting the right element from the DOM, we can change the CSS style that applies to it. We can do this using the `style` property. This is how to do it:

1. Select the right element from the DOM.
2. Change the right property of the style property of this element.

We are going to make a button that will toggle the appearing and disappearing of a line of text. To hide something using CSS, we can set the `display` property of the element to `none`, like this for a p (paragraph) element:

```
p {
    display: none;
}
```

And we can toggle it back to visible using:

```
p {
    display: block;
}
```

We can add this style using JavaScript as well. Here is a little HTML and JavaScript snippet that will toggle the displaying of a piece of text:

```
<!DOCTYPE html>
<html>
```

```
<body>
  <script>
    function toggleDisplay(){
      let p = document.getElementById("magic");
      if(p.style.display === "none") {
        p.style.display = "block";
      } else {
        p.style.display = "none";
      }
    }
  </script>
  <p id="magic">I might disappear and appear.</p>
  <button onclick="toggleDisplay()">Magic!</button>
</body>
</html>
```

As you can see, in the `if` statement we are checking for whether it is currently hiding, if it is hiding, we show it. Otherwise, we hide it. If you click the button and it is currently visible, it will disappear. If you click the button when the text is gone, it will appear.

You can do all sorts of fun things using this style element. What do you think this does when you click the button?

```
<!DOCTYPE html>
<html>
  <body>
    <script>
      function rainbowify(){
        let divs = document.getElementsByTagName("div");
        for(let i = 0; i < divs.length; i++) {
          divs[i].style.backgroundColor = divs[i].id;
        }
      }
    </script>
    <style>
      div {
        height: 30px;
        width: 30px;
        background-color: white;
      }
    </style>
```

```
        <div id="red"></div>
        <div id="orange"></div>
        <div id="yellow"></div>
        <div id="green"></div>
        <div id="blue"></div>
        <div id="indigo"></div>
        <div id="violet"></div>
        <button onclick="rainbowify()">Make me a rainbow</button>
    </body>
</html>
```

This is what you see when you first open the page:

Figure 10.2: A button that will do wonderful things when it is clicked

And when you click the button:

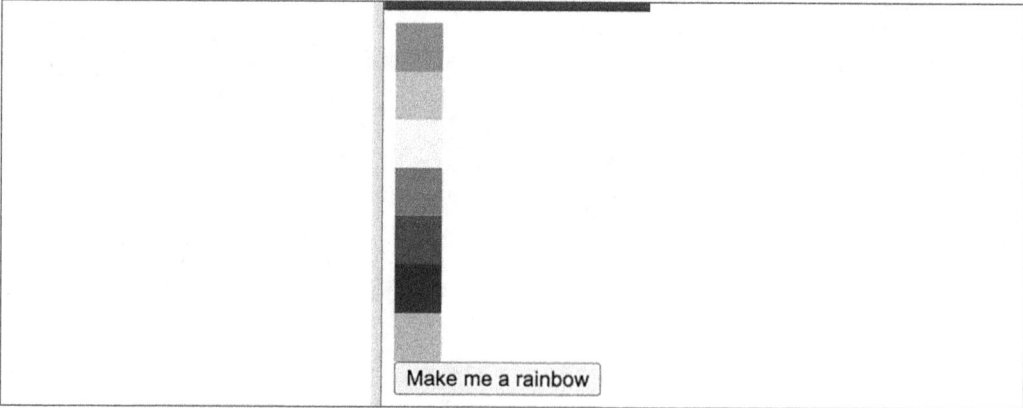

Figure 10.3: Beautiful rainbow made by JavaScript at the click of a button

Let's go over this script to see how works. First of all, there are a few `div` tags in the HTML that all have the ID of a certain color. There is a `style` tag specified in HTML, which gives a default layout to these `div` tags of 30px by 30px and a white background.

When you click the button, the `rainbowify()` JavaScript function is executed. In this function the following things are happening:

1. All the `div` elements get selected and stored in an array, `divs`.

2. We loop over this `divs` array.

3. For every element in the `divs` array, we are setting the `backgroundColor` property of style to the ID of the element. Since all the IDs represent a color, we see a rainbow appear.

As you can imagine, you can really have a lot of fun playing around with this. With just a few lines of code, you can make all sorts of things appear on the screen.

Changing the classes of an element

HTML elements can have classes, and as we have seen, we can select elements by the name of the class. As you may remember, classes are used a lot for giving elements a certain layout using CSS.

With JavaScript, we can change the classes of HTML elements, and this might trigger a certain layout that is associated with that class in CSS. We are going to have a look at adding classes, removing classes, and toggling classes.

Adding classes to elements

This might sound a bit vague, so let's have a look at an example where we are going to add a class to an element, which in this case will add a layout and make the element disappear.

```
<!DOCTYPE html>
<html>
  <body>
    <script>
        function disappear(){
           document.getElementById("shape").classList.add("hide");
        }
    </script>
```

```
    <style>
      .hide {
        display: none;
      }

      .square {
        height: 100px;
        width: 100px;
        background-color: yellow;
      }

      .square.blue {
        background-color: blue;
      }
    </style>
    <div id="shape" class="square blue"></div>

    <button onclick="disappear()">Disappear!</button>
  </body>
</html>
```

In this example, we have some CSS specified in the style tag. Elements with the hide class have a display: none style, meaning they are hidden. Elements with the square class are 100 by 100 pixels and are yellow. But when they have both the square and blue class, they are blue.

When we click on the **Disappear!** button, the disappear() function gets called. This one is specified in the script tag. The disappear() function changes the classes by getting the classList property of the element with the ID shape, which is the square we are seeing. We are adding the hide class to the classList and because of this, the elements get the display: none layout and we can no longer see it.

Removing classes from elements

We can also remove a class. If we remove the hide class from the classList, for example, we could see our element again because the display: none layout no longer applies.

In this example, we are removing another class. Can you figure out what will happen if you press the button by looking at the code?

```
<!DOCTYPE html>
<html>
  <body>
    <script>
      function change(){
        document.getElementById("shape").classList.remove("blue");
      }
    </script>
    <style>
      .square {
        height: 100px;
        width: 100px;
        background-color: yellow;
      }

      .square.blue {
        background-color: blue;
      }
    </style>
    <div id="shape" class="square blue"></div>

    <button onclick="change()">Change!</button>
  </body>
</html>
```

When the button gets pressed, the change function gets triggered. This function removes the `blue` class, which removes the blue background color from the layout, leaving us with the yellow background color and the square will turn yellow.

You may wonder why the square was blue in the first place since it had two layouts for `background-color` assigned to it with the CSS. This happens with a points system. When a styling is more specific, it gets more points. So, specifying two classes with no space in between means that it applies to elements with these two classes. This is more specific than pointing at one class.

 Referring to an ID in CSS, #nameId, gets even more points and would be prioritized over class-based layouts. This layering allows for less duplicate code, but it can become messy, so always make sure to combine the CSS and the HTML well to get the desired layout.

Toggling classes

In some cases, you would want to add a class when it doesn't already have that particular class, but remove it when it does. This is called toggling. There is a special method to toggle classes. Let's change our first example to toggle the hide class so the class will appear when we press the button the second time, disappear the third time, and so on. The blue class was removed to make it shorter; it's not doing anything in this example other than making the square blue.

```html
<!DOCTYPE html>
<html>
  <body>
    <script>
      function changeVisibility(){
        document.getElementById("shape").classList.toggle("hide");
      }
    </script>
    <style>
      .hide {
        display: none;
      }

      .square {
        height: 100px;
        width: 100px;
        background-color: yellow;
      }
    </style>
    <div id="shape" class="square"></div>

    <button onclick="changeVisibility()">Magic!</button>
  </body>
</html>
```

Pressing the Magic! button will add the class to the classList when it isn't there and remove it when it is there. This means that you can see the result every time you press the button. The square keeps appearing and disappearing.

Manipulating attributes

We have seen already that we can change the class and style attributes, but there is a more general method that can be used to change any attribute. Just a quick reminder, attributes are the parts in HTML elements that are followed by equals signs. For example, this HTML link to Google:

```
<a id="friend" class="fancy boxed" href="https://www.google.com">Ask my
friend here.</a>
```

The attributes in this example are id, class, and href. Other common attributes are src and style, but there are many others out there.

With the setAttribute() method, we can add or change attributes on an element. This will change the HTML of the page. If you inspect the HTML in the browser you will see that the changed attributes are visible. You can do this from the console and see the result easily, or write another HTML file with this built in as a function. In this HTML snippet, you will see it in action:

```
<!DOCTYPE html>
<html>
  <body>
    <script>
      function changeAttr(){
        let el = document.getElementById("shape");
        el.setAttribute("style", "background-color:red;border:1px solid
black");
        el.setAttribute("id", "new");
        el.setAttribute("class", "circle");


      }
    </script>
    <style>
      div {
        height: 100px;
        width: 100px;
        background-color: yellow;
      }
```

```
      .circle {
        border-radius: 50%;
      }
    </style>
    <div id="shape" class="square"></div>

    <button onclick="changeAttr()">Change attributes...</button>
  </body>
</html>
```

This is the page before clicking the button:

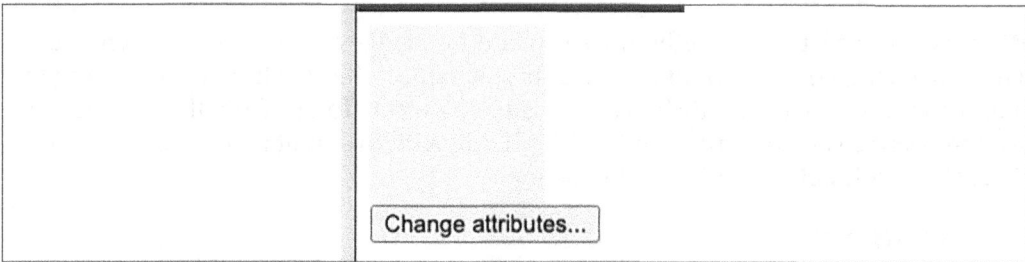

Figure 10.4: Page with a yellow square div

After clicking the button, the HTML of the div becomes:

```
<div id="new" class="circle" style="background-color:red;border:1px
solid black"></div>
```

As you can see, the attributes are changed. The id has changed from shape to new. The class has changed from square to circle and a style has been added. It will look like this:

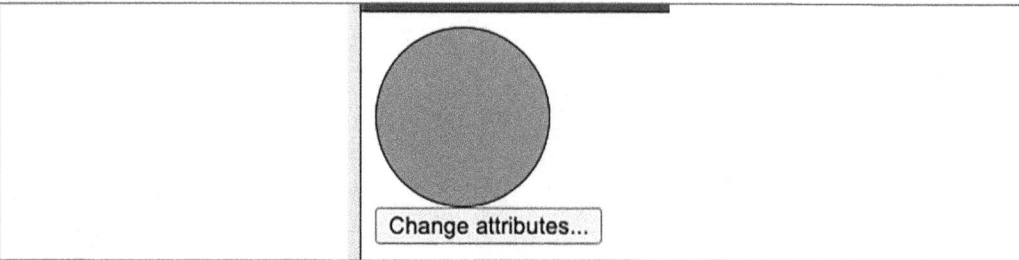

Figure 10.5: Page with a red circle with a black line around it

This is a very powerful tool that can be used to interact with the DOM in very many ways. Think, for example, of a tool that can be used to create images, or even postcards. Beneath the surface, there is a lot of manipulating going on.

It is important to note here that JavaScript interacts with the DOM and not with the HTML file—therefore, the DOM is the one that gets changed. If you click the button again, you'll get an error message in the console because no element with `id="shape"` is found in the DOM, and as a result we try to call a method on a null value.

Practice exercise 10.8

Creating custom attributes: using an array of names, the following code will update the element's HTML, adding HTML code using the data from the array. The items within the array will be output to the page as HTML code. The user will be able to click the page elements and they will display the page element attribute values.

My Friends Table

Laurence	1
Mike	2
John	3
Larry	4
Kim	5
Joanne	6
Lisa	7
Janet	8
Jane	9

Figure 10.6: Creating custom attributes with an array of names

As the HTML will start getting more complex from now on, and we're only trying to test your JavaScript, we will provide HTML templates to use where needed. You can use the following HTML template and provide your answer as the completed `script` element:

```
<!DOCTYPE html>
<html>
<head>
    <title>Complete JavaScript Course</title>
</head>
<body>
```

```
        <div id="message"></div>
        <div id="output"></div>
        <script>

        </script>
    </body>
</html>
```

Take the following steps:

1. Create an array of names. You can add as many as you want—all the string values will be output onto the page within a table.

2. Select the page elements as JavaScript objects.

3. Add a function and also invoke that function within the JavaScript code. The function can be called `build()` as it will be building the page content. Within the `build` function, you will be setting up the HTML in a table.

4. Create a table named `html`, and within the tags, loop through the contents of the array and output the results into the `html` table.

5. Add a class called `box` to one of the cells that has the index value of the item from the array, adding the same class to the elements for each additional row.

6. As you create the HTML for the elements within the `tr` element, create an attribute called `data-row` in the main row element that includes the index value of the item from the array. In addition, add another attribute within the element called `data-name` that will contain the text output.

7. Within the attribute of the same `tr` element, also add `onclick` to invoke a function named `getData` passing the current element object as `this` into the function parameter.

8. Add the table of HTML code to the page.

9. Create a function named `getData` that will be invoked once the HTML `tr` elements are clicked. Once the `tr` element is clicked, use `getAttribute` to get the attribute values of the row value and the contents of the text output and store them in different variables.

10. Using the values in the attributes stored in the preceding step, output the values into the `message` element on the page.

11. Once the user clicks the element on the page, it will display the details coming from the element attributes within the element with the `id` of `message`.

Event listeners on elements

Events are things that happen on a web page, like clicking on something, moving the mouse over an element, changing an element, and there are many more. We have seen how to add an onclick event handler already. In the same way, you can add an onchange handler, or an onmouseover handler. There is one special condition, though; one element can only have one event handler as an HTML attribute. So, if it has an onclick handler, it cannot have an onmouseover handler as well. At this point, we have only seen how to add event listeners using HTML attributes like this:

```
<button onclick="addRandomNumber()">Add a number</button>
```

There is a way to register event handlers using JavaScript as well. We call these event listeners. Using event listeners, we can add multiple events to one element. This way, JavaScript is constantly checking, or listening, for certain events to the elements on the page. Adding event listeners is a two-step process:

1. Select the element you want to add an event to
2. Use the addEventListener("event", function) syntax to add the event

Even though it is two steps, it can be done in one line of code:

```
document.getElementById("square").addEventListener("click",
changeColor);
```

This is getting the element with the ID square and adding the changeColor function as the event for whenever it gets clicked. Note that when using event listeners, we remove the on prefix from the event type. For example, click here references the same event type as onclick, but we have removed the on prefix.

Let's consider another way to add an event listener (don't worry, we will review these methods in detail in *Chapter 11, Interactive Content and Event Listeners*) by setting the event property of a certain object to a function.

 There is a fun fact here—event listeners often get added during other events!

We could reuse our trusty `onclick` listener in this context, but another common one is when the web page is done loading with `onload`:

```
window.onload = function() {
    // whatever needs to happen after loading
    // for example adding event listeners to elements
}
```

This function will then be executed. This is common for `window.onload`, but less common for many others, such as `onclick` on a `div` (it is possible though). Let's look at an example of the first event listener we looked at on a web page. Can you figure out what it will be doing when you click on the square?

```
<!DOCTYPE html>
<html>
  <body>
    <script>
      window.onload = function() {
        document.getElementById("square").addEventListener("click",
changeColor);
      }
      function changeColor(){
        let red = Math.floor(Math.random() * 256);
        let green = Math.floor(Math.random() * 256);
        let blue = Math.floor(Math.random() * 256);
        this.style.backgroundColor = `rgb(${red}, ${green}, ${blue})`;
      }
    </script>
    <div id="square" style="width:100px;height:100px;background-
color:grey;">Click for magic</div>
  </body>
</html>
```

The web page starts with a gray square with the text `Click for magic` in it. After the web page is done loading, an event gets added for this square. Whenever it gets clicked, the `changeColor` function will be executed. This function uses random variables to change the color using RGB colors. Whenever you click the square, the color gets updated with random values.

You can add events to all sorts of elements. We have only used the `click` event so far, but there are many more. For example, `focus`, `blur`, `focusin`, `focusout`, `mouseout`, `mouseover`, `keydown`, `keypress`, and `keyup`. These will be covered in the next chapter, so keep going!

Practice exercise 10.9

Try an alternative way to implement similar logic to *Practice exercise 10.7*. Use the following HTML code as a template for this exercise, and add the contents of the script element:

```
<!doctype html>
<html>
<head>
    <title>JS Tester</title>
</head>
<body>
    <div>
        <button>Button 1</button>
        <button>Button 2</button>
        <button>Button 3</button>
    </div>
    <script>

    </script>
</body>
</html>
```

Take the following steps:

1. Select all the page buttons into a JavaScript object.
2. Loop through each button, and create a function within the button scope called output.
3. Within the output() function, add a console.log() method that outputs the current object's textContent. You can reference the current parent object using the this keyword.
4. As you loop through the buttons attach an event listener that when clicked invokes the output() function.

Creating new elements

In this chapter, you have seen so many cool ways to manipulate the DOM already. There is still an important one missing, the creation of new elements and adding them to the DOM. This consists of two steps, first creating new elements and second adding them to the DOM.

This is not as hard as it may seem. The following JavaScript does just that:

```javascript
let el = document.createElement("p");
el.innerText = Math.floor(Math.random() * 100);
document.body.appendChild(el);
```

It creates an element of type p (paragraph). This is a `createElement()` function that is on the `document` object. Upon creation, you need to specify what type of HTML element you would want to create, which in this case is a p, so something like this:

```html
<p>innertext here</p>
```

And as `innerText`, it is adding a random number. Next, it is adding the element as a new last child of the body. You could also add it to another element; just select the element you want to add it to and use the `appendChild()` method.

Here, you can see it incorporated in a HTML page. This page has a button, and whenever it gets pressed, the p gets added.

```html
<!DOCTYPE html>
<html>
  <body>
    <script>
      function addRandomNumber(){
        let el = document.createElement("p");
        el.innerText = Math.floor(Math.random() * 100);
        document.body.appendChild(el);
      }
    </script>
    <button onclick="addRandomNumber()">Add a number</button>
  </body>
</html>
```

Here is a screenshot of this page after having pressed the button five times.

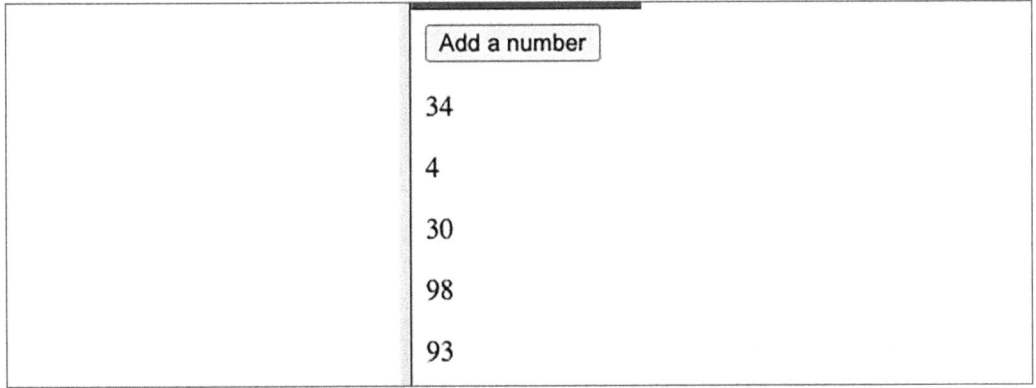

Figure 10.7: Random numbers after pressing the button five times

Once we refresh the page, it's empty again. The file with the source code doesn't change and we're not storing it anywhere.

Practice exercise 10.10

Shopping list: Using the following HTML template, update the code to add new items to the list of items on the page. Once the button is clicked, it will add a new item to the list of items:

```
<!DOCTYPE html>
<html>
<head>
    <title>Complete JavaScript Course</title>
    <style>
    </style>
</head>
<body>
    <div id="message">Complete JavaScript Course</div>
    <div>
        <input type="text" id="addItem">
        <input type="button" id="addNew" value="Add to List"> </div>
```

```
    <div id="output">
        <h1>Shopping List</h1>
        <ol id="sList"> </ol>
    </div>
    <script>

    </script>
</body>
</html>
```

Take the following steps:

1. Select the page elements as JavaScript objects.

2. Add an onclick event listener to the add button. Once the button is clicked, it should add the contents of the input field to the end of the list. You can call the function addOne().

3. Within addOne(), create li elements to append to the main list on the page. Add the input value to the list item text content.

4. Within the addOne() function, get the current value of the addItem input field. Use that value to create a textNode with that value, adding it to the list item. Append the textNode to the list item.

Chapter projects

Collapsible accordion component

Build a collapsing and expanding accordion component that will open page elements, hiding and showing content when the title tab is clicked. Using the following HTML as a template, add the completed script element and create the desired functionality with JavaScript:

```
<!doctype html>
<html>
<head>
    <title>JS Tester</title>
    <style>
        .active {
            display: block !important;
        }
```

```
        .myText {
            display: none;
        }
        .title {
            font-size: 1.5em;
            background-color: #ddd;

        }
    </style>
</head>
<body>
    <div class="container">
        <div class="title">Title #1</div>
        <div class="myText">Just some text #1</div>
        <div class="title">Title #2</div>
        <div class="myText">Just some text #2</div>
        <div class="title">Title #3</div>
        <div class="myText">Just some text #3</div>
    </div>
    <script>

    </script>
</body>
</html>
```

Take the following steps:

1. Using querySelectorAll(), select all the elements with a class of title.

2. Using querySelectorAll(), select all the elements with a class of myText. This should be the same number of elements as the title elements.

3. Iterate through all the title elements and add event listeners that, once clicked, will select the next element siblings.

4. Select the element on the click action and toggle the classlist of the element with the class of active. This will allow the user to click the element and hide and show the below content.

5. Add a function that will be invoked each time the elements are clicked that will remove the class of active from all the elements. This will hide all the elements with myText.

Interactive voting system

The below code will create a dynamic list of people that can be clicked, and it will update the corresponding value with the number of times that name was clicked. It also includes an input field that will allow you to add more users to the list, each of which will create another item in the list that can be interacted with the same as the default list items.

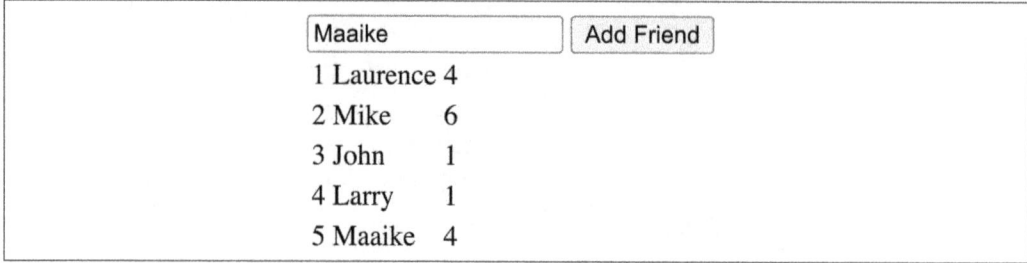

Figure 10.8: Creating an interactive voting system

Use the following HTML code as a template to add JavaScript to, and provide your answer as the completed `script` element.

```
<!DOCTYPE html>
<html>
<head>
    <title>Complete JavaScript Course</title>
</head>
<body>
    <div id="message">Complete JavaScript Course</div>
    <div>
        <input type="text" id="addFriend">
        <input type="button" id="addNew" value="Add Friend">
    </div>
    <table id="output"></table>
    <script>

    </script>
</body>
</html>
```

Take the following steps:

1. Create an array of people's names called `myArray`. This will be the default original list of names.

2. Select the page elements as JavaScript objects so they can easily be selected within the code.

3. Add event listener to the **Add Friend** button. Once clicked, this will get the value from the input field and pass the values to a function that will add the friend list to the page. Additionally, add the new friend's name into the people's names array you created. Get the current value in the input field and push that value into the array so the array matches the values on the page.

4. Run a function to build the content on the page, using the `forEach()` loop get all the items within the array and add them to the page. Include 0 as a default for the vote count, as all individuals should start on zero votes.

5. Create a main function that will create the page elements, starting with the parent table row, `tr`. Then create three table cell, `td`, elements. Add content to the table cells, including the vote count in the last column, the person name in the middle, and the index plus 1 in the first column.

6. Append the table cells to the table row and append the table row to the output area on the page.

7. Add an event listener that will increase the vote counter for that row when the user clicks.

8. Get the text content from the last column in the row. It should be the value of the current counter. Increment the counter by one and make sure the datatype is a number so you can add to it.

9. Update the last column with the new click counter.

Hangman game

Create a Hangman game using arrays and page elements. You can use the following HTML template:

```
<!doctype html>
<html><head>
    <title>Hangman Game</title>
    <style>
        .gameArea {
```

```
                text-align: center;
                font-size: 2em;
            }
            .box,
            .boxD {
                display: inline-block;
                padding: 5px;
            }
            .boxE {
                display: inline-block;
                width: 40px;
                border: 1px solid #ccc;
                border-radius: 5px;
                font-size: 1.5em;
            }
        </style>
    </head>
    <body>
        <div class="gameArea">
            <div class="score"> </div>
            <div class="puzzle"></div>
            <div class="letters"></div>
            <button>Start Game</button>
        </div>
        <script>

        </script>
    </body>
</html>
```

Take the following steps:

1. Set up an array that contains some words or phrases that you want to use in the game.

2. In JavaScript, create a main game object containing a property to contain the current word solution, and another property to contain the array of letters of the solution. It should also create an array to contain the page elements and correspond with the values of the index values of each letter from the solution, and finally add a property to count the number of letters left to solve and end the game when needed.

3. Select all the page elements into variables so they are easier to access in the code.

4. Add an event listener to the **Start Game** button, making it clickable, and when it gets clicked it should launch a function called startGame().

5. Within startGame(), check if the words array has any words left. If it does, then hide the button by setting the .display object to none. Clear the game contents and set the total to 0. Within the current word in the game object, assign a value, which should be the response of shift() from the array containing the in-game words.

6. In the game solution, convert the string into an array of all the characters in the word solution using split().

7. Create a function called builder() that can be used to build the game board. Invoke the function within the startGame() function once all the game values are cleared and set.

8. Create a separate function that you can use to generate page elements. In the parameters, get the type of element, the parent that the new element will be appended to, the output content for the new element, and a class to add to the new element. Using a temporary variable, create the element, add the class, append to the parent, set the textContent, and return the element.

9. In the builder() function, which will also get invoked once startGame() is run, clear the innerHTML from the letters and puzzle page elements.

10. Iterate through the game solution array, getting each letter of the solution. Use the builder() function to generate page elements, add an output value of -, set a class, and append it to the main puzzle page element.

11. Check if the value is blank, and if it is, clear textContent and update the border to white. If it's not blank, increment the total so that it reflects the total number of letters that must be guessed. Push the new element into the game puzzle array.

12. Create a new function to update the score so that you can output the current number of letters left. Add it to the builder() function.

13. Create a loop to represent the 26 letters of the alphabet. You can generate the letter by using an array containing all the letters. The string method fromCharCode() will return the character from the numeric representation.

14. Create elements for each letter, adding a class of box and appending it to the letters page element. As each element gets created, add an event listener that runs a function called checker().

15. Once the letter gets clicked, we need to invoke the checker() function, which will remove the main class, add another class, remove the event listener, and update the background color. Also invoke a function called checkLetter(), passing the value of the clicked letter into the argument.

16. The `checkLetter()` function will loop through all the solution letters. Add a condition to check if the solution letter is equal to the letter selected by the player. Make sure to convert the inputted letter to uppercase so that you can match the letters accurately. Update the matching letters in the puzzle using the game puzzle array and the index from the letter in the solution. The index values will be the same on each, which provides an easy way to match the visual representation with what is in the array.

17. Subtract one from the game global object that tracks the total letters left to be solved, invoke the `updatescore()` function to check if the game is over, and update the score. Set the `textContent` of the puzzle to the letter removing the original dash.

18. In the `updatescore()` function, set the score to the number of letters left. If the total left is less than or equal to zero, the game is over. Show the button so that the player has an option for the next phrase.

Self-check quiz

1. What output will the following code produce?

```
<div id="output">Complete JavaScript Course </div>
<script>
    var output = document.getElementById('output');
    output.innerText = "Hello <br> World";
</script>
```

2. What output will be seen within the browser page?

```
<div id="output">Complete JavaScript Course </div>
<script>
    document.getElementById('output').innerHTML = "Hello
<br> World";
</script>
```

3. What will be seen in the input field from the following code?

```
<div id="output">Hello World</div>
<input type="text" id="val" value="JavaScript">
<script>
    document.getElementById('val').value = document.
getElementById('output').innerHTML;
</script>
```

4. In the following code, what is output into the console when the element with the word three gets clicked? What is the output when the element with the word one gets clicked?

```
<div class="holder">
    <div onclick="output('three')">Three
        <div onclick="output('two')">Two
            <div onclick="output('one')">One</div>
        </div>
    </div>
</div>
<script>
    function
    output(val) {
        console.log(val);
    }
</script>
```

5. What line of code needs to be added to remove the event listener when the button is clicked in the following code?

```
<div class="btn">Click Me</div>
<script>
    const btn = document.querySelector(".btn");
    btn.addEventListener("click", myFun);
    function myFun() {
        console.log("clicked");


    }
</script>
```

Summary

In this chapter, we really took our web skills to the next level. Manipulating the DOM allows all kinds of interactions with the web page, meaning that the web page is no longer a static event.

We started off by explaining the dynamic web and how to traverse the DOM. After having walked over the elements manually, we learned that there's an easier way to select elements in the DOM with the getElementBy...() and the querySelector() methods. After having selected them, we had the power to modify them, add new elements to them, and do all sorts of things using the elements we selected. We started with some more basic HTML handlers, and we could assign a function to, for example, the onclick attribute of the HTML element.

We also accessed the clicked element using the `this` argument that was sent in as a parameter, and we could modify it in different ways, for example, by changing the `style` property. We also saw how to add classes to an element, create new elements, and add them to the DOM. And finally, we worked with event listeners on elements that really took our dynamic web pages to the next level. With event listeners, we can specify more than one event handler for a certain element. All these new skills allow us to create amazing things in the web browser. You can actually create complete games now!

The next chapter will take your event handler skills to the next level and will enhance your ability to create interactive web pages even further (and make it a bit easier as well!).

Join our book's Discord space

Join the book's Discord workspace for a monthly *Ask me Anything* session with the authors: `https://packt.link/JSBook`

11
Interactive Content and Event Listeners

You are now familiar with the basic manipulation of the **Document Object Model** (**DOM**). In the last chapter, we had a look at events, and we saw that event listeners are constantly monitoring for whether a certain event is taking place; when it does occur, the specified event (a function) gets invoked.

In this chapter, we are going to take this knowledge one step further and use event listeners to create interactive web content. This chapter is really going to complete your DOM knowledge. We are going to cover the following topics:

- Interactive content
- Specifying events
- The onload event handler
- The mouse event handler
- The event target property
- DOM event flow
- onchange and onblur
- The key event handler
- Drag and drop elements
- Form submission
- Animating elements

Note: exercise, project and self-check quiz answers can be found in the *Appendix*.

Introducing interactive content

Interactive content is content that responds to the actions of a user. Think, for example, of a web app in which you can create postcards dynamically, or play a game on a website in a web browser.

This interactive content is made possible by changing the DOM based on user interactions. These interactions could be anything: entering text in an input field, clicking somewhere on the page, hovering over a certain element with the mouse, or a certain input with the keyboard. All these are called events. We have seen events already. But there is actually more to it!

Specifying events

There are three ways to specify events. We have seen each of these in the previous chapter, but let's run through them again now. One is HTML-based and the other two are JavaScript-based. For this example, we are going to use the `click` event as an example.

Specifying events with HTML

First, the HTML way:

```
<p id="unique" onclick="magic()">Click here for magic!</p>
```

The great thing about specifying events this way is that it's quite easy to read this code and predict what it is going to do. As soon as you click on the paragraph, the function `magic()` will be triggered. There are some downsides too: you can only specify one event this way, and you cannot change the event dynamically either.

Specifying events with JavaScript

Here is the first way to do it using JavaScript.

```
document.getElementById("unique").onclick = function() { magic(); };
```

What is happening here is that we are getting the property that represents the selected event and assigning our function to it. So, in this case, we are selecting the p shown in the previous section by its attribute value unique, grabbing the onclick property, and assigning the magic() function to it by wrapping it in an anonymous function. We could also specify the exact function on the spot here. We can overwrite this with another function anytime, making the event that can be fired more dynamic.

We can also specify different events now, which we cannot do with HTML. So we could also give it a keyup, keydown, or mouseover event, for example – we will consider each of these event types in this chapter.

 If we wanted to specify event triggers for all the elements of the page, we could do so in a loop for a cleaner coding style.

Practice exercise 11.1

Personalize your web pages. Allow users to change the theme of the page display between regular mode and dark mode.

1. Within a simple HTML document, set up a Boolean value variable to use that will toggle the color modes.
2. Use window.onclick to set up a function that outputs a message in the console when clicked. You can use the value of the Boolean variable.
3. Within the function, add a condition that checks whether the darkMode variable is true or false.
4. If false, then update the page style to a background color of black and a font color of white.
5. Add an else response that changes the color of the background to white and the color of the text to black. Also, update the value of the darkMode variable accordingly.

Specifying events with event listeners

The last method is using the addEventListener() method to add an event to an element. With this, we can specify multiple functions for the same event, for example, when an element gets clicked.

What is striking for both methods we have looked at—using HTML events and assigning to properties—is that the event gets prefixed with on. For example, onclick, onload, onfocus, onblur, onchange, etc. This is not the case when we use the addEventListener() method, where we specify the event type within the event listener *without* the on prefix, as here, with an alternative to onclick:

```
document.getElementById("unique").addEventListener("click", magic);
```

Please note that we are leaving out the parentheses behind the magic function here. We cannot send in parameters like this. If that is something you have to do, you'd have to wrap the functionality in an anonymous function, like this:

```
document.getElementById("unique").addEventListener("click", function()
{ magic(arg1, arg2) });
```

In this chapter, we may use any of these ways to specify an event. We will mostly be using one of the JavaScript options, though.

Practice exercise 11.2

Create several divs with color names in textContent. Add JavaScript to add click event listeners to each element, and as each element is clicked, update the background color of the body to match the color name in the div.

The onload event handler

We briefly saw this event handler in the previous chapter. The onload event gets fired after a certain element is loaded. This can be useful for a number of reasons. For example, if you want to select an element using getElementById, you'll have to be sure this element is loaded in the DOM already. This event is most commonly used on the window object, but it can be used on any element. When you use it on window, this event gets started when the window object is done loading. Here is how to use it:

```
window.onload = function() {
    // whatever needs to happen after the page loads goes here
}
```

onload is similar, but it's different for the window and document objects. The difference depends on the web browser you are using. The load event fires at the end of the document loading process. Therefore, you will find that all the objects in the document are in the DOM and the assets have finished loading.

You can also use the `addEventListener()` method on any element to handle any event. And it can also be used for the event that all the content in the DOM is loaded. There is a special built-in event for this: `DOMContentLoaded()`. This event can be used to handle the event of the DOM loading, which will get fired immediately after the DOM for the page has been constructed when the event is set. Here is how to set it:

```
document.addEventListener("DOMContentLoaded", (e) => {
    console.log(e);
});
```

This will log to the console when all the DOM content has been loaded. As an alternative, you will also often see it in the body tag, like this:

```
<body onload="unique()"></body>
```

This is assigning a function called `unique()` to the body, and it will fire off when the body is done loading. You cannot combine `addEventListener()` and the HTML by using them together. One will overwrite the other, depending on the order of the web page. If you need two events to happen when the DOM is loaded, you will need two `addEventListener()` calls in your JavaScript.

Practice exercise 11.3

Using a basic HTML file, the below exercise will demonstrate the order of loading for the `window` object and the `document` object using `DOMContentLoaded`, which is an event that fires once the `document` object content is loaded in the browser. The window object will load afterward, even if the `window.onload` statement comes first.

1. Within a basic HTML file, create a function named `message` that requires two parameters, the first one being a string value for the message and the second an event object. Within the function, output into the console using `console.log` the event and the message.

2. Using the `window` object, attach an `onload` function to the event object. Invoke the function, passing a string value of `Window Ready` and the event object to the `message` function for output.

3. Create a second function to capture the DOM content loading, and add an event listener listening for `DOMContentLoaded` to the document object. Once that event is triggered, pass the event object and a string value of `Document Ready` to the `message` output function.

4. Change the order of the event listeners, placing the document event statement prior to the window `onload`: does it make a difference in the output?

5. Using the document object, add the `DOMContentLoaded` event listener, which will send to the function the arguments of `Document Ready` and the event object that was triggered.

6. Run the script and see which event is triggered first; change the order of the events to see if the output sequence changes.

Mouse event handlers

There are different mouse event handlers. Mouse events are actions of the mouse. These are the ones we have:

- `ondblclick`: when the mouse is double-clicked
- `onmousedown`: when the mouse clicks on top of an element without the click being released
- `onmouseup`: when the mouse click on top of an element is released
- `onmouseenter`: when the mouse moves onto an element
- `onmouseleave`: when the mouse leaves an element and all of its children
- `onmousemove`: when the mouse moves over an element
- `onmouseout`: when the mouse leaves an individual element
- `onmouseover`: when the mouse hovers over an element

Let's have a look at one of these in practice. What do you think this does?

```
<!doctype html>
<html>
  <body>
    <div id="divvy" onmouseover="changeColor()" style="width: 100px;
height: 100px; background-color: pink;">
    <script>
      function changeColor() {
        document.getElementById("divvy").style.backgroundColor =
"blue";
      }
    </script>
  </body>
</html>
```

If you go with your mouse over the pink square (the div with id `divvy`), it turns blue immediately. This is because `onmouseover` is added in the HTML and points to the JavaScript function that changes the color of the square.

Let's look at a similar slightly more complicated example.

```
<!doctype html>
<html>
  <body>
    <div id="divvy" style="width: 100px; height: 100px; background-
color: pink;">
    <script>
      window.onload = function donenow() {
        console.log("hi");
        document.getElementById("divvy").addEventListener("mousedown",
function() { changeColor(this, "green"); });
        document.getElementById("divvy").addEventListener("mouseup",
function() { changeColor(this, "yellow"); });
        document.getElementById("divvy").addEventListener("dblclick",
function() { changeColor(this, "black"); });
        document.getElementById("divvy").addEventListener("mouseout",
function() { changeColor(this, "blue"); });
      }
      console.log("hi2");

      function changeColor(el, color) {
        el.style.backgroundColor = color;
      }
    </script>
  </body>
</html>
```

We are still starting with the pink square. There are four event listeners connected to this div:

- mousedown: when the button is pressed on the mouse but is not yet released, the square will turn green.

- mouseup: as soon as the mouse button gets released, the square will turn yellow.

- dblclick: this is a favorite. What do you think will happen upon a double-click? A double-click contains two mousedown events and two mouseup events. Before the second mouseup, it is not a double-click. So, the square will get the colors green, yellow, green, black (and then stay black until another event is fired).

- mouseout: when the mouse leaves the square, it turns blue and stays blue until one of the three above events is fired again.

This allows for a lot of interaction. You can do so many things with this. Just to give you an example of a thing you can do, say you want to have a very dynamic, mouseover-driven, product-help decision tool. It will consist of four columns, and the content of the last three columns (from the right) is dynamic content. The first column is for categories. The second column contains some more specific product categories for each category. The third column consists of individual products, and the fourth column shows product information. This requires a lot of event listeners, and lots of deletion and addition of listeners.

Practice exercise 11.4

Our aim is to change the background color of the element on the page as the various mouse events occur. On mousedown over the element, the element will turn green. When the mouse is over the element, it will turn red. As the mouse moves out of the element boundaries, the color will turn yellow. When the mouse is clicked, the color will go green, and when the mouse is released, it will change to blue. The actions also be logged in the console.

1. Create a blank element on the page and assign a class to it.
2. Select the element using its class name.
3. Assign a variable to the element object from the page.
4. Update the content of the element to say hello world.
5. Using the style properties of the element, update the height and width, then add a default background color to it.
6. Create a function to handle two arguments, the first being a color value as a string and the second being the event object of the trigger.
7. In the function, output the color value to the console, and for the event, output the event type to the console.
8. Add event listeners to the element: mousedown, mouseover, mouseout, and mouseup. For each of these events, send two arguments to the function that you created: a color value and the event object.
9. Run the code and try it in your browser.

The event target property

Whenever an event gets fired, an event variable becomes available. It has many properties, and you can check it out by using this command in the function that gets fired for the event:

```
console.dir(event);
```

This will show many properties. One of the most interesting properties for now is the `target` property. The target is the HTML element that fired the event. So, we can use it to get information from a web page. Let's look at a simple example.

```
<!doctype html>
<html>
  <body>
    <button type="button" onclick="triggerSomething()">Click</button>
    <script>
      function triggerSomething() {
        console.dir(event.target);
      }
    </script>
  </body>
</html>
```

In this case, `event.target` is the button element. In the console, the button element and all its properties will be logged, including potential siblings and parents.

A use case where parent properties can come in handy is in the case of HTML forms, where there are multiple input fields and a button. A button in a form would often have the form as its direct parent. Via this parent, data from the input fields can be fetched. This is demonstrated in the following example:

```
<!doctype html>
<html>
  <body>
    <div id="welcome">Hi there!</div>
    <form>
      <input type="text" name="firstname" placeholder="First name" />
      <input type="text" name="lastname" placeholder="Last name" />
      <input type="button" onclick="sendInfo()" value="Submit" />
    </form>
    <script>
      function sendInfo() {
        let p = event.target.parentElement;
        message("Welcome " + p.firstname.value + " " + p.lastname.
value);
      }

      function message(m) {
        document.getElementById("welcome").innerHTML = m;
      }
```

```
        </script>
    </body>
</html>
```

This results in a little form, like this:

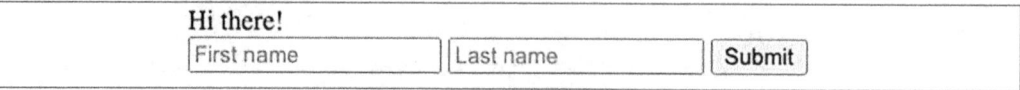

Figure 11.1: Basic HTML form

And once you enter data in the fields and hit **Submit**, this is what it looks like:

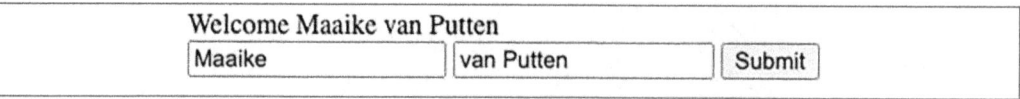

Figure 11.2: Data entered in the basic HTML form with a dynamic welcome message

With this command, event.target[CIT] is the HTML button:

```
let p = event.target.parentElement;
```

The parent element of the button, the form in this case, gets stored in the p variable. p is the parent and it represents the form element. So, this command will get the value of the input box:

```
p.firstname.value;
```

Similarly, p.lastname.value gets the last name. We haven't seen this yet, but with the value property, you can get the values of input elements.

Next, both input values are combined and sent to the message() function. This function changes the inner HTML of the div to a personalized welcome message, which is why **Hi there!** changes to **Welcome Maaike van Putten**.

Practice exercise 11.5

Change the text in a div element on the page. This exercise will demonstrate how you can get the value from an input field and place it within a page element. It also covers tracking button clicks and details about the event target. You can use the following HTML document as a template, to which you can add JavaScript:

```
<!doctype html>
<html>
<head>
```

```
    <title>JS Tester</title>
</head>
<body>
    <div class="output"></div>
    <input type="text" name="message" placeholder="Your Message">
    <button class="btn1">Button 1</button>
    <button class="btn2">Button 2</button>
    <div>
        <button class="btn3">Log</button>
    </div>
    <script>

    </script>
</body>
</html>
```

Take the following steps:

1. Using the above HTML as a template, add the JavaScript code, selecting each page element, including the div, the input field, and the button element. Assign these element objects to variables in your code.

2. Create an empty array called log, which will be used to track and log all the events.

3. Create a function that will capture the event object details in an object, adding it to the log array. Get the event target and create an object, adding it to the array that stores the input value at the time, the type of event, the class name of the target element, and the tag name of the target element.

4. Within the logging function, get the value of the content within the input and assign that value to the textContent of the div.

5. Clear the div content after the information is added to the log array.

6. Add an event listener to both of the first two buttons that sends the event object to the tracking function created in the earlier steps.

7. Attach an event listener to the third button that outputs the log content to the console.

DOM event flow

Let's go over what happens when you click on an element that has multiple elements associated with it.

We are going to create nested div elements. In order to illustrate this, there is a style added to the body. It is actually better to add this style in a head tag, and even better to have a separate CSS file, but this is a bit shorter to read. This is what the nested div elements will look like:

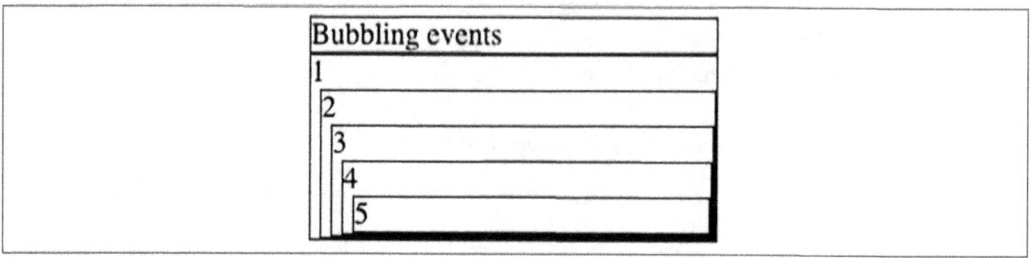

Figure 11.3: Event bubbling in web page

And below is the code associated with it. The script is on the bottom and will be executed when the parts on top are done. It is going to add event listeners to every div, and what it will do is log the innerText. For the outermost element of the nested div elements, this would be 12345, with a new number on every line.

So the question here is, how will it trigger the events? Say we click on the 5, what will be executed? The event of all of the nested div elements, or only the one from 5? And if it is going to execute all of them, will it execute them from inner to outer event or the other way around?

```
<!DOCTYPE html>
<html>
  <body>
    <style>
      div {
        border: 1px solid black;
        margin-left: 5px;
      }
    </style>
    <div id="message">Bubbling events</div>
    <div id="output">
      1
      <div>
        2
        <div>
          3
          <div>
            4
```

```
            <div>5</div>
          </div>
        </div>
      </div>
    </div>
    <script>
      function bubble() {
        console.log(this.innerText);
      }
      let divs = document.getElementsByTagName("div");
      for (let i = 0; i < divs.length; i++) {
        divs[i].addEventListener("click", bubble);
      }
    </script>
  </body>
</html>
```

In this case, it has the default behavior. It will execute all five events, so each one of every nested div. And it will execute them inside out. So it will start with the innerText of only **5**, then **45**, until the last one, **12345**:

Figure 11.4: Console output event bubbling

This is called **event bubbling**. It's what happens when you trigger the handlers on an element. It runs its own events first, then its parents, and so on. It is called bubbling because it goes up from the inner event to the outer, like water bubbles going up.

You can alter this behavior by adding `true` as a third argument when you add the event listener like this:

```
divs[i].addEventListener("click", bubble, true);
```

This would be the result:

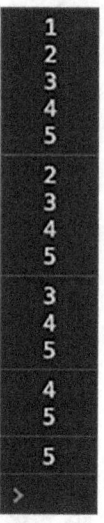

Figure 11.5: Console output event capturing

This moving from the outer element to the inner element is called **event capturing**. It is not used a lot anymore nowadays, but if you do need to implement it, you can use the `useCapture` argument of `addEventListener()` (the third argument) and set it to `true`. It is `false` by default.

The event capturing and bubbling allows us to apply a principle called **event delegation**. Event delegation is the concept where instead of adding event handlers to every element in a certain block of HTML, we define a wrapper and add the event to this wrapper element, and it then applies to all the child elements as well. You'll apply this principle in the next exercise.

Practice exercise 11.6

This example will demonstrate event capturing and the delegation of page elements. By adding event listeners to the parent and children within the main element, this example will order the console messages according to the event capture properties.

All of the `div` elements with a `class` of `box` will have the same event object. We can add the event target, `textcontent`, as well into the console so that we can tell which element was clicked.

Use the following template:

```
<!doctype html>
<html>
<head>
    <title>JS Tester</title>
    <style>
        .box {
            width: 200px;
            height: 100px;
            border: 1px solid black
        }
    </style>
</head>
<body>
    <div class="container">
        <div class="box" id="box0">Box #1</div>
        <div class="box" id="box1">Box #2</div>
        <div class="box" id="box2">Box #3</div>
        <div class="box" id="box3">Box #4</div>
    </div>
    <script>

    </script>
</body>
</html>
```

Take the following steps:

1. In the JavaScript code, select all the elements with the classes, and separately select the main container element.

2. Add event listeners to the main container, outputting to the console value of 4 for the `useCapture` argument set to `false`, and 1 for the `useCapture` argument set to `true`.

3. For each of the nested elements, add `click` event listeners with a `console.log()` value of 3 for the `useCapture` argument set to `false`, and 2 for `useCapture` set to `true`.

4. Click the page elements to see the event delegation and order of output on the page.

5. Within the box elements on both click events, add to the console an output for the event target's textContent value.

onchange and onblur

Two other events that are often combined with input boxes are onchange and onblur. onchange gets triggered when an element changes, for example, when the value of an input box changes. onblur gets triggered when an object goes out of focus; for example, when you have the cursor in one input box and the cursor goes to another input box, the onblur event of the first input box will get triggered.

Here is an example of both in practice; it's an HTML snippet of the body of a web page. The inputs contain onblur and onchange, and there is an extra function.

```
<!DOCTYPE html>
<html>
  <body>
    <div id="welcome">Hi there!</div>
    <form>
      <input type="text" name="firstname" placeholder="First name"
onchange="logEvent()" />
      <input type="text" name="lastname" placeholder="Last name"
onblur="logEvent()" />
      <input type="button" onclick="sendInfo()" value="Submit" />
    </form>
    <script>
      function logEvent() {
        let p = event.target;
        if (p.name == "firstname") {
          message("First Name Changed to  " + p.value);
        } else {
          message("Last Name Changed to  " + p.value);
        }
      }

      function sendInfo() {
        let p = event.target.parentElement;
        message("Welcome " + p.firstname.value + " " + p.lastname.
value);
      }
```

```
        function message(m) {
            document.getElementById("welcome").innerHTML = m;
        }
    </script>
  </body>
</html>
```

The `firstname` input box has an onchange event. If the value of the data in the input box gets changed, this event gets triggered as soon as the input box loses focus. If the input box loses focus when the value has not changed, nothing happens for onchange. This is not true for onblur, which is assigned to the `lastname` input box. Even when the value hasn't changed, the event will get triggered.

Another event that is often used with input boxes is onfocus, or simply focus when used in combination with an event listener. This event is associated with the cursor entering the input box, and it gets fired when the input box gets focused on by the cursor and input can be entered.

Practice exercise 11.7

With two input fields on the page, JavaScript will listen for changes to the content in the input field. Once the input field is not in focus, if the value has been changed, the change event will be invoked. blur and focus are also added to the input fields and will get logged to the console as those events occur. Both input elements will have the same event listeners, and as you change the content of the input fields and remove focus, the output text content will update using the values of the input field that triggered the event.

Use the following HTML template:

```
<!doctype html>
<html>
<head>
    <title>JS Tester</title>
</head>
<body>
    <div class="output1">
    </div>

    <input type="text" placeholder="First Name" name="first"><br>
    <input type="text" placeholder="Last Name" name="last"><br>
    <script>
```

```
        </script>
    </body>
    </html>
```

Now take the following steps:

1. Within the JavaScript code, put the HTML output element into a variable object that you can use to display content on the page.

2. Select both input fields. You can use `querySelector()` and `"input[name='first']"`, which will allow you to make your selection using the input field name.

3. Add an event listener to the first input and the second input. The event listener should be a change event to track changed values. This will only be invoked if the value in the field is changed and you click off the input field.

4. Create a separate function to handle the output of the content to the page, updating the `textContent` of the output element.

5. Send the values of the input fields as they get changed to the output element `textContent`.

6. Add four additional event listeners and listen for `blur` and `focus` on each input. Once the event gets triggered, output in the console the value of the event type.

Key event handler

There are several key events. One of them is `onkeypress`. `onkeypress` gets triggered, well, you may have guessed this, whenever a key gets pressed. Pressing means here when the button is pressed and released. If you want an event to happen as soon as the button is pressed (so before releasing), you can use the `onkeydown` event. If you want the event to happen on release, you can use the `onkeyup` event.

There are many things we can do with key events. For example, we can restrict what characters can be entered in an input box. Every time a key gets pressed, we can check the character and decide whether it gets to stay.

We can get the key that triggered the event using:

```
event.key;
```

The following HTML code has two input boxes. Can you see what is happening here?

```
<!doctype html>
<html>
  <body>
    <body>
      <div id="wrapper">JavaScript is fun!</div>
      <input type="text" name="myNum1" onkeypress="numCheck()">
      <input type="text" name="myNum2" onkeypress="numCheck2()">
      <script>
        function numCheck() {
            message("Number: " + !isNaN(event.key));
            return !isNaN(event.key);
        }

        function numCheck2() {
            message("Not a number: " + isNaN(event.key));
            return isNaN(event.key);
        }

        function message(m) {
            document.getElementById('wrapper').innerHTML = m;
        }
      </script>
    </body>
  </body>
</html>
```

The first one checks if a value is a number, and if it is a number, it will write `Number: true` at the top; else, it will write `Number: false` at the top. The second one is checking for if a value is not a number; if it is not a number, it will write `Not a number: true`; else, it will write `Not a number: false`.

So this is one way of using the onkeypress event, but we can do even more. We can add a return statement to our onkeypress event, like this:

```
onkeypress="return numCheck2()";
```

If `true` is returned, the key value gets added to the input box; if `false` is returned, the key value is not added.

The following code snippet only allows numbers to be entered in the input box. Whenever the user tries to type something else, the function restricts it.

```html
<!doctype html>
<html>
  <body>
    <body>
      <div id="wrapper">JavaScript is fun!</div>
      <input type="text" name="myNum1" onkeypress="return numCheck()"
onpaste="return false">
      <input type="text" name="myNum2" onkeypress="return numCheck2()"
onpaste="return false">
      <script>
        function numCheck() {
            message(!isNaN(event.key));
            return !isNaN(event.key);
        }

        function numCheck2() {
            message(isNaN(event.key));
            return isNaN(event.key);
        }

        function message(m) {
            document.getElementById("wrapper").innerHTML = m;
        }
      </script>
    </body>
  </html>
```

As you can see, `return` gets included in onkeypress to ensure that only numbers can be entered. One other thing might have caught your eye: `onpaste="return false"`. This is to deal with smart people who copy and paste numbers to a non-numeric field or other characters to a numeric field and still manage to get illegal characters in there.

Practice exercise 11.8

By recognizing key presses and detecting the values of characters as key presses occur with the element in focus, we can also detect if content is pasted into an input field.

1. Create two input fields within your HTML. Add an element to output content too.

2. Using JavaScript, select the page elements. You can assign a variable called output to the element with a class of output. Create another variable, eles, and select all the input fields (using querySelectorAll()) as its value. This way, we can loop through the node list and assign the same events to all the matching elements.

3. Using forEach(), iterate through all the input elements from the page. Add the same event listeners to all of them.

4. Add a keydown event listener and check if the value is a number. If it is a number, then add it to the output area.

5. On keyup, output to the console the value of the key.

6. Check if there was a paste in the input field; if there was, then you can output the word paste to the console.

Drag and drop elements

There are also special event handlers for dragging and dropping. We need a starting point to be able to drag and drop something. Let's create the CSS and HTML for a dragging and dropping area.

```
<!doctype>
<html>
  <head>
    <style>
      .box {
        height: 200px;
        width: 200px;
        padding: 20px;
        margin: 0 50px;
        display: inline-block;
        border: 1px solid black;
      }

      #dragme {
        background-color: red;
      }
    </style>
  </head>
```

```
  <body>
    <div class="box">1</div>
    <div class="box">2</div>
  </body>
</html>
```

Now we are also going to include an element that is going to be dragged and dropped. In order to mark an element as something that can be dragged, we need to add the attribute draggable. This is the code we are going to include in our second div, with the first div around it:

```
<div class="box"> 1
  <div id="dragme" draggable="true">
    Drag Me Please!
  </div>
</div>
```

Then we need to decide what we are going to do when we drop the draggable element. We need to specify this within the box it can be dragged to. We are going to add the functionality to both boxes, so it can be dragged over to one and back to the other.

```
<div class="box" ondrop="dDrop()" ondragover="nDrop()">
    1
  <div id="dragme" ondragstart="dStart()" draggable="true">
    Drag Me Please!
  </div>
  </div>
<div class="box" ondrop="dDrop()" ondragover="nDrop()">2</div>
```

And here is the script that will be added to the end of the body:

```
<script>
  let holderItem;

  function dStart() {
    holderItem = event.target;
  }

  function nDrop() {
    event.preventDefault();
  }
```

```
    function dDrop() {
      event.preventDefault();
      if (event.target.className == "box") {
        event.target.appendChild(holderItem);
      }
    }
  }
</script>
```

We start by specifying a variable in the script for the item that we want to hold when dragging. When the `ondragstart` event gets triggered, we are going to store the element that is being dragged in the `holderItem` variable. Normally, when you drag, dropping is not allowed by the design of HTML. In order to allow the drop, you'll have to prevent the default event that means the item you want to drop cannot be dropped. You can do this with:

```
event.preventDefault();
```

Usually, before you prevent the default behavior, you would do some checks to see whether the element that is being dropped can be accepted at that place. In the example above, we check whether the class name of the element that it is being dropped to is box. If that's the case, we append `holderItem` as a child to the box.

We have created a page that allows moving an HTML element from one box to another. If you try to release it anywhere else, the element goes back instead to its previous location.

Practice exercise 11.9

This will be an "I'm not a robot" check. Drag and drop can be used to ensure that it's a live user that is acting on a page rather than a robot. This exercise will demonstrate how to create a visual dragging effect on an active element, in which the user clicks the mouse down to create a drag action, and once the mouse button is released, the drop event occurs. The successful actions are logged to the console.

You can use the following template:

```
<!doctype html>
<html>
<head>
    <title>JS Tester</title>
    <style>
        .box {
```

```
                width: 100px;
                height: 100px;
                border: 1px solid black;
                background-color: white;
            }
            .red {
                background-color: red;
            }
        </style>
    </head>
    <body>
        <div class="box">1
            <div id="dragme" draggable="true">
                Drag Me Please!
            </div>
        </div>
        <div class="box">2</div>
        <script>
        </script>
    </body>
</html>
```

The preceding HTML creates styles for an element that will be used for dropping, and sets a width, height, and border. It creates another class called red and adds a red background to the active element so that it shows as active, along with two div elements that will have classes of the box element for dropoff. Finally, we create a div nested in one of the boxes that has an id of dragme and an attribute of draggable set to true, with some instructive text added to aid the user. Complete the script by taking the following steps:

1. Select the draggable element as an object in your JavaScript code.

2. Add an event listener of dragstart, where it updates the draggable element to 0.5 opacity.

3. Add another event listener of dragend that removes the value for the opacity.

4. Using querySelectorAll(), select all the dropoff boxes.

5. Add event listeners to all the dropoff boxes, setting things such that the red class is added to an element whenever the user triggers the dragenter event. This will indicate to the user that the action is taking place.

6. Set dragover, adding a preventDefault() method to the element to disable any actions that might already exist.

7. On dragleave, remove the red class.

8. Adding the event listener of drop to the box, append the draggable element to the event target.

9. To work across all elements in the same way, remove the default action of the element. You can use the preventDefault() method to this event to disable any actions that might already exist.

10. You can add console log messages to any of these events to better track them.

Form submission

When a form gets submitted, an event can be triggered. This can be achieved in different ways, and one of them is to add to the form element the onsubmit attribute.

```
<form onsubmit="doSomething()">
```

The function that is listed there will get triggered whenever input of type submit is submitted.

```
<input type="submit" value="send">
```

We can do more with the HTML of the form element; for example, we can redirect to another page. We have to specify the way we want to send the form values using the method attribute and the location page using the action attribute.

```
<form action="anotherpage.html" method="get" onsubmit="doStuff()">
```

Don't worry about the get for now; this just means that values get sent via the URL. URLs look like this when you use get:

```
www.example.com/anotherpage.html?name=edward
```

After the question mark, the variables that are sent along are shown in key-value pairs. This is the form that created the URL when edward was inserted for name.

```
<!doctype html>
<html>
  <body>
    <form action="anotherpage.html" method="get">
      <input type="text" placeholder="name" name="name" />
      <input type="submit" value="send" />
    </form>
  </body>
</html>
```

anotherpage.html can use the variables from the URL. This can be done in the
JavaScript of anotherpage.html doing something like this:

```
<!doctype html>
<html>
  <body>
    <script>
      let q = window.location.search;
      let params = new URLSearchParams(q);
      let name = params.get("name");
      console.log(name);
    </script>
  </body>
</html>
```

So far we have been submitting forms using the action and onsubmit attributes.
action redirects to another location. This could be the API endpoint of a different
page. onsubmit specifies an event that is fired when the form gets submitted.

There are more cool things we can do with the onsubmit event of forms. Remember
the use of return for onkeypress? We can do something similar here! If we make the
called function return a Boolean, the form will only get submitted when the Boolean
is true.

This comes in very handy if we want to do some form validation before sending it.
Have a look at this code and see if you can figure out when it can be submitted.

```
<!doctype html>
<html>
  <body>
    <div id="wrapper"></div>
    <form action="anotherpage.html" method="get" onsubmit="return
valForm()">
      <input type="text" id="firstName" name="firstName"
placeholder="First name" />
      <input type="text" id="lastName" name="lastName"
placeholder="Last name" />
      <input type="text" id="age" name="age" placeholder="Age" />
      <input type="submit" value="submit" />
    </form>
    <script>
      function valForm() {
        var p = event.target.children;
```

```
            if (p.firstName.value == "") {
                message("Need a first name!!");
                return false;
            }
            if (p.lastName.value == "") {
                message("Need a last name!!");
                return false;
            }
            if (p.age.value == "") {
                message("Need an age!!");
                return false;
            }
            return true;
        }

        function message(m) {
            document.getElementById("wrapper").innerHTML = m;
        }
    </script>
  </body>
</html>
```

This form contains three input fields and one input button. The fields are for last name, first name, and age. When one of them is missing, the form will not submit, because the function will return `false`. A message will also be added to the `div` above the form, explaining what went wrong.

Practice exercise 11.10

This will be about creating a form validator. In this exercise, you will be checking to ensure that the desired values are entered into the input fields. The code will check the input values that are entered by the user to match predetermined conditions for those field values.

1. Set up a form, adding three input fields inside: `First`, `Last`, and `Age`. Add a submit button.
2. Within the JavaScript code, select the form as an element object.
3. Add an submit event listener to the form.
4. Set up the default value for `error` as `false`.
5. Create a function named `checker()`, which will check to see the length of a string and output the string length to the console.

6. Add conditions to each of the field values, first checking if the value is there and then returning an error if the response is `false`, before changing the error variable to `true`.

7. Use `console.log()` to log the details about the error.

8. For the age input value, check the value to see if the age provided is 19 or over, otherwise cause an error.

9. At the end of the validation, check if `error` is `true`; if it is, use `preventDefault()` to stop the form submission. Log the errors to the console.

Animating elements

Lastly, we want to show you that you can animate using HTML, CSS, and JavaScript. This allows us to do even cooler things with our web page. For example, we can trigger an animation as an event. This can be used for many different purposes, for example, to illustrate an explanation, to draw the user's eyes to a certain location, or to play a game.

Let's show you a very basic example. We can use the `position` key and set it to `absolute` in CSS. This makes the position of the element relative to its nearest positioned parent. Here, that would be the body. This is the code for a purple square that moves from left to right when a button is clicked.

```
<!doctype html>
<html>
  <style>
    div {
      background-color: purple;
      width: 100px;
      height: 100px;
      position: absolute;
    }
  </style>
  <body>
    <button onclick="toTheRight()">Go right</button>
    <div id="block"></div>

    <script>
      function toTheRight() {
        let b = document.getElementById("block");
        let x = 0;
        setInterval(function () {
```

```
        if (x === 600) {
          clearInterval();
        } else {
          x++;
          b.style.left = x + "px";
        }
      }, 2);


    }
  </script>
</body>
</html>
```

We need to give the div block an absolute position, because we rely on the CSS left property to make it move. In order to be to the left of something, that something needs to be absolute, else the left property cannot be positioned relative to it. In this case, we need to be a certain number of pixels to the left of the div; this is why we need the position of the div to be absolute, so the position of the moving box can be relative to that of its parent.

When we click the button, the function toTheRight() gets triggered. This function grabs block and stores it in b. It sets x to 0. Then we use a very powerful built-in JavaScript function: setInterval(). This function keeps on evaluating an expression until clearInterval() gets called. This is done when x, the measure of how far we are to the left, reaches 600. It repeats it every 2 milliseconds, which gives it the sliding look.

You can at the same time also set different positions, like style.top, style.bottom, and style.right, or append new elements to create a snow effect, or show constantly driving cars. With this in your toolbox, the sky is the limit.

Practice exercise 11.11

Here we will click the purple square and watch it move on the page. This exercise will demonstrate creating the events for a simple interactive element on the page. The purple square will move every time it's clicked; once it reaches the boundaries of the page, it will change direction from left to right and right to left, depending on what side it hits.

1. Set up styling for an element, setting height and width before setting position to absolute.

2. Create an element that you want to move on the page.

3. Select and store the element using JavaScript.

4. Set up an object with values for speed, direction, and position.

5. Add an event listener for if the element is clicked on.

6. Set a default value of 30 for the value of the interval counter.

7. If the counter is less than 1, then end the interval and clear it.

8. Once the interval has run 30 times using the value of x, the element will stand still and wait to be clicked again.

9. While in motion, check if the position value is greater than 800 or less than 0, which means it needs to change direction. The direction value will provide the direction of movement. If the movement takes the box outside the boundaries of the container, we need to send it in the other direction. This can be done by multiplying by negative one. If the value is positive, it will become negative, sending the element to the left. If the value is negative, it will become positive, sending the element to the right.

10. Update the style.left position value of the element, assigning the value of the position that was updated. Add px, as the assigned value of the style is a string.

11. Output the result to the console.

Chapter projects

Build your own analytics

Figure out which elements are clicked on in a page and record their IDs, tags, and class name.

1. Create a main container element within your HTML.

2. Add four elements inside the main element, each having a class of box and a unique ID with unique text content.

3. Set up your JavaScript code to contain an array that you can use for tracking, adding details from each click into it.

4. Select the main container element as a variable object in your code.

5. Add an event listener to capture clicks on the element.

6. Create a function to handle the clicks. Get the target element from the event object.

7. Check if the element has an ID, so that you don't track clicks on the main container.

8. Set up an object to track the values; include the element `textContent`, `id`, `tagName`, and `className`.

9. Add the temporary object to your tracking array.

10. Output the values captured in your tracking array to your console.

Star rating system

Create a star rating component that is fully interactive and dynamic using JavaScript.

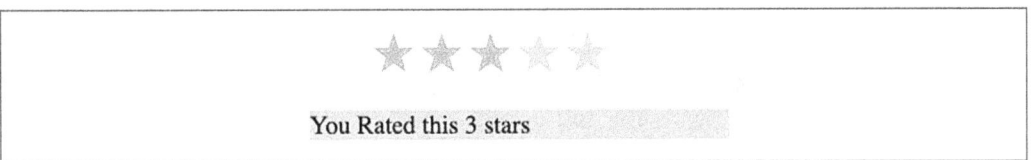

Figure 11.6: Creating a star rating system

You can use the following HTML and CSS as a starting template. Provide the completed script element as your answer.

```
<!DOCTYPE html>
<html>
<head>
    <title>Star Rater</title>
    <style>
        .stars ul {
            list-style-type: none;
            padding: 0;
        }
        .star {
            font-size: 2em;
            color: #ddd;
            display: inline-block;
        }
        .orange {
            color: orange;
        }
        .output {
            background-color: #ddd;
        }
```

```
        </style>
    </head>
    <body>
        <ul class="stars">
            <li class="star">&#10029;</li>
            <li class="star">&#10029;</li>
            <li class="star">&#10029;</li>
            <li class="star">&#10029;</li>
            <li class="star">&#10029;</li>
        </ul>
        <div class="output"></div>
        <script>

        </script>
    </body>
</html>
```

Take the following steps:

1. Select all the stars within the ul that have a class of stars into an object, and create another object for the output element.

2. Create another object to contain the results of calling querySelectorAll() on elements with a class of star.

3. Loop through the resulting node list, adding to the element object the value of the index plus 1, and adding an event listener listening for a click. Attach a function called starRate() to the click event of each star element.

4. Within the starRate() function, add to the output the value of the star using the event target and the element object's star value, which was set in the previous step.

5. Loop through all the stars using forEach() to check if the index value of the star element is less than the star value; if it is, apply a class of orange. Otherwise, remove the class of orange from the classList element.

Mouse position tracker

Track your mouse's x and y position within an element. As you move the mouse within the element, the x position and y position values will update.

1. Create a page element and add sizing to it, including height and width. Create a class style named active that has a background-color property of red. Finally, create an output element that will contain your text.

2. Select the main container element and add event listeners to it. Listen for mouseover, mouseout, and mousemove.

3. On mouseover, add the active class, and on mouseout, remove the active class.

4. On mousemove, call a function that tracks the event element clientX and clientY positions, embeds them in a human-readable sentence, and outputs it into the output element.

Box clicker speed test game

The objective here is to click on the red box as quickly as possible once it appears. The box will be randomly placed within a container and positioned with random values. The box will have an event listener that will track the start and click times to calculate the duration of the click events. You can use the following template, as the HTML gets a little complex here—just add the <script> element to make the HTML interactive!

```
<!DOCTYPE html>
<html>

<head>
    <title>Click Me Game</title>
    <style>
        .output {
            width: 500px;
            height: 500px;
            border: 1px solid black;
            margin: auto;
            text-align: center;
        }

        .box {
            width: 50px;
            height: 50px;
            position: relative;
            top: 50px;
            left: 20%;
            background-color: red;
        }

        .message {
            text-align: center;
```

```
                padding: 10px;
                font-size: 1.3em;
            }
        </style>
    </head>

    <body>
        <div class="output"></div>
        <div class="message"></div>
        <script>

        </script>
    </body>
</html>
```

Work with the above HTML code using JavaScript.

1. There are two div elements, one with a class of output for the gameplay area and another with a class of message to provide instructions to the player. Select those main elements as objects using JavaScript.

2. Using JavaScript, create another element within the output element, and create a div that will be the main clickable object. Attach a style called box to the new element and append it to the output element.

3. Using JavaScript, add to the message area instructions for the user: Press to Start. They will need to click the newly created div with a class of box to start the game.

4. Create a global object called game to track the timer and the start time values. This is to be used to calculate the duration in seconds between when the element is shown and when the player clicks it. Set start to null.

5. Create a function that will generate a random number and return a random value, with the argument being the maximum value you want to use.

6. Add an event listener to the box element. Once clicked, this should start the gameplay. Set the display of the box element to none. Using the setTimeout() method, invoke a function called addBox() and set the timeout to a random millisecond value. You can adjust as needed; this will be the time between the click object box being shown and it disappearing. If the start value is null, then add text content to the message area of loading.

7. If start has a value, then get the Unix time value using getTime() of the current date object, subtract the game start time from the current time value in milliseconds, and then divide by 1,000 to get the value in seconds. Output the result to the message element for the player to see their score.

8. Create a function to handle the clicks, adding the box once the timer is up. Update the message text content to say `Click it...`. Set the game `start` value to the current time in milliseconds. Apply the style of `block` to the element so it shows on the page.

9. From the available space (500 total container width minus the 50 box width) set a random position above and to the left of the element using the `Math.random()`.

10. Play the game and update the styling as needed.

Self-check quiz

1. Where can you find `window.innerHeight` and `window.innerWidth`?

2. What does `preventDefault()` do?

Summary

In this chapter, we have dealt with quite a few topics to increase the interactivity of web pages. We saw the different ways to specify events and then we dived into some different event handlers in more detail. The onload event handler gets fired when the element it was specified on, often the document object, is fully loaded. This is great to wrap other functionality in, because it avoids selecting DOM content that is not there yet.

We also saw the mouse event handlers, for responding to all the different things that can be done with a mouse on a web page. The use of all these event handlers is very similar, but they each enable a different type of interaction with the user. We also saw that we can access the element that fired an event by calling event.target. This property holds the element that fired an event.

We also dived into onchange, onblur, and the key event handlers in more detail. After that, we saw how to trigger interaction when forms are submitted. We looked at the HTML action attribute, which redirects the handling of submission, and the onsubmit event, which deals with form submission. We then saw some things that we can do with all these events, such as specifying a drag and drop on a page and animating elements.

In the next chapter, we will move on to some more advanced topics that will take your existing JavaScript skills to the next level!

Join our book's Discord space

Join the book's Discord workspace for a monthly *Ask me Anything* session with the authors: `https://packt.link/JSBook`

12
Intermediate JavaScript

The concepts and solution approaches presented up to this point in the book are not the only way to think about solving issues. In this chapter, we will challenge you to look a little deeper, be curious, and practice the good habit of optimizing solutions.

In previous chapters, you were promised great things about this chapter because the optimal use of some built-in methods require knowledge of regular expressions, which we will cover in this chapter. There is a lot more fun to be had though—here is a list of topics that we'll cover:

- Regular expressions
- Functions and the arguments object
- JavaScript hoisting
- Strict mode
- Debugging
- Using cookies
- Local storage
- JSON

As you can see, a selection of diverse topics, but all advanced and fun. The sections in this chapter are not as related to each other as you might have gotten used to by now. They are mostly individual topics that can help to really enhance your understanding and improve your JavaScript knowledge a lot.

Note: exercise, project and self-check quiz answers can be found in the *Appendix*.

Regular expressions

Regular expressions, also known as **regex**, are simply ways to describe text patterns. You can consider them next-level strings. There are different regex implementations. This means that depending on the interpreter, regex might differ a bit in the way they're written. However, they are somewhat standardized, so you write them (almost) the same for all versions of regex. We are going to use regex for JavaScript.

Regex can be very useful in many situations, for example when you need to look for errors in a large file or retrieve the browser agent a user is using. They can also be used for form validation, as with regex you can specify valid patterns for field entries such as email addresses or phone numbers.

Regex is not only useful for finding strings, but can also be used for replacing strings. By now you might think, *so regex is amazing, but is there a catch?* And yes, unfortunately, there is a catch. At first, regex might kind of look like your neighbor's cat walked over your keyboard and just typed some random characters by accident. This regex checks for a valid email, for example:

```
/([a-zA-Z0-9._-]+@[a-zA-Z0-9._-]+\.[a-zA-Z0-9._-]+)/g
```

Fear not, after this section, you will be able to decipher the secret patterns within the regex. We are not going to go through everything there is to say about regex, but we will establish a solid level of familiarity that will allow you to work with them and expand your knowledge as you go.

Let's start off easy. The regex pattern is specified between two slashes. This is a valid regex expression:

```
/JavaScript/
```

The above expression will match if a given string contains the word `JavaScript`. When it matches, this means the result is positive. And this can be used to do many things.

We can use the JavaScript built-in `match()` function for this. This function returns the regex match on the result (if there is one) in the form of the substring that matched the starting position of this string and the input string.

There are actually other built-in functions that use regex, but we will see them later. `match()` is just a convenient function to demonstrate how regex works. You can see it in action here:

```
let text = "I love JavaScript!";
console.log(text.match(/javascript/));
```

This logs null because it is case-sensitive by default and therefore is not a match. If we had looked for /ava/ or simply /a/, it would have matched because it contains ava and a. If you want it to be case-insensitive, you can specify this using an i after the slash. In this case-insensitive example, the expression will match the previous string:

```
console.log(text.match(/javascript/i));
```

This will actually log the result, because it is now case-insensitive, and from that point of view, our string does contain `javascript`. Here is the result:

```
[
  'JavaScript',
  index: 7,
  input: 'I love JavaScript!',
  groups: undefined
]
```

The result is an object, containing the found match and the index it started on, as well as the input that was looked through. The groups are undefined. You can create groups with round parentheses, as you'll see when we get to the section on groups.

You can often find regex in JavaScript in combination with the built-in search and replace method on strings, which we'll cover next.

Specifying multiple options for words

In order to specify a certain range of options, we can use this syntax:

```
let text = "I love JavaScript!";
console.log(text.match(/javascript|nodejs|react/i));
```

Here, the expression matches either `javascript`, `nodejs`, or `react`. At this point, we are only matching for the first encounter and then we quit. So this is not going to find two or more matches right now — it will output the same thing as before:

```
let text = "I love React and JavaScript!";
console.log(text.match(/javascript|nodejs|react/i));
```

It logs this:

```
[
  'React',
  index: 7,
  input: 'I love React and JavaScript!',
  groups: undefined
]
```

If we wanted to find all matches, we could specify the global modifier, g. It is very similar to what we did for case-insensitive searches. In this example, we are checking for all matches, and it is case-insensitive. All the modifiers are behind the last slash. You can use multiple modifiers at the same time as we do below, or you could decide to only use g:

```
let text = "I love React and JavaScript!";
console.log(text.match(/javascript|nodejs|react/gi));
```

This returns both `React` and `JavaScript` as a result:

```
[ 'React', 'JavaScript' ]
```

As you can see, the result looks very different now. As soon as you specify g, the match function will just return an array of the matching words. This is not too exciting in this case, since these are the words we asked for. But it can be more of a surprise with a more complex pattern. This is exactly what we'll learn next.

Character options

So far, our expressions are quite readable, right? The character options are where things start to look, well, intense. Say we want to search for a string of only one character equal to a, b, or c. We would write it like this:

```
let text = "d";
console.log(text.match(/[abc]/));
```

This will return `null` because d is not a, b, or c. We can include d like this:

```
console.log(text.match(/[abcd]/));
```

This will log:

```
[ 'd', index: 0, input: 'd', groups: undefined ]
```

Since this is a range of characters, we can write it shorter, like this:

```
let text = "d";
console.log(text.match(/[a-d]/));
```

And if we wanted any letter, lowercase or uppercase, we would write this:

```
let text = "t";
console.log(text.match(/[a-zA-Z]/));
```

We could actually also use the case-insensitive modifier to achieve the same thing, but this would apply to the regex pattern as a whole, and you might only need it to apply for the specific character:

```
console.log(text.match(/[a-z]/i));
```

We would get a match on both of the preceding options. If we wanted to include numbers as well, we would write:

```
console.log(text.match(/[a-zA-Z0-9]/));
```

As you can see, we can just concatenate ranges to specify one character, much like we could concatenate possible options for that specific character, like [abc]. The example above specifies three possible ranges. It will match any lowercase or uppercase letter from a to z and all numeric characters as well.

It doesn't mean that it can only match a one-character string by the way; it will just match the first matching character in this case because we didn't add the global modifier. However, these special characters won't match:

```
let text = "äé!";
console.log(text.match(/[a-zA-Z0-9]/));
```

To address the difficulty of complex characters not matching an expression, the dot functions as a special wildcard character in regex that can match any character. So what do you think this does?

```
let text = "Just some text.";
console.log(text.match(/./g));
```

Since it has the global modifier, it is going to match any character. This is the result:

```
[
  'J', 'u', 's', 't',
  ' ', 's', 'o', 'm',
```

```
    'e', ' ', 't', 'e',
    'x', 't', '.'
]
```

But what if you only wanted to find a match for the dot character itself? If you want a special character (one that is used in regex to specify a pattern) to have a normal meaning, or a normal character to have a special meaning, you can escape it using the backslash:

```
let text = "Just some text.";
console.log(text.match(/\./g));
```

In this example, we escape the dot by adding a preceding backslash. Therefore, it doesn't function as a wildcard and it is going to look for a literal match. This is what it will return:

```
[ '.' ]
```

There are some normal characters that get a special meaning by adding a backslash before them. We are not going to cover them in depth, but let's have a look at some examples:

```
let text = "I'm 29 years old.";
console.log(text.match(/\d/g));
```

If we escape the d, \d, it matches any digit. We are doing a global search so it will specify any digit. This is the result:

```
[ '2', '9' ]
```

We can also escape the s, \s, which matches all whitespace characters:

```
let text = "Coding is a lot of fun!";
console.log(text.match(/\s/g));
```

The above example will just return a few spaces, but tabs and other types of whitespace are also included:

```
[ ' ', ' ', ' ', ' ', ' ' ]
```

A very useful one is \b, which matches text only when it's at the beginning of a word. So, in the following example, it is not going to match the instances of in in beginning:

```
let text = "In the end or at the beginning?";
console.log(text.match(/\bin/gi));
```

This is what it will end up logging:

```
[ 'In' ]
```

Even though you can check for characters being numbers, the `match()` method belongs to the `string` object, so you implement it on numeric variables. For example, try the following:

```
let nr = 357;
console.log(nr.match(/3/g));
```

You should receive a `TypeError` saying that `nr.match()` is not a function.

Groups

There are many reasons to group your regex. Whenever you want to match a group of characters, you can surround them with parentheses. Have a look at this example:

```
let text = "I love JavaScript!";
console.log(text.match(/(love|dislike)\s(javascript|spiders)/gi));
```

Here it is going to look for either `love` or `dislike`, followed by a whitespace character, followed by `javascript` or `spiders`, and it will do so for all occurrences while ignoring whether they are in uppercase or lowercase. This is what it will log:

```
[ 'love JavaScript' ]
```

Let's just say we can match on roughly four combinations here. Two of them seem to make more sense to me personally:

- Love spiders
- Dislike spiders
- Love JavaScript
- Dislike JavaScript

Groups are very powerful when we know how to repeat them. Let's see how to do that. Very often, you'll find yourself in need of repeating a certain regex piece. We have several options for this. For example, if we want to match any four alphanumeric characters in a sequence, we could just write this:

```
let text = "I love JavaScript!";
console.log(text.match(/[a-zA-Z0-9][a-zA-Z0-9][a-zA-Z0-9][a-zA-Z0-
9]/g));
```

This will produce the following as output:

```
[ 'love', 'Java', 'Scri' ]
```

This is a terrible way to go about repeating a block: let's look for better options. If we only want it to be present 0 or 1 times, we can use the question mark. So this is for optional characters, for example:

```
let text = "You are doing great!";
console.log(text.match(/n?g/gi));
```

This looks for a g character that may or not may be preceded by an n. Therefore, this will log:

```
[ 'ng', 'g' ]
```

Arguably, one time is not really an example of repeating. Let's look at getting more repetitions. If you want something at least once, but optionally more often, you can use the plus sign: +. Here is an example:

```
let text = "123123123";
console.log(text.match(/(123)+/));
```

This is going to match for the group 123 one or more times. And since this string is present, it will find a match. This is what will be logged:

```
[ '123123123', '123', index: 0, input: '123123123', groups: undefined ]
```

It matches the whole string in this case, since it is just 123 repeated. There are also situations where you want to have a certain piece of regex match any number of times, which can be indicated with the asterisk: *. Here is an example regex pattern:

```
/(123)*a/
```

It will match with any a preceded by 123 any number of times. So it will match on the following, for example:

- 123123123a
- 123a
- a
- ba

The last thing to note about repeating is that we can be more specific as well. We do this using this syntax {min, max}. Here is an example:

```
let text = "abcabcabc";
console.log(text.match(/(abc){1,2}/));
```

This will log:

```
[ 'abcabc', 'abc', index: 0, input: 'abcabcabc', groups: undefined ]
```

It does this because it will match on abc both once and twice. As you can see, we have been using groups, but groups is still undefined in the output. In order to specify groups, we'll have to name them. Here's an example of how to do it:

```
let text = "I love JavaScript!";
console.log(text.match(/(?<language>javascript)/i));
```

This will output:

```
[
  'JavaScript',
  'JavaScript',
  index: 7,
  input: 'I love JavaScript!',
  groups: [Object: null prototype] { language: 'JavaScript' }
]
```

There is more to say about regex, but this should already enable you to do quite a lot of cool things with it. Let's have a look at some practical examples.

Practical regex

Regex can be of great use in many situations—anywhere you need to match certain string patterns, regex will come in handy. We are going to discuss how you can use regex in combination with other string methods, and how you can use it to validate email addresses and IPv4 addresses.

Searching and replacing strings

In *Chapter 8, Built-In JavaScript Methods*, we saw the search and replace methods on strings. We would have liked our search to be case-insensitive, though. Guess what—we can use regex for this!

```
let text = "That's not the case.";
console.log(text.search(/Case/i));
```

Adding the i modifier here ignores the distinction between uppercase and lowercase. This code returns 15, which is the starting index position of the match. This cannot be done using the normal string input.

How do you think we can alter the behavior of the replace method using regex in such a way that we can replace all instances rather than the first instance of a string? Again, with a modifier! We use the global modifier (g) for this. To get a feel for the difference, look at this expression without g:

```
let text = "Coding is fun. Coding opens up a lot of opportunities.";
console.log(text.replace("Coding", "JavaScript"));
```

This is what it outputs:

```
JavaScript is fun. Coding opens up a lot of opportunities.
```

Without regex, it only replaces the first encounter. This time, let's see it with the g global modifier:

```
let text = "Coding is fun. Coding opens up a lot of opportunities.";
console.log(text.replace(/Coding/g, "JavaScript"));
```

The result is as follows:

```
JavaScript is fun. JavaScript opens up a lot of opportunities.
```

As you can see, all occurrences are replaced.

Practice exercise 12.1

Find and replace strings. The following exercise involves replacing characters in a specified string value. The first input field will indicate which character string will be replaced, and the second input field will indicate which characters will replace them once the button is clicked.

Use the HTML below as a template, and add the JavaScript needed to complete the task:

```
<!doctype html>
<html>

<head>
    <title>Complete JavaScript Course</title>
</head>

<body>
    <div id="output">Complete JavaScript Course</div>
    Search for:
    <input id="sText" type="text">
    <br> Replace with:
    <input id="rText" type="text">
    <br>
    <button>Replace</button>
    <script>

    </script>
</body>

</html>
```

Take the following steps:

1. Select each of the three page elements using JavaScript and assign the element objects as variables so that they can be easily referenced in your code.

2. Add an event listener to the button to invoke a function when clicked.

3. Create a function named lookup() that will find and replace the text in the output element. Assign the output element's text content to a variable named s, and then assign the value of the input we are replacing to another variable named rt.

4. Create a new regex with the value of the first input field, which will allow you to replace the text. Using the regex, check for a match with the match() method. Wrap this with a condition that will execute a block of code if matches are found.

5. If the match is found, use replace() to set the new value.

6. Update the output area with the newly created and updated text output.

Email validation

In order to create a regex pattern, we need to be able to describe the pattern with words first. Email addresses consist of five parts, in the form of [name]@[domain].[extension].

Here are the five parts explained:

1. name: One or more alphanumerical characters, underscores, dashes, or dots
2. @: Literal character
3. domain: One or more alphanumerical characters, underscores, dashes, or dots
4. .: Literal dot
5. extension: One or more alphanumerical characters, underscores, dashes, or dots

So, let's do the steps for regex:

1. [a-zA-Z0-9._-]+
2. @
3. [a-zA-Z0-9._-]+
4. \. (remember, the dot is a special character in regex, so we need to escape it)
5. [a-zA-Z0-9._-]+

Putting it all together:

/([a-zA-Z0-9._-]+@[a-zA-Z0-9._-]+\.[a-zA-Z0-9._-]+)/g

Let's look at this regex in action:

```
let emailPattern = /([a-zA-Z0-9._-]+@[a-zA-Z0-9._-]+\.[a-zA-Z0-9._-
]+)/g;
let validEmail = "maaike_1234@email.com";
let invalidEmail = "maaike@mail@.com";
console.log(validEmail.match(emailPattern));
console.log(invalidEmail.match(emailPattern));
```

We tested the pattern on both a valid and an invalid email address, and this is the output:

```
[ 'maaike_1234@email.com' ]
null
```

As you can see, it returns a result for the valid email and it returns null (no match) for the invalid email.

Practice exercise 12.2

Create an application that uses JavaScript to check whether the string value of an input is a validly formatted email using regex. Look at the following template:

```
<!doctype html>
<html>
<head>
    <title>JavaScript Course</title>
</head>
<body>
    <div class="output"></div>
    <input type="text" placeholder="Enter Email">
    <button>Check</button>
    <script>

    </script>
</body>
</html>
```

Take the following steps:

1. Use the above template code to start creating your application. Within the JavaScript code, select the input, output, and button elements from the page as JavaScript objects.

2. Add an event listener to the button to run a block of code when clicked that will get the current value in the input field. Create a blank response value that will populate the output div element contents.

3. Add a test with the string value from the input field and the expression for email format. If the test result is false, update the response output to say Invalid Email and change the output color to red.

4. If the condition of the test returns true, add a response that confirms the email format is correct and change the text color of output to green.

5. Output the response value into the output element.

Functions and the arguments object

JavaScript deals with arguments in functions by adding them to a custom object called arguments. This object works a lot like an array, and we can use it instead of using the name of the parameter. Consider the following code:

```
function test(a, b, c) {
  console.log("first:", a, arguments[0]);
  console.log("second:", b, arguments[1]);
  console.log("third:", c, arguments[2]);
}

test("fun", "js", "secrets");
```

This outputs:

```
first: fun fun
second: js js
third: secrets secrets
```

When you update one of the parameters, the argument gets changed accordingly. The same goes for the other way around;

```
function test(a, b, c) {
  a = "nice";
  arguments[1] = "JavaScript";
  console.log("first:", a, arguments[0]);
  console.log("second:", b, arguments[1]);
  console.log("third:", c, arguments[2]);
}

test("fun", "js", "secrets");
```

This is going to change both arguments[0] and b, as they are related to a and arguments[1], respectively, as you can see in the output:

```
first: nice nice
second: JavaScript JavaScript
third: secrets secrets
```

If the function is called with more arguments than were declared in the function signature, this is the way to access them. However, the modern way is to use the rest parameter (...param) instead of the arguments object.

In case you've forgotten what the rest parameter is, you can revisit the rest parameter in *Chapter 6, Functions*.

Practice exercise 12.3

This exercise will demonstrate using the array-like `arguments` object and extracting values from it. Using the `arguments` length property, we will iterate through the items in the arguments and return the last item in the list:

1. Create a function without any parameters. Create a loop to iterate through the length of the `arguments` object. This will allow an iteration of each item of the arguments in the function.

2. Set up a variable called `lastOne` with a blank value.

3. As you loop through the arguments, set `lastOne` to the current value of the argument using the index of `i` to return the argument value. The argument will have an index value that can be used to reference the value as you iterate through the `arguments` object.

4. Return the value of `lastOne`, which should only return the last argument value as the response.

5. Output the response from the function, pass a number of arguments into the function, and console log the response result. You should see only the last item in the list. If you want to see each one, you can output them separately to the console as you look through the values, or construct an array that can then be returned, adding each one as you go through the arguments.

JavaScript hoisting

In *Chapter 6, Functions*, we discussed that we have three different variables, `const`, `let`, and `var`, and we highly recommended that you should use `let` instead of `var` because of their different scopes. JavaScript **hoisting** is why. Hoisting is the principle of moving declarations of variables to the top of the scope in which they are defined. This allows you to do things that you cannot do in many other languages, and for good reason by the way. This should look normal:

```
var x;
x = 5;
console.log(x);
```

It just logs 5. But thanks to hoisting, so does this:

```
x = 5;
console.log(x);
var x;
```

If you try to do this with `let`, you'll get a `ReferenceError`. This is why it is better to use `let`. Because clearly, this behavior is very hard to read, unpredictable, and you don't really need it.

The reason this happens is that the JavaScript interpreter moves all the var declarations to the top of the file before processing the file. Only the declarations, not the initializations. This is why you get a result of `undefined` if you use it before having initialized it. And this is why it should be initialized before it has been declared. It was designed this way for memory allocation, but the side effects are undesirable.

However, there is a way to turn this behavior off. Let's see how we can do so in the next section!

Using strict mode

We can change the understanding and forgiving behavior of JavaScript to some extent using strict mode. You can switch on strict mode with the following command in your code. This needs to be the first command of your code:

```
"use strict";
```

Here is something that works when we don't use strict mode:

```
function sayHi() {
    greeting = "Hello!";
    console.log(greeting);
}

sayHi();
```

We forgot to declare `greeting`, so JavaScript did it for us by adding a `greeting` variable to the top level and it will log `Hello!`. If we enable strict mode, however, this will give an error:

```
"use strict";

function sayHi() {
```

```
    greeting = "Hello!";
    console.log(greeting);
}

  sayHi();
```

The error:

```
ReferenceError: greeting is not defined
```

You can also use strict mode only in a particular function: simply add it to the top of the function and it gets enabled for that function only. Strict mode alters a few other things too; for example, when using strict mode, there are fewer words that can be used as names for your variables and functions because they are likely to become reserved keywords in the future that JavaScript will need for its own language.

Using strict mode is a great way of getting used to using JavaScript in the setting of frameworks or even for writing TypeScript later. It is typically considered a good practice nowadays, so we would encourage you to use this in your own code when you have the chance. This is often not an (easy) option when working with existing older code though.

Now we have seen strict mode, it's time to dive into a whole different mode: debug mode! Debug mode is for when you are not busy writing or running your application, but are running it in a special way to spot the locations of any errors.

Debugging

Debugging is a delicate art. In the beginning, it usually is very hard to spot what's wrong with your code. If you are using JavaScript in the browser and it is not behaving as you would expect, step 1 is always to open the console in the browser. Often it will contain errors that can help you further.

If that doesn't solve it, you can log to the console in every step of your code, and also log the variables. This will give you some insight as to what is going on. It might just be that you are relying on a certain variable that happens to be undefined. Or perhaps you are expecting a certain value from a mathematical computation, but you've made an error and the result is something completely different from what you thought. Using `console.log()` during development to see what's happening is rather common.

Breakpoints

A more professional way to go about debugging is to use breakpoints. This can be done from most browsers and IDEs. You click on the line before your code (in the **Sources** panel in Chrome, but this may be different for different browsers), and a dot or arrow will appear. When your application is running, it will pause at this point to give you the opportunity to inspect the values of variables and walk through the code line by line from there.

This way, you will get a good clue of what is going on and how to fix it. Here is how to use breakpoints in Chrome, and most other browsers have something like this. In Chrome, go to the **Sources** tab of the **Inspect** panel. Select the file you want to set a breakpoint in. Then you just click on the line number and it sets the breakpoint:

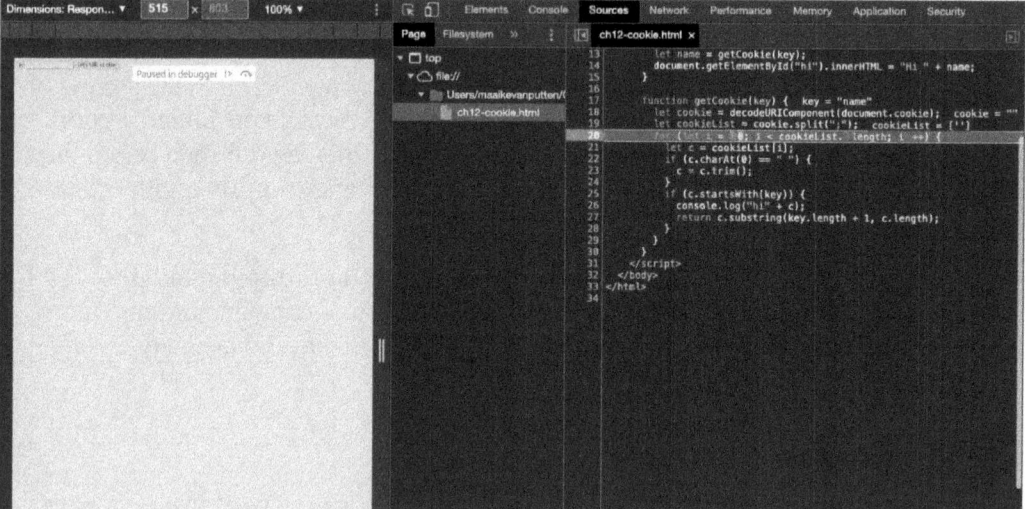

Figure 12.1: Breakpoints in the browser

Then try to trigger the line of code, and when it gets triggered, it pauses. On the very right of the screen I can inspect all the variables and values:

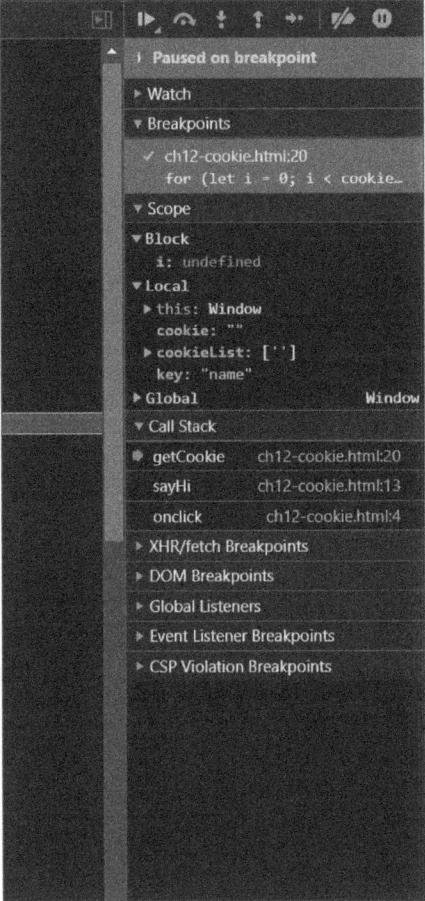

Figure 12.2: Inspecting breakpoint variables

You can now go through your code with a fine-toothed comb: with the play icon on top, you can resume script execution (until it hits the next breakpoint or runs in to the same breakpoint again). With the round arrow icon at the top, I can go to the next line and inspect the values on the next line again.

> There are many options with breakpoints that we don't have space to cover here. For more detail on how you can debug your code with breakpoints, look in your chosen code editor's documentation or check the relevant Google Chrome documentation here: `https://developer.chrome.com/docs/devtools/javascript/breakpoints/`.

Practice exercise 12.4

Variable values can be tracked in the editor while debugging. The following exercise will demonstrate how to use the editor's breakpoints to check a value of a variable at a certain point in the running of the script. This is a simple example, but the same process can be used to find out information about larger scripts at specific points during execution, or establish where a problem may lie.

> There are minor differences and nuances in the way breakpoints operate in different editors, so please refer to the documentation of your environment for more of a detailed walk-through — this is intended to give you an idea of what breakpoints offer when it comes to debugging.

You can use the following short script as an example:

```
let val = 5;
val += adder();
val += adder();
val += adder();
console.log(val);
function adder(){
    let counter = val;
    for(let i=0;i<val;i++){
        counter++;
    }
return counter ;
}
```

Remember to add <script> tags and open the script as an HTML document if you're testing this in your browser console.

This exercise has been tested in a desktop editor but it is equally relevant to browser consoles and other environments. Take the following steps:

1. Open your script in your chosen editor, or the **Sources** tab of your browser's **Inspect** panel. Click to the left of the line of code where you want to add a breakpoint. A dot or other indicator will appear to indicate the breakpoint is set:

```
 1    let val = 5;
 2    val += adder();
 3    val += adder();
 4    val += adder();
 5    console.log(val);
 6    function adder(){
 7        let counter = val;
 8        for(let i=0;i<val;i++){
 9            counter++;
10        }
11        return counter ;
12    }
```

Figure 12.3: Setting breakpoints

2. Run the code with your new breakpoints: I have selected **Run | Start Debugging**, but this will vary depending on your editor. You can simply reload the web page if you're using the browser console to rerun the code with your new breakpoints accounted for:

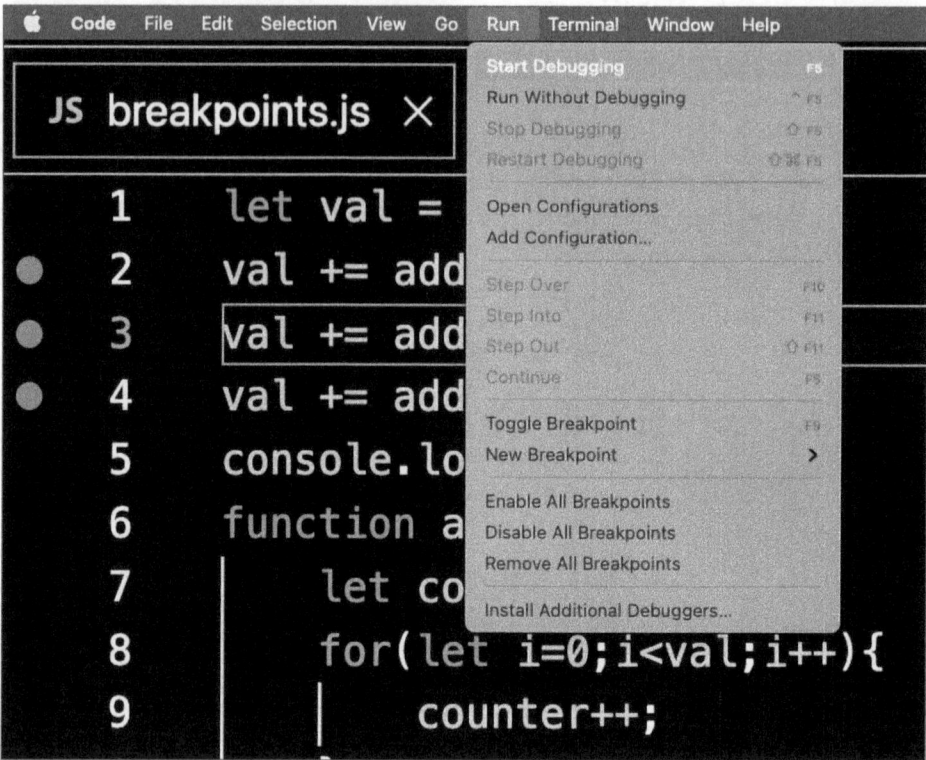

Figure 12.4: Running code with breakpoints added

3. You should now see the debugging console. There will be a tab that lists the variables in the code and the current values at the first breakpoint. It's called **VARIABLES** in my editor, but it's the **Scope** tab in the Chrome browser console.

4. You can use the menu options to move to the next breakpoint, stop debugging, or restart the breakpoint sequence. Press the play icon to move to the next breakpoint. It will update to have a value of 5, as specified by line 1, and pause at the first breakpoint. Note that the highlighted line has not been run yet:

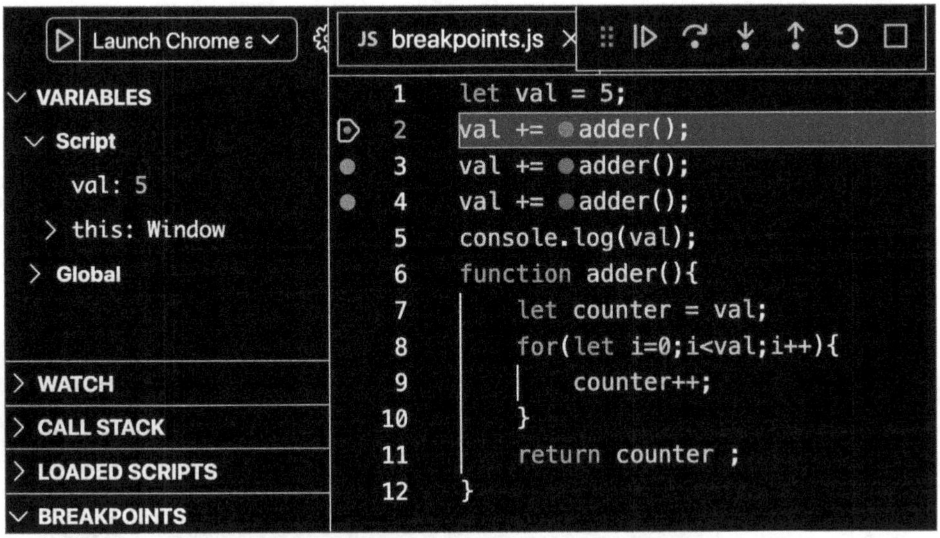

Figure 12.5: Viewing variables in the console

5. Press the play icon once more, and the script will run until it hits the next breakpoint, at which point the value of the variable will update as a result of the code on line 2:

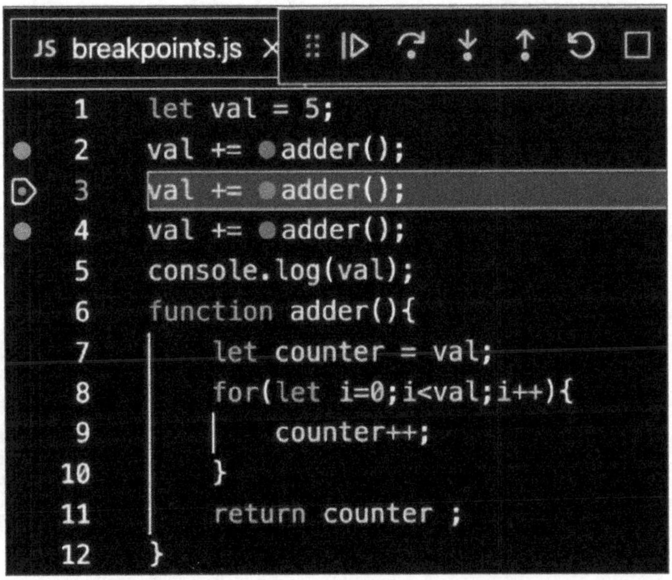

Figure 12.6: Progressing through breakpoints in a script

6. Press play again to move to the next breakpoint, which increases the value of val once more:

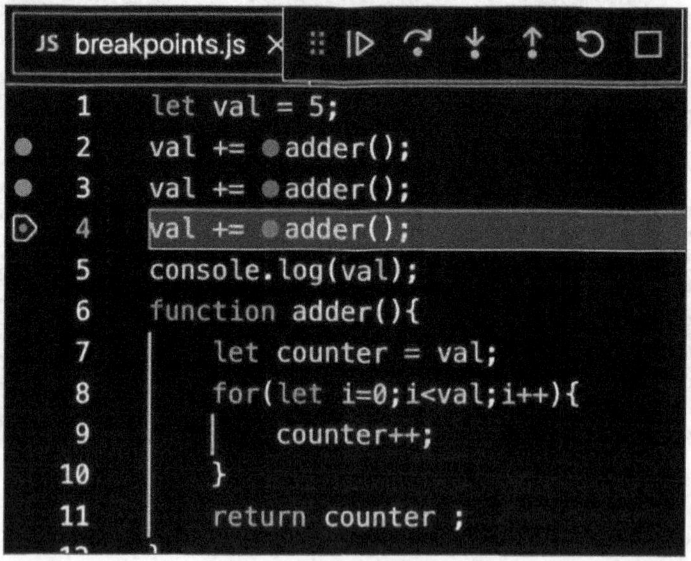

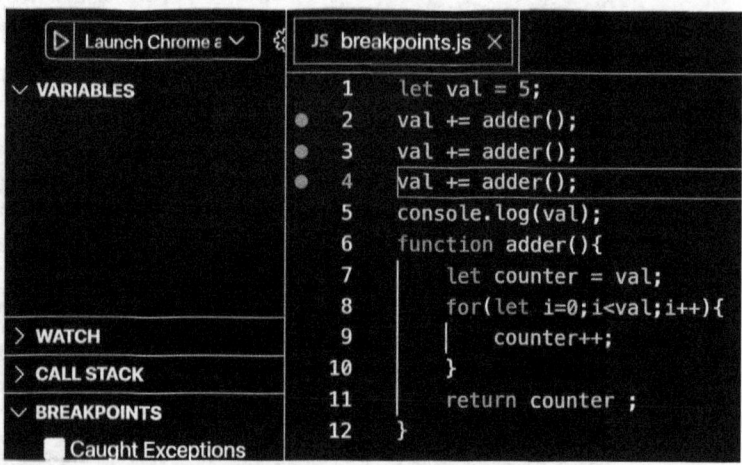

Figure 12.7: The final breakpoint

7. Once the last breakpoint is reached you will only see options to restart or stop the debugger. If you press stop, it will end the debugging process:

Figure 12.8: Breakpoints in the browser

The final value of val after the third breakpoint was revealed as 135. Write down the values of val after the first and second calls to the adder() function, which were revealed to you by using breakpoints.

This was a basic exercise, but we invite you to test out using breakpoints on some larger scripts and get more comfortable in your understanding of how your code works during runtime.

Error handling

We have seen a lot of errors appear already. Until now, we let the program crash when it encountered an error. There are other ways to deal with errors. When we are dealing with code that depends on some sort of outside input, such as an API, user input, or a file we will need to deal with the errors that this input can cause.

If we expect a certain piece of code to throw an error, we can surround this code with a catch block. The error it might throw will be caught in this block.

You have to be careful not to use this too much, and you usually don't want to do this when you can just write better code to avoid the error in the first place.

Here is an example of a piece of code that throws an error, and is surrounded with a try and catch block. Let's assume the somethingVeryDangerous() function might throw errors:

```
try {
  somethingVeryDangerous();
} catch (e) {
  if (e instanceof TypeError) {
    // deal with TypeError exceptions
  } else if (e instanceof RangeError) {
    // deal with RangeError exceptions
  } else if (e instanceof EvalError) {
    // deal with EvalError exceptions
  } else {
    //deal with all other exceptions
    throw e; //rethrow
  }
}
```

If it throws an error, it will end up in the catch block. Since Error could mean many different errors, we are going to check for the exact error we are dealing with and write a specific handling of this error. We check the exact error class with the instanceof operator. After the error handling, the rest of the code will continue to execute normally.

You can do one more thing with a try catch block, and that is add a finally block. This finally block gets executed irrespective of whether errors are thrown. This is great for cleanup purposes. Here is a simple example:

```
try {
    trySomething();
} catch (e) {
    console.log("Oh oh");
} finally {
    console.log("Error or no error, I will be logged!");
}
```

We don't know the output of this code, since trySomething() is not defined. If it were to throw an error, it would log Oh oh to the console and then Error or no error, I will be logged!. If trySomething() didn't throw an error, it would only log the last part.

Lastly, if, for whatever reason, you need to throw an error, you can do so with the throw keyword, like this:

```
function somethingVeryDangerous() {
    throw RangeError();
}
```

This can be of great use whenever you need to deal with things out of your control, such as an API response, user input, or input from reading a file. If unexpected things happen, sometimes you'll have to throw an error to deal with it appropriately.

Practice exercise 12.5

1. Using throw, try, and catch, check if the value is a number, and if it's not, then create a custom error.

2. Create a function with one argument called val.

3. Use try, and within it add a condition that checks whether val is a number using isNaN. If true, then throw an error that states that it is not a number. Otherwise, output Got a number to the console.

4. Use `catch` to catch any errors and output the error values to the console.

5. Add `finally` to run and output the value, and when the function has completed, also include the value of `val`.

6. Create one request to the function with a string argument and another with a number. See the results in the console.

Using cookies

Cookies are small data files that are stored on your own computer and used by websites. Cookies were invented to store things about the user of the website. Cookies are strings with a special pattern. They contain key-value pairs, and these key-value pairs are separated by semi-colons.

You can create a cookie and use it again later. Here is how you can create a cookie:

```
document.cookie = "name=Maaike;favoriteColor=black";
```

This does not work in all browsers when you run it on the client side (such as in your `<script>` tag). In Chrome, for example, you cannot set the cookies from the client side. You have to run the code from a server. (I have used Safari instead to do this here, but there are no guarantees about future support.) An alternative is the web storage API.

It is also possible to start Chrome from the command line with certain settings enabled, or to enable the cookies in the settings under privacy preferences. Careful to turn this off afterward if you don't want it, though. This is how you can read from the cookie:

```
let cookie = decodeURIComponent(document.cookie);
let cookieList = cookie.split(";");
for (let i = 0; i < cookieList.length; i++) {
  let c = cookieList[i];
  if (c.charAt(0) == " ") {
    c = c.trim();
  }
  if (c.startsWith("name")) {
    alert(c.substring(5, c.length));
  }
}
```

This example gets all the cookies using `decodeURIComponent()`, and then splits them on the `;`. This leaves us with an array, `cookieList`, with key-value pairs as strings. Next, we loop over all the key-value pairs. Trim them (remove the whitespace in front and at the back), and see whether they start with name. This was the name of our cookie key.

If we want to get the value, we have to start reading after the key, so at least the length of the key, which is 4 (name) in this case. This brings us to index 3 already. We also want to skip the equal sign on index 4, so we start at index 5. In this case, we are adding an alert to the name. Here is an example of a simple website that uses a cookie to greet the user:

```html
<!DOCTYPE html>
<html>
  <body>
    <input onchange="setCookie(this)" />
    <button onclick="sayHi('name')">Let's talk, cookie!</button>
    <p id="hi"></p>

    <script>
      function setCookie(e) {
        document.cookie = "name=" + e.value + ";";
      }

      function sayHi(key) {
        let name = getCookie(key);
        document.getElementById("hi").innerHTML = "Hi " + name;
      }

      function getCookie(key) {
        let cookie = decodeURIComponent(document.cookie);
        let cookieList = cookie.split(";");
        for (let i = 0; i < cookieList.length; i++) {
          let c = cookieList[i];
          if (c.charAt(0) == " ") {
            c = c.trim();
          }
          if (c.startsWith(key)) {
            console.log("hi" + c);
            return c.substring(key.length + 1, c.length);
          }
        }
      }
```

```
        </script>
    </body>
</html>
```

If you are writing a new website, you probably should not be using this. However, whenever you need to work with older code, chances are you'll come across this. And now you know what it means and how to adjust it. Good for you!

Practice exercise 12.6

Let's make a cookie builder. Create several functions that will allow you to interact with page cookies, including reading a cookie value by name, creating a new cookie using a name and setting it for a set number of days, and deleting a cookie. You can use the following HTML template to get you started:

```
<!doctype html>
<html>
<head>
    <title>Complete JavaScript Course</title>
</head>
<body>
    <script>

    </script>
</body>
</html>
```

Take the following steps:

1. Set up your webpage, and in the JavaScript code, output the value of `document.cookie`. It should be blank.

2. Create a function that will take the parameters for `cookieName`, `cookieValue`, and the number of days you want to set the cookie.

3. Check if `days` is valid, and within the block of valid code, get the current date. Set a `setTime` value for the cookie to expire in milliseconds by multiplying the days into milliseconds.

4. Change the date object of milliseconds until the cookie expires to a UTC string value.

5. Set `document.cookie` to `cookieName` = `cookieValue`, plus add the expiry details and lastly specify `path=/`.

6. Create a function to create a test cookie with a value and expiry set after a number of days. Create a second cookie the same way, and when you refresh your page, you should see at least two cookies in the console.

7. Create a second function to read a cookie value, set the value as `false`, and then create an array of the cookies split by semi-colons.

8. Loop through all the cookies and split again where the equal signs are. This will give you the first item with index 0 as the name of the cookie. Add a condition to check if the name is equal to the name that was requested in the function parameters. If it matches, assign the value of the second item in the index, which will be the value of the cookie with the selected name. Return `cookievalue` in the function.

9. Add two console log messages using the function to read both cookies you have set earlier. Output the values of the cookies in the console.

10. To delete a cookie, you need to set a date prior to the current date. You can create a cookie with a `-1` date and send the cookie with its selected name to be deleted by invoking the cookie creation function.

11. Try deleting a cookie by name.

Local storage

We have looked at cookies as a way to save user data, but there is actually a more modern way to do this: **local storage**. Local storage is an amazing fun topic that will add to your ability to make smart websites. With local storage, we can save key-value pairs in our web browser and use them again in a new session (when the browser is opened again later). The information is typically stored in a folder on the computer of the user, but this differs a bit by browser.

This allows the website to store some information and retrieve it later, even after refreshing the page or closing the browser. The advantage of local storage over cookies is that they don't need to be passed around with every HTTP request, which is the case with cookies. Local storage just lives there and waits to be accessed.

The `localStorage` object is a property of the `window` object that we have seen before. There are a few methods on the `localStorage` object that we need to know to use it effectively. First of all, we need to be able to get and set key-value pairs on local storage. We use `setItem()` whenever we want to save something and `getItem()` whenever we want to retrieve the value later. Here is how to do it:

```
<!DOCTYPE html>
<html>
  <body>
```

```
    <div id="stored"></div>
    <script>
      let message = "Hello storage!";
      localStorage.setItem("example", message);

      if (localStorage.getItem("example")) {
        document.getElementById("stored").innerHTML =
          localStorage.getItem("example");
      }
    </script>
  </body>
</html>
```

This code snippet outputs Hello storage! on the page. You can add items to
storage by specifying a key and a value with the setItem method. You can access
localStorage directly or via the window object. Here we specify example as the key
and Hello storage! as the value and save it to local storage. Then we check whether
the example key is set in local storage and output the data by writing it to the
innerHTML of the div with the ID stored.

If you go back to your code and turn off the setItem() line before loading the page
a second time, it still will output that value, since the information was stored when
running the script the first time and never got deleted. Local storage doesn't expire,
though it can be manually deleted.

We can also retrieve a key using the index. This is useful whenever we need to loop
through the key-value pairs and we don't know the names of the keys. This is how to
retrieve a key by index:

```
window.localStorage.key(0);
```

In this case, the key is name. In order to get the associated value, we can do this:

```
window.localStorage.getItem(window.localStorage.key(0));
```

We can also remove key-value pairs like this:

```
window.localStorage.removeItem("name");
```

And we can remove all the key-value pairs from the local storage in one call:

```
window.localStorage.clear();
```

So, with local storage you can save values even after closing the browser. This allows for a lot of "smart" behavior, since your app is now able to remember things, such as what you've entered in a form, which settings you've toggled on a website, and what you've looked at previously.

Please don't see this as an alternative that you can use to bypass the problems with cookies and privacy. Local storage raises the exact same issues as cookies, it's just less known. You will still have to mention on your website that you are tracking users and storing information, just like you need to do for cookies.

Practice exercise 12.7

Let's create a local storage shopping list that will store values in the browser's local storage. This is an example of using JavaScript to convert from strings to useable JavaScript objects and back to strings that can be stored in local storage. You can use the following template:

```html
<!doctype html>
<html>
<head>
    <title>JavaScript</title>
    <style>
        .ready {
            background-color: #ddd;
            color: red;
            text-decoration: line-through;
        }
    </style>
</head>
<body>
    <div class="main">
        <input placeholder="New Item" value="test item" maxlength="30">
        <button>Add</button>
    </div>
    <ul class="output">
    </ul>
    <script>

    </script>
</body>
</html>
```

Take the following steps:

1. In the JavaScript code, select all the page elements as JavaScript objects.
2. Create a `tasks` array with a value of the local `tasklist` storage if it exists, otherwise set the `tasks` array to an empty array. Using `JSON.parse`, you can convert the string value to a useable object in JavaScript.
3. Loop through all the items in the `tasklist` array; they will be stored as objects, with a name and a Boolean value for their checked status. Create a separate function to build the task item, adding it to the page from the list.
4. In the task generation function, create a new list item and a `textNode`. Append `textNode` to the list item. Append the list item to the page output area. If the task is marked complete with a Boolean value of `true`, then add the `style` class of ready.
5. Add an event listener to the list item that will toggle the ready class when clicked. Every time there is a change to any list item, you will also need to store that to the local storage. Create a task builder function that will store and ensure the visual list is the same as the local storage list. You will need to clear the current task list array and rebuild from the visual data, so create a function to handle the list building.
6. The task builder function will clear the current `tasks` array, and select all the `li` elements on the page. Loop through all the list items, getting the text value from the element, and checking if it contains the class of ready. If it contains the ready class, then mark the checked condition as true. Add the results to the `tasks` array, and this will rebuild the array to ensure it matches with what the user sees visually. Send to a save tasks function to save the `tasks` array in local storage, so if the page is refreshed, you will see the same list.
7. In the save tasks function, set the `localstorage` item to the tasks array. You will need to stringify the object so that it can go into the string parameter of local storage.
8. Now, when you refresh the page, you will see the list of tasks. They can be crossed out by clicking them and new items can be added in the input field by pressing the button to submit new items.

JSON

JSON stands for **JavaScript Object Notation**, which is nothing more than a data format. We saw this notation when we were creating our objects in JavaScript; however, JSON doesn't mean JavaScript objects, it's just a way of representing data using a similar format as JavaScript objects. It can also be easily converted to a JavaScript object.

JSON is a standard used to communicate with APIs, including APIs that aren't written in JavaScript! APIs can accept data, for example, the data from a form on a website, in JSON format. And nowadays, APIs almost always send data back in JSON. Sending data from an API happens, for example, when you enter a web shop—the products typically come from a call to an API that is connected to a database. This data gets converted to JSON and is sent back to the website. Here is an example of JSON:

```json
{
    "name" : "Malika",
    "age" : 50,
    "profession" : "programmer",
    "languages" : ["JavaScript", "C#", "Python"],
    "address" : {
      "street" : "Some street",
      "number" : 123,
      "zipcode" : "3850AA",
      "city" : "Utrecht",
      "country" : "The Netherlands"
    }
}
```

This is an object that seems to describe a person. It has key-value pairs. The keys always have to be between quotes, but the values only have to be between quotes when they are strings. So, the first key is name and the first value is Malika.

Lists of values (or JavaScript arrays) are indicated with [ ]. The JSON object contains a list of languages, which has the square brackets, and another object, address. You can tell this by the curly brackets.

There are actually only a few flavours in JSON:

- Key-value pairs with values of the following types: string, number, Boolean, and null
- Key-value pairs with lists, which have [and] that contain the items in the list
- Key-value pairs with other objects, which have { and } that contain other JSON elements

These three options can be combined, so an object can contain other objects and a list can contain other lists. We saw this already in the above example. Our object contained a nested address object.

But this can be nested even further. A list can also contain objects, which can contain lists with objects, with lists, and so on. This might sound a bit complicated and that's exactly the point. Even though it is very simple, nesting all these options can still complicate JSON a bit. There is a reason we've placed it in our advanced topic chapter.

Let's now have a look at a slightly more complex example:

```
{
    "companies": [
        {
            "name": "JavaScript Code Dojo",
            "addresses": [
                {
                    "street": "123 Main street",
                    "zipcode": 12345,
                    "city" : "Scott"
                },
                {
                    "street": "123 Side street",
                    "zipcode": 35401,
                    "city" : "Tuscaloosa"
                }
            ]
        },
        {
            "name": "Python Code Dojo",
            "addresses": [
                {
                    "street": "123 Party street",
                    "zipcode": 68863,
                    "city" : "Nebraska"
                },
                {
                    "street": "123 Monty street",
                    "zipcode": 33306,
                    "city" : "Florida"
                }
            ]
        }
    ]
}
```

This is a list of companies, with two company objects on it. The companies have two key-value pairs: a name and an address list. Each of the address lists contains two addresses, and each address consists of three key-value pairs: `street`, `zipcode` and `city`.

Practice exercise 12.8

This exercise will demonstrate how you can create a valid JSON object that can be used as a JavaScript object. You will create a simple list of names and statuses that can be looped through and output the results to the console. You will load JSON data to JavaScript and output the results of the object's contents:

1. Create a JavaScript object that contains JSON formatted data. The object should contain at least two items and each item should be an object with at least two paired values.

2. Create a function that can be invoked that will loop through each item in the JavaScript JSON object and output the result to the console. Output each item of data to the console using `console.log`.

3. Invoke the function and launch the JavaScript code.

Parsing JSON

There are many libraries and tools available for parsing a JSON string into an object. A JavaScript string can be converted to a JSON object using the `JSON.parse()` function. Data that is received from another place is always of value `string`, so in order to treat it as an object, it needs to be converted. This is how to do it:

```
let str = "{\"name\": \"Maaike\", \"age\": 30}";
let obj = JSON.parse(str);
console.log(obj.name, "is", obj.age);
```

After parsing, it can be treated as an object. Therefore it will log `Maaike is 30` to the console.

The other way around is also necessary sometimes. Objects can be converted to a JSON string using the `JSON.stringify()` method. It converts the object or value from JavaScript to a JSON string. You can see it in action here:

```
let dog = {
    "name": "wiesje",
    "breed": "dachshund"
};
```

```
let strdog = JSON.stringify(dog);
console.log(typeof strdog);
console.log(strdog);
```

The type of strdog becomes a string because it is being stringified. And it no longer has the properties name and breed. These will be undefined. This code snippet will log the following to the console:

```
string
{"name":"wiesje","breed":"dachshund"}
```

This can be useful for storing JSON data directly in a database, for example.

Practice exercise 12.9

This exercise will demonstrate the use of JSON methods to parse JSON and convert string values to JSON. Using JSON methods with JavaScript, convert a JSON formatted string value to a JavaScript object and convert a JavaScript object into a string representation of the JSON object:

1. Create a JSON object with several items and objects. You can use the JSON object from the previous lesson.

2. Using the JSON stringify() method, convert the JSON JavaScript object into a string version and assign it to a variable named newStr [{"name":"Learn JavaScript","status":true},{"name":"Try JSON","status":false}].

3. Using JSON.parse(), convert the newStr value back into an object and assign it to a variable named newObj.

4. Iterate through the items in the newObj and output the results to the console.

Practice exercise 12.9 answers

```
let myList = [{
    "name": "Learn JavaScript",
    "status": true
},
{
    "name": "Try JSON",
    "status": false
}
];
```

```
const newStr = JSON.stringify(myList);
const newObj = JSON.parse(newStr);
newObj.forEach((el)=>{
    console.log(el);
});
```

Chapter projects

Email extractor

Use the following HTML as a starter template and add the JavaScript code to make an email extractor function:

```
<!doctype html>
<html>
<head>
    <title>Complete JavaScript Course</title>
</head>
<body>
    <textarea name="txtarea" rows=2 cols=50></textarea> <button>Get
Emails</button>
    <textarea name="txtarea2" rows=2 cols=50></textarea>
    <script>

    </script>
</body>
</html>
```

Take the following steps:

1. In JavaScript, select both text areas and the button and set them as JavaScript objects.

2. Add an event listener to the button that will invoke a function that gets the content of the first textarea and filters it to only accept email addresses.

3. Within the extracting function, get the content of the first input field. Using match(), return an array of the email addresses that were matched from within the content from the first textarea.

4. To remove any duplicates, create a separate array that will hold only unique values.

5. Loop through all the email addresses found and check whether each one is already in the `holder` array, and if not, add it.

6. Using the `join()` array method, you can now join together the results of the email addresses found within the content and output it into the second `textarea`.

Form validator

This project is an example of a typical form structure where you check the values inputted into the form and validate them before the content gets submitted. A response is returned to the user if the values do not meet the validation criteria in the code. Use the following HTML and CSS as a starting template:

```
<!doctype html>
<html>
<head>
    <title>JavaScript Course</title>
    <style>
        .hide {
            display: none;
        }
        .error {
            color: red;
            font-size: 0.8em;
            font-family: sans-serif;
            font-style: italic;
        }
        input {
            border-color: #ddd;
            width: 400px;
            display: block;
            font-size: 1.5em;
        }
    </style>
</head>
<body>
    <form name="myform"> Email :
        <input type="text" name="email"> <span class="error hide"></
span>
```

```
        <br> Password :
        <input type="password" name="password"> <span class="error
hide"></span>
        <br> User Name :
        <input type="text" name="userName"> <span class="error hide"></
span>
        <br>
        <input type="submit" value="Sign Up"> </form>
    <script>

    </script>
</body>
</html>
```

Take the following steps:

1. Using JavaScript, select all the page elements and set them as JavaScript objects so they are easier to select within the code. Also select all the page elements that have the error class as an object.

2. Add an event listener to submit and capture the click, preventing the default form action.

3. Loop through all the page elements that have a class error and add the hide class, which will remove them from view since this is a new submission.

4. Using the regular expression for valid emails, test the results against the input value of the email field.

5. Create a function to respond to errors, which removes the hide class from the element next to the element that triggered the event. Apply focus to that element within the function.

6. If there is an error that an input does not match the desired regex, pass the parameters to the error handling function you just created.

7. Check the password field input value to ensure only letters and numbers are used. Also check the length to ensure that it is 3-8 characters. If either are false, then add the error with the error function and create a message for the user. Set the error Boolean to true.

8. Add in an object to track the form data creation and add values to the object by looping through all the inputs, setting the property name to be the same as the input name, and the value the same as the input value.

9. Before the end of the validation function, check if an error is still present, and if it is not, submit the form object.

Simple math quiz

In this project, we will create a math quiz that will allow the user to respond to math questions. The application will check the responses and score the accuracy of the user's answers to the questions. You can use the following HTML template:

```html
<!doctype html>
<html>
<head>
    <title>Complete JavaScript Course</title>
</head>
<body>
    <span class="val1"></span> <span>+</span> <span class="val2"></span> = <span>
        <input type="text" name="answer"></span><button>Check</button>
    <div class="output"></div>
</body>
</html>
```

Take the following steps:

1. In JavaScript, wrap the code within a function, app. Within the app function, create variable objects to contain all the page elements so they can be used in the script, and create a blank object called game.

2. Add a DOMContentLoaded event listener that invokes the app initialization once the page loads.

3. Within an init() function, add an event listener to the button, listen for a click, and track the event into a function called checker. Also within the init function, load another function called loadQuestion().

4. Create a function to load the questions, and another function that can generate a random number from min and max values in the arguments.

5. In the loadQuestion() function, generate two random values and add them to the game object. Calculate the result of both values added together and assign that value within the game object as well.

6. Assign and update the textContent of the page elements that require the dynamic number values for the calculation question.

7. When the button is clicked, use a ternary operator to determine whether the answer to the question was correct or incorrect. Set the color to green for correct, and to red for incorrect.

8. Create a page element to output all the questions and keep track of the results. Within the `checker()` function, append a new element to the HTML with a style color to indicate a correct or incorrect response. Display the first and second values as well as the answer, and show the user's response within brackets.

9. Clear the input field and load the next question.

Self-check quiz

1. What will the following regex expression return from the following words?

    ```
    Expression / ([a-e])\w+/g
    "Hope you enjoy JavaScript"
    ```

2. Are cookies part of the document object?

3. What will the following code do to a JavaScript cookie?

    ```
    const mydate = new Date();
    mydate.setTime(mydate.getTime() - 1);
    document.cookie = "username=; expires=" + mydate.toGMTString();
    ```

4. What is the output in the console from the following code?

    ```
    const a = "hello world";
    (function () {
        const a = "JavaScript";
    })();
    console.log(a);
    ```

5. What is the output in the console from the following code?

    ```
    <script>
    "use strict";
    myFun();
    console.log(a);
    function myFun() {
        a = "Hello World";
    }
    </script>
    ```

6. What is the output of the following code?

```
console.log("a");
setTimeout(() => {
    console.log("b");
}, 0);
console.log("c");
```

Summary

In this chapter, we had some important, more advanced topics that we still had to cover, but that you were probably not ready for earlier in the book. After this chapter, you should have deepened your understanding of JavaScript in several areas, first and foremost, regular expressions. With regex, we can specify patterns of strings and we can use these to search other strings for matches to our patterns.

We also considered functions and the `arguments` object, with which we can access arguments by their index. We continued with a look at JavaScript hoisting and strict mode, which enables us to use JavaScript with a few more rules. Getting used to JavaScript in strict mode is generally a good practice and is great preparation for working with JavaScript frameworks.

Debugging and tweaking were also discussed: we can use breakpoints or log our output to the console to get an idea of what is going on. Handling errors well can prevent unnecessary crashes of our program. Finally, we looked at JavaScript cookie creation and the use of local storage, along with the use of JSON, a syntax for sending data around. We saw the different types of key-value pairs and how to parse JSON. We also saw how to store key-value pairs in the `localStorage` object of `window`.

This chapter has deepened our understanding of JavaScript, and we learned some new things we need to know for modern JavaScript, but also a lot for when dealing with old (legacy) code. In the next chapter, we'll dive into an even more advanced topic: concurrency. This topic is about multitasking with your JavaScript code.

Join our book's Discord space

Join the book's Discord workspace for a monthly *Ask me Anything* session with the authors: https://packt.link/JSBook

13
Concurrency

It's time for a more advanced topic. You're ready! We are going to deal with the topic of asynchronous code and some options for multitasking with code. This concept is called concurrency. Don't worry if you find this chapter a bit of a struggle; this is programming in JavaScript at a high level. These are the topics we'll be dealing with:

- Concurrency
- Callbacks
- Promises
- `async`/`await`
- Event loop

Yes, this is tough, but understanding how to leverage concurrency can really enhance the performance of your program by speeding up the process, which is more than enough reason to dive into this advanced topic!

 Note: exercise, project, and self-check quiz answers can be found in the *Appendix*.

Introducing concurrency

Concurrency is whenever things are happening "at the same time" or *in parallel*. To give a non-code example, let's talk about managing my household. When I come home on a Friday night, I have a series of tasks: the kids need to eat, to shower, and to be brought to bed, the laundry needs to be folded and laundry needs to be put in the machine, and to be fair, a lot more, but this is enough to illustrate the example.

If I were to do this without being able to do multiple things at once, it would be a very tough night and get very late. I would first make dinner — put a pizza in the oven and wait next to it — feed the kids, shower them afterward, then bring them to bed, and then fold the laundry afterward, turn the machine on again, and wait until it's done. Luckily, I can multitask, so it looks more like this: I put the pizza in the oven, in the meantime, I turn the washing machine on and maybe fold a few pieces of laundry, then I feed the kids, do the rest of the laundry while they shower, and I'm done a lot quicker.

This is the same for your computer and the applications that you use. If it weren't able to do multiple things at the same time, you would probably be very annoyed. You wouldn't be able to check your mail while you are writing code, you wouldn't be able to listen to music while writing code, and a lot more. This is your computer switching between different tasks. The same thing can happen at the application level. For example, we can do a call to some API and not wait for the reply but do something useful in the meantime instead. We can do so using the concept of **concurrency**.

There are three strategies in JavaScript that you'll need to know of when working with concurrency: **callbacks**, **Promises**, and the **async** and **await** keywords.

Callbacks

Callbacks are the first thing we should understand when we are talking about concurrency. The good news is that the `callback` principle is not too hard to understand. It is just a function that takes another function as an argument, which is then called when the rest of the initial function has finished. In other words, it's just a function calling a function, like this:

```
function doSomething(callback) {
    callback();
}

function sayHi() {
```

```
            console.log("Hi!");
    }


    doSomething(sayHi);
```

The doSomething() function, which is created with the parameter callback, is just calling whatever function is being passed in as an argument. We call it using the sayHi() function as an argument, so this code snippet is just a very complicated way to get Hi! printed to the console.

Here is an example of the callback principle actually doing something:

```
    function judge(grade) {
        switch (true) {
            case grade == "A":
                console.log("You got an", grade, ": amazing!");
                break;
            case grade == "B":
                console.log("You got a", grade, ": well done!");
                break;
            case grade == "C":
                console.log("You got a", grade, ": alright.");
                break;
            case grade == "D":
                console.log("You got a", grade, ": hmmm...");
                break;
            default:
                console.log("An", grade, "! What?!");
        }
    }


    function getGrade(score, callback) {
        let grade;
        switch (true) {
            case score >= 90:
                grade = "A";
                break;
            case score >= 80:
                console.log(score);
                grade = "B";
                break;
            case score >= 70:
```

```
                    grade = "C";
                    break;
                case score >= 60:
                    grade = "D";
                    break;
                default:
                    grade = "F";
        }
        callback(grade);
    }

    getGrade(85, judge);
```

There are two functions here: `judge()` and `getGrade()`. We call the function `getGrade()` with two arguments: 85 and the function `judge()`. Note that when calling the function as an argument, we do not include the parantheses. The `judge()` function gets stored in a `callback`. After determining the grade, the function that is stored in a callback (`judge()` in this case) gets called with the grade.

This could also be another function that does something more useful than judging, for example, sending a certain email based on test results. If we wanted that, we actually wouldn't need to change the `getGrade()` function; we just need to write a new function to do this and call `getGrade()` with the new function as a second argument.

You might be very disappointed right now, because this is not too exciting. Callbacks become really valuable in an asynchronous context, for example, when one function is still waiting for the results of a call to the database before calling the `callback` function that is going to process the data.

Some JavaScript built-in functions work with this callback principle, for example, the `setTimeOut()` and `setInterval()` functions. They will take a function that is executed after a certain time in the case of a timeout and every certain amount of time for the specified interval. We have seen these already, but just as a reminder:

```
setInterval(encourage, 500);

function encourage() {
    console.log("You're doing great, keep going!");
}
```

The functions that are inserted as arguments are called callbacks here. Understanding concurrency really starts with callbacks, but multiple nested callbacks make code difficult to read.

When this is all written as one function with anonymous functions inside, this gets very indented as well. We call this **callback hell** or the **Christmas tree problem** (because the code gets nested so much, it looks like a Christmas tree on its side).

Callbacks are a great concept, but they can create ugly code very fast. There is often a better solution, we promise.

Practice exercise 13.1

This exercise will demonstrate how to use a callback function, creating a way to pass a value from one function to another by invoking a callback function. We will create a greeting callback using a full name in a string.

1. Create a function named greet() that takes one argument, fullName. That argument should be an array. Output the items of the array into the console interpolated into a greeting message string.
2. Create a second function that has two arguments: the first one is a string for the user's full name, and the second is the callback function.
3. Split the string into an array using the split() method.
4. Send the full-name array to the greet() function created in the first step.
5. Invoke the process of the callback function.

Promises

With **Promises**, we can organize the sequence of our code in a slightly easier-to-maintain way. A Promise is a special object that connects code that needs to produce a result and the code that needs to use this result in the next step.

When we create a Promise, we give it a function. In the following example, we use a convention that we have seen a lot; we are creating a function on the spot. So, inside the argument list we are defining the function, often done using arrow functions as well. This function needs two parameters, and these parameters are callbacks. We have called them resolve and reject here.

 You can call these parameters anything you want, but resolve or res and reject or rej are most common.

When `resolve()` is called, the Promise is presumed to be successful and whatever is between the arrows is returned and used as input for the then method on the `Promise` object. If `reject()` is called, the `Promise` failed and the `catch()` method on the `Promise` object (if present) is executed with the argument of the `reject()` function.

This is a lot of information that can be hard to understand at first, so here is an example of a Promise to help you:

```
let promise = new Promise(function (resolve, reject) {
    // do something that might take a while
    // let's just set x instead for this example
    let x = 20;
    if (x > 10) {
        resolve(x); // on success
    } else {
        reject("Too low");  // on error
    }
});

promise.then(
    function (value) {
        console.log("Success:", value);
    },
    function (error) {
        console.log("Error:", error);
    }
);
```

We first create a Promise. When creating a `Promise`, we don't know what the value of the Promise is going to be. This value is whatever is sent as an argument to the resolve function. It is a sort of placeholder.

So when we call then on the Promise, we basically say: figure out what the value of the Promise is, and when you know, execute one function if the Promise was resolved or a different function if it was rejected. When a Promise is neither resolved nor rejected, we say that the Promise is pending.

then() is a Promise itself, so when it returns we can use the result for the next then() instance. This means we can chain the then() instances, which can look like this:

```
const promise = new Promise((resolve, reject) => {
    resolve("success!");
})
```

```
    .then(value => {
        console.log(value);
        return "we";
    })
    .then(value => {
        console.log(value);
        return "can";
    })
    .then(value => {
        console.log(value);
        return "chain";
    })
    .then(value => {
        console.log(value);
        return "promises";
    })
    .then(value => {
        console.log(value);
    })
    .catch(value => {
        console.log(value);
    })
```

This will log:

```
success!
we
can
chain
promises
```

The resolve functions are implemented with an arrow function. The `return` statement is the `value` input for the next function. You can see that the last block is a `catch()` function. If any of the functions were to result in a rejection and the Promise were therefore rejected, this `catch()` block would be executed and print whatever the `reject()` function sent to the `catch()` method. For example:

```
const promise = new Promise((resolve, reject) => {
    reject("oops... ");
})
    .then(value => {
        console.log(value);
        return "we";
    })
```

```
    .then(value => {
        console.log(value);
        return "can";
    })
    .then(value => {
        console.log(value);
        return "chain";
    })
    .then(value => {
        console.log(value);
        return "promises";
    })
    .then(value => {
        console.log(value);
    })
    .catch(value => {
        console.log(value);
    })
```

This will just log oops... because the first Promise was rejected instead of resolved. This is great for creating asynchronous processes that need to wait till another process is complete. We can try to do a certain set of actions and when something goes wrong, use a catch() method to deal with it.

Practice exercise 13.2

In this exercise, you will create a counter that will output the values in sequence using Promises.

1. Set up a Promise that resolves with a value of Start Counting.

2. Create a function named counter() that has one argument that gets the value and outputs it into the console.

3. Set up the next function in the Promise with four then() instances, which should output a value into the counter function, and return a value which will provide input for the subsequent then() instance. The returned values should be one, then two, then three. The screen output in the console should be the following:

```
Start Counting
One
Two
Three
```

async and await

We have just seen the Promise syntax. With the async keyword, we can make a function return a Promise. This makes the Promises nicer to read and look a lot like synchronous (non-concurrent) code. We can use this Promise just like we learned in the previous section, or we can use the more powerful await keyword to wait until the Promise is done. await only works in an asynchronous function.

In an asynchronous context, we can await other Promises as well, as can be seen in this example:

```
function saySomething(x) {
    return new Promise(resolve => {
        setTimeout(() => {
            resolve("something" + x);
        }, 2000);
    });
}

async function talk(x) {
    const words = await saySomething(x);
    console.log(words);
}

talk(2);
talk(4);
talk(8);
```

Can you figure out what this code does? We call the asynchronous function talk() three times in a row with no break. Each of these function calls is awaiting the saySomething() function. The saySomething() function contains a new Promise that is being resolved with a setTimeout() function that waits two seconds before resolving with the value of something plus x. So after two seconds, the three functions are done at the same time (or so it seems to the human eye).

If the talk() function were not asynchronous, it would throw a SyntaxError because of the await keyword. await is only valid in asynchronous functions, so talk() must be asynchronous. Without the async and the await in this example, it would store the result of the function saySomething(), a pending Promise, in words and log that once for every function call:

```
Promise { <pending> }
Promise { <pending> }
Promise { <pending> }
```

We have now seen the basic building blocks of concurrency. This should prepare you for working with concurrency in real life. Concurrency really is an advanced topic; debugging it is troublesome, but it is really worth while in terms of performance when applied at the right moment.

Practice exercise 13.3

This exercise will demonstrate how to use `await` to wait on a `Promise` inside an `async` function. Using `await` and `async`, create a counter with `timeout()`, and increment a global counter value.

1. Create a global value for a counter.
2. Create a function that takes one argument. Return the result of a new Promise, setting a `setTimeout()` function that will contain the resolve instance.
3. Increment the counter within `setTimeout()`, adding one every second. Resolve the Promise with the value of the counter and the value of the variable that was in the function argument.
4. Create an asynchronous function that outputs into the console the value of the global counter and the value of the argument of the function.
5. Create a variable to capture the returned resolve value from the `await` function. Output that result into the console.
6. Create a loop to iterate 10 times, incrementing the value and invoking the async function, passing the value of the increment variable as the parameter in the function.

The results should look like the following:

```
ready 1 counter:0
ready 2 counter:0
ready 3 counter:0
x value 1 counter:1
x value 2 counter:2
x value 3 counter:3
```

Event loop

We would like to end this chapter by explaining how JavaScript handles asynchrony and concurrency under the hood. JavaScript is a single-threaded language. A thread in this context means a *path of execution*. If there is only a single path, this means that tasks will have to wait for one another and only one thing can happen at a time.

This single executor is the **event loop**. It's a process that executes the actual work. You may wonder about this, because you've just learned about concurrency and doing things asynchronously and at the same time. Well, even though JavaScript is single-threaded, it doesn't mean that it cannot outsource some tasks and wait for them to come back. This is exactly how JavaScript manages to do things in a multithreaded manner.

Call stack and callback queue

JavaScript works with a **call stack**, and all the actions that it has to execute are queued up here. The event loop is a process that is constantly monitoring this call stack, and whenever there are tasks to do, the event loop does them one by one. The tasks on top get executed first.

Here's a tiny script:

```
console.log("Hi there");
add(4,5);

function add(x, y) {
    return x + y;
}
```

Here's a visualization of the call stack and event loop for this script.

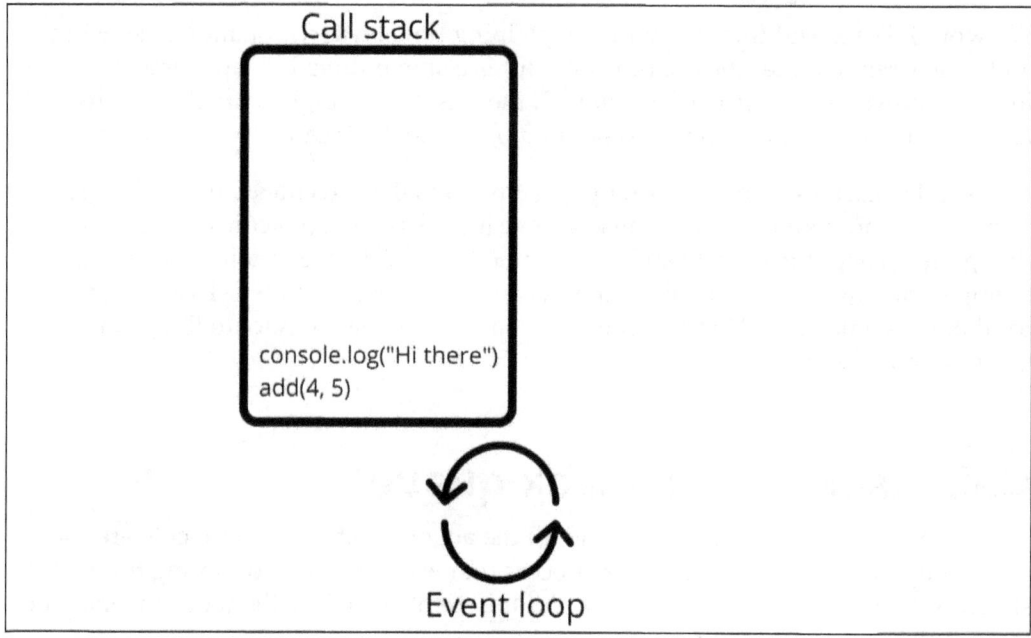

Figure 13.1: Visualization of the event loop and the call stack

No multithreading is going on here. But it is here:

```
console.log("Hi there");
setTimeout(() => console.log("Sorry I'm late"), 1000);
console.log(add(4, 5));

function add(x, y) {
    return x + y;
}
```

The setTimeout() task gets outsourced to the browser's web API (more on APIs in *Chapter 15, Next Steps*). When it's done, this appears in a special place: the **callback queue**. When the call stack is empty (and only then!), the event loop will check the callback queue for work to do. If there are any callbacks waiting, they'll be executed, one by one. After every action, the event loop will check the call stack for work first.

Here's a visualization of the situation with the outsourcing of setTimeout():

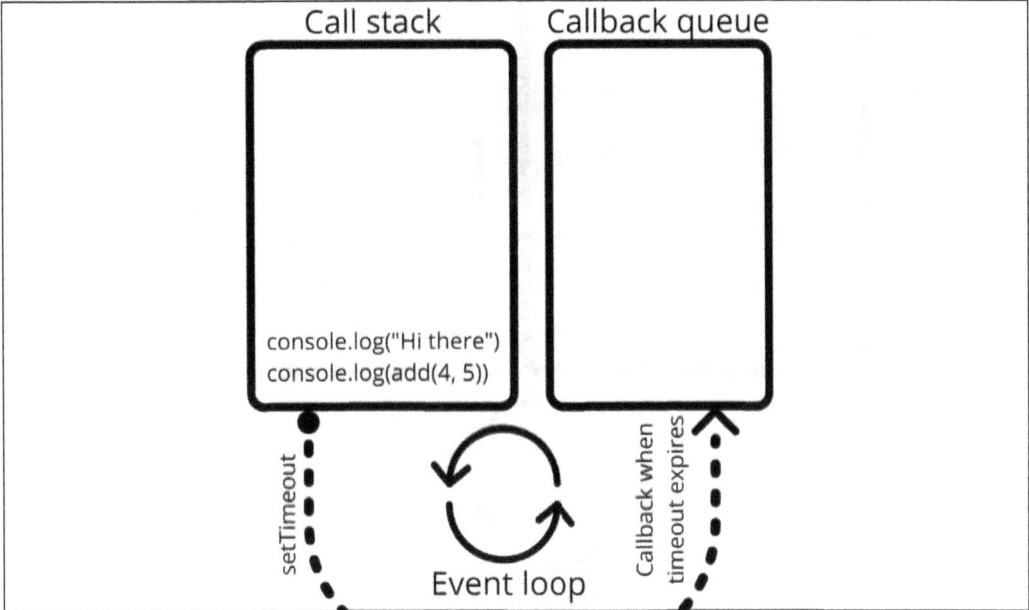

Figure 13.2: Visualization of the setTimeout being outsourced

When `setTimeout()` expires, the event loop will have done whatever was on the **call stack** already, and will check the callback queue and execute any tasks on there:

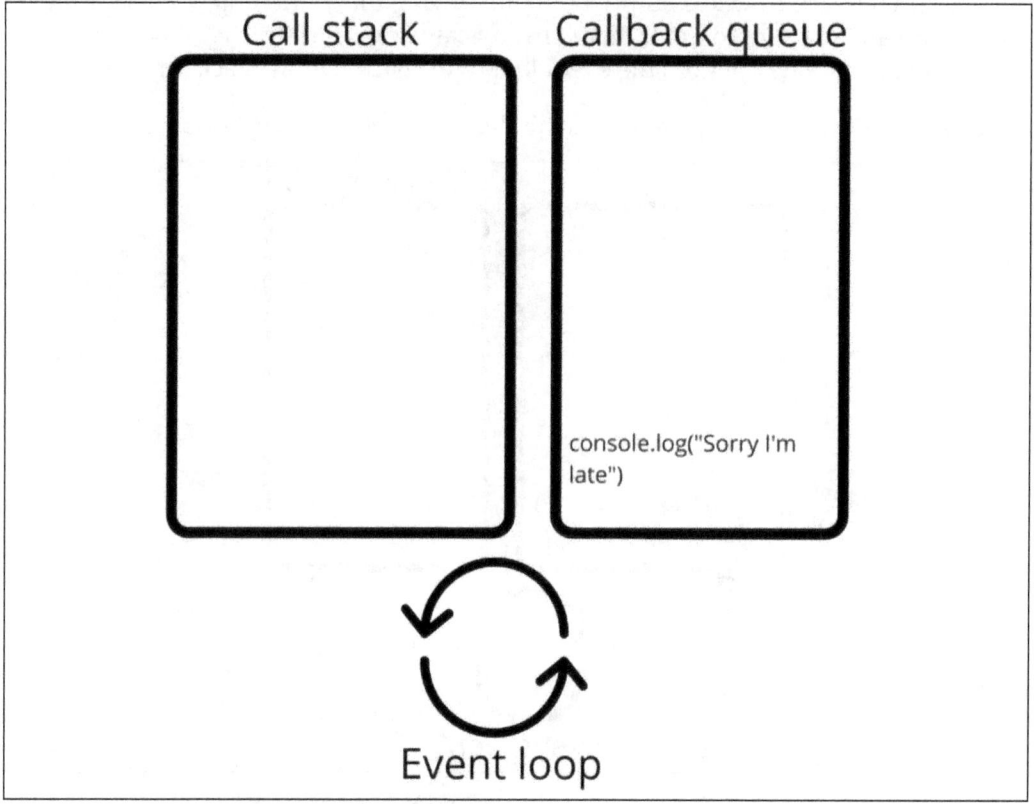

Figure 13.3: Visualization of the task on the callback queue

And this is what it will output:

```
Hi there
9
Sorry I'm late
```

Let's see if you read the above text well. What do you think will happen when we set the timer to `0`, like here?

```
console.log("Hi there");
setTimeout(() => console.log("Sorry I'm late"), 0);
console.log(add(4,5));
```

```
function add(x, y) {
    return x + y;
}
```

This will output the exact same thing. setTimeout() will also be outsourced when the timer is at 0. The callback is placed in the callback queue right away, but the event loop won't even check the callback queue until the callstack is empty. So it will still print Sorry I'm late after 9, even though the timer is at 0.

Chapter project

Password checker

Using an array of allowed passwords, this exercise will create an application to check if one of these password string values exists in an array that lists all the accepted passwords. Set a Promise to check if the password is valid, and upon the result either resolve with the status of true or reject with the status of false. Return the check results.

1. Create an array of allowed passwords.

2. Create a login function that will check if the argument is a value that is included in the passwords array. You can use indexof() or the includes() method to check the array for a value and return a Boolean value of the result.

 The includes() method is an array method that can check whether a certain value is included among the items in the array. It will return a Boolean value depending on the result.

3. Add a function that returns a Promise. Using resolve and reject, return a JavaScript object with the Boolean of true or false to indicate the password validity status.

4. Create a function that checks the password, sending it to the login function, and using then() and catch(), outputs the result of either the rejected password or the resolved password.

5. Send several passwords, some within the array, others not, to the checker function.

Self-check quiz

1. Fix the error in the following code to use the `callback` function:

    ```
    function addOne(val){
       return val + 1;
    }
    function total(a, b, callback){
       const sum = a + b;
       return callback(sum);
    }
    console.log(total(4, 5, addOne()));
    ```

2. Write down the result of the following code:

    ```
    function checker(val) {
       return new Promise((resolve, reject) => {
          if (val > 5) {
             resolve("Ready");
          } else {
             reject(new Error("Oh no"));
          }
       });
    }
    checker(5)
       .then((data) => {console.log(data); })
       .catch((err) => {console.error(err); });
    ```

3. What line(s) of code need to be added to the preceding function so that there is always a result after the function runs that ensures the word done is output into the console?

4. Update the below code to make the function return a Promise:

    ```
    function myFun() {
       return "Hello";
    }
    myFun().then(
       function(val) { console.log(val); },
       function(err) { conole.log(err); }
    );
    ```

Summary

In this chapter, we've discussed concurrency. Concurrency enables our code to do multiple things at the same time and we can determine the order of things using callbacks, Promises, and the `async` and `await` keywords. Implementing these in your applications and pages will improve the user experience a lot! Users are quite demanding nowadays; if a website isn't loading fast enough, they bounce (go back to, for example, Google). Concurrency helps to deliver results faster.

The next two chapters are about using JavaScript for modern web development and will be dealing with HTML5 and JavaScript and modern JavaScript frameworks that are real game-changers.

Join our book's Discord space

Join the book's Discord workspace for a monthly *Ask me Anything* session with the authors: `https://packt.link/JSBook`

14
HTML5, Canvas, and JavaScript

HTML5 was released in 2012 and became standardized in 2014, which caused browsers to support all sorts of new features. The introduction of HTML5 impacted the realm of possibilities that are available through JavaScript. The options for graphics, videos, interaction with graphics, and a lot more with JavaScript have increased tremendously since the introduction of HTML5, and have been so revolutionary that in fact, they led to the end of support of Flash by web browsers.

HTML5 allows web page(s) to be better structured by adding new elements, such as `<header>`. And also the DOM has improved quite a bit, which has led to increased performance. There are quite a few other additions and you'll see some of them in the chapter. Another fun (and useful) addition worth mentioning here is the `<canvas>` element, which we'll cover in this chapter as well.

JavaScript gives us a lot of amazing features already, but together with HTML5 there is a lot more possible when it comes to creating dynamic interactive web apps. This combination enables us to level up our content presentation game. We can work with files in the browser now, as well as drawing on the HTML5 canvas and adding images and text to it.

In this chapter, we will be examining some of the amazing things HTML5 has brought us. The topics don't all relate to one another directly, but they have in common that they were made possible by the powerful team of HTML5 and JavaScript, and of course, that they are all fun and useful. They will allow you to create an even more dynamic and interactive experience for the users of your app.

These are the topics that will be covered in this chapter:

- Introducing HTML5 with JavaScript
- Local file reader
- GeoLocation
- HTML5 canvas
- Dynamic canvas
- Drawing on the canvas with the mouse
- Saving dynamic images
- Media on the page
- Digital accessibility

 Note: exercise, project and self-check quiz answers can be found in the *Appendix*.

Introducing HTML5 with JavaScript

HTML5 is formally a version of HTML. It is a huge step up compared to its predecessor and enables us to make full applications in the web browser that are even accessible offline. When you read HTML5 in a job description, it often means more than just HTML. Usually, the combination of HTML5 with JavaScript, CSS, JSON, and others is included here as well.

Since HTML5 the structure of our page has improved. We have new elements such as <header>, <nav>, and <article>. And we can play videos with the <video> element, which means we no longer need Flash since HTML5. And as we already mentioned we can work with the <canvas> element to create visuals on the page or to represent visuals such as animation, graphs, and others. Some things that had to be done with JavaScript in the past can now be done solely with HTML, such as adding video and audio to a webpage.

Changes to the DOM also improved the loading time of web page(s). We are going to dive into some of the HTML5-specific features in this chapter. Let's start with accessing files from the browser.

Local file reader

Since HTML5 we can finally interact with local files using the JavaScript that runs in our browser, which is really an amazing feature. Using this feature, we can upload files from our device to our web app and read from them in our app. This means that we can attach files to forms for example, which is great in many cases whenever we need to upload some sort of file for whatever purpose, for example, adding a résumé to your online job application.

Let's first make sure that the browser you are using supports this. We can run a simple script to check whether it does:

```
<!DOCTYPE html>
<html>
  <body>
    <div id="message"></div>
    <script>
      let message = document.getElementById("message");
      if (window.FileReader) {
        message.innerText = "Good to go!";
      } else {
        message.innerText = "No FileReader :(";
      }
    </script>
  </body>
</html>
```

If you open this file in your browser it should say **Good to go!** when your browser supports file reading. Try updating your browser or using another one if it says **No FileReader :(**. Browsers that will work are, for example, Chrome and Firefox.

Uploading files

Uploading files is actually easier than you might think. We indicate we want to upload a file by adding an input of type `file`. Here is a basic script that does just that:

```
<!DOCTYPE html>
<!DOCTYPE html>
<html>
  <body>
    <input type="file" onchange="uploadFile(this.files)" />
    <div id="message"></div>
```

```
    <script>
      let message = document.getElementById("message");

      function uploadFile(files) {
        console.log(files[0]);
        message.innerText = files[0].name;
      }
    </script>
  </body>
</html>
```

It gives a blank HTML page with a **Choose file** button and the **No file chosen** comment behind it. Clicking on the button pops up the filesystem and you can select a file. After selecting the file, the JavaScript gets triggered. And as you can see, we are sending in the property files that are active in our body. This is a list of files. Therefore, we are grabbing the 0th index, the first element in the list. Files are represented as objects.

The file object gets logged to the console here, which enables you to see all the properties and associated values. Some of the important properties are the name, size, type, and lastModified, but there are many more.

We are putting the name of our file in the innerText of our div message. So, on the screen, you will see the name of the file appear in the div. We can do something similar for multiple files. Here is how to upload multiple files at the same time:

```
<html>
  <body>
    <input type="file" multiple onchange="uploadFile(this.files)" />
    <div id="message"></div>
    <script>
      let message = document.getElementById("message");

      function uploadFile(files) {
        for (let i = 0; i < files.length; i++) {
          message.innerHTML += files[i].name + "<br>";
        }
      }
    </script>
  </body>
</html>
```

We have added the multiple attribute to our input element. This changes the text on the button; instead of **Choose file** it now says **Choose files**, and we can select more than one file as a result.

We have changed our upload function a bit as well by adding a loop. And instead of `innerText`, we are now using `innerHTML`, because then we could insert a break using the HTML break. It will output the names of all the selected files below the input box on the screen.

Reading files

There is a special JavaScript object for reading files. It has a very suitable name: `FileReader`. Here is how we can use it to read a file.

```
<!DOCTYPE html>
<html>
  <body>
    <input type="file" onchange="uploadAndReadFile(this.files)" />
    <div id="message"></div>
    <script>
      let message = document.getElementById("message");

      function uploadAndReadFile(files) {
        let fr = new FileReader();
        fr.onload = function (e) {
          message.innerHTML = e.target.result;
        };
        fr.readAsText(files[0]);
      }
    </script>
  </body>
</html>
```

As you can see, we have to specify what needs to happen in order to connect our HTML and JavaScript to a file. We do this by adding the `onload` event as an anonymous function that is sending on the event data.

Reading the data can then be done using one of the `readAs()` methods on the `FileReader` object. We have used `readAsText()` here, because we are dealing with a text file. This triggers the actual reading and the onload function that comes with it gets triggered when it's done, adding the result of the reading to our message. This accepts all file types, but not all file types will make sense.

In order to see something sensible, we will have to upload something that contains plain text, such as `.txt`, `.json`, and `.xml`. With this we can also send a file to the server or process the contents of a log file.

Practice exercise 14.1

This exercise will demonstrate the process of uploading and displaying local image files in your webpage. Use the following HTML and CSS as a starting template:

```
<!doctype html>
<html>
<head>
    <title>Complete JavaScript Course</title>
    <style>
        .thumb {
            max-height: 100px;
        }
    </style>
</head>
<body>
    <input type="file" multiple accept="image/*" />
    <div class="output"></div>
    <script>

    </script>
</body>
</html>
```

Take the following steps to complete the script element:

1. Select your page elements as values within variable objects in your JavaScript code.
2. Add an event listener to the `input` field. The event trigger should be changed so that it immediately invokes a reader function.
3. Create a function to handle the reading of the selected files.
4. Using the event object, select the target element that triggered the event. Get the files selected within that input and assign them to the `files` variable.
5. Loop through all the files that were selected.
6. Set the files by index within the loop to a variable named `file`.

7. Set the image file as the file within the loop selected from the user input field files.

8. Add the newly created img tag to the page, create an area on the page that you can output the content to, and append the new page element to it.

9. Create a new FileReader object.

10. Add an onload event listener to the fileReader object to create and invoke an anonymous function that sets the source of the image as the result from the target element. Pass in the image object you just created as an argument into the function.

11. Using readAsDataURL(), get the current file object and pass it into the file reader object so that it can be used once the onload completes and is added to the page.

12. You can now select multiple image files from your computer and have them show on your webpage.

Getting position data with GeoLocation

We are going to look at the window object navigator now to see whether we can locate the user of the browser. This can be useful for many things, for example, suggesting restaurant locations nearby the user. We can have a look at the GeoLocation by inspecting navigator.geolocation. This is one way to do it:

```
<!DOCTYPE html>
<html>
  <body>
    <script>
      window.onload = init;

      function init() {
        console.dir(navigator.geolocation);
      }
    </script>
  </body>
</html>
```

If you check out the log, you can see what the GeoLocation object contains, and one of these methods is to get the current position of the user. Here is how to use it:

```
<!DOCTYPE html>
<html>
  <body>
    <script>
      window.onload = init;

      function init() {
        navigator.geolocation.getCurrentPosition(showGeoPosition);
      }

      function showGeoPosition(data) {
        console.dir(data);
      }
    </script>
  </body>
</html>
```

This might look a bit more complicated than you'd expect, and this is because the getCurrentPosition() method takes another method as an argument. The position data gets sent to this function and that function will use the data as input. Therefore, we will have to wrap console.dir() in an external function (called showGeoPosition()) that takes a parameter and outputs this data so that we can see the data in the console. We can then send this function to the getCurrentPosition() function and see the data.

If you run this, you should get a GeolocationPosition object, with a coords property containing your latitude and longitude. The browser might prompt whether you're okay with sharing your location. And if it doesn't show anything, make sure the preferences and settings of your computer allow the browser to use your location.

Using this, you can get the location of the user and show personalized content based on it or gather data about their location for other purposes, such as analyzing where visitors are located or displaying suggestions for the user based on their location.

HTML5 canvas

Did we already mention that the <canvas> element is new in HTML5? This is an amazing tool that will help you create dynamic web apps. Here is how to set up the canvas:

```
<!DOCTYPE html>
<html>
  <body>
    <canvas id="c1"></canvas>
    <script></script>
  </body>
</html>
```

And when you open this page, you will see nothing. Why? Well, the canvas element is, by default, a white rectangle that you cannot see against the white background. You could add some CSS to add a border to the canvas or a background color to the body and your canvas will be revealed.

But, we probably want to put something on it and we need JavaScript to make that happen. Let's create a "drawing" on it using JavaScript:

```
<!DOCTYPE html>
<html>
  <head>
    <style>
      canvas {
        border: 1px solid black;
      }
    </style>
  </head>
  <body>
    <canvas id="c1"></canvas>
    <script>
      let canvas = document.getElementById("c1");
      let ctx = canvas.getContext("2d");
      canvas.width = 500; //px
      canvas.height = 500; //px
      ctx.fillRect(20, 40, 100, 100);
    </script>
  </body>
</html>
```

The context of the canvas is read and stored in the `ctx` variable (a common shortened version of context). We need this to be able to draw on the canvas. We change the dimensions of the canvas to `500` by `500` pixels. This is not the same as using CSS for width and height; this adds the HTML attributes' `width` and `height`.

With the `fillRect()` method on the context of the canvas, we can draw a rectangle on the canvas. It takes four parameters. The first two are the *x* and *y* coordinates of where the figure should be added to the canvas. The last two are the width and height of the rectangle. In our case, it's a square. Here is what the result looks like:

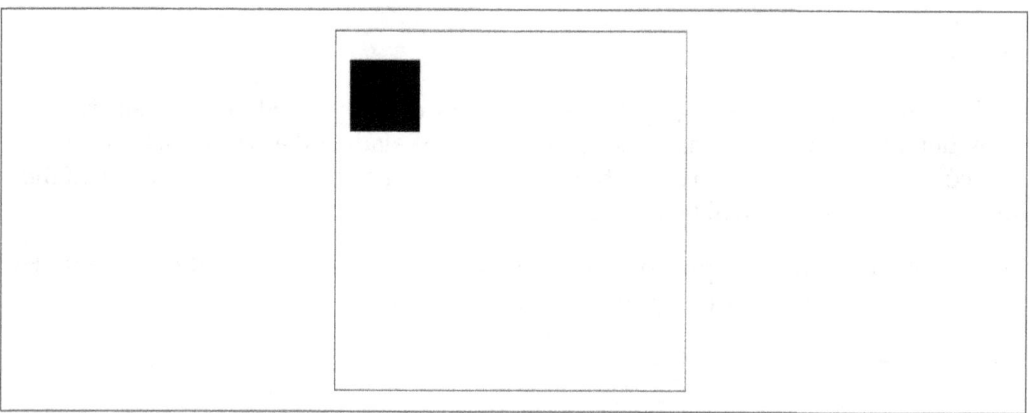

Figure 14.1: Result of the fillRect() method on our 500 px by 500 px canvas

We can also change the color we are drawing with. You can get a pink square instead by replacing the JavaScript of the previous HTML document with the following:

```
<script>
    let canvas = document.getElementById("c1");
    let ctx = canvas.getContext("2d");
    canvas.width = 500; //px
    canvas.height = 500; //px
    ctx.fillStyle = "pink";
    ctx.fillRect(20, 40, 100, 100);
</script>
```

 We have now just used the word *pink*, but you can also work with hexadecimal color codes for the `fillStyle` property, which could look like this for pink: `#FFC0CB`. The first two characters specify the amount of red (`FF` here), the third and fourth the amount of green (`C0`), and the last two the amount of blue (`CB`). The values differ from `00` to `FF` (0 to 255 in decimal numbers).

There are more things you can do with the canvas than just drawing. Let's have a look at adding text to our canvas.

Practice exercise 14.2

We will be implementing shapes and using the HTML5 canvas element to draw on a webpage with JavaScript. Draw a rectangle using JavaScript. The output will resemble the following:

Figure 14.2: Exercise outcome

Take the following steps:

1. Add the canvas element to the page.
2. Set the width and height to 640 px and, using CSS, add a 1 pc border to the element.
3. Within the JavaScript, select the canvas element and set the Context to 2d.
4. Set the fill style to red.
5. Create an output of the shape by using a rectangle.
6. Set the outline of the rectangle.
7. Clear the rectangle inside to make it transparent and the color of the background.

Dynamic canvas

We can draw more advanced shapes, add images, and add text. This enables us to take our canvas skills to the next level.

Adding lines and circles to the canvas

Here we will see how to draw a line and a circle. Here is a piece of sample code that draws a line:

```html
<!DOCTYPE html>
<html>
  <head>
    <style>
      #canvas1 {
        border: 1px solid black;
      }
    </style>
  </head>
  <body>
    <canvas id="canvas1"></canvas>
    <script>
      let canvas = document.getElementById("canvas1");
      let ctx = canvas.getContext("2d");
      canvas.width = 100;
      canvas.height = 100;
      ctx.lineWidth = 2;
      ctx.moveTo(0, 20);
      ctx.lineTo(50, 100);
      ctx.stroke();
    </script>
  </body>
</html>
```

The line width is set to 2 pixels. This first puts the focus to 0 (*x*) and 20 (*y*). This means it is at the very left edge of the canvas, 20 pixels from the top. This canvas is smaller; it is 100 by 100 pixels. The second point is at 50 (*x*) and 100 (*y*). This is what the line looks like:

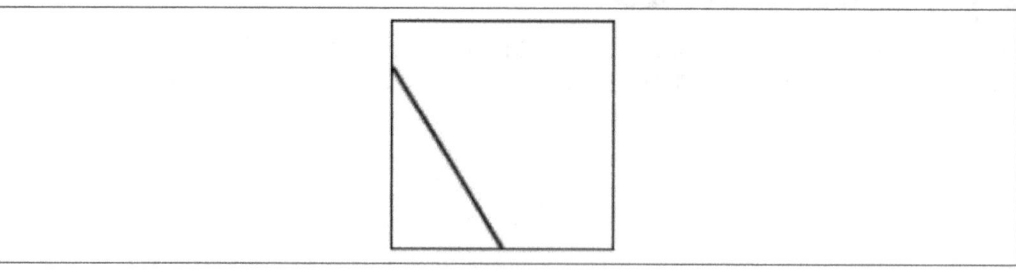

Figure 14.3: Outcome of drawing a line to the canvas

And before we move over to text, here is how to draw a circle.

```
<!DOCTYPE html>
<html>
  <head>
    <style>
      #canvas1 {
        border: 1px solid black;
      }
    </style>
  </head>
  <body>
    <canvas id="canvas1"></canvas>
    <script>
      let canvas = document.getElementById("canvas1");
      let ctx = canvas.getContext("2d");
      canvas.width = 150;
      canvas.height = 200;
      ctx.beginPath();
      ctx.arc(75, 100, 50, 0, Math.PI * 2);
      ctx.stroke();
    </script>
  </body>
</html>
```

We use the `arc()` method to create a curve or a circle. It takes five parameters:

- start position x on canvas
- start position y on canvas
- radius of the circle
- starting angle in radians
- ending angle in radians

So, if we don't want a circle, but a semicircle, for example, we'll have to specify a different starting and end angle in radians. This time we used the `stroke()` method to do the actual drawing instead of the `fill()` method:

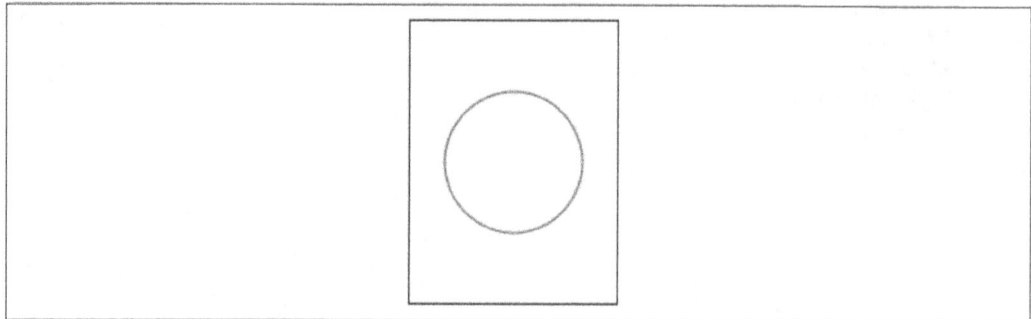

Figure 14.4: Outcome of drawing a circle using the arc() method

`stroke()` is only drawing the line, whereas `fill()` colors the full shape.

In the canvas, the shapes and lines will be added on top of each other, based on the order in which they're drawn. The first one you draw is underneath the latter ones. Exactly what happens when you paint on a real canvas. You will be seeing this in the next practice exercise.

Practice exercise 14.3

In this exercise, you will be drawing a stick person using canvas:

Figure 14.5: Exercise result within the web browser canvas element

1. Create the page elements and prepare to draw on the canvas.

2. Begin the path with an arc roughly at the top center of your canvas object.

3. Using `arc()`, set a position for the left eye, roughly at the top left of the center of the arc you just drew, then add another arc for the right eye. Create a half arc for the mouth (the radian angle for a semicircle is pi) and fill all.

4. Move the draw position to the center and draw a line for the nose.

5. Draw the body with a line down from the center of the arc, create the left arm, and then move the draw position to do the right arm, which will be twice the width of the left arm. Move back to the center and continue down to draw the left leg, move back to the center, and draw the line for the right leg.

6. Move to the top, set the colour to blue, and draw a triangle for a hat.

Adding text to the canvas

We can add text to the canvas in a similar fashion as well. In this example, we set a font and a font size, and then write our text to the canvas:

```html
<!DOCTYPE html>
<html>
  <head>
    <style>
      #canvas1 {
        border: 1px solid black;
      }
    </style>
  </head>
  <body>
    <canvas id="canvas1"></canvas>
    <script>
      let canvas = document.getElementById("canvas1");
      let ctx = canvas.getContext("2d");
      canvas.width = 200;
      canvas.height = 200;
      ctx.font = "24px Arial";
      let txt = "Hi canvas!";
      ctx.fillText(txt, 10, 35);
    </script>
  </body>
</html>
```

The `fillText()` method is used to add text. We have to specify three parameters: the text, the *x* position, and the *y* position. Here is the result:

Figure 14.6: Result of using the fillText() method

We have specified 35 px from the top for the text to start. We can specify other aspects of the text, for example, like this:

```
ctx.textAlign = "center";
```

Here, we use the `textAlign` property on the canvas to specify how the text should be aligned.

Practice exercise 14.4

We will work with text and add text to your canvas element. The following exercise will demonstrate how to dynamically add text and position it within your canvas element. The result from the exercise code will look similar to this diagram:

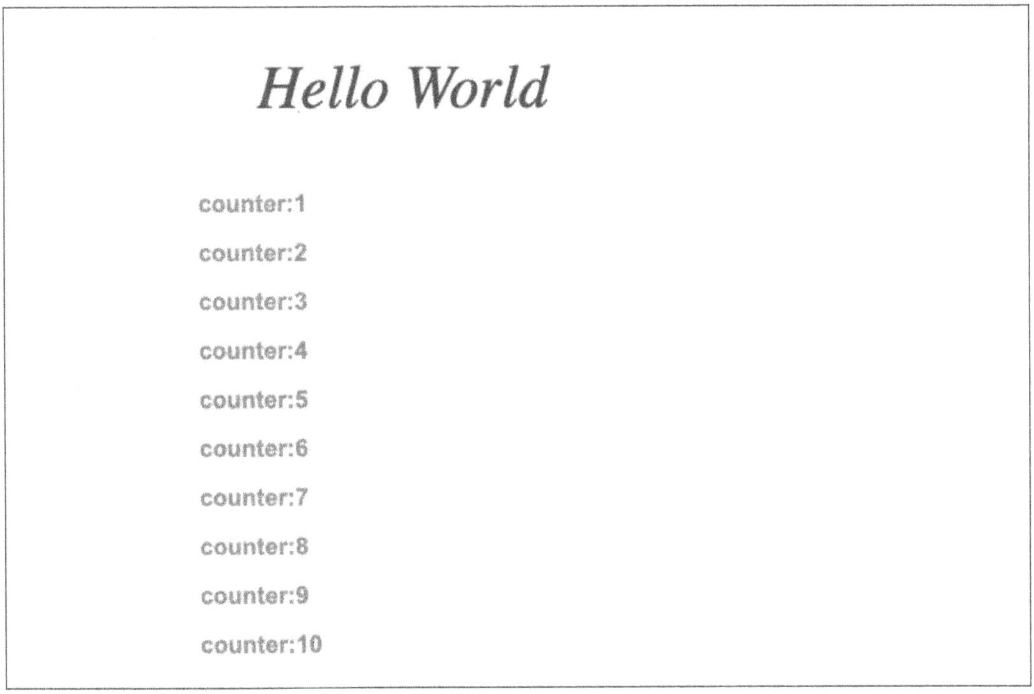

Hello World

counter:1

counter:2

counter:3

counter:4

counter:5

counter:6

counter:7

counter:8

counter:9

counter:10

Figure 14.7: Exercise outcome

Take the following steps:

1. Create a simple HTML document, and add the canvas element to your page. Set the height and width to 640, and add a 1 px border to the element so you can see it on the page.

2. Select the page elements as values within JavaScript variables.

3. Create a string variable with the message Hello World.

4. Set a font style using the font property and a blue fill color using the fillStyle property. You can also align the text to the left.

5. Add the text to the canvas with fillText and set the *x* and *y* positions of the text.

6. Set a new font and color of red.

7. Create a loop and, using the value of the loop variable, add text to the page canvas element.

Adding and uploading images to the canvas

We can add an image to the canvas. We can simply get an image from our page, and add it to our canvas:

```
<!DOCTYPE html>
<html>
  <head>
    <style>
      canvas {
        border: 1px solid black;
      }
    </style>
  </head>
  <body>
    <canvas id="c1"></canvas>
    <img id="flower" src="flower.jpg" />
    <script>
      window.onload = function () {
        let canvas = document.getElementById("c1");
        canvas.height = 300;
        canvas.width = 300;
        let ctx = canvas.getContext("2d");
        let myImage = document.getElementById("flower");
        ctx.drawImage(myImage, 10, 10);
      };
    </script>
  </body>
</html>
```

We wrap it all in an `onload` event listener here because we want to be sure that the image is loaded before getting it from the DOM, else the canvas will remain empty. We use the `drawImage()` method to add an image to the canvas. It takes three arguments: the *image,* the *x* position, and the *y* position.

We can use one canvas inside another canvas as well. We do this exactly like we did when we were using the image. This is a very powerful feature, because it enables us to use a part of the drawing from the user input, for example. Let's look at an example of how to do this:

```
<!DOCTYPE html>
<html>
  <head>
    <style>
```

```
      canvas {
        border: 1px solid black;
      }
    </style>
  </head>
  <body>
    <canvas id="canvas1"></canvas>
    <canvas id="canvas2"></canvas>
    <canvas id="canvas3"></canvas>
    <script>
      let canvas1 = document.getElementById("canvas1");
      let ctx1 = canvas1.getContext("2d");
      ctx1.strokeRect(5, 5, 150, 100);

      let canvas2 = document.getElementById("canvas2");
      let ctx2 = canvas2.getContext("2d");
      ctx2.beginPath();
      ctx2.arc(60, 60, 20, 0, 2 * Math.PI);
      ctx2.stroke();

      let canvas3 = document.getElementById("canvas3");
      let ctx3 = canvas3.getContext("2d");
      ctx3.drawImage(canvas1, 10, 10);
      ctx3.drawImage(canvas2, 10, 10);
    </script>
  </body>
</html>
```

We create three canvases, to two we add shapes, and the third one is a combination of the first two. Here is what it looks like:

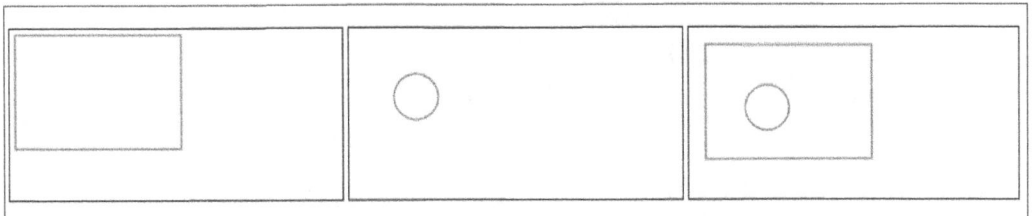

Figure 14.8: The result: three canvases with shapes

We also can upload images to the canvas. This can be of great use when you want to show a preview to your user of something that was just uploaded, for example, a profile picture. This is very similar to grabbing the <img> element from the webpage and using that element, but this time we need to read our data from the uploaded file, create a new image element, and then draw that image to the canvas.

The below code does just that:

```html
<html>
  <head>
    <style>
      canvas {
        border: 1px solid black;
      }
    </style>
  </head>
  <body>
    <input type="file" id="imgLoader" />
    <br>
    <canvas id="canvas"></canvas>
    <script>
      let canvas = document.getElementById("canvas");
      let ctx = canvas.getContext("2d");
      let imgLoader = document.getElementById("imgLoader");
      imgLoader.addEventListener("change", upImage, false);
      function upImage() {
        let fr = new FileReader();
        fr.readAsDataURL(event.target.files[0]);
        fr.onload = function (e) {
          let img = new Image();
          img.src = event.target.result;
          img.onload = function () {
            canvas.width = img.width;
            canvas.height = img.height;
            ctx.drawImage(img, 0, 0);
          };
          console.log(fr);
        };
      }
    </script>
  </body>
</html>
```

Every time the input of the input field changes, the upImage() method gets executed. This method does a few things, so let's break them down. First of all, we create a new FileReader and add the uploaded file. There is only one in this case, so we use index 0. Instead of readAsText() that we have already seen, we are now using readAsDataURL(), which we can use to read images.

This will trigger the `onload` event. And in our case, this creates a new image that can be added to the canvas later. As a source, we add the result of our read action and when the image is loaded, we change the size of our canvas to the size of our picture and then add the picture in there.

These new skills will enable you to work with images on canvases, draw your own images, upload images from elsewhere, and even re-use the ones on the webpage. This can come in handy for many situations, for example, to create basic animation, or to create the functionality to upload a new profile picture to a user's profile.

Practice exercise 14.5

We will practice uploading a local image to the canvas. The following exercise will demonstrate how to upload images from your local computer and have them displayed within the canvas element within your browser.

1. Set up the page elements and add an input field to upload an image. Add the canvas element to the page.

2. In JavaScript, select the input field and the canvas elements as JavaScript objects.

3. Add an event listener to invoke an upload function once there is a change in the input field contents.

4. Create the aforementioned function to handle the upload of the image to the canvas. Using `FileReader`, create a new `FileReader` object. In the `reader.onload` event, create a new image object.

5. Add an `onload` listener to the image object so that when the image is loaded, set the canvas height and width to match half the image size height and width. Using `ctx.drawImage()`, add the image to the canvas.

6. Set the img source to the result from the input value.

7. Use the reader object and invoke `readAsDataURL()` to convert the file input value to a readable format of base64 image data that can be used within the canvas.

Adding animations to the canvas

With the methods we have seen so far, we can already start creating animations. We do this by using loops and recursion, combined with `timeout()`. These drawings with (short) time intervals result in an animation. Let's start with a basic animation:

```
<!DOCTYPE html>
<html>
```

```
<head>
  <style>
    canvas {
      border: 1px solid black;
    }
  </style>
</head>

<body>
  <canvas id="canvas"></canvas>
  <script>
    window.onload = init;
    var canvas = document.getElementById("canvas");
    var ctx = canvas.getContext("2d");
    canvas.height = 500;
    canvas.width = 500;
    var pos = {
      x: 0,
      y: 50,
    };

    function init() {
      draw();
    }

    function draw() {
      pos.x = pos.x + 5;
      if (pos.x > canvas.width) {
        pos.x = 0;
      }
      if (pos.y > canvas.height) {
        pos.y = 0;
      }

      ctx.fillRect(pos.x, pos.y, 100, 100);
      window.setTimeout(draw, 50);
    }
  </script>
</body>
</html>
```

This will start drawing a square at position 5, 50. And after 50 ms, it will draw another square at position 10, 50, and after that at 15, 50. And it will keep on changing this x value by 5 up to the point that x gets bigger than the width of the canvas, when it is then set to zero. This way, the last bit of white canvas on that line gets colored black too.

Right now, it is more creating a line, and not a moving square. This is because we keep on adding the colored part to the canvas, but not resetting it to the previous color. We can do this with the `clearRect()` method. This method takes four parameters. The first two are the starting point to draw the rectangle to be cleared (so x, y). The third one is the `width` of the rectangle to be cleared and the last one is the `height`. In order to clear the full canvas, we'll have to write:

```
ctx.clearRect(0, 0, canvas.width, canvas.height);
```

Adding this to the beginning of the draw function in our previous example results in a moving square instead of a fat line being drawn because the previous square is not kept, but the canvas resets every time and the square gets drawn from scratch.

Practice exercise 14.6

We will practice animating shapes and moving objects on the page. This exercise will demonstrate how to move an object on the page using the HTML5 canvas element and JavaScript.

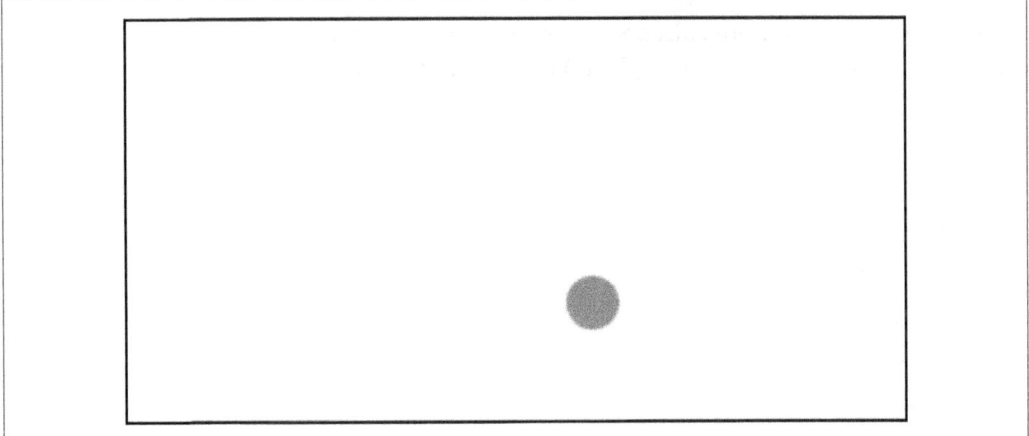

Figure 14.9: Red circle moving within the boundaries of the canvas object

Take the following steps to create a red circle that will then be moved within the canvas boundaries, appearing to be bouncing off the sides:

1. Create the canvas and apply a border of 1 px to it.

2. Select the canvas page elements with JavaScript and prepare to draw on the canvas.

3. Create variables to track the x and y positions, as well as the x-direction speed and the y-direction speed. You can set these as a default of 1 and the x and y starting positions can be half of the canvas dimensions.

4. Create a function to draw the ball. This will draw the ball as a red ball arc in the x and y positions. Also, the size for the ball should be set as a variable so that the boundaries can be calculated from it. Fill and close the path.

5. Create a function to move the ball and set the interval on that function to 10 milliseconds.

6. In the aforementioned movement function, clear the current rectangle and draw the ball using the draw ball function.

7. Check the position of the ball. If the ball is outside the canvas boundaries, you need to change direction. This can be done by multiplying the direction by -1. Update the x and y positions with the new values.

Drawing on canvas with a mouse

We have all the ingredients already to create a canvas on which we can draw with our mouse. Let's walk you through it. We'll start by setting up the canvas:

```html
<!DOCTYPE html>
<html>
  <head>
    <style>
      canvas {
        border: 1px solid black;
      }
    </style>
  </head>
  <body>
    <canvas id="canvas"></canvas>
    <input type="color" id="bgColor" />
```

```
    <script>
      let canvas = document.getElementById("canvas");
      let ctx = canvas.getContext("2d");
      canvas.width = 700;
      canvas.height = 700;
    </script>
  </body>
</html>
```

In our script element, we are going to add a method for when the window has loaded. When the window has loaded, we need to add some event listeners:

```
window.onload = init; // add this line to the start of the script

function init() {
  canvas.addEventListener("mousemove", draw);
  canvas.addEventListener("mousemove", setPosition);
  canvas.addEventListener("mouseenter", setPosition);
}
```

We want to draw when the mouse is moving, and we want to change the current position on the canvas when the mouse is moving. This is also something we want to do on mouseenter. Let's write the code for setting the position. This will be added to the script element as well. We will also have to add the position variable, which again should be declared at the start of the script:

```
let pos = {
  x: 0,
  y: 0,
};
```

And the function for setting the position:

```
function setPosition(e) {
  pos.x = e.pageX;
  pos.y = e.pageY;
}
```

This function gets triggered on mousemove and on mouseenter. The event that triggers this has a pageX and a pageY property we can use to get the current position of the mouse.

The last must-have ingredient for drawing on the canvas is the draw() method. Here is what it could look like:

```
function draw(e) {
    if (e.buttons !== 1) return;
    ctx.beginPath();
    ctx.moveTo(pos.x, pos.y);
    setPosition(e);
    ctx.lineTo(pos.x, pos.y);
    ctx.lineWidth = 10;
    ctx.lineCap = "round";
    ctx.stroke();
}
```

We start with something that might look strange, but it is a great trick to make sure that the mouse is actually being clicked. We don't want to be drawing when no button on the mouse is clicked. This method prevents that by returning from the method if it is not being clicked.

Then we start to begin a path. We always have a current x and y, so they are set as coordinate one, and then we set them again and use these new coordinates for the line. We give it a round linecap to achieve smooth lines and a line width of 10. Then we draw the line, and as long as the mouse is moving, the draw() function gets called again.

The app can now be opened and used as a functioning drawing tool. We can also give the user more options here, for example, adding a color picker to change the color that the user is drawing with. In order to do that, we'll have to add a color picker to the HTML, like this:

```
<input type="color" id="bgColor" />
```

And change the selected color in JavaScript by adding an event listener for when the value of that input box changes:

```
let bgColor = "pink";
let bgC = document.getElementById("bgColor");
bgC.addEventListener("change", function () {
    bgColor = event.target.value;
});
```

We start with the color pink, and overwrite it with whatever the user selects in the color picker.

Practice exercise 14.7

We will create an online drawing board, and include a dynamic value for width, color, and ability to erase the current drawing. Use the following HTML as a template for this project to add JavaScript code to:

```
<!doctype html>
<html>
<head>
    <style>
        canvas {
            border: 1px solid black;
        }
    </style>
</head>
<body>
    <div class="controls">
        <button class="clear">Clear</button> <span>Color
            <input type="color" value="#ffff00" id="penColor"></span>
<span>Width
            <input type="range" min="1" max="20" value="10"
id="penWidth"></span> </div>
    </div>
    <canvas id="canvas"></canvas>
    <script>

    </script>
</body>
</html>
```

Take the following steps:

1. Select the page elements as variable objects in JavaScript. Get the input field and select the button as an object.

2. Add an event listener to the button that will run a function to clear the current canvas. Within the clear function, use the `confirm()` method to check if the user wants to erase the canvas drawing. If they then confirm using `clearRect()`, delete the contents of the canvas element.

3. Set a global position object for x and y and by adding event listeners to the mouse events, update the position. If the mouse move is triggered, invoke a draw function. Set the position to update the mouse position, setting the global position values to that of the mouse x and y.

4. Within the draw function, check if the mouse button is pressed, and if not, then add `return`. If it is pressed, we can then draw on the canvas. Set the new path and move to the positions *x* and *y*. Start a new line, get the `strokestyle` value from the color input field, and set the `linewidth` value from the input width value. Add the `stroke()` method to add the new line to the page.

Saving dynamic images

We can convert the canvas to an image, and this image can then be saved as a next step. In order to convert it to an image, we need to add the following to our script element:

```
let dataURL = canvas.toDataURL();
document.getElementById("imageId").src = dataURL;
```

We are changing our canvas to a data URL, which then becomes the source of our image. We want this to happen whenever a save button gets clicked. Here is the button:

```
<input type="button" id="save" value="save" />
```

And the event listener:

```
document.getElementById("save").addEventListener("click", function () {
    let dataURL = canvas.toDataURL();
    document.getElementById("holder").src = dataURL;
});
```

Now whenever the save button gets clicked, it is going to update the image with the generated data URL from the canvas. Whatever content is within the canvas element will be turned into a base64 data image value and added to the page within an img tag.

In the following example, there is a canvas of 200 by 200 pixels and an empty image of the same size. When a color gets selected, a square of 100 by 100 pixels in that color is drawn on the canvas. When the save button gets clicked, this canvas gets converted to an image. This image can then be saved. Here is the code for the example:

```html
<!doctype html>
<html>
<head>
    <style>
        canvas {
            border: 1px solid black;
        }
    </style>
</head>
<body>
    <canvas id="canvas"></canvas>
    <input type="color" id="squareColor" />
    <br>
    <img src="" width="200" height="200" id="holder" />
    <input type="button" id="save" value="save" />
    <script>
        const canvas = document.getElementById("canvas");
        const ctx = canvas.getContext("2d");
        canvas.width = 200;
        canvas.height = 200;
        const penColor = document.getElementById("squareColor");
        penColor.addEventListener("change", function () {
            color = event.target.value;
            draw(color);
        });
        document.getElementById("save").addEventListener("click",
function () {
            let dataURL = canvas.toDataURL();
            document.getElementById("holder").src = dataURL;
        });
        function draw(color) {
            ctx.fillStyle = color;
            ctx.fillRect(70, 70, 100, 100);
        }
    </script>
</body>
</html>
```

Here is what it looks like after saving the image:

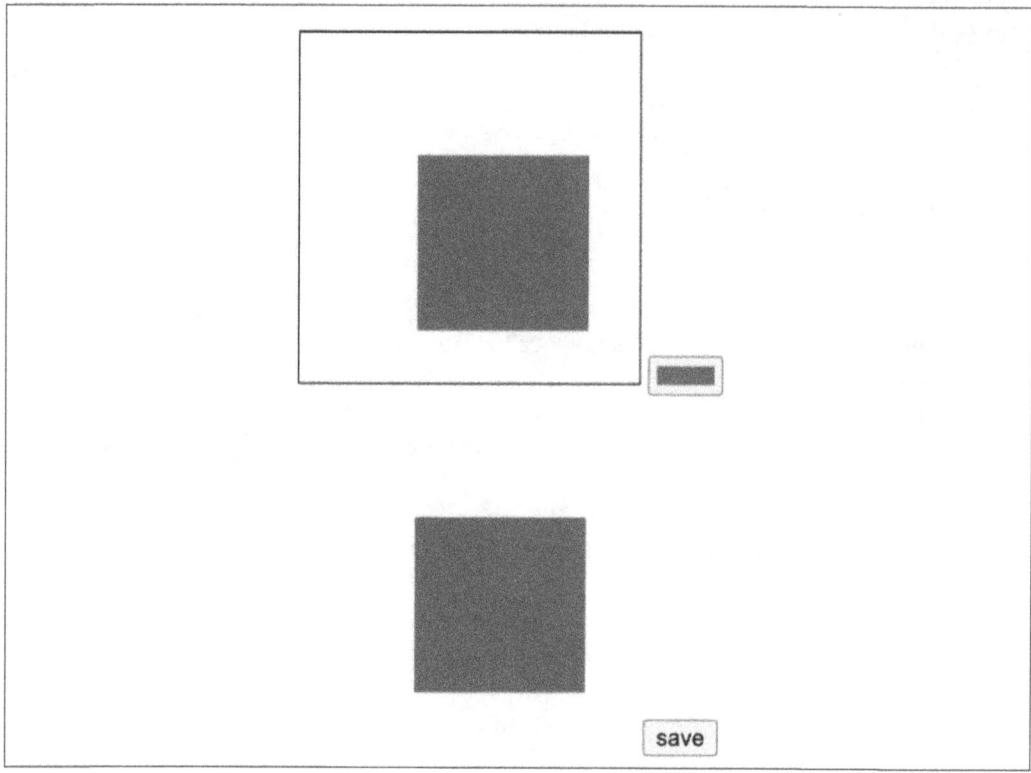

Figure 14.10: Result of saving the image

Media on the page

There are special elements for media on the page. We are going to show you how to add audio and video and how to embed YouTube on a webpage.

Adding an audio player to a page is very simple:

```
<!DOCTYPE html>
<html>
  <body>
    <audio controls>
      <source src="sound.ogg" type="audio/ogg">
      <source src="sound.mp3" type="audio/mpeg">
    </audio>
  </body>
</html>
```

You specify the controls attribute if you want the user to be able to control pause and play and the volume. If you want it to start automatically, you'll have to add the attribute autoplay. With the source element, you specify the audio files that can be played. The browser will choose only one and will choose the first one (from top to bottom) that it supports.

Adding a video to a webpage is very similar to adding audio. Here's how to do it:

```
<video width="1024" height="576" controls>
    <source src="movie.mp4" type="video/mp4">
    <source src="movie.ogg" type="video/ogg">
</video>
```

Often you would want to link to YouTube instead. Here's how to do that:

```
<iframe
    width="1024"
    height="576"
    src="https://www.youtube.com/embed/v6VTv7czb1Y"
>
</iframe>
```

You will have to use the iframe element. This is a special element that allows another webpage inside the current webpage. And you can then add the YouTube embed link as a source. The last code after embed comes from the video URL.

The height and width attributes of the video can be changed to make the video bigger or smaller. If you want to show it fullscreen, you can change the width and height like this:

```
<iframe
  width="100%"
  height="100%"
  src="https://www.youtube.com/embed/v6VTv7czb1Y"
>
</iframe>
```

If you want it to be only a part of the screen, you can adjust the width and height attributes accordingly.

You can autoplay these as well with the autoplay attribute. If you use autoplay on more than one, none of them will autoplay to protect the visitor from getting all that noise from the webpage. It is typically considered annoying if your video starts making noise in the browser. Adding the attribute muted will avoid this.

Digital accessibility in HTML

Digital accessibility is of huge importance for visually impaired people or those unable to use a mouse. In order to use the internet with little or no vision, screen readers are in place. This is a special piece of software that reads what is on the screen or converts it to braille using special devices connected to the computer. People that cannot use a mouse will often rely on speech to give the computer instructions.

Early web applications were terrible in terms of accessibility. Luckily, WAI-ARIA created a technical specification of how to make the internet digitally accessible. Dynamic parts can be recognized if implemented correctly, and by adding semantics and metadata to the HTML, it's better useable for external tooling.

Semantics might be one of the most important parts here. This comes down to using the right HTML element for the right purpose. If something should be clicked, it is best to make it a <button> element and not a <span>, for example. If it is a button, it is possible to navigate to it with the *Tab* key and click it using *Enter*.

The same goes for headers. You can create something that looks like a header using a special class and give it a layout, but the screen readers are looking for h1, h2, and h3. You should always use the header elements for headers. This helps the screen readers and improves the accessibility of your website. And as a bonus, it helps you rank higher in Google as well because bots also check out the headers to see what is important on your site.

It is also important to use labels and link text that is descriptive. If the link part is only **Click here**, that is not helpful. Something like **Click here to sign up for the summer event** is much better.

Throughout this book, we have also done something wrong with our input boxes. In order to make input fields accessible, you'll have to add a label element. This will make it easier for screen readers to pick up on what the input box is about. So this is generally bad practice:

```
<input type="text" id="address" />
```

And this is much better, because now screen readers can read it too (and therefore visually impaired people can understand it):

```
<label for="address">Address:</label>
<input type="text" id="address" />
```

One last one that you may know already is the `alt` attribute for images. If the screen reader encounters an image, it will read the `alt` description. So make sure that these are descriptive, even if the image is not important. Since there is clearly no way to know it's not important if you cannot see the image, all you'll know is that you cannot see some picture. Here is how to add `alt` text:

```
<img src="umbrella.jpg" width="200" height="200" alt="rainbow colored
umbrella" />
```

These tips are not that important for practicing and testing purposes, but they are of great use when you are going to create professional apps. Taking accessibility into account will make your app more accessible for everyone. And as I said, Google will (currently) reward this good behavior by ranking you more highly and your app will be more profitable since more people can use it!

Chapter projects

Create a Matrix effect

This exercise will create a continuous animation of text moving from top to bottom. The final effect produced will show characters moving down the screen within the canvas element and appearing to disappear and fade as they approach the bottom of the screen as more new characters will be added to the canvas in their place. The random character can be either a 0 or 1, and will be in place in the position according to the number, which will represent the vertical position of where the character is drawn.

The canvas will be filled with a black background, which is going to use opacity to create the fading effect once it's redrawn:

Figure 14.11: Matrix effect desired outcome

Take the following steps:

1. Create a simple HTML document, and in JavaScript create a canvas element and add the getContent element as 2d.

2. Select that canvas element and set the attribute height and width to 500x400. Prepend it to the body of your document.

3. Create an empty array named colVal and create a loop to add a number of items into the array that will have a value of 0. The number of items you need to add to the array can be determined by dividing the width by ten, which should be the width between each column. The values in the array will be the starting vertical position of the content for the fillText() method that you will set up.

4. Create the main Matrix function to run at 50 millisecond intervals.

5. Set the fillStyle to be black with .05 opacity, so that when it layers on top of the existing elements it will produce a fading effect.

6. Set the canvas font color to be green.

7. Using an array map, iterate all the current items in the colVal array, which holds the vertical position for the output text.

8. Within the map, set the characters to display. We want it to alternate between 0 and 1 so, using `Math.random()`, generate a value of either 0 or 1 for the text output. You can use a ternary operator to do this.

9. Set the position of x using the index value multiplied by 10, which is the start of each new letter. Using the index from the `colVal` array, this will create separate columns of moving characters.

10. Create the character within the canvas using the ctx `fillText()` method, setting the output character to the random 0 or 1 value, using `posX` for the column *x* position, and `posY`, which is the value in the `colVal` array for the item, as the position of the *y* axis for the output.

11. Add a condition that checks if the position of *y* is greater than 100 plus a random value of 0-300. The larger the number, the longer the number will fall on the *y* position. This is random so not all numbers end at the same spot. This will create a staggered effect after the initial drop.

12. If the position of *y* is not past the random value and 100, increment the value of the index item by 10. Assign this value of *y* back to the item in the `colVal` array, which can then be used in the next iteration. This will move the letter down 10 pixels on the canvas within the next draw round.

Countdown clock

This exercise will produce a real-time countdown clock that will display the amount of time in days, hours, minutes, and seconds left until the date value within the input date field. Adjusting the input date field will update the countdown clock. It will also use local storage to capture and save the value in the input field, so if the page is refreshed, the input field will still retain the date value and the countdown clock can continue to count down to that date value from the input field. You can use the following HTML template:

```
<!doctype html>
<html>
<head>
    <title>JavaScript</title>
    <style>
        .clock {
            background-color: blue;
            width: 400px;
            text-align: center;
            color: white;
            font-size: 1em;
        }
```

```css
        .clock>span {
            padding: 10px;
            border-radius: 10px;
            background-color: black;
        }
        .clock>span>span {
            padding: 5px;
            border-radius: 10px;
            background-color: red;
        }
        input {
            padding: 15px;
            margin: 20px;
            font-size: 1.5em;
        }
    </style>
</head>
<body>
    <div>
        <input type="date" name="endDate">
        <div class="clock"> <span><span class="days">0</span> Days</
span> <span><span class="hours">0</span>
                Hours</span> <span><span class="minutes">0</span>
Minutes</span> <span><span class="seconds">0</span>
                Seconds</span>
        </div>
    </div>
    <script>

    </script>
</body>
</html>
```

We have created page elements including input with a type of date, a main clock container, and added spans for days, hours, minutes, and seconds. They have been labeled and CSS applied as needed.

You can take the following steps:

1. Select the page elements as JavaScript objects, as well as selecting the main clock output area as the value of a JavaScript object.

2. Create variables for the `timeInterval` and a global Boolean value that can be used to stop the clock timer.

3. Check the local storage if there is an item for countdown already set. If there is, use that value.

4. Create a condition and function to start the clock as the saved value and set the input field date value to the local storage saved value.

5. Add an event listener to invoke a function if the value of the input field is changed. Clear the interval if it has changed and set the new `endDate` value in the local storage.

6. Start the clock with the start clock function from that new `endDate` input value.

7. Create a function to start the clock that is used to start the counter. Within that function, you can create a function that updates the counter and outputs the new clock time values into the page clock container area.

8. Within this function, check if `timeLeft` is less than the counter time. Create a separate function to handle this. If it's less, stop the timer.

9. If the time left is more and has a value within the object, then output the object by property names and match the property names you use in the time left function object to the class names you use in your webpage elements so they match and you can save time rewriting them. Loop through all the object values and assign the values within the `innerHTML` page element.

10. In the time left function, get the current date. Using `Date.parse()`, parse the date and calculate the total milliseconds left until the counter ends. Return the values of the total days, hours, minutes, and seconds as a response object to use in the update function.

11. If the counter is false and has passed the end time, then clear the interval. If the counter is still valid, set the interval to run the update function every 1,000 milliseconds.

Online paint app

Create a drawing application where the user can draw using their mouse in the canvas element. When the user is within the canvas element and clicks down on the mouse button, holding the button down will add lines, producing a drawing effect within the canvas element. The color and width of the drawing pencil can be changed dynamically for more functionality. In addition, this app will include a button to save and download the image from the canvas element, as well as clearing the current canvas content.

You can use the following template and add the JavaScript code:

```html
<!doctype html>
<html>
<head>
    <title>Canvas HTML5</title>
    <style>
        #canvas {
            border: 1px solid black;
        }
    </style>
</head>
<body>
    <canvas id="canvas" width="600" height="400"></canvas>
    <div>
        <button class="save">Save</button>
        <button class="clear">clear</button>
        <span>Color: <input type="color" value="#ffff00"
id="penColor"></span>
        <span>Width: <input type="range" min="1" max="20" value="10"
id="penWidth"></span>
    </div>
    <div class="output"></div>
    <script>

    </script>
</body>
</html>
```

We have created a button to save and a button to clear, an input for color using the HTML5 color type, and the range type to get a numeric value for the pen width. We have also added page elements for the canvas and an output area.

Take the following steps:

1. Using JavaScript, select all the page elements as JavaScript objects and set up the canvas element to draw into.

2. Set a variable to track the location of the pen.

3. On the canvas, add an event listener to track mouse movement. Update the pen position to the lastX and lastY positions, and then set the location position to clientX and clientY. Create a function to draw at the pen position and invoke the draw function.

4. For mousedown, set draw to true, and for mouseup and mouseout, set draw to false.

5. Within the draw function, begin the move path at the pen location values and set the stroke style to the pen color and stroke width to the pen width. These can be changed by clicking the inputs and updating their HTML values. Add the stroke and close the drawing path.

6. Add an event listener to the clear button. If clicked, create a function that confirms that the user wants to remove and clear the drawing, and then if true, invoke clearRect() to clear the canvas contents.

7. Add another event listener to save the image. When clicked, it should invoke a function that gets the canvas object using toDataURL as base64 image data. You can log it into the console to see what it looks like.

8. Create an img element and prepend it to the output area element. Set the src path to the dataURL value.

9. To set a download of the image, create an anchor tag, append it to anywhere within the HTML page elements, and create a filename. You can generate a unique filename with Math.random(). Set the hyperlink to the download attribute and the href path to the dataURL path, and trigger a click with the click() method. Once clicked, remove the link element.

Self-check quiz

1. Which statements below are the correct way to prepare to draw?

```
const canvas = document.getElementById("canvas");
const ctx = canvas.getContext("2d");
var canvas = document.getElementById("canvas");
var ctx = getContext("canvas");
var ctx = canvas.getContext("canvas");
```

2. What will the following code do?

```
<canvas id="canvas"></canvas>
<script>
    var canvas = document.getElementById("canvas");
    var ctx = canvas.getContext("2d");
    canvas.height = 600;
    canvas.width = 500;
    ctx.beginPath();
    ctx.fillStyle = "red";
    ctx.arc(50, 50, 50, 0, Math.PI * 2);
    ctx.fill();
    ctx.closePath();
</script>
```

- Nothing, the code has errors
- Draws a red square
- Draws a red circle
- Draws half a circle

3. What are all three methods required to draw a line within the canvas element, and in what order?

Summary

We have discussed a lot of great additions to our JavaScript toolbox using HTML5 in this chapter. These new skills will really enhance our capabilities to build interactive web apps. We started off with the local file reader, which enabled us to upload and read files using several methods, such as the `readAsText()` method. Then we saw how to get the `GeoLocation` of a user. This can be great to personalize suggestions, for example, for restaurants or parking spots.

The canvas was yet another amazing addition to what we can do with web page(s). Canvases allow us to draw, write text, add images (by drawing and uploading), and create complete animations. This all can be done using the methods on the canvas.

We then had a look at media on the page and how to add audio and video. Finally, we discussed the topic of digital accessibility and how to make sure your website is accessible for everybody, with and without a screen reader.

And at this point, we can say, you did it! You've worked your way through so many basic and advanced web development topics. In the final chapter, we are going to be exploring the next steps for you to take your skills to the next level beyond pure JavaScript, which is what this book has focused on.

Join our book's Discord space

Join the book's Discord workspace for a monthly *Ask me Anything* session with the authors: `https://packt.link/JSBook`

15

Next Steps

You've come very far already! At this point, you should have the building blocks of JavaScript down. And you are able to create apps, write clever scripts, and read a lot of code. This is a great foundation for some serious next steps. In this chapter, we will be taking what you've learned to the next step by practicing and figuring out what interests you out of the endless possibilities that JavaScript offers.

We won't go into too much detail about all the topics here. The details will be outdated soon and there is an endless supply of very well-crafted tutorials and information on the internet for each one of them. Chances are that by the time you are reading this, the frameworks and libraries we are recommending are hopelessly old. The good news is that the likelihood that the next big thing will use the same concepts is huge.

This chapter will serve as a starting point for your next steps with JavaScript. We will cover the following topics:

- Libraries and frameworks
- Learning the backend
- Next steps

 Note: exercise, project and self-check quiz answers can be found in the *Appendix*.

Libraries and frameworks

Let's start with libraries and frameworks. Libraries are basically pre-programmed JavaScript modules that you can use to speed up your development process. They typically do one specific thing for you. Frameworks are very similar, they are also pre-programmed, but instead of doing only one thing for you, they arrange a whole list of things. This is why it is called a framework, it really is providing you a solid place to start from and usually demands a certain structure for your files in order to do so. A framework is often a bundle of libraries that provide an all-in-one solution. Or at least a many-in-one. You'll eventually even find yourself using external libraries on top of the frameworks.

To give a non-code example, if we started building a car, we could do so from scratch and make every single piece of this car ourselves. This is pretty much what we've been doing in this book so far. With libraries, we get ready-made parts — in our car example, we could get fully built chairs that we only would have to install onto the car frame we've built. If we used a framework to make a car, we would get the skeleton of the car itself, with all the essential parts in it already, and it would probably be capable of driving already. We would only need to focus on customizing the car and making sure it includes all the special things for our wants and needs. While doing that, we would have to keep in mind the skeleton of the car we already have and continue in that style.

As you can imagine, we would be done with our car project a lot faster using libraries and frameworks. Also, we would run into less trouble using libraries and frameworks, since the pre-made parts would have been well tested by many others already. If we were to make our own car chairs from scratch, chances are that after a year of driving they are no longer comfortable, whereas the standard solution has been thoroughly checked already.

So, libraries and frameworks don't just speed up the process, they also provide you with a more stable and better-tested solution. Are there no downsides? Well, of course there are. The most important one is probably flexibility, as you will have to stick to the structure of the framework you are using. To some extent, this could also be an advantage because it usually requires a well-structured coding style from you, which will improve the code quality.

Another downside is that you'll have to keep on updating your app whenever the framework or library you are using is updated. This is very important, especially when the updates are fixes to security issues. On the one hand, frameworks and libraries are very reliable, but because they're so commonly used, it is not unusual for hackers to find weaknesses. If they find one, this will give them opportunities on many apps, including your own. On the other hand, your own code is probably weaker than an average framework, by a lot.

However, in many cases, hacking your custom app might be too costly. For example, when you just have a hobby project online, you are probably not going to pay a huge amount of ransom money to hackers and the data in your app also won't be worth the hackers' effort. Whereas a script that just tries to exploit a weakness of an often-used framework for apps on a random number of websites is common. To minimize the risk, update your dependencies often and keep an eye out for reported weaknesses by the owner of your library or framework.

Libraries

Technically, we cannot do anything more with frameworks and libraries than we can do without them. That is, if you leave time out of the equation. Frameworks and libraries allow us to develop to a higher quality a lot faster, and this is why they are so popular.

We will be discussing a few of the most popular libraries here. This is definitely not an exclusive list, and it is also very dynamic, so other libraries or frameworks might be more popular in a year's time. This is why we are not going to be covering full tutorials and how to get started here. We will just explain the basic principles and show some code snippets. However, this is still a solid foundation for the next big step in your development career.

Many of the libraries can be included in a page by adding a script tag to the head of the HTML, like this:

```
<script src="https://linktolibrary.com/librarycode.js"></script>
```

We will start by discussing a few common libraries.

jQuery

jQuery is arguably the most famous JavaScript library. It was great to use in the past, when it would be compiled into the latest version of JavaScript for the specific browser. Nowadays, it is just a different way of writing some of the things we have seen in the book. You can recognize jQuery easily by the amount of dollar signs in the code. You can also tell if a website is using jQuery if you type $ or jQuery into the console of the website, and it returns the jQuery object. The jQuery library is mainly focused on selecting HTML elements from the DOM and interacting with and manipulating them. It roughly looks like this:

```
$(selector).action();
```

With the dollar sign you indicate that you want to start jQuery, and with the selector you can select the element in HTML. The signs here are a bit like CSS:

- Just a simple string value targets an HTML element: `$("p")`
- A period before a word or phrase indicates you want to select all elements with a certain class: `$(".special")`
- A hashtag targets an element with a certain ID: `$("#unique")`
- You can also use any other CSS selector, including the more complicated chained ones

Here is an example where the jQuery library is imported in the `script` element starting on line 3:

```
<html>
  <head>
    <script src="https://ajax.googleapis.com/ajax/libs/jquery/3.6.0/
jquery.min.js"></script>
  </head>
  <body>
    <p>Let's play a game!</p>
    <p>Of hide and seek...</p>
    <p class="easy">I'm easy to find!</p>
    <button id="hidebutton">Great idea</button>
    <button id="revealbutton">Found you!</button>
    <script>
      $(document).ready(function () {
        $("#hidebutton").click(function () {
          $("p").hide();
        });
        $("#revealbutton").click(function () {
          $(".easy").show();
        });
      });
    </script>
  </body>
</html>
```

This is what the page looks like:

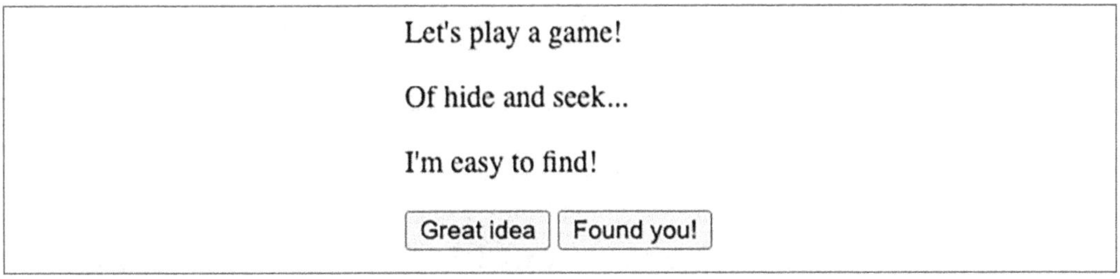

Let's play a game!

Of hide and seek...

I'm easy to find!

| Great idea | Found you! |

Figure 15.1: Page with a simple jQuery script

When you click the **Great idea** button, all the paragraphs will be hidden. This is done inside the event that's been added using jQuery. First, we selected the button with the ID hidebutton, next we call the click function on it, which specifies what will happen on click. In that function, we state that we'll select all p elements and hide them. hide is a special jQuery function that adds the display:none style to the HTML element.

So, after clicking, all the paragraphs are gone. When we click on **Found you!**, only one comes back, the last one reading **I'm easy to find**. This is because when the button with the ID revealbutton gets clicked, it selects all elements with class easy and removes the display:none from the style using the jQuery show function.

This is what jQuery really comes down to:

• Getting the selectors down
• Knowing some extra or differently named functions to manipulate the elements

You can use jQuery in your code, but this won't expand your possibilities to do more with JavaScript. It will just allow you to do the same thing with fewer characters of code. The reason jQuery was so popular is that it added a lot of value when browsers were less standardized, in which case using jQuery would actually provide the solution to standardizing JavaScript across multiple browsers. This is of little use nowadays, and if you are going to write new code, you would be better just using JavaScript. However, whenever you are working on older code, it is very likely you'll run into jQuery so knowing how it works will definitely help you in these cases.

At the time of writing, you can find the jQuery docs here:
`https://api.jquery.com/`.

D3

D3 stands for three Ds: **data-driven documents**. It is a JavaScript library that helps manipulate documents based on data and it can be used to visualize data using HTML, SVG, and CSS. It comes in very handy for dashboards that need to contain any sort of data representation.

You can make pretty much any kind of graph you could want with a lot of features using D3. It can look rather intimidating, because all the settings for the graph figure need to be set. Diving into it and breaking it up in pieces will ensure you'll overcome any hurdles. Below you'll find a very basic example to add three spheres to an SVG using D3:

```
<!DOCTYPE html>
<html>
<head>
    <script src="https://d3js.org/d3.v7.min.js"></script>
    <style>
        svg {
            background-color: lightgrey;
        }
    </style>
</head>
<body>
    <svg id="drawing-area" height=100 width=500></svg>
    <script>
        let svg = d3.select("#drawing-area");
        svg.append("circle")
            .attr("cx", 100).attr("cy", 50).attr("r", 20).style("fill",
"pink");
        svg.append("circle")
            .attr("cx", 200).attr("cy", 20).attr("r", 20).style("fill",
"black");
        svg.append("circle")
            .attr("cx", 300).attr("cy", 70).attr("r", 20).style("fill",
"grey");
```

```
        </script>
    </body>

    </html>
```

The D3 library gets imported in the first `script` tag. And the `svg` variable gets created using the `d3.select` method on the `svg` with ID `drawing-area`.

We are not doing the possibilities of D3 any justice—in this case, this isn't a lot more useful than just doing this with a canvas. However, you can make beautiful animations of the data, such as a zoom effect, a sortable bar graph, a spin effect on a sphere, and so much more. That code would take up multiple pages of the book though.

 At the time of writing, you can find the full documentation here: `https://devdocs.io/d3~4/`.

Underscore

Underscore is a JavaScript library that can be summarized as a toolkit for functional programming. Functional programming can be considered a programming paradigm, it revolves around using descriptive functions in a sequence rather than separate examples. **Object-oriented programming (OOP)** is also a programming paradigm, which is all about objects and their state, and the data can be encapsulated and hidden from the outside code. In functional programming the functions are very important, but there is less state to be concerned about. These functions do the same thing with different arguments all the time, and they can be easily chained.

The Underscore library offers a lot of functions for everyday programming, such as `map`, `filter`, `invoke`, and functions for testing. Here is a little code snippet showing some Underscore, which makes an alert pop-up box for all the items in the array—in this case, it is making a pop-up for 1, 2, and 3:

```
<!DOCTYPE html>
<html>

<head>
    <script src="https://cdn.jsdelivr.net/npm/underscore@1.13.1/
underscore-umd-min.js"></script>
```

```
    </head>

    <body>
        <script>
            _.each([1, 2, 3], alert);
        </script>
    </body>

    </html>
```

There are many other functions for filtering, grouping elements, transforming elements, getting a random value, getting the current time, and a lot more.

This snippet probably explains the name as well, since we access Underscore functions using an underscore. You will have to install Underscore first though, else the interpreter won't understand the syntax.

 At the time of writing, you can find the full documentation here: https://devdocs.io/underscore/.

React

React is the last frontend library we are going to discuss. If you would rather say React is a framework you are not completely wrong, but not right either. The reason that we consider React a library is that you'll need to use some other libraries to get to the point where it feels like a framework.

React is used to build beautiful and dynamic user interfaces. It splits up pages into different components and the data gets sent and updated between components as it changes. Here is a very basic example that only scratches the very surface of what React can do. This HTML will give this sentence on the page: **Hi Emile, what's up?**:

```
<div id="root"></div>
```

It will do this when the following JavaScript is associated with it:

```
ReactDOM.render(
    <p> Hi Emile, what's up?</p>,
    document.getElementById('root');
);
```

This will only work when the React library is available. And it will render the DOM, replacing the innerHTML of the div with the first argument of the render function. We can do this by adding React in a script element in the header and not installing anything on our system. The completed script looks like this:

```
<!DOCTYPE html>
<html>

<head>
    <script src="https://unpkg.com/react@17/umd/react.development.js"
crossorigin></script>
    <script src="https://unpkg.com/react-dom@17/umd/react-dom.
development.js" crossorigin></script>
</head>

<body>
    <div id="root"></div>
    <script>
        let p = React.createElement("p", null, "Hi Emile, what's up?");
        ReactDOM.render(
            p,
            document.getElementById("root");
        );
    </script>
</body>

</html>
```

This will write **Hi Emile, what's up?** to the page using React elements created manually in the script tag. This is not something you should be doing for large projects though. It is way more valuable to set up React and everything you need using a package manager such as **Node Package Manager** (**NPM**). This will allow you to easily manage all the dependencies and keep your code organized.

 At the time of writing, more can be found here: `https://reactjs.org/docs/getting-started.html`.

Frameworks

The frameworks are more complex and usually you'll have to install them on your computer. How to do this can be found in the online documentation of the specific framework. And whenever you are done coding and you want to run your code, you'll have to run a command that will process your code into something the browser will understand. We are "serving" the application when we do this.

Vue.js

Vue.js is a lightweight JavaScript framework. It can be used to build user interfaces and **single-page applications (SPAs)**. The way user interfaces are written with Vue.js can be hard to get your head around the first time you encounter it. Have a look at this code sample:

```html
<!DOCTYPE html>
<html>
  <script src="https://cdn.jsdelivr.net/npm/vue"></script>

  <body>
    <div id="app">
      <p v-if="!hide">
        Let's play hide and seek. <br />
        Go to the console and type: <br />
        obj._data.hide = true <br />
      </p>
    </div>

    <script>
      let obj = new Vue({
        el: "#app",
        data: {
          hide: false,
        },
      });
    </script>
  </body>
</html>
```

This is a simple HTML page, importing a JavaScript link from Vue. There is something weird going on in the HTML of the <p> tag: there is a v-if element. This element will only be displayed when the condition in that v-if is true.

In this case, it is looking at the `hide` property of our data object in our Vue instance. If you change the value of this `hide` to `true`, the negated `hide` statement will become `false`, and the element will disappear. This is something that we could have done without Vue as well, but we would then have specified a JavaScript event for the change of the value and used JavaScript to edit the CSS to hide the paragraph.

You can even see HTML elements that are new to you. That is because these are not regular HTML elements, but rather from Vue, which lets you define your own elements. You can run into HTML that looks like this:

```
<div id="custom-component">
  <maaike></maaike>
</div>
```

And when you open the webpage associated with it, it shows:

```
Maaike says: good job!
```

This is not because HTML knows how to do that. This is because there is a snippet that defines the `maaike` component. Here is the snippet:

```
<script>
    Vue.component("maaike", {
        template: "<p>Maaike says: good job!</p>",
    });

    new Vue({ el: "#app" });
</script>
```

In the preceding code, a new Vue component is created, and it can actually hold data and have a function too, but this one is very basic and just to illustrate we can add HTML templates in the `template` property. There is a paragraph specified. When the webpage gets loaded, the `<maaike>` component will be replaced with whatever is in the template.

The content of one page can come from many files. Usually these components all have their own file. There is a lot more official Vue tooling that you will get to know once you dive into Vue.js. It is actually a great framework for beginners with frameworks, as it is rather clear what is going on and is a great starting point for comprehending frameworks in general.

At the time of writing, you can find the full Vue docs here: https://v3.vuejs.org/guide/introduction.html.

Angular

Angular is a framework that originates from and is (currently) maintained by Google. Angular is a lot heavier than Vue.js, but it can be considered a complete package. This means that Angular takes up more disk space, and more disk space usually means it is slower to compile and install. Looking at Angular code isn't really that much different from Vue.js. However, Angular uses TypeScript instead of JavaScript. TypeScript is a superset of JavaScript and gets transpiled to JavaScript, but it is stricter and has a different syntax as well.

Angular can be recognized by the ng attributes in the HTML. We are not going to show a full example, but here is the HTML that will show all the tasks on a to-do list (when the code around it is set correctly):

```
<ul>
  <li ng-repeat="task in tasks">
    {{task}}<span ng-click="deleteTask($index)">Done</span>
  </li>
</ul>
```

The ng-repeat attribute is specifying the repeat action that for every task on the task list, it should create a <li> element. And task can be used as a variable inside <li> as well, as indicated by {{ task }}.

There's one more Angular-specific thing going on, ng-click, which tells Angular what to do when an element gets clicked. This is similar to the onclick event of JavaScript, but it can now be dynamically binded. This means that when writing the code, you don't need to know about onclick yet. Clearly, you can achieve the same thing in JavaScript by specifying events that will lead to changes of the onclick attribute (and the complete element if necessary), but this is a lot more code that needs to be written. This goes for anything in Angular: it can be done with just JavaScript but it is a lot more work (and that might actually be an understatement, depending on the complexity of the situation).

At the time of writing, you can find the full docs here: `https://angular.io/docs`.

Learning to work with libraries and frameworks such as React, Angular, or Vue is a very logical and even must-have next step if you seek to be a frontend developer. In the authors' view, the difficulty of these options doesn't really differ that much. Which one is the best choice depends on the place you want to work and the region that you are in, because there are regional preferences for these frameworks and libraries.

Learning the backend

So far, we have only been dealing with the frontend. The frontend is the part that is running on the client side, which could be any device that the user is using, such as a phone, laptop, or tablet. In order for websites to do interesting stuff, we also need a backend. For example, if you want to log on to a website, this website somehow needs to know whether this user exists.

This is the job of the server-side code, the backend. This is code that is running not on the device of the user, but on some sort of server elsewhere, which is often owned or leased by the company hosting the website. Hosting the website usually means that they make it available to the world wide web by placing it on a server that can take outside requests via a URL.

The code on the server does many things, all related to deeper logic and data. For example, an e-commerce store has a bunch of items in the shop that come from a database. The server gets the items from the database, parsing the HTML template and sending the HTML, CSS, and JavaScript over to the client.

The same goes for logging in: when you enter your username and password on a website and you click on login, the code on the server gets triggered. This code is going to verify the details you entered with those in the database. If you have the correct details, it will send you back the page of your portal for logged-in users. And if you have entered incorrect details, it will send back the error to the client.

In this section, we will cover the basics of communication between the frontend and backend, and we will show you how you can use JavaScript to write backend code as well using Node.js.

APIs

An **API (Application Programming Interface)** is essentially an interface for code, written with more code. A request can be made to an API using (for example) a URL. This will trigger a certain piece of code and this piece of code will give a certain response back.

This is all very abstract, so let's use an example. If we had a website for a hotel, it would make sense for people to be able to make bookings online. This would require us to have some sort of API. Whenever a user has filled out all the fields and clicks on **Submit booking**, the API will get triggered by calling the URL and sending all the data that the user has entered to that endpoint (a specific URL), for example: www.api.hotelname.com/rooms/book. This API will process and validate our data and when everything is fine, it will store the room booking in our database and probably send a confirmation mail to our guest.

Whenever one of the hotel clerks goes to check out the reservations, another API call will be made using one of the endpoints. It could be an endpoint that looks like this for example: www.api.hotelname.com/reservations. This would first go ahead and check whether our employee is logged in with the right role, and if so, it will fetch all the reservations for the selected date range from the database and send the page with the results back to our employee, who can then see all the bookings. So APIs are the connection points between the logic, database, and frontend.

APIs work with **Hypertext Transfer Protocol (HTTP)** calls. HTTP is just a protocol for communication between two parties: a client and a server, or a server and another server (in which the requesting server acts like the client). This means that it has to stick to certain conventions and rules that the other party expects, and the other party will respond in a certain way. For example, this means using a specific format to specify headers, using GET methods for getting information, using POST methods for creating new information on the server, and using PUT methods to change information on the server.

 There can be more done with APIs, for example, your computer and printer communicate via an API as well. However, this is not too relevant from a JavaScript point of view.

You will see how to consume these APIs in the *AJAX* section. You can also write your own APIs, and the ultimate basics of how to do this can be found in the *Node.js* section.

AJAX

AJAX stands for **Asynchronous JavaScript and XML,** which is a misnomer, because nowadays it is more common to use JSON instead of XML. We use it to make calls from the frontend to the backend, without refreshing the page (asynchronously). AJAX is not a programming language or a library, it is a combination of the built-in `XMLHttpRequest` object in the browser and the JavaScript language.

You probably won't be using plain AJAX in your day-to-day life as a frontend developer nowadays, but it is being used beneath the surface so it won't hurt to know how it works. Here is an example of calling the backend using AJAX:

```
let xhttp = new XMLHttpRequest();
let url = "some valid url";
xhttp.load = function () {
    if (this.status == 200 && this.readyState == 4) {
        document.getElementById("content").innerHTML = this.responseText;
    }
};
xhttp.open("GET", url, true);
xhttp.send();
```

This is not a working example, because there is no valid URL, but it demonstrates how AJAX works. It sets up what it needs to do when the request has been loaded, in this case, replacing the HTML inside the element with ID `content` with whatever the link returns. This could be a link to a file, or to some API that calls a database. It can give different responses when there is other (or no) data in the database. This response is in JSON, but it could also be in XML. This depends on how the server was coded.

More common now is the use of the **Fetch API** for AJAX requests. This is similar to what we can do with `XMLHttpRequest` but it provides a more flexible and powerful set of features. For example, in the following code we get the data from the URL, convert it to JSON with the `json()` method, and output it to the console:

```
let url = "some valid url";
fetch(url)
   .then(response => response.json())
   .then(data => console.log(data));
```

The Fetch API works with promises, which should look familiar at this point. So after the promise is resolved, a new one gets created with `then`, and when that one is resolved, the next `then` gets executed.

At the time of writing, more information can be found here: `https://developer.mozilla.org/en-US/docs/Web/Guide/AJAX/Getting_Started`.

Practice exercise 15.1

Create a JSON file and using `fetch`, return the results as a usable object into your JavaScript code:

1. Create a JSON object and save it in a file called `list.json`.
2. Using JavaScript, assign the filename and path to a variable named `url`.
3. Using `fetch`, make the request to the file URL. Return the results as JSON.
4. Once the response object is ready, iterate through the data and output the results into the console of each item in the JSON file.

Node.js

We can write APIs in JavaScript using Node.js. Node.js is a very clever runtime environment that has taken the Google JavaScript engine, expanded it, and made it possible to run JavaScript on servers, interacting with the filesystem protocol and HTTP using JavaScript. Because of this, we can use JavaScript for the backend. This means that you can write both the backend and the frontend with only one language (along with HTML and CSS). Without Node.js, you would have to use another language such as PHP, Java, or C# for the backend.

In order to run Node.js, you first have to set it up and then run the `node nameOfFile.js` command. You can find out how to set it up on your system in the official Node.js documentation. Often it requires downloading and installing something, and then you are done.

At the time of writing, the download instructions are accessible at `https://nodejs.org/en/download/`.

Here is an example of some code that will receive HTTP calls that can be written for Node.js:

```
const http = require("http");

http.createServer(function(req, res){
    res.writeHead(200, {"Content-Type": "text/html"}); //header status
    let name = "Rob";
    res.write(`Finally, hello ${name}`); //body
    res.end();
}).listen(8080); //Listen to port 8080

console.log("Listening on port 8080... ");
```

We start by importing the `http` module. This is an external code file that needs to be imported in order to run. The `http` module comes with Node.js, but other modules might need to be installed. You will use a package manager for this, such as NPM, which will help to install all the dependencies and be able to manage all the different versions of the external modules.

The code above sets up a server that is listening to port `8080`, and whenever it gets accessed, it will return `Finally, hello Rob`. We create the server with the `createServer` method on the imported `http` module. We then say what needs to happen for a call to our server. We respond with a 200 status (indicating "OK") and write `Finally, hello Rob` to the response. We then specify the default port `8080` as the listening port.

This example uses the built-in `http` module for Node.js, which is very powerful for creating APIs. This is definitely something that's worth having some experience with. Being able to write your own APIs will enable you to write full applications yourself. This gets even easier when we add Express to the mix.

Using the Express Node.js framework

Node.js is not a framework, nor a library. It is a runtime environment. This means that it can run and interpret the JavaScript code written. There are frameworks for Node.js and currently Express is the most popular one.

Here is a very basic Express application—again, you will have to set up Node.js first, then add the Express module (if you are using NPM, `npm install express` will do) and run it using the `node nameOfRootFile.js` command:

```
const express = require('express');
const app = express();

app.get('/', (request, response) => {
```

```
    response.send('Hello Express!');
});

app.listen(3000, () => {
    console.log('Express app at http://localhost:3000');
});
```

After running this and going to `localhost:3000` (assuming you are running it on localhost), you will get the message **Hello Express!** in your browser. In the terminal where you are running your `Node` app, it will print the console log message after loading.

> You can find more in the Node.js documentation, which at the time of writing is at the following address: `https://nodejs.org/en/docs/`.
>
> For the Express module, you can go to `https://expressjs.com/en/5x/api.html`.

Next steps

You have learned a lot about JavaScript in this book and with this chapter you should have an idea of possible next steps you can take. This chapter hasn't taught you all of these topics in depth, as entire books could be (and have been) written about each of them, but you should have a good idea of where to look for your next steps and what to consider while deciding which next step to take.

The best way to learn is by doing. So we highly recommend you just come up with a fun project idea and go ahead and try to make it. Alternatively, with this knowledge, you may feel ready for an entry-level JavaScript position! You can also do tutorials online or even work in a project team as a junior, using freelance platforms such as Upwork or Fiverr to get a project. These are hard to find though, and we can imagine that you'll learn a framework or get a bit more experience with Node.js first. However, this is often possible on the job if you can show your skills and potential in the hiring process.

Chapter projects

Working with JSON

Create a JSON file locally, connect to the JSON and data, and output the data from the JSON file into your console:

1. Create a file with the extension JSON name it `people.json`.

2. Within `people.json` create an array that contains multiple objects. Each item in the array should be an object that has the same structure, using `first`, `last`, and `topic` as the property names. Make sure you use double quotes around the property names and values as this is the proper JSON syntax.

3. Add three or more entries into the array using the same object structure for each item.

4. Create an HTML file and add a JavaScript file. Within the JavaScript file use `people.json` as the URL. Using `fetch` connect to the URL and retrieve the data. Since this is a JSON-formatted file, once you get the response data it can be formatted into JSON using the `.json()` method in `fetch`.

5. Output the full contents of the data into the console.

6. Using `foreach`, loop through the items in the data and output the values into the console. You can use a template literal and output each value.

List-making project

Create a list that saves to local storage so even if the page is refreshed, the data will persist within the browser. If the local storage is empty on the first load of the page, set up a JSON file that will be loaded to the local storage and saved as a default list to start the list:

1. Set up an HTML file, adding a `div` to output the list results to, and an input field with a button that can be clicked.

2. Using JavaScript, add the page elements as objects that can be used within the code.

3. Create your default JSON file (which can be empty) and add the path to the file into your JavaScript code using a variable called url.

4. Add an event listener to the button element that will run a function called addToList().

5. In addToList(), check if the value of the input field has a length of 3 or more. If it does then create an object with a name and the value of the input field. Create a global variable named myList to hold the list, and within addToList() push the new object data into myList.

6. Create a function called maker(), which will create the page element and add text into the element, appending it to the output element. Invoke maker() to add the new item within the addToList() function.

7. Also, save the item to local storage so that the visual content of myList will be synced with the local storage saved value. To do this, create a function called savetoStorage() and invoke it every time you update the myList in the script.

8. Within the savetoStorage() function, set the value of myList into localStorage using setItem. You will need to convert myList into a string value to save it into localStorage.

9. Add to the code getItem() to retrieve a value of myList from localStorage. Set up a global variable for the myList array.

10. Add an event listener to listen for DOMContentLoaded. Within that function, check if the localstorage loaded a value. If it did then get myList from local storage and convert it from a string to a JavaScript object. Clear the output element contents. Loop through the items in myList and add them to the page with the maker() function created earlier.

11. If localStorage does not have content, load the JSON file with the default values using fetch. Once the data is loaded, assign it to the global myList value. Loop through the items in myList and using maker(), output them to the page. Don't forget to invoke savetoStorage() after so that the storage will contain the same list items as are visible on the page.

Self-check quiz

1. What are JavaScript libraries and frameworks?

2. How can you tell if a webpage is using the jQuery library?

3. Which library contains a lot of functionality for manipulating data?

4. When Node.js is installed, how can you run a Node.js file?

Summary

In this chapter, we have explored a few of the possibilities to continue your JavaScript journey and keep on improving yourself. We started off by discussing the frontend and what libraries and frameworks are. Libraries and frameworks are both pre-made code that you can use in your project, but libraries typically solve one problem while frameworks provide a standard solution that usually controls the way you structure your application and will come with some limitations. On the other hand, frameworks are great fits for very many things you might want to do with your web apps.

We then moved on to looking at the backend. The backend is the code that runs on the server and we can write this code in JavaScript when we use Node.js. Node.js is a runtime engine that can process JavaScript and has some additional features for JavaScript that we don't have when using JavaScript in the browser.

And that's it. You have a very solid understanding of JavaScript at this point. You have seen all the major building blocks, and had a lot of practice with smaller exercises and bigger projects. There are a few things for certain: you'll never be done with learning as a JavaScript programmer, and you will keep on amazing yourself with the things you can make as you keep on progressing.

Don't forget to have fun!

Join our book's Discord space

Join the book's Discord workspace for a monthly *Ask me Anything* session with the authors: `https://packt.link/JSBook`

Appendix – Practice Exercise, Project, and Self-Check Quiz Answers

Chapter 1, Getting Started with JavaScript

Practice exercises

Practice exercise 1.1

```
4 + 10
14

console.log("Laurence");
Laurence
undefined
```

Practice exercise 1.2

```
<!DOCTYPE html>
<html>

<head>
  <title>Tester</title>
</head>

<body>
```

```
  <script>
    console.log("hello world");
  </script>
</body>

</html>
```

Practice exercise 1.3

```
<!DOCTYPE html>
<html>

<head>
  <title>Tester</title>
</head>

<body>
  <script src="app.js"></script>
</body>

</html>
```

Practice exercise 1.4

```
let a = 10; // assign a value of 10 to variable a
console.log(a); // This will output 10 into the console
/*
This is a multi-line
Comment
*/
```

Projects

Creating an HTML file and a linked JavaScript file

```
<!doctype html>
<html>
  <head>
    <title>JS Tester</title>
  </head>
```

```
  <body>
    <script src="myJS.js"></script>
  </body>
</html>

// console.log("Laurence");
/*
This is my comment
Laurence Svekis
*/
```

Self-check quiz

1. `<script src="myJS.js"></script>`.
2. No.
3. By opening and closing it with /* and */.
4. Comment out the line with //.

Chapter 2, JavaScript Essentials

Practice exercises

Practice exercise 2.1

```
console.log(typeof(str1));
console.log(typeof(str2));
console.log(typeof(val1));
console.log(typeof(val2));
console.log(typeof(myNum));
```

Practice exercise 2.2

```
const myName = "Maaike";
const myAge = 29;
const coder = true;
const message = "Hello, my name is " + myName + ", I am " + myAge+"
years old and I can code JavaScript: " + coder + ".";
console.log(message);
```

Practice exercise 2.3

```
let a = window.prompt("Value 1?");
let b = window.prompt("Value 2?");
a = Number(a);
b = Number(b);
let hypotenuseVal = ((a * a) + (b * b))**0.5;
console.log(hypotenuseVal);
```

Practice exercise 2.4

```
let a = 4;
let b = 11;
let c = 21;
a = a + b;
a = a / c;
c = c % b;
console.log(a, b, c);
```

Projects

Miles-to-kilometers converter

```
//Convert miles to kilometers.
//1 mile equals 1.60934 kilometers.
let myDistanceMiles = 130;
let myDistanceKM = myDistanceMiles * 1.60934;
console.log("The distance of " + myDistanceMiles + " miles is equal to
" + myDistanceKM + " kilometers");
```

BMI calculator

```
//1 inch = 2.54 centimetres.
//2.2046 pounds in a kilo
let inches = 72;
let pounds = 180;
let weight = pounds / 2.2046; // in kilos
let height = inches * 2.54; // height in centimetres
console.log(weight, height);
let bmi = weight/(height/100*height/100);
console.log(bmi);
```

Self-check quiz

1. String
2. Number
3. Line 2
4. `world`
5. `Hello world!`
6. Whatever the user enters in
7. `71`
8. `4`
9. 16 and 536
10. `true`

    `false`

    `true`

    `true`

    `false`

Chapter 3, JavaScript Multiple Values

Practice exercises

Practice exercise 3.1

```
const myList = ["Milk", "Bread", "Apples"];
console.log(myList.length);
myList[1] = "Bananas";
console.log(myList);
```

Practice exercise 3.2

```
const myList = [];
myList.push("Milk", "Bread", "Apples");
myList.splice(1, 1, "Bananas", "Eggs");
const removeLast = myList.pop();
console.log(removeLast);
```

```
myList.sort();
console.log(myList.indexOf("Milk"));
myList.splice(1, 0, "Carrots", "Lettuce");
const myList2 = ["Juice", "Pop"];
const finalList = myList.concat(myList2, myList2);
console.log(finalList.lastIndexOf("Pop"));
console.log(finalList);
```

Practice exercise 3.3

```
const myArr = [1, 2, 3];
const bigArr = [myArr, myArr, myArr];
console.log(bigArr[1][1]);
console.log(bigArr[0][1]);
console.log(bigArr[2][1]);
```

Practice exercise 3.4

```
const myCar = {
    make: "Toyota",
    model: "Camry",
    tires: 4,
    doors: 4,
    color: "blue",
    forSale: false
};

let propColor = "color";
myCar[propColor] = "red";
propColor = "forSale";
myCar[propColor] = true;
console.log(myCar.make + " " + myCar.model);
console.log(myCar.forSale);
```

Practice exercise 3.5

```
const people = {friends:[]};
const friend1 = {first: "Laurence", last: "Svekis", id: 1};
const friend2 = {first: "Jane", last: "Doe", id: 2};
const friend3 = {first: "John", last: "Doe", id: 3};
people.friends.push(friend1, friend2, friend3);
console.log(people);
```

Projects

Manipulating an array

```
theList.pop();
theList.shift();
theList.unshift("FIRST");
theList[3] = "hello World";
theList[2] = "MIDDLE";
theList.push("LAST");
console.log(theList);
```

Company product catalog

```
const inventory = [];
const item3 = {
    name: "computer",
    model: "imac",
    cost: 1000,
    qty: 3
}
const item2 = {
    name: "phone",
    model: "android",
    cost: 500,
    qty: 11
}
const item1 = {
    name: "tablet",
    model: "ipad",
    cost: 650,
    qty: 1
}
inventory.push(item1, item2, item3);
console.log(inventory);
console.log(inventory[2].qty);
```

Self-check quiz

1. Yes. You can reassign values within an array declared with const, but cannot redeclare the array itself.

2. `Length`

3. The outputs are as follows:

```
-1
1
```

4. You can do the following:

```
const myArr = [1,3,5,6,8,9,15];
myArr.splice(1,1,4);
console.log(myArr);
```

5. The output is as follows:

```
[empty × 10, "test"]
undefined
```

6. The output is as follows:

```
undefined
```

Chapter 4, Logic Statements

Practice exercises

Practice exercise 4.1

```
const test = false;
console.log(test);
if(test){
    console.log("It's True");
}
if(!test){
    console.log("False now");
}
```

Practice exercise 4.2

```
let age = prompt("How old are you?");
age = Number(age);
let message;
if(age >= 21){
    message = "You can enter and drink.";
}else if(age >= 19){
    message = "You can enter but not drink.";
}else{
    message = "You are not allowed in!";
}
console.log(message);
```

Practice exercise 4.3

```
const id = true;
const message = (id) ? "Allowed In" : "Denied Entry";
console.log(message);
```

Practice exercise 4.4

```
const randomNumber = Math.floor(Math.random() * 6);
let answer = "Something went wrong";
let question = prompt("Ask me anything");
switch (randomNumber) {
    case 0:
        answer = "It will work out";
        break;
    case 1:
        answer = "Maybe, maybe not";
        break;
    case 2:
        answer = "Probably not";
        break;
    case 3:
        answer = "Highly likely";
        break;
    default:
```

```
            answer = "I don't know about that";
        }
        let output = "You asked me " + question + ". I think that " + answer;
        console.log(output);
```

Practice exercise 4.5

```
let prize = prompt("Pick a number 0-10");
prize = Number(prize);
let output = "My Selection: ";
switch (prize){
    case 0:
        output += "Gold ";
    case 1:
        output += "Coin ";
        break;
    case 2:
        output += "Big ";
    case 3:
        output += "Box of ";
    case 4:
        output += "Silver ";
    case 5:
        output += "Bricks ";
        break;
    default:
        output += "Sorry Try Again";
}
console.log(output);
```

Projects

Evaluating a number game answers

```
let val = prompt("What number?");
val = Number(val);
let num = 100;
let message = "nothing";
if (val > num) {
    message = val + "  was greater than " + num;
} else if (val === num) {
```

```
    message = val + "  was equal to " + num;
} else {
    message = val + " is less than " + num;
}
console.log(message);
console.log(message);
```

Friend checker game answers

```
let person = prompt("Enter a name");
let message;
switch (person) {
    case "John" :
    case "Larry" :
    case "Jane" :
    case "Laurence" :
    message = person + " is my friend";
    break;
    default :
    message = "I don't know " + person;
}
console.log(message);
```

Rock paper scissors game answers

```
const myArr = ["Rock", "Paper", "Scissors"];
let computer = Math.floor(Math.random() * 3);
let player = Math.floor(Math.random() * 3);
let message = "player " + myArr[player] + " vs computer " +
myArr[computer] + " ";
if (player === computer) {
    message += "it's a tie";
} else if (player > computer) {
    if (computer == 0 && player == 2) {
        message += "Computer Wins";
    } else {
        message += "Player Wins";
    }
} else {
    if (computer == 2 && player == 0) {
        message += "Player Wins";
    } else {
```

```
        message += "Computer Wins";
    }
}
console.log(message);
```

Self-check quiz

1. one
2. this is the one
3. login
4. Welcome, that is a user: John
5. Wake up, it's morning
6. Result:
   - true
   - false
   - true
   - true

7. Result:

```
100 was LESS or Equal to 100
100 is Even
```

Chapter 5, Loops

Practice exercises

Practice exercise 5.1

```
const max = 5;
const ranNumber = Math.floor(Math.random() * max) + 1;
//console.log(ranNumber);
let correct = false;
while (!correct) {
    let guess = prompt("Guess a Number 1 - " + max);
    guess = Number(guess);
    if (guess === ranNumber) {
```

```
        correct = true;
        console.log("You got it " + ranNumber);
    } else if (guess > ranNumber) {
        console.log("Too high");
    } else {
        console.log("Too Low");
    }
}
```

Practice exercise 5.2

```
let counter = 0;
let step = 5;
do {
    console.log(counter);
    counter += step;
}
while (counter <= 100);
```

Practice exercise 5.3

```
const myWork = [];
for (let x = 1; x < 10; x++) {
    let stat = x % 2 ? true : false;
    let temp = {
        name: `Lesson ${x}`, status: stat
    };
    myWork.push(temp);
}
console.log(myWork);
```

Practice exercise 5.4

```
const myTable = [];
const rows = 4;
const cols = 7;
let counter = 0;
for (let y = 0; y < rows; y++) {
    let tempTable = [];
    for (let x = 0; x < cols; x++) {
        counter++;
```

```
        tempTable.push(counter);
    }
    myTable.push(tempTable);
}
console.table(myTable);
```

(index)	0	1	2	3	4	5	6
0	1	2	3	4	5	6	7
1	8	9	10	11	12	13	14
2	15	16	17	18	19	20	21
3	22	23	24	25	26	27	28

```
▼ Array(4) ⓘ
  ▶ 0: (7) [1, 2, 3, 4, 5, 6, 7]
  ▶ 1: (7) [8, 9, 10, 11, 12, 13, 14]
  ▶ 2: (7) [15, 16, 17, 18, 19, 20, 21]
  ▶ 3: (7) [22, 23, 24, 25, 26, 27, 28]
    length: 4
  ▶ [[Prototype]]: Array(0)
‹ undefined
```

Practice exercise 5.5

```
const grid = [];
const cells = 64;
let counter = 0;
let row;
for (let x = 0; x < cells + 1; x++) {
    if (counter % 8 == 0) {
        if (row != undefined) {
            grid.push(row);
        }
        row = [];
    }
    counter++;
    let temp = counter;
    row.push(temp);

}
console.table(grid);
```

(index)	0	1	2	3	4	5	6	7
0	1	2	3	4	5	6	7	8
1	9	10	11	12	13	14	15	16
2	17	18	19	20	21	22	23	24
3	25	26	27	28	29	30	31	32
4	33	34	35	36	37	38	39	40
5	41	42	43	44	45	46	47	48
6	49	50	51	52	53	54	55	56
7	57	58	59	60	61	62	63	64

```
▼ Array(8) ▣
  ▶ 0: (8) [1, 2, 3, 4, 5, 6, 7, 8]
  ▶ 1: (8) [9, 10, 11, 12, 13, 14, 15, 16]
  ▶ 2: (8) [17, 18, 19, 20, 21, 22, 23, 24]
  ▶ 3: (8) [25, 26, 27, 28, 29, 30, 31, 32]
  ▶ 4: (8) [33, 34, 35, 36, 37, 38, 39, 40]
  ▶ 5: (8) [41, 42, 43, 44, 45, 46, 47, 48]
  ▶ 6: (8) [49, 50, 51, 52, 53, 54, 55, 56]
  ▶ 7: (8) [57, 58, 59, 60, 61, 62, 63, 64]
    length: 8
  ▶ [[Prototype]]: Array(0)
◌ undefined
>
```

Practice exercise 5.6

```
const myArray = [];
for (let x = 0; x < 10; x++) {
    myArray.push(x + 1);
}
console.log(myArray);

for (let i = 0; i < myArray.length; i++) {
    console.log(myArray[i]);
}
for (let val of myArray) {
    console.log(val);
}
```

Practice exercise 5.7

```
const obj = {
    a: 1,
    b: 2,
    c: 3
};
```

```
for (let prop in obj) {
    console.log(prop, obj[prop]);
}
const arr = ["a", "b", "c"];
for (let w = 0; w < arr.length; w++) {
    console.log(w, arr[w]);
}

for (el in arr) {
    console.log(el, arr[el]);
}
```

Practice exercise 5.8

```
let output = "";
let skipThis = 7;
for (let i = 0; i < 10; i++) {
  if (i === skipThis) {
    continue;
  }
  output += i;
}
console.log(output);
```

Alternatively, the following code could be used, replacing continue with break:

```
let output = "";
let skipThis = 7;
for (let i = 0; i < 10; i++) {
  if (i === skipThis) {
    break;
  }
  output += i;
}

console.log(output);
```

Project

Math multiplication table

```
const myTable = [];
const numm = 10;
for(let x=0; x<numm; x++){
    const temp = [];
    for(let y = 0; y<numm; y++){
        temp.push(x*y);
    }
    myTable.push(temp);
}


console.table(myTable);
```

(index)	0	1	2	3	4	5	6	7	8	9
0	0	0	0	0	0	0	0	0	0	0
1	0	1	2	3	4	5	6	7	8	9
2	0	2	4	6	8	10	12	14	16	18
3	0	3	6	9	12	15	18	21	24	27
4	0	4	8	12	16	20	24	28	32	36
5	0	5	10	15	20	25	30	35	40	45
6	0	6	12	18	24	30	36	42	48	54
7	0	7	14	21	28	35	42	49	56	63
8	0	8	16	24	32	40	48	56	64	72
9	0	9	18	27	36	45	54	63	72	81

```
▼ Array(10) 🔢
  ▶ 0: (10) [0, 0, 0, 0, 0, 0, 0, 0, 0, 0]
  ▶ 1: (10) [0, 1, 2, 3, 4, 5, 6, 7, 8, 9]
  ▶ 2: (10) [0, 2, 4, 6, 8, 10, 12, 14, 16, 18]
  ▶ 3: (10) [0, 3, 6, 9, 12, 15, 18, 21, 24, 27]
  ▶ 4: (10) [0, 4, 8, 12, 16, 20, 24, 28, 32, 36]
  ▶ 5: (10) [0, 5, 10, 15, 20, 25, 30, 35, 40, 45]
  ▶ 6: (10) [0, 6, 12, 18, 24, 30, 36, 42, 48, 54]
  ▶ 7: (10) [0, 7, 14, 21, 28, 35, 42, 49, 56, 63]
  ▶ 8: (10) [0, 8, 16, 24, 32, 40, 48, 56, 64, 72]
  ▶ 9: (10) [0, 9, 18, 27, 36, 45, 54, 63, 72, 81]
    length: 10
  ▶ [[Prototype]]: Array(0)
< undefined
```

Self-check quiz

1. Result:

```
0
3
6
9
```

2. Result:

```
0
5
1
6
2
7
[1, 5, 7]
```

Chapter 6, Functions

Practice exercises

Practice exercise 6.1

```
function adder(a, b) {
return a + b;
}
const val1 = 10;
const val2 = 20;
console.log(adder(val1, val2));
console.log(adder(20, 30));
```

Practice exercise 6.2

```
const adj = ["super", "wonderful", "bad", "angry", "careful"];

function myFun() {
    const question = prompt("What is your name?");
    const nameAdj = Math.floor(Math.random() * adj.length);
    console.log(adj[nameAdj] + " " + question );
```

```
}
myFun();
```

Practice exercise 6.3

```
const val1 = 10;
const val2 = 5;
let operat = "-";
function cal(a, b, op) {
  if (op == "-") {
    console.log(a − b);
  } else {
    console.log(a + b);
  }
}
cal(val1, val2, operat);
```

Practice exercise 6.4

```
const myArr = [];

for(let x=0; x<10; x++){
  let val1 = 5 * x;
  let val2 = x * x;
  let res = cal(val1, val2, "+");
  myArr.push(res);
}
console.log(myArr);
function cal(a, b, op) {
  if (op == "-") {
    return a - b;
  } else {
    return a + b;
  }
}
```

Practice exercise 6.5

```
let val = "1000";

(function () {
    let val = "100"; // local scope variable
```

```
        console.log(val);
})();

let result = (function () {
    let val = "Laurence";
    return val;
})();
console.log(result);
console.log(val);

(function (val) {
    console.log(`My name is ${val}`);
})("Laurence");
```

Practice exercise 6.6

```
function calcFactorial(nr) {
    console.log(nr);
    if (nr === 0) {
        return 1;
    }
    else {
        return nr * calcFactorial(--nr);
    }
}
console.log(calcFactorial(4));
```

Practice exercise 6.7

```
let start = 10;
function loop1(val) {
    console.log(val);
    if (val < 1) {
        return;
    }
    return loop1(val - 1);
}
loop1(start);
function loop2(val) {
    console.log(val);
    if (val > 0) {
```

```
        val--;
        return loop2(val);
    }
    return;
}
loop2(start);
```

Practice exercise 6.8

```
const test = function(val){
    console.log(val);
}
test('hello 1');

function test1(val){
    console.log(val);
}
test1("hello 2");
```

Projects

Create a recursive function

```
const main = function counter(i) {
    console.log(i);
    if (i < 10) {
        return counter(i + 1);
    }
    return;
}
main(0);
```

Set timeout order

```
const one   = ()=> console.log('one');
const two   = ()=> console.log('two');
const three = () =>{
    console.log('three');
    one();
    two();
}
```

```
const four = () =>{
    console.log('four');
    setTimeout(one,0);
    three();
}
four();
```

Self-check quiz

1. `10`

2. `Hello`

3. Answer:

    ```
    Welcome
    Laurence
    My Name is Laurence
    ```

4. `19`

5. `16`

Chapter 7, Classes

Practice exercises

Practice exercise 7.1

```
class Person {
    constructor(firstname, lastname) {
    this.firstname = firstname;
    this.lastname = lastname;
    }
}
let person1 = new Person("Maaike", "van Putten");
let person2 = new Person("Laurence", "Svekis");
console.log("hello " + person1.firstname);
console.log("hello " + person2.firstname);
```

Practice exercise 7.2

```
class Person {
    constructor(firstname, lastname) {
    this.firstname = firstname;
    this.lastname = lastname;
    }
    fullname(){
        return this.firstname + " " + this.lastname;
    }
}
let person1 = new Person("Maaike", "van Putten");
let person2 = new Person("Laurence", "Svekis");
console.log(person1.fullname());
console.log(person2.fullname());
```

Practice exercise 7.3

```
class Animal {
    constructor(species, sounds) {
        this.species = species;
        this.sounds = sounds;
    }
    speak() {
        console.log(this.species + " " + this.sounds);
    }
}
Animal.prototype.eat = function () {
    return this.species + " is eating";
}
let cat = new Animal("cat", "meow");
let dog = new Animal("dog", "bark");
cat.speak();
console.log(dog.eat());
console.log(dog);
```

Projects

Employee tracking app

```
class Employee {
    constructor(first, last, years) {
        this.first = first;
        this.last = last;
        this.years = years;
    }
}
const person1 = new Employee("Laurence", "Svekis", 10);
const person2 = new Employee("Jane", "Doe", 5);
const workers = [person1, person2];

Employee.prototype.details = function(){
    return this.first + " " + this.last + " has worked here " +
            this.years + " years";
}

workers.forEach((person) => {
    console.log(person.details());
});
```

Menu items price calculator

```
class Menu {
    #offer1 = 10;
    #offer2 = 20;
    constructor(val1, val2) {
        this.val1 = val1;
        this.val2 = val2;
    }
    calTotal(){
        return (this.val1 * this.#offer1) + (this.val2 * this.#offer2);
    }
    get total(){
        return this.calTotal();
    }
}
```

```
const val1 = new Menu(2,0);
const val2 = new Menu(1,3);
const val3 = new Menu(3,2);
console.log(val1.total);
console.log(val2.total);
console.log(val3.total);
```

Self-check quiz

1. class

2. Using the following syntax:

```
class Person {
    constructor(firstname, lastname) {
        this.firstname = firstname;
        this.lastname = lastname;
    }
}
```

3. Inheritance

4. Answers:

   - True
   - False
   - True
   - True
   - False

5. B

Chapter 8, Built-In JavaScript Methods

Practice exercises

Practice exercise 8.1

```
const secretMes1 = "How's%20it%20going%3F";
const secretMes2 = "How's it going?";
const decodedComp = decodeURIComponent(secretMes1);
console.log(decodedComp);
```

```
const encodedComp = encodeURIComponent(secretMes2);
console.log(encodedComp);
const uri = "http://www.basescripts.com?=Hello World";
const encoded = encodeURI(uri);
console.log(encoded);
```

Practice exercise 8.2

```
const arr = ["Laurence", "Mike", "Larry", "Kim", "Joanne", "Laurence",
"Mike", "Laurence", "Mike", "Laurence", "Mike"];
const arr2 = arr.filter ( (value, index, array) => {
    console.log(value,index,array.indexOf(value));
    return array.indexOf(value) === index;
});
console.log(arr2);
```

Practice exercise 8.3

```
const myArr = [1,4,5,6];
const myArr1 = myArr.map(function(ele){
    return ele * 2;
});
console.log(myArr1);

const myArr2 = myArr.map((ele)=> ele*2);
console.log(myArr2);
```

Practice exercise 8.4

```
const val = "thIs will be capiTalized for each word";
function wordsCaps(str) {
    str = str.toLowerCase();
    const tempArr = [];
    let words = str.split(" ");
    words.forEach(word => {
        let temp = word.slice(0, 1).toUpperCase() + word.slice(1);
        tempArr.push(temp);
    });
    return tempArr.join(" ");
}
console.log(wordsCaps(val));
```

Practice exercise 8.5

```
let val = "I love JavaScript";
val = val.toLowerCase();
let vowels = ["a","e","i","o","u"];
vowels.forEach((letter,index) =>{
    console.log(letter);
    val = val.replaceAll(letter,index);
});
console.log(val);
```

Practice exercise 8.6

```
console.log(Math.ceil(5.7));
console.log(Math.floor(5.7));
console.log(Math.round(5.7));
console.log(Math.random());
console.log(Math.floor(Math.random()*11)); // 0-10
console.log(Math.floor(Math.random()*10)+1); // 1-10;
console.log(Math.floor(Math.random()*100)+1); // 1-100;
function ranNum(min, max) {
    return Math.floor(Math.random() * (max - min + 1)) + min;
}
for (let x = 0; x < 100; x++) {
    console.log(ranNum(1, 100));
}
```

Practice exercise 8.7

```
let future = new Date(2025, 5, 15);
console.log(future);
const months = ["January", "February", "March", "April", "May", "June",
"July", "August", "September", "October", "November", "December"];
let day = future.getDate();
let month = future.getMonth();
let year = future.getFullYear();
let myDate = `${months[month-1]} ${day} ${year}`;
console.log(myDate);
```

Projects

Word scrambler

```
let str = "JavaScript";

function scramble(val) {
    let max = val.length;
    let temp = "";
    for(let i=0;i<max;i++){
        console.log(val.length);
        let index = Math.floor(Math.random() * val.length);
        temp += val[index];
        console.log(temp);
        val = val.substr(0, index) + val.substr(index + 1);
        console.log(val);
    }
    return temp;
}
console.log(scramble(str));
```

Countdown timer

```
const endDate = "Sept 1 2022";

function countdown() {
    const total = Date.parse(endDate) - new Date();
    const days = Math.floor(total / (1000 * 60 * 60 * 24));
    const hrs = Math.floor((total / (1000 * 60 * 60)) % 24);
    const mins = Math.floor((total / 1000 / 60) % 60);
    const secs = Math.floor((total / 1000) % 60);
    return {
        days,
        hrs,
        mins,
        secs
    };
}

function update() {
    const temp = countdown();
```

```
    let output = "";
    for (const property in temp) {
        output += (`${property}: ${temp[property]} `);
    }
    console.log(output);
    setTimeout(update, 1000);
}

update();
```

Self-check quiz

1. `decodeURIComponent(e)`
2. `4`
3. `["Hii", "hi", "hello", "Hii", "hi", "hi World", "Hi"]`
4. `["hi", "hi World"]`

Chapter 9, The Document Object Model

Practice exercises

Practice exercise 9.1

Practice exercise 9.2

```
console.log(window.location.protocol);
console.log(window.location.href);
```

Practice exercise 9.3

```
<script>
    const output = document.querySelector('.output');
    output.textContent = "Hello World";
    output.classList.add("red");
    output.id = "tester";
    output.style.backgroundColor = "red";
    console.log(document.URL);
    output.textContent = document.URL;
</script>
```

Projects

Manipulating HTML elements with JavaScript

```
const output = document.querySelector(".output");
const mainList = output.querySelector("ul");
mainList.id = "mainList";
```

```
console.log(mainList);
const eles = document.querySelectorAll("div");
for (let x = 0; x < eles.length; x++) {
    console.log(eles[x].tagName);
    eles[x].id = "id" + (x + 1);
    if (x % 2) {
        eles[x].style.color = "red";
    } else {
        eles[x].style.color = "blue";
    }
}
```

Self-check quiz

1. You should see an object representing the list of elements contained within body object of the HTML page.

    ```
    >  document.body
    ⟨·  ▼ <body>
          ▶ <ul>…</ul>
          ▶ <div class="output">…</div>
          ▶ <script>…</script>
            <!-- Code injected by live-server -->
          ▶ <script type="text/javascript">…</script>
          </body>
    ```

2. `document.body.textContent = "Hello World";`

3. The code is as follows:

    ```
    for (const property in document) {
        console.log(`${property}: ${document[property]}`);
    }
    ```

4. The code is as follows:

    ```
    for (const property in window) {
        console.log(`${property}: ${document[window]}`);
    }
    ```

5. The code is as follows:

    ```
    <!doctype html>
    <html>
    <head>
    ```

```
        <title>JS Tester</title>
    </head>
    <body>
        <h1>Test</h1>

        <script>
            const output = document.querySelector('h1');
            output.textContent = "Hello World";
        </script>
    </body>
</html>
```

Chapter 10, Dynamic Element Manipulation Using the DOM

Practice exercises

Practice exercise 10.1

```
>  console.dir(document)
   ▶ #document
<  undefined
>  document.body.children
<  ▼ HTMLCollection [div.main] 🛈
      ▶ 0: div.main
        length: 1
      ▶ [[Prototype]]: HTMLCollection
>  document.body.children[0].children[0]
<  ▶ <div>…</div>
>  document.body.children[0].children[0].nextSibling
<  ▶ #text
```

Practice exercise 10.2

```
<!doctype html>
<html>
<head>
    <title>Canvas HTML5</title>
</head>
<body>
    <div id="one">Hello World</div>
    <script>
        const myEle = document.getElementById("one");
        console.log(myEle);
    </script>
</body>
</html>
```

Practice exercise 10.3

```
<!doctype html>
<html>
<head>
    <title>Dynamic event manipulation</title>
</head>
<body>
    <div>Hello World 1</div>
    <div>Hello World 2</div>
    <div>Hello World 3</div>
    <script>
        const myEles = document.getElementsByTagName("div");
        console.log(myEles[1]);
    </script>
</body>
</html>
```

Practice exercise 10.4

```
<!doctype html>
<html>
<head>
    <title>Canvas HTML5</title>
</head>
<body>
```

```
    <body>
        <h1 class="ele">Hello World</h1>
        <div class="ele">Hello World 1</div>
        <div class="ele">Hello World 3</div>
    <script>
        const myEles = document.getElementsByClassName("ele");
        console.log(myEles[0]);
    </script>
</html>
```

Practice exercise 10.5

```
<!doctype html>
<html>
<head>
    <title>Canvas HTML5</title>
</head>
<body>
    <body>
        <h1 class="ele">Hello World</h1>
        <div class="ele">Hello World 1</div>
        <div class="ele">Hello World 3</div>
        <p class="ele">Hello World 4</p>
    <script>
        const myEle = document.querySelector(".ele");
        console.log(myEle);
    </script>
</html>
```

Practice exercise 10.6

```
<!doctype html>
<html>
<head>
    <title>JS Tester</title>
</head>
<body>
    <div class="container">
        <div class="myEle">One</div>
        <div class="myEle">Two</div>
        <div class="myEle">Three</div>
```

```
        <div class="myEle">Four</div>
        <div class="myEle">Five</div>
    </div>
    <script>
        const eles = document.querySelectorAll(".myEle");
        console.log(eles);
        eles.forEach((el) => {
            console.log(el);
        });
    </script>
</body>
</html>
```

Practice exercise 10.7

```
<!doctype html>
<html>
<head>
    <title>JS Tester</title>
</head>
<body>
    <div>
        <button onclick="message(this)">Button 1</button>
        <button onclick="message(this)">Button 2</button>
    </div>
    <script>
        function message(el) {
            console.dir(el.textContent);
        }
    </script>
</body>
</html>
```

Practice exercise 10.8

```
    <script>
        const message = document.querySelector("#message");
        const myArray = ["Laurence", "Mike", "John", "Larry", "Kim",
                        "Joanne", "Lisa", "Janet", "Jane"];
        build();
        //addClicks();
```

```
        function build() {
            let html = "<h1>My Friends Table</h1><table>";
            myArray.forEach((item, index) => {
                html += `<tr class="box" data-row="${index+1}"
                          data-name="${item}" onclick="getData(this)">
                          <td>${item}</td>`;
                html += `<td >${index + 1}</td></tr>`;
            });
            html += "</table>";
            document.getElementById("output").innerHTML = html;
        }

        function getData(el) {
            let temp = el.getAttribute("data-row");
            let tempName = el.getAttribute("data-name");
            message.innerHTML = `${tempName } is in row #${temp}`;
        }
    </script>
```

Practice exercise 10.9

```
    <script>
        const btns = document.querySelectorAll("button");
        btns.forEach((btn)=>{
            function output(){
                console.log(this.textContent);
            }
            btn.addEventListener("click",output);
        });
    </script>
```

Practice exercise 10.10

```
    <script>
        document.getElementById("addNew").onclick = function () {
            addOne();
        }
        function addOne() {
            var a = document.getElementById("addItem").value;
            var li = document.createElement("li");
            li.appendChild(document.createTextNode(a));
```

```
            document.getElementById("sList").appendChild(li);
        }
    </script>
```

Projects

Collapsible accordion component

```
    <script>
        const menus = document.querySelectorAll(".title");
        const openText = document.querySelectorAll(".myText");
        menus.forEach((el) => {
            el.addEventListener("click", (e) => {
                console.log(el.nextElementSibling);
                remover();
                el.nextElementSibling.classList.toggle("active");
            })
        })
        function remover() {
            openText.forEach((ele) => {
                ele.classList.remove("active");
            })
        }
    </script>
```

Interactive voting system

```
    <script>
        window.onload = build;
        const myArray = ["Laurence", "Mike", "John", "Larry"];
        const message = document.getElementById("message");
        const addNew = document.getElementById("addNew");
        const newInput = document.getElementById("addFriend");
        const output = document.getElementById("output");
        addNew.onclick = function () {
            const newFriend = newInput.value;
            adder(newFriend, myArray.length, 0);
            myArray.push(newFriend);
        }
        function build() {
```

```
        myArray.forEach((item, index) => {
            adder(item, index, 0);
        });
    }
    function adder(name, index, counter) {
        const tr = document.createElement("tr");
        const td1 = document.createElement("td");
        td1.classList.add("box");
        td1.textContent = index + 1;
        const td2 = document.createElement("td");
        td2.textContent = name;
        const td3 = document.createElement("td");
        td3.textContent = counter;
        tr.append(td1);
        tr.append(td2);
        tr.append(td3);
        tr.onclick= function () {
            console.log(tr.lastChild);
            let val = Number(tr.lastChild.textContent);
            val++;
            tr.lastChild.textContent = val;
        }
        output.appendChild(tr);
    }
</script>
```

Hangman game

```
<script>
    const game = { cur: "", solution: "", puzz: [], total: 0 };
    const myWords = ["learn Javascript", "learn html",
                     "learn css"];
    const score = document.querySelector(".score");
    const puzzle = document.querySelector(".puzzle");
    const letters = document.querySelector(".letters");
    const btn = document.querySelector("button");
    btn.addEventListener("click", startGame);
    function startGame() {
        if (myWords.length > 0) {
            btn.style.display = "none";
            game.puzz = [];
```

```
                game.total = 0;
                game.cur = myWords.shift();
                game.solution = game.cur.split("");
                builder();
            } else {
                score.textContent = "No More Words.";
            }
        }
    }
    function createElements(elType, parentEle, output, cla) {
        const temp = document.createElement(elType);
        temp.classList.add("boxE");
        parentEle.append(temp);
        temp.textContent = output;
        return temp;
    }
    function updateScore() {
        score.textContent = `Total Letters Left : ${game.total}`;
        if (game.total <= 0) {
            console.log("game over");
            score.textContent = "Game Over";
            btn.style.display = "block";
        }
    }
    function builder() {
        letters.innerHTML = "";
        puzzle.innerHTML = "";
        game.solution.forEach((lett) => {
            let div = createElements("div", puzzle, "-", "boxE");
            if (lett == " ") {
                div.style.borderColor = "white";
                div.textContent = " ";
            } else {
                game.total++;
            }
            game.puzz.push(div);
            updateScore();
        })
        for (let i = 0; i < 26; i++) {
            let temp = String.fromCharCode(65 + i);
            let div = createElements("div", letters, temp,"box");
```

```
                let checker = function (e) {
                    div.style.backgroundColor = "#ddd";
                    div.classList.remove("box");
                    div.classList.add("boxD");
                    div.removeEventListener("click", checker);
                    checkLetter(temp);
                }
                div.addEventListener("click", checker);
            }
        }
        function checkLetter(letter) {
            console.log(letter);
            game.solution.forEach((ele, index) => {
                if (ele.toUpperCase() == letter) {
                    game.puzz[index].textContent = letter;
                    game.total--;
                    updateScore();
                };
            };
            )
        }
    </script>
```

Self-check quiz

1. Hello
 World

2. Hello

   World

3. Hello World

4. When three gets clicked, the output is three. When one gets clicked, the output is:

   one

   two

   three

5. btn.removeEventListener("click", myFun);

Chapter 11, Interactive Content and Event Listeners

Practice exercises

Practice exercise 11.1

```
<!DOCTYPE html>
<html>

<head>
    <title>Laurence Svekis</title>
</head>

<body>
    <script>
        let darkMode = false;
        window.onclick = () => {
            console.log(darkMode);
            if (!darkMode) {
                document.body.style.backgroundColor = "black";
                document.body.style.color = "white";
                darkMode = true;
            } else {
                document.body.style.backgroundColor = "white";
                document.body.style.color = "black";
                darkMode = false;
            }
        }
    </script>
</body>

</html>
```

Practice exercise 11.2

```
<!doctype html>
<html>
<body>
    <div>red</div>
    <div>blue</div>
    <div>green</div>
    <div>yellow</div>
    <script>
        const divs = document.querySelectorAll("div");
        divs.forEach((el)=>{
            el.addEventListener("click",()=>{
                document.body.style.backgroundColor = el.textContent;
            });
        })
    </script>
</body>
</html>
```

Practice exercise 11.3

```
<!doctype html>
<html>
<head>
    <title>JS Tester</title>
</head>
<body>
    <script>
        document.addEventListener("DOMContentLoaded", (e) => {
            message("Document ready", e);
        });
        window.onload = (e) => {
            message("Window ready", e);
        }
        function message(val, event) {
            console.log(event);
            console.log(val);
        }
    </script>
</body>
</html>
```

Practice exercise 11.4

```
<!doctype html>
<html>
<head>
    <title>JS Tester</title>
</head>
<body>
    <div class="output"></div>
    <script>
        const output = document.querySelector(".output");
        output.textContent = "hello world";
        output.style.height = "200px";
        output.style.width = "400px";
        output.style.backgroundColor = "red";
        output.addEventListener("mousedown", function (e) {
            message("green", e);
        });
        output.addEventListener("mouseover", function (e) {
            message("red", e);
        });
        output.addEventListener("mouseout", function (e) {
            message("yellow", e);
        });
        output.addEventListener("mouseup", function (e) {
            message("blue", e);
        });
        function message(elColor, event) {
            console.log(event.type);
            output.style.backgroundColor = elColor;
        }
    </script>
</body>
</html>
```

Practice exercise 11.5

```
    <script>
        const myInput = document.querySelector("input[name='message']");
        const output = document.querySelector(".output");
        const btn1 = document.querySelector(".btn1");
```

```
            const btn2 = document.querySelector(".btn2");
            const btn3 = document.querySelector(".btn3");
            const log = [];
            btn1.addEventListener("click", tracker);
            btn2.addEventListener("click", tracker);
            btn3.addEventListener("click", (e) => {
                console.log(log);
            });
            function tracker(e) {
                output.textContent = myInput.value;
                const ev = e.target;
                console.dir(ev);
                const temp = {
                    message: myInput.value,
                    type: ev.type,
                    class: ev.className,
                    tag: ev.tagName
                };
                log.push(temp);
                myInput.value = "";
            }
        </script>
```

Practice exercise 11.6

```
        <script>
            const main = document.querySelector(".container");
            const boxes = document.querySelectorAll(".box");
            main.addEventListener("click", (e) => {
                console.log("4");
            },false);
            main.addEventListener("click", (e) => {
                console.log("1");
            },true);

            boxes.forEach(ele => {
                ele.addEventListener("click", (e) => {
                    console.log("3");
                    console.log(e.target.textContent);
                },false);
```

```
        ele.addEventListener("click", (e) => {
            console.log("2");
            console.log(e.target.textContent);
        },true);

    });
</script>
```

Practice exercise 11.7

```
<script>
    const output = document.querySelector(".output1");

    const in1 = document.querySelector("input[name='first']");
    const in2 = document.querySelector("input[name='last']");
    in1.addEventListener("change", (e) => {
        console.log("change");
        updater(in1.value);
    });
    in1.addEventListener("blur", (e) => {
        console.log("blur");
    });
    in1.addEventListener("focus", (e) => {
        console.log("focus");
    });
    in2.addEventListener("change", (e) => {
        console.log("change");
        updater(in2.value);
    });
    in2.addEventListener("blur", (e) => {
        console.log("blur");
    });
    in2.addEventListener("focus", (e) => {
        console.log("focus");
    });
    function updater(str) {
        output.textContent = str;
    }
</script>
```

Practice exercise 11.8

```
<!doctype html>
<html>
<head>
    <title>JS Tester</title>
</head>
<body>
    <div class="output"></div>
        <input type="text" name="myNum1">
        <input type="text" name="myNum2">
    <script>
        const eles = document.querySelectorAll("input");
        const output = document.querySelector(".output");
        eles.forEach(el => {
            el.addEventListener("keydown", (e) => {
                if (!isNaN(e.key)) {
                    output.textContent += e.key;
                }
            });
            el.addEventListener("keyup", (e) => {
                console.log(e.key);
            });
            el.addEventListener("paste", (e) => {
                console.log('pasted');
            });
        });
    </script>
</body>
</html>
```

Practice exercise 11.9

```
<script>
    const dragme = document.querySelector("#dragme");
    dragme.addEventListener("dragstart", (e) => {
        dragme.style.opacity = .5;
    });
    dragme.addEventListener("dragend", (e) => {
        dragme.style.opacity = "";
    });
    const boxes = document.querySelectorAll(".box");
```

```
        boxes.forEach(box => {
            box.addEventListener("dragenter", (e) => {
                e.target.classList.add('red');
            });
            box.addEventListener("dragover", (e) => {
                e.preventDefault();
            });
            box.addEventListener("dragleave", (e) => {
                //console.log("leave");
                e.target.classList.remove('red');
            });
            box.addEventListener("drop", (e) => {
                e.preventDefault();
                console.log("dropped");
                e.target.appendChild(dragme);
            });
        });
        function dragStart(e) {
            console.log("Started");
        }
    </script>
```

Practice exercise 11.10

```
<!doctype html>
<html>
<head>
    <title>JS Tester</title>
</head>
<body>
    <form action="index2.html" method="get">
        First: <input type="text" name="first">
        <br>Last: <input type="text" name="last">
        <br>Age: <input type="number" name="age">
        <br><input type="submit" value="submit">
    </form>
    <script>
        const form = document.querySelector("form");
        const email = document.querySelector("#email");
        form.addEventListener("submit", (e) => {
            let error = false;
```

```
            if (checker(form.first.value)) {
                console.log("First Name needed");
                error = true;
            }
            if (checker(form.last.value)) {
                console.log("Last Name needed");
                error = true;
            }
            if (form.age.value < 19) {
                console.log("You must be 19 or over");
                error = true;
            }
            if (error) {
                e.preventDefault();
                console.log("please review the form");
            }
        });
        function checker(val) {
            console.log(val.length);
            if (val.length < 6) {
                return true;
            }
            return false;
        }
    </script>
</body>
</html>
```

Practice exercise 11.11

```
<!doctype html>
<html>
<style>
    div {
        background-color: purple;
        width: 100px;
        height: 100px;
        position: absolute;
    }
</style>
<body>
```

```
    <div id="block"></div>
    <script>
        const main = document.querySelector("#block");
        let mover = { speed: 10, dir: 1, pos: 0 };
        main.addEventListener("click", moveBlock);
        function moveBlock() {
            let x = 30;
            setInterval(function () {
                if (x < 1) {
                    clearInterval();
                } else {
                    if (mover.pos > 800 || mover.pos < 0) {
                        mover.dir *= -1;
                    }
                    x--;
                    mover.pos += x * mover.dir;
                    main.style.left = mover.pos + "px";
                    console.log(mover.pos);
                }
            }, 2);
        }
    </script>
</body>
</html>
```

Projects

Build your own analytics

```
<!doctype html >
<html>
<head>
    <title>JS Tester</title>
    <style>.box{width:200px;height:100px;border:1px solid black}</
style>
</head>
<body>
    <div class="container">
        <div class="box" id="box0">Box #1</div>
        <div class="box" id="box1">Box #2</div>
        <div class="box" id="box2">Box #3</div>
```

```
            <div class="box" id="box3">Box #4</div>
        </div>
        <script>
            const counter = [];
            const main = document.querySelector(".container");
            main.addEventListener("click",tracker);
            function tracker(e){
                const el = e.target;
                if(el.id){
                const temp = {};
                temp.content = el.textContent;
                temp.id = el.id;
                temp.tagName = el.tagName;
                temp.class = el.className;
                console.dir(el);
                counter.push(temp);
                console.log(counter);
                }
            }
        </script>
    </body>
</html>
```

Star rater system

```
    <script>
        const starsUL = document.querySelector(".stars");
        const output = document.querySelector(".output");
        const stars = document.querySelectorAll(".star");
        stars.forEach((star, index) => {
            star.starValue = (index + 1);
            star.addEventListener("click", starRate);
        });
        function starRate(e) {
            output.innerHTML =
                `You Rated this ${e.target.starValue} stars`;
            stars.forEach((star, index) => {
                if (index < e.target.starValue) {
                    star.classList.add("orange");
                } else {
                    star.classList.remove("orange");
                }
```

```
        });
    }
    </script>
```

Mouse position tracker

```
<!DOCTYPE html>
<html>
<head>
    <title>Complete JavaScript Course</title>
    <style>
        .holder {
            display: inline-block;
            width: 300px;
            height: 300px;
            border: 1px solid black;
            padding: 10px;
        }

        .active {
            background-color: red;
        }
    </style>
</head>
<body>
    <div class="holder">
        <div id="output"></div>
    </div>
    <script>
        const ele = document.querySelector(".holder");
        ele.addEventListener("mouseover",
            (e) => { e.target.classList.add("active"); });
        ele.addEventListener("mouseout",
            (e) => { e.target.classList.remove("active"); });
        ele.addEventListener("mousemove", coordin);
        function coordin() {
            let html = "X:" + event.clientX + " | Y:" + event.clientY;
            document.getElementById("output").innerHTML = html;
        }
    </script>
</body>
</html>
```

Box clicker speed test game

```
<script>
    const output = document.querySelector('.output');
    const message = document.querySelector('.message');
    message.textContent = "Press to Start";
    const box = document.createElement('div');
    const game = {
        timer: 0,
        start: null
    };
    box.classList.add('box');
    output.append(box);

    box.addEventListener('click', (e) => {
        box.textContent = "";
        box.style.display = 'none';
        game.timer = setTimeout(addBox, ranNum(3000));
        if (!game.start) {
            message.textContent = 'Loading....';
        } else {
            const cur = new Date().getTime();
            const dur = (cur - game.start) / 1000;
            message.textContent = `It took ${dur} seconds to click`;
        }
    });

    function addBox() {
        message.textContent = 'Click it...';
        game.start = new Date().getTime();
        box.style.display = 'block';
        box.style.left = ranNum(450) + 'px';
        box.style.top = ranNum(450) + 'px';
    }

    function ranNum(max) {
        return Math.floor(Math.random() * max);
    }
</script>
```

Self-check quiz

1. `Window Object Model`.
2. The `preventDefault()` method cancels the event if it can be canceled. The default action that belongs to the event will not occur.

Chapter 12, Intermediate JavaScript

Practice exercises

Practice exercise 12.1

```
<script>
    const output = document.getElementById("output");
    const findValue = document.getElementById("sText");
    const replaceValue = document.getElementById("rText");
    document.querySelector("button").addEventListener("click", lookUp);

    function lookUp() {
        const s = output.textContent;
        const rt = replaceValue.value;
        const re = new RegExp(findValue.value, "gi");
        if (s.match(re)) {
            let newValue = s.replace(re, rt);
            output.textContent = newValue;
        }
    }
</script>
```

Practice exercise 12.2

```
<script>
    const output = document.querySelector(".output");
    const emailVal = document.querySelector("input");
    const btn = document.querySelector("button");
    const emailExp =
        /([A-Za-z0-9._-]+@[A-Za-z0-9._-]+\.[A-Za-z0-9]+)\w+/;
    btn.addEventListener("click", (e) => {
```

```
            const val = emailVal.value;
            const result = emailExp.test(val);
            let response = "";
            if (!result) {
                response = "Invalid Email";
                output.style.color = "red";
            } else {
                response = "Valid Email";
                output.style.color = "green";
            }
            emailVal.value = "";
            output.textContent = response;
        });
    </script>
```

Practice exercise 12.3

```
function showNames() {
    let lastOne = "";
    for (let i = 0; i < arguments.length; i++) {
        lastOne = arguments[i];
    }
    return lastOne;
}
console.log(showNames("JavaScript", "Laurence", "Mike", "Larry"));
```

Practice exercise 12.4

```
15
45
```

Practice exercise 12.5

```
function test(val) {
    try {
        if (isNaN(val)) {
            throw "Not a number";
        } else {
            console.log("Got number");
        }
```

```
    } catch (e) {
        console.error(e);
    } finally {
        console.log("Done " + val);
    }
}
test("a");
test(100);
```

Practice exercise 12.6

```
<script>
    console.log(document.cookie);
    console.log(rCookie("test1"));
    console.log(rCookie("test"));
    cCookie("test1", "new Cookie", 30);
    dCookie("test2");
    function cCookie(cName, value, days) {
        if (days) {
            const d = new Date();
            d.setTime(d.getTime() + (days * 24 * 60 * 60 * 1000));
            let e = "; expires=" + d.toUTCString();
            document.cookie = cName + "=" + value + e + "; path=/";
        }
    }
    function rCookie(cName) {
        let cookieValue = false;
        let arr = document.cookie.split("; ");
        arr.forEach(str => {
            const cookie = str.split("=");
            if (cookie[0] == cName) {
                cookieValue = cookie[1];
            }
        });
        return cookieValue;
    }
    function dCookie(cName) {
        cCookie(cName, "", -1);
    }
</script>
```

Practice exercise 12.7

```
<script>
    const userTask = document.querySelector(".main input");
    const addBtn = document.querySelector(".main button");
    const output = document.querySelector(".output");
    const tasks = JSON.parse(localStorage.getItem("tasklist")) || [];
    addBtn.addEventListener("click", createListItem);
    if (tasks.length > 0) {
        tasks.forEach((task) => {
            genItem(task.val, task.checked);
        });
    }
    function saveTasks() {
        localStorage.setItem("tasklist", JSON.stringify(tasks));
    }
    function buildTasks() {
        tasks.length = 0;
        const curList = output.querySelectorAll("li");
        curList.forEach((el) => {
            const tempTask = {
                val: el.textContent,
                checked: false
            };
            if (el.classList.contains("ready")) {
                tempTask.checked = true;
            }
            tasks.push(tempTask);
        });
        saveTasks();
    }
    function genItem(val, complete) {
        const li = document.createElement("li");
        const temp = document.createTextNode(val);
        li.appendChild(temp);
        output.append(li);
        userTask.value = "";
        if (complete) {
            li.classList.add("ready");
        }
```

```
            li.addEventListener("click", (e) => {
                li.classList.toggle("ready");
                buildTasks();
            });
            return val;
        }
        function createListItem() {
            const val = userTask.value;
            if (val.length > 0) {
                const myObj = {
                    val: genItem(val, false),
                    checked: false
                };
                tasks.push(myObj);
                saveTasks();
            }
        }
    </script>
```

Practice exercise 12.8

```
let myList = [{
        "name": "Learn JavaScript",
        "status": true
    },
    {
        "name": "Try JSON",
        "status": false
    }
];

reloader();
function reloader() {
    myList.forEach((el) => {
    console.log(`${el.name} = ${el.status}`);
    });
}
```

Practice Exercise 12.9

```
let myList = [{
    "name": "Learn JavaScript",
    "status": true
},
{
    "name": "Try JSON",
    "status": false
}
];

const newStr = JSON.stringify(myList);
const newObj = JSON.parse(newStr);
newObj.forEach((el)=>{
    console.log(el);
});
```

Projects

Email extractor

```
<script>
    const firstArea = document.querySelector(
        "textarea[name='txtarea']");
    const secArea = document.querySelector(
        "textarea[name='txtarea2']");
    document.querySelector("button").addEventListener("click", lookUp);
    function lookUp() {
        const rawTxt = firstArea.value;
        const eData = rawTxt.match(
            /([a-zA-Z0-9._-]+@[a-zA-Z0-9._-]+\.[a-zA-Z0-9._-]+)/gi);
        const holder = [];
        for (let x = 0; x < eData.length; x++) {
            if (holder.indexOf(eData[x]) == -1) {
                holder.push(eData[x]);
            }
        }
        secArea.value = holder.join(',');
    }
</script>
```

Form validator

```
<script>
    const myForm = document.querySelector("form");
    const inputs = document.querySelectorAll("input");
    const errors = document.querySelectorAll(".error");
    const required = ["email", "userName"];
    myForm.addEventListener("submit", validation);
    function validation(e) {
        let data = {};
        e.preventDefault();
        errors.forEach(function (item) {
            item.classList.add("hide");
        });
        let error = false;
        inputs.forEach(function (el) {
            let tempName = el.getAttribute("name");
            if (tempName != null) {
                el.style.borderColor = "#ddd";
                if (el.value.length == 0 &&
                required.includes(tempName)) {
                    addError(el, "Required Field", tempName);
                    error = true;
                }
                if (tempName == "email") {
                    let exp = /([A-Za-z0-9._-]+@[A-Za-z0-9._-]+\.
[A-Za-z0-9]+)\w+/;
                    let result = exp.test(el.value);
                    if (!result) {
                        addError(el, "Invalid Email", tempName);
                        error = true;
                    }
                }
                if (tempName == "password") {
                    let exp = /[A-Za-z0-9]+$/;
                    let result = exp.test(el.value);
                    if (!result) {
                        addError(el, "Only numbers and Letters",
                                tempName);
                        error = true;
                    }
```

```
                    if (!(el.value.length > 3 &&
                    el.value.length < 9)) {
                        addError(el, "Needs to be between 3-8 " +
                                "characters", tempName);
                        error = true;
                    }
                }
                data[tempName] = el.value;
            }
        });
        if (!error) {
            myForm.submit();
        }
    }

    function addError(el, mes, fieldName) {
        let temp = el.nextElementSibling;
        temp.classList.remove("hide");
        temp.textContent = fieldName.toUpperCase() + " " + mes;
        el.style.borderColor = "red";
        el.focus();
    }
</script>
```

Simple math quiz

```
<!doctype html>
<html>
<head>
    <title>Complete JavaScript Course</title>
</head>
<body>
    <span class="val1"></span> <span>+</span>
    <span class="val2"></span> = <span>
        <input type="text" name="answer"></span><button>Check</button>
    <div class="output"></div>
    <script>
        const app = function () {
            const game = {};
            const val1 = document.querySelector(".val1");
            const val2 = document.querySelector(".val2");
            const output = document.querySelector(".output");
```

```
    const answer = document.querySelector("input");
    function init() {
        document.querySelector("button").addEventListener(
            "click", checker);
        loadQuestion();
    }
    function ranValue(min, max) {
        return Math.floor(Math.random() * (max - min + 1) +
                            min);
    }
    function loadQuestion() {
        game.val1 = ranValue(1, 100);
        game.val2 = ranValue(1, 100);
        game.answer = game.val1 + game.val2;
        val1.textContent = game.val1;
        val2.textContent = game.val2;
    }
    function checker() {
        let bg = answer.value == game.answer ? "green" : "red";
        output.innerHTML +=
            `<div style="color:${bg}">${game.val1} +
            ${game.val2} = ${game.answer} (${answer.value})
            </div>`;
        answer.value = "";
        loadQuestion();
    }
    return {
        init: init
    };
}();
document.addEventListener('DOMContentLoaded', app.init);
    </script>
</body>
</html>
```

Self-check quiz

1. The range matched is from a to e and is case sensitive. It will return the rest of the word: enjoy avaScript.

2. Yes.

3. It will clear cookies from the site.

4. hello world

5. a is not defined.

6. a

   c

   b

Chapter 13, Concurrency

Practice exercises

Practice exercise 13.1

```
function greet(fullName){
    console.log(`Welcome, ${fullName[0]} ${fullName[1]}`)
}
function processCall(user, callback){
    const fullName = user.split(" ");
    callback(fullName);
}

processCall("Laurence Svekis", greet);
```

Practice exercise 13.2

```
const myPromise = new Promise((resolve, reject) => {
    resolve("Start Counting");
});

function counter(val){
    console.log(val);
}

myPromise
  .then(value => {counter(value); return "one"})
  .then(value => {counter(value); return "two"})
  .then(value => {counter(value); return "three"})
  .then(value => {counter(value);});
```

Practice exercise 13.3

```
let cnt = 0;
function outputTime(val) {
    return new Promise(resolve => {
        setTimeout(() => {
            cnt++;
            resolve(`x value ${val} counter:${cnt}`);
        }, 1000);
    });
}
async function aCall(val) {
    console.log(`ready ${val} counter:${cnt}`);
    const res = await outputTime(val);
    console.log(res);
}
for (let x = 1; x < 4; x++) {
    aCall(x);
}
```

Projects

Password checker

```
const allowed = ["1234", "pass", "apple"];

function passwordChecker(pass) {
    return allowed.includes(pass);
}

function login(password) {
    return new Promise((resolve, reject) => {
        if (passwordChecker(password)) {
            resolve({
                status: true
            });
        } else {
            reject({
                status: false
            });
        }
```

```
        });
    }

    function checker(pass) {
        login(pass)
            .then(token => {
                console.log("Approve:");
                console.log(token);
            })
            .catch(value => {
                console.log("Reject:");
                console.log(value);
            })
    }
    checker("1234");
    checker("wrong");
```

Self-check quiz

1. The updated code is as follows:

```
    function addOne(val){
      return val + 1;
    }
    function total(a, b, callback){
      const sum = a + b;
      return callback(sum);
    }
    console.log(total(4, 5, addOne));
```

2. The console will show the error message `Error: Oh no`.

3. The updated code is as follows:

```
    function checker(val) {
      return new Promise((resolve, reject) => {
        if (val > 5) {
          resolve("Ready");
        } else {
          reject(new Error("Oh no"));
        }
      });
    }
```

```
checker(5)
  .then((data) => {console.log(data); })
  .catch((err) => {console.error(err); })
  .finally(() => { console.log("done");});
```

4. The updated code is as follows:

```
async function myFun() {
  return "Hello";
}
myFun().then(
  function(val) { console.log(val); },
  function(err) { conole.log(err); }
```

Chapter 14, HTML5, Canvas, and JavaScript

Practice exercises

Practice exercise 14.1

```
<script>
  const message = document.getElementById("message");
  const output = document.querySelector(".output");
  const myInput = document.querySelector("input");
  myInput.addEventListener("change", uploadAndReadFile);
  function uploadAndReadFile(e) {
    const files = e.target.files;
    for (let i = 0; i < files.length; i++) {
      const file = files[i];
      const img = document.createElement("img");
      img.classList.add("thumb");
      img.file = file;
      output.appendChild(img);
      const reader = new FileReader();
      reader.onload = (function (myImg) {
        return function (e) {
          myImg.src = e.target.result;
        };
```

```
            })(img);
            reader.readAsDataURL(file);
        }
    }
</script>
```

Practice exercise 14.2

```
<!doctype html>
<html>
<head>
    <title>Canvas HTML5</title>
    <style>
        #canvas {
            border: 1px solid black;
        }
    </style>
</head>
<body>
    <canvas id="canvas" width="640" height="640">Not Supported</canvas>
    <script>
        const canvas = document.querySelector('#canvas');
        const ctx = canvas.getContext("2d");
        ctx.fillStyle = "red";
        ctx.fillRect(100, 100, 500, 300); //filled shape
        ctx.strokeRect(90, 90, 520, 320); // outline
        ctx.clearRect(150, 150, 400, 200); //transparent
    </script>
</body>
</html>
```

Practice exercise 14.3

```
<!doctype html>
<html>
<head>
    <title>Canvas HTML5</title>
    <style>
        #canvas {
            border: 1px solid black;
        }
```

```
        </style>
</head>
<body>
    <canvas id="canvas" width="640" height="640">Not Supported</canvas>
    <script>
        const canvas = document.querySelector("#canvas");
        const ctx = canvas.getContext("2d");
        ctx.beginPath();
        ctx.fillStyle = "red";
        ctx.arc(300, 130, 100, 0, Math.PI * 2);
        ctx.fill();
        ctx.beginPath();
        ctx.fillStyle = "black";
        ctx.arc(250, 120, 20, 0, Math.PI * 2);
        ctx.moveTo(370, 120);
        ctx.arc(350, 120, 20, 0, Math.PI * 2);
        ctx.moveTo(240, 160);
        ctx.arc(300, 160, 60, 0, Math.PI);
        ctx.fill();
        ctx.moveTo(300, 130);
        ctx.lineTo(300, 150);
        ctx.stroke();
        ctx.beginPath();
        ctx.moveTo(300, 230);
        ctx.lineTo(300, 270);
        ctx.lineTo(400, 270);
        ctx.lineTo(200, 270);
        ctx.lineTo(300, 270);
        ctx.lineTo(300, 350);
        ctx.lineTo(400, 500);
        ctx.moveTo(300, 350);
        ctx.lineTo(200, 500);
        ctx.stroke();
        ctx.beginPath();
        ctx.fillStyle = "blue";
        ctx.moveTo(200, 50);
        ctx.lineTo(400, 50);
        ctx.lineTo(300, 20);
        ctx.lineTo(200, 50);
        ctx.fill();
        ctx.stroke();
```

```
            </script>
    </body>
    </html>
```

Practice exercise 14.4

```
<html>
<head>
    <title>Canvas HTML5</title>
    <style>
        #canvas {
        border: 1px solid black;
        }
    </style>
</head>
<body>
    <canvas id="canvas" width="640" height="640">Not Supported</canvas>
    <script>
        const canvas = document.querySelector('#canvas');
        const ctx = canvas.getContext('2d');
        const str = "Hello World";
        ctx.font = 'italic 50px Comic';
        ctx.fillStyle = 'blue';
        //ctx.textAlign = 'left';
        ctx.fillText(str, 100, 100);
        ctx.font = 'bold 20px Arial';
        ctx.fillStyle = 'red';
        for (let x = 1; x < 11; x++) {
            ctx.fillText("counter:" + x, 50, (200 + (40 * x)));
        }
    </script>
</body>
</html>
```

Practice exercise 14.5

```
<!doctype html>
<html>
<head>
    <title>Canvas HTML5</title>
```

```
    <style>
        #canvas {
            border: 1px solid black;
        }
    </style>
</head>
<body>
    <div><label>Image</label>
        <input type="file" id="imgLoader" name="imgLoader">
    </div>
    <div><canvas id="canvas"></canvas></div>
    <script>
        const canvas = document.querySelector("#canvas");
        const ctx = canvas.getContext("2d");
        const imgLoader = document.querySelector("#imgLoader");
        imgLoader.addEventListener("change", handleUpload);
        function handleUpload(e) {
            console.log(e);
            const reader = new FileReader();
            reader.onload = function (e) {
                console.log(e);
                const img = new Image();
                img.onload = function () {
                    canvas.width = img.width / 2;
                    canvas.height = img.height / 2;
                    ctx.drawImage(img, 0, 0, img.width / 2,
                                  img.height / 2);
                }
                img.src = e.target.result;
            }
            reader.readAsDataURL(e.target.files[0]);
        }
    </script>
</body>
</html>
```

Practice exercise 14.6

```
<!doctype html>
<html>
<head>
```

```
    <title>Canvas HTML5</title>
    <style>
        #canvas {
            border: 1px solid black;
        }
    </style>
</head>
<body>
    <div><canvas id="canvas"></canvas></div>
    <script>
        const canvas = document.getElementById("canvas");
        const ctx = canvas.getContext("2d");
        const ballSize = 10;
        let x = canvas.width / 2;
        let y = canvas.height / 2;
        let dirX = 1;
        let dirY = 1;
        function drawBall() {
            ctx.beginPath();
            ctx.arc(x, y, ballSize, 0, Math.PI * 2);
            ctx.fillStyle = "red";
            ctx.fill();
            ctx.closePath();
        }
        function move() {
            ctx.clearRect(0, 0, canvas.width, canvas.height);
            drawBall();
            if (x > canvas.width - ballSize || x < ballSize) {
                dirX *= -1;
            }
            if (y > canvas.height - ballSize || y < ballSize) {
                dirY *= -1;
            }
            x += dirX;
            y += dirY;
        }
        setInterval(move, 10);
    </script>
</body>
</html>
```

Practice exercise 14.7

```
<script>
    window.onload = init;
    const canvas = document.getElementById("canvas");
    const ctx = canvas.getContext("2d");
    canvas.style.border = "1px solid black";
    const penColor = document.querySelector("#penColor");
    const penWidth = document.querySelector("#penWidth");
    document.querySelector(".clear").addEventListener(
        "click", clearImg);
    canvas.width = 700;
    canvas.height = 700;
    let pos = {
        x: 0,
        y: 0,
    };
    function init() {
        canvas.addEventListener("mousemove", draw);
        canvas.addEventListener("mousemove", setPosition);
        canvas.addEventListener("mouseenter", setPosition);
    }
    function draw(e) {
        if (e.buttons !== 1) return;
        ctx.beginPath();
        ctx.moveTo(pos.x, pos.y);
        setPosition(e);
        ctx.lineTo(pos.x, pos.y);
        ctx.strokeStyle = penColor.value;
        ctx.lineWidth = penWidth.value;
        ctx.lineCap = "round";
        ctx.stroke();
    }
    function setPosition(e) {
        pos.x = e.pageX;
        pos.y = e.pageY;
    }
    function clearImg() {
        const temp = confirm("Clear confirm?");
        if (temp) {
            ctx.clearRect(0, 0, canvas.offsetWidth,
```

```
                                        canvas.offsetHeight);
            }
        }
    </script>
```

Projects

Create a Matrix effect

```
<!doctype html>
<html>
<head>
    <title>Canvas HTML5</title>
</head>
<body>
    <div class="output"></div>
    <script>
        const canvas = document.createElement("canvas");
        const ctx = canvas.getContext("2d");
        canvas.setAttribute("width", "500");
        canvas.setAttribute("height", "300");
        document.body.prepend(canvas);
        const colVal = [];
        for(let x=0;x<50;x++){
            colVal.push(0);
        }
        function matrix() {
            ctx.fillStyle = "rgba(0,0,0,.05)";
            ctx.fillRect(0, 0, canvas.width, canvas.height);
            ctx.fillStyle = "green";
            colVal.map((posY, index) => {
                let output = Math.random()<0.5?0:1;
                let posX = (index * 10) + 10;
                ctx.fillText(output, posX, posY);
                if (posY > 100 + Math.random() * 300) {
                    colVal[index] = 0;

                } else {
                    colVal[index] = posY + 10;
                }
            });
```

```
        }
        setInterval(matrix, 50);
    </script>
</body>
</html>
```

Countdown clock

```
<script>
        const endDate = document.querySelector("input[name='endDate']");
        const clock = document.querySelector(".clock");
        let timeInterval;
        let timeStop = true;
        const savedValue = localStorage.getItem("countdown") || false;
        if (savedValue) {
            startClock(savedValue);
            let inputValue = new Date(savedValue);
            endDate.valueAsDate = inputValue;
        }
        endDate.addEventListener("change", function (e) {
            e.preventDefault();
            clearInterval(timeInterval);
            const temp = new Date(endDate.value);
            localStorage.setItem("countdown", temp);
            startClock(temp);
            timeStop = true;
        });
        function startClock(d) {
            function updateCounter() {
                let tl = (timeLeft(d));
                if (tl.total <= 0) {
                    timeStop = false;
                }
                for (let pro in tl) {
                    let el = clock.querySelector("." + pro);
                    if (el) {
                        el.innerHTML = tl[pro];
                    }
                }
            }
            updateCounter();
            if (timeStop) {
```

```
                    timeInterval = setInterval(updateCounter, 1000);
            } else {
                clearInterval(timeInterval);
            }
        }
        function timeLeft(d) {
            let currentDate = new Date();
            let t = Date.parse(d) - Date.parse(currentDate);
            let seconds = Math.floor((t / 1000) % 60);
            let minutes = Math.floor((t / 1000 / 60) % 60);
            let hours = Math.floor((t / (1000 * 60 * 60)) % 24);
            let days = Math.floor(t / (1000 * 60 * 60 * 24));
            return {
                "total": t,
                "days": days,
                "hours": hours,
                "minutes": minutes,
                "seconds": seconds
            };
        }

</script>
```

Online paint app

```
<script>
    const canvas = document.querySelector("#canvas");
    const ctx = canvas.getContext("2d");
    const penColor = document.querySelector("#penColor");
    const penWidth = document.querySelector("#penWidth");
    const btnSave = document.querySelector(".save");
    const btnClear = document.querySelector(".clear");
    const output = document.querySelector(".output");
    const mLoc = {
        draw: false,
        x: 0,
        y: 0,
        lastX: 0,
        lastY: 0
    };
    canvas.style.border = "1px solid black";
```

```
btnSave.addEventListener("click", saveImg);
btnClear.addEventListener("click", clearCanvas);
canvas.addEventListener("mousemove", (e) => {
    mLoc.lastX = mLoc.x;
    mLoc.lastY = mLoc.y;
    //console.log(e);
    mLoc.x = e.clientX;
    mLoc.y = e.clientY;
    draw();
});
canvas.addEventListener("mousedown", (e) => {
    mLoc.draw = true;
});
canvas.addEventListener("mouseup", (e) => {
    mLoc.draw = false;
});
canvas.addEventListener("mouseout", (e) => {
    mLoc.draw = false;
});
function saveImg() {
    const dataURL = canvas.toDataURL();
    console.log(dataURL);
    const img = document.createElement("img");
    output.prepend(img);
    img.setAttribute("src", dataURL);
    const link = document.createElement("a");
    output.append(link);
    let fileName = Math.random().toString(16).substr(-8) +
        ".png"
    link.setAttribute("download", fileName);
    link.href = dataURL;
    link.click();
    output.removeChild(link);
}
function clearCanvas() {
    let temp = confirm("clear canvas?");
    if (temp) {
        ctx.clearRect(0, 0, canvas.width, canvas.height);
    }
}
function draw() {
```

```
            if (mLoc.draw) {
                ctx.beginPath();
                ctx.moveTo(mLoc.lastX, mLoc.lastY);
                ctx.lineTo(mLoc.x, mLoc.y);
                ctx.strokeStyle = penColor.value;
                ctx.lineWidth = penWidth.value;
                ctx.stroke();
                ctx.closePath();
            }
        }
    </script>
```

Self-check quiz

1. ```
   const canvas = document.getElementById('canvas');
   const ctx = canvas.getContext('2d');
   ```

2. Draws a red circle.

3. `moveTo()`, `lineTo()`, `stroke()`

   ```
   ctx.moveTo(100, 0);
   ctx.lineTo(100, 100);
   ctx.stroke();
   ```

Chapter 15, Next Steps

Practice exercises

Practice exercise 15.1

```
[
    {
        "name": "Learn JavaScript",
        "status" : true
    },
    {
        "name": "Try JSON",
        "status" : false
    }
```
```

```
]

const url = "list.json";
fetch(url).then(rep => rep.json())
.then((data) => {
data.forEach((el) => {
        console.log(`${el.name} = ${el.status}`);
    });
});
```

Projects

Working with JSON

```
<!DOCTYPE html>
<html>
    <head><title>Working with JSON Project</title></head>
    <body>
        <script src="myscript.js"></script>
    </body>
</html>


// myscript.js

let url = "people.json";
fetch(url)
.then(response => response.json())
.then(data => {
    console.log(data);
    data.forEach(person => {
        console.log(`${person.first} ${person.last} - ${person.topic}`);
    });
});


// people.json
[
    {
        "first": "Laurence",
        "last": "Svekis",
        "topic": "JavaScript"
```

```
    },
    {
        "first": "John",
        "last": "Smith",
        "topic": "HTML"
    },
    {
        "first": "Jane",
        "last": "Doe",
        "topic": "CSS"
    }
]
```

List-making project

```html
<!DOCTYPE html>
<html>
<head>
    <title>JavaScript List Project</title>
</head>
<body>
    <div class="output"></div>
    <input type="text"><button>add</button>
    <script>
        const output = document.querySelector(".output");
        const myValue = document.querySelector("input");
        const btn1 = document.querySelector("button");
        const url = "list.json";
        btn1.addEventListener("click", addToList);
        let localData = localStorage.getItem("myList");
        let myList = [];
        window.addEventListener("DOMContentLoaded", () => {
            output.textContent = "Loading......";
            if (localData) {
                myList = JSON.parse(localStorage.getItem("myList"));
                output.innerHTML = "";
                myList.forEach((el, index) => {
                    maker(el);
                });
            } else {
                reloader();
            }
```

```
        });

        function addToList() {
            if (myValue.value.length > 3) {
                const myObj = {
                    "name": myValue.value
                }
                myList.push(myObj);
                maker(myObj);
                savetoStorage();
            }
            myValue.value = "";
        }

        function savetoStorage() {
            console.log(myList);
            localStorage.setItem("myList", JSON.stringify(myList));
        }

        function reloader() {
            fetch(url).then(rep => rep.json())
            .then((data) => {
                myList = data;
                myList.forEach((el, index) => {
                    maker(el);
                });
                savetoStorage();
            });
        }

        function maker(el) {
            const div = document.createElement("div");
            div.innerHTML = `${el.name}`;
            output.append(div);
        }
    </script>
</body>
</html>
```

Self-check quiz

1. Pre-programmed JavaScript modules that you can use to speed up your development process.

2. Open the console and type $ or jQuery, and if you get a jQuery object as a response, the page has reference to the $ or jQuery.

3. UnderscoreJS.

4. Type node and the filename into the terminal within the file directory.

Join our book's Discord space

Join the book's Discord workspace for a monthly *Ask me Anything* session with the authors: https://packt.link/JSBook

packt.com

Subscribe to our online digital library for full access to over 7,000 books and videos, as well as industry leading tools to help you plan your personal development and advance your career. For more information, please visit our website.

Why subscribe?

- Spend less time learning and more time coding with practical eBooks and Videos from over 4,000 industry professionals
- Improve your learning with Skill Plans built especially for you
- Get a free eBook or video every month
- Fully searchable for easy access to vital information
- Copy and paste, print, and bookmark content

At www.packt.com, you can also read a collection of free technical articles, sign up for a range of free newsletters, and receive exclusive discounts and offers on Packt books and eBooks.

Other Books You May Enjoy

If you enjoyed this book, you may be interested in these other books by Packt:

Responsive Web Design with HTML5 and CSS - Third Edition

Ben Frain

ISBN: 9781839211560

- Integrate CSS media queries into your designs; apply different styles to different devices
- Load different sets of images depending upon screen size or resolution
- Leverage the speed, semantics, and clean markup of accessible HTML patterns
- Implement SVGs into your designs to provide resolution-independent images

- Apply the latest features of CSS like custom properties, variable fonts, and CSS Grid

- Add validation and interface elements like date and color pickers to HTML forms

- Understand the multitude of ways to enhance interface elements with filters, shadows, animations, and more

Learn Python Programming - Third Edition

Fabrizio Romano

Heinrich Kruger

ISBN: 9781801815093

- Get Python up and running on Windows, Mac, and Linux
- Write elegant, reusable, and efficient code in any situation
- Avoid common pitfalls like duplication, complicated design, and over-engineering
- Understand when to use the functional or object-oriented approach to programming
- Build a simple API with FastAPI and program GUI applications with Tkinter
- Get an initial overview of more complex topics such as data persistence and cryptography
- Fetch, clean, and manipulate data, making efficient use of Python's built-in data structures

Dancing with Python

Robert S. Sutor

ISBN: 9781801077859

- Explore different quantum gates and build quantum circuits with Qiskit and Python
- Write succinct code the Pythonic way using magic methods, iterators, and generators
- Analyze data, build basic machine learning models, and plot the results
- Search for information using the quantum Grover Search Algorithm
- Optimize and test your code to run efficiently

Packt is searching for authors like you

If you're interested in becoming an author for Packt, please visit authors.packtpub.com and apply today. We have worked with thousands of developers and tech professionals, just like you, to help them share their insight with the global tech community. You can make a general application, apply for a specific hot topic that we are recruiting an author for, or submit your own idea.

Share Your Thoughts

Now you've finished *JavaScript from Beginner to Professional*, we'd love to hear your thoughts! Scan the QR code below to go straight to the Amazon review page for this book and share your feedback or leave a review on the site that you purchased it from.

https://packt.link/r/1800562527

Your review is important to us and the tech community and will help us make sure we're delivering excellent quality content.

Index

stick man, drawing 376, 377
text, adding to 377-379
dynamic images
saving 390-392

E

ECMAScript 6 (ES6) 5
element click handler 237, 238
elements
animating 292, 293
class, adding to 243, 244
class, modifying 243
class, removing 244, 245
class, toggling 246
creating 253, 254
dragging 285-287
dropping 285-287
exercise 255
mouse position, tracking 296
element style
manipulating 240-243
else-if statements 74, 75
email extractor 338
employee tracking app 163
encapsulation 158
encodeUri() 170
encodeUriComponent() 171, 172
equal operator 40
error handling 325, 326
escape()
encoding with 172
escape characters 22
eval()
used, for executing JavaScript 175, 176
event bubbling 278
event capturing 278
event delegation 278
event listeners
exercise 253
on element 251, 252
event loop 355
events
specifying 266
specifying, with event listeners 267, 268
specifying, with HTML 266
specifying, with JavaScript 267

event target property 272-274
exponent 196
exponentiation operator 34
Express module
reference link 420
Express Node.js framework
using 419

F

Fetch API 417
Fibonacci sequence 90
floats
making, with parseFloat() 174, 175
foreach 87
for in loop 103
used, for looping over object 103
for loops 92-94
formatting code 11
indentations and whitespace 11, 12
semicolon 12
form submission 289-291
form validator 339, 340
for of loop 101, 102
frameworks 404, 412
Angular 414
Vue.js 412, 413
friend checker game 83
function callbacks 143, 144
functions 314
basic functions 118
invoking 118
local variables 130, 131
naming 119
return value 128
writing 118, 119
function values
returning 127

G

GeoLocation
used, for obtaining data position 369, 370
get keyword 158
getters 157-159
global JavaScript methods 169
global variables 134-136
greater than operator 41

undefined data type 26
Underscore.js
  reference link 410
Underscore library 409, 410
unescape()
  encoding with 172
uniform resource identifier (URI)s
  decoding 169, 170
  encoding 169, 170
uniform resource locator (URL) 169
unsuitable parameters 122, 123

V

values
  mapping, of array 179
variables 18
  declaring 18
  naming 20
var keyword 19
  global scope 19
var variables
  versus let variables 132, 133
Vue.js 412, 413
  reference link 414

W

web browser
  for JavaScript coding environment 4
  recognizing, JavaScript 4, 5
web browser console
  using 5-7
  working with 7
web page
  JavaScript, adding to 8
while loop 88-90
window browser object 211
window history object 214
window location object 216, 217
window navigator object 215
word scrambler 201, 202

Download a free PDF copy of this book

Thanks for purchasing this book!

Do you like to read on the go but are unable to carry your print books everywhere? Is your eBook purchase not compatible with the device of your choice?

Don't worry, now with every Packt book you get a DRM-free PDF version of that book at no cost.

Read anywhere, any place, on any device. Search, copy, and paste code from your favorite technical books directly into your application.

The perks don't stop there, you can get exclusive access to discounts, newsletters, and great free content in your inbox daily

Follow these simple steps to get the benefits:

1. Scan the QR code or visit the link below

https://packt.link/free-ebook/9781800562523

2. Submit your proof of purchase
3. That's it! We'll send your free PDF and other benefits to your email directly